Elementary Statistics for Public Administration

Taking a simplified approach to statistics, this textbook teaches students the skills required to conduct and understand quantitative research. It provides basic mathematical instruction without compromising on analytical rigor, covering the essentials of research design; descriptive statistics; data visualization; and statistical tests including t-tests, chi-squares, ANOVAs, Wilcoxon tests, OLS regression, and logistic regression. Step-by-step instructions with screenshots are used to help students master the use of the freely accessible software R Commander. Ancillary resources include a solutions manual and figure files for instructors, and datasets and further guidance on using STATA and SPSS for students. Packed with examples and drawing on real-world data, this is an invaluable textbook for both undergraduate and graduate students in public administration and political science.

Daniel S. Scheller is Associate Professor of Public Administration and Director of the Master of Public Administration (MPA) program in the Department of Political Science at Texas Tech University, USA. His research interests are in urban policy, neighborhood development, housing, and civic participation.

"Daniel Scheller's *Elementary Statistics for Public Administration* is the long-awaited successor to Meier and Brudney's *Applied Statistics for Public Administration*. Perfectly pitched to MPA and MPP students, this textbook walks students through research design, measurement, and data collection with many relevant examples for public administrators and presents the full panoply of statistical techniques and tests including central tendency and dispersion, ANOVA, Chi-square and Wilcoxon tests, bivariate and multivariate regression models, and, for the more ambitious student, logistic regression. At every juncture, Scheller shows students how to perform statistical tests with R Commander, the most user-friendly version of R available today, and provides students with datasets on which to practice their newly acquired skills. Of particular note is the emphasis on graphs, charts, and data visualization – all critical skills for today's public administrator. I recommend this book highly for students of public and nonprofit administration, urban affairs and planning, and public policy more broadly."

Jonathan Engel, *CUNY*

"*Elementary Statistics for Public Administration* is an invaluable resource for students and teachers of public administration. This textbook seamlessly integrates elementary statistical theory with practical application using R Commander. Its focus on public administration examples adds real-world relevance and practicality for current or aspiring public officials seeking to enhance their statistical skills in today's data-driven world."

Eva Marín Hlynsdóttir, *University of Iceland*

"This is an exceptional textbook that ties together research methodology in a way that is accessible to both students and practitioners. The book is well organized and thorough in its coverage, and I appreciate the care the author takes in demonstrating how to conduct research using R Commander which can seem intimidating to many students. I would highly recommend this textbook to faculty and would use this resource in my own courses at the graduate level."

Thaddieus Conner, *New Mexico State University*

"With this textbook, education in Public Administration finally has a solid basic work regarding quantitative methods. Students and their instructors find guidance concerning the analysis of quantitative data and the author emphasizes the logic behind establishing a basic research design and good data collection practices. Various statistical techniques are systematically introduced in a logical manner allowing students to become familiar with the primary analysis techniques in the field of Public Administration.

An absolute advantage of this textbook is the integration of an accessible introduction to using R as statistical software via R commander. This helps to overcome a hurdle for many students in mastering basic data analysis skills. By incorporating numerous databases from the political-administrative reality, students gain a practical understanding of their field. The inclusion of documentation for those using STATA and SPSS in the companion site is a significant asset to this handbook.

In short, this is an indispensable guide to familiarize students in public administration with quantitative data analysis. This textbook is not only useful during their studies but also afterwards."

Dries Verlet, *Ghent University, Belgium*

Elementary Statistics for Public Administration

An Applied Perspective

DANIEL S. SCHELLER
Texas Tech University

CAMBRIDGE
UNIVERSITY PRESS

CAMBRIDGE
UNIVERSITY PRESS

Shaftesbury Road, Cambridge CB2 8EA, United Kingdom

One Liberty Plaza, 20th Floor, New York, NY 10006, USA

477 Williamstown Road, Port Melbourne, VIC 3207, Australia

314–321, 3rd Floor, Plot 3, Splendor Forum, Jasola District Centre,
New Delhi – 110025, India

103 Penang Road, #05–06/07, Visioncrest Commercial, Singapore 238467

Cambridge University Press is part of Cambridge University Press & Assessment,
a department of the University of Cambridge.

We share the University's mission to contribute to society through the pursuit of
education, learning and research at the highest international levels of excellence.

www.cambridge.org
Information on this title: www.cambridge.org/highereducation/isbn/9781009439947

DOI: 10.1017/9781009439930

When citing this work, please include a reference to the DOI 10.1017/9781009439930

First published 2025

Printed in the United Kingdom by CPI Group Ltd, Croydon, CR0 4YY

A catalogue record for this publication is available from the British Library

Library of Congress Cataloging-in-Publication Data
Names: Scheller, Daniel S. (Daniel Staton) author.
Title: Elementary statistics for public administration : an applied
perspective / Daniel S. Scheller, Texas Tech University.
Description: New York, NY : Cambridge University Press, 2025. |
Includes bibliographical references and index.
Identifiers: LCCN 2023052223 | ISBN 9781009439947 (hardback) |
ISBN 9781009439930 (ebook)
Subjects: LCSH: Public administration – Statistical methods. |
Public administration – Study and teaching. | R (Computer program
language) – Study and teaching.
Classification: LCC JA71.7 .S34 2025 | DDC 351.072/7–dc23/eng/20240131
LC record available at https://lccn.loc.gov/2023052223

ISBN 978-1-009-43994-7 Hardback
ISBN 978-1-009-43995-4 Paperback

Additional resources for this publication at www.cambridge.org/scheller.

Contents

Preface

Two trends continue to develop in public administration for both scholars and practitioners: the growth of quantitative empirical analysis, and the desire of employers for researchers and employees to have statistical software literacy. Advertisements for public sector jobs increasingly require knowledge of basic statistics to interpret government reports and studies. Preferred and even required qualifications for positions like policy analysts, program evaluators, budget managers, economic development associates, research directors, etc., elicit a desire for employee ability to collect and analyze data using statistical software. Students with these skills retain an advantage on the job market over other applicants without statistics training.

Quantitative methods using statistics have seen a growth in importance not only in the academic study of public administration, but also for use in the public sector among practitioners. Government departments and nonprofit organizations at all levels in the federal system are increasingly demanding empirical and quantitative skills from employees, as they seek to hire individuals that can analyze and make sense of "big data" to solve departmental and public policy problems. Students graduating from public administration undergraduate programs and especially from Master of Public Administration (MPA) programs with the skills to at least understand technical quantitative reports have an advantage over their employment competition. Additionally, those students that have the ability to take thousands of pieces of data over numerous variables and synthesize and explain them using graphs, tables, and unique numbers have a skillset in high demand.

Aim of the Book

Statistics is an often dirty and avoided word among public administration and social science students. Many students interested in political and social issues often wonder what is the point of understanding data and statistics for their field of study. In fact, many students may come to social science disciplines specifically to *avoid* mathematics and statistics! To be sure, courses in political science, public administration, and sociology may have fewer mathematics requirements than majors like economics, finance, and those in the hard sciences, but understanding basic research design and statistics in these fields will likely yield major career benefits for students. If this is where you find yourself – interested in social phenomena, especially as applied to public administration and policy issues – yet deterred by mathematics, statistics, and complicated equations, do not worry. The aim of this textbook is to "demystify" statistics and statistics software for public administration students. My goal in writing this textbook is for students to first understand when and why to use particular statistical tests. Second, I seek to instruct students to understand the basic mathematics behind common statistics and statistical tests. Finally, and most important, I aim to provide instruction on how to use a free statistics software program that students can continue to use in their future studies and in their applied careers.

Motivation

The main, overarching motivation in writing this textbook is to present students and instructors with a public administration statistics textbook that combines both basic mathematical instruction with statistics software instruction *without* sacrificing the instructional rigor students need to master key statistics concepts. To be sure, there are a number of excellent public administration statistics textbooks. However, I have found that textbooks with excellent mathematical instruction often lack software instruction. Textbooks with excellent software instruction often cut back on the mathematical background of the statistical tests. Finally, few, if any public administration statistics textbooks use the free R Commander software. SPSS and STATA are the typical non-Excel software used in public administration textbooks, and they are not free. Students have to rent or purchase the software or find a computer lab to access SPSS and STATA. Excel is often difficult to learn for running statistics tests, even though it is widely available. The R Commander software is free, allowing students to easily access a software program from anywhere at no cost. The accessibility of the R Commander allows traditional in-person students and online learners the ability to have free software wherever they are as long as they have computer access.

Intended Audience

The typical public administration student graduating with an MPA or an undergraduate degree is not going to conduct academic research for publication purposes or even need to gain the skills to move into a PhD program. However, they may be asked to produce reports or white papers concerning public or departmental policies that require data collection and analysis.

This textbook focuses on the most important statistical concepts for students seeking careers in the public sector. It covers common statistical tests used to analzye data and answer research questions common among public administration practitioners. Attention is paid to when and how to conduct particular statistical tests to understand patterns in data in order to produce empirically sound research for white papers, memorandums, and oral presentations. Finally, I hope that this textbook can serve as a reference for students as they continue their studies and in their careers if they are ever called to use statistics. The software instruction hopefully provides the skills needed for students to conduct future research.

Structure of the Book

The text is divided into four parts. Part 1 focuses on principles of research design. While this section of the textbook is not a perfect substitute for a formal course in research design and the philosophy of science, it provides students with the necessary information needed to answer research questions and to set up the testing of hypotheses. For many MPA students, especially those students in programs requiring a stand-alone research design course, Chapters 2–3 will be good chapters for review. For students in programs without a separate research design course, Chapters 2–3 will provide enough information for students to understand the basics of research design to allow them to comprehend the lessons in later chapters involving specific statistical tests as they apply to the level of measurement of dependent and independent variables. Chapter 4 is unique to most public administration statistics textbooks in that it describes good practices for data collection and data entry. Most textbooks simply assume that students have data ready for analysis; however, statistical analyses and their interpretation cannot be conducted without bias and severe error unless the data are organized correctly. This chapter explains how and why to organize data in various formats. Chapter 5 introduces students to the R statistical software and how to download it, along with uploading data.

Part 2 focuses on the descriptive statistics of data. Knowing the characteristics of data or what the data "look like" is important for all students and practitioners of statistics. Chapter 6 focuses on central tendency of variables in datasets (mean, median, mode, etc.), and Chapter 7 covers dispersion (principally the standard deviation and issues dealing with skewness). Chapter 8 is unique in that it provides in-depth instruction on how to visualize data based upon the level of measurement. Students need to know how to present data visually for publications and presentations, and the most common graphics are discussed like histograms, bar graphs, and scatterplots, among others. Finally, Chapter 9 covers the important concept of sampling and how a sample can be used to better understand population characteristics. It also introduces students to the concept of probability in the form of Z-scores and their importance for describing normally distributed data.

Part 3 covers the various statistical models used to conduct hypothesis tests. Each chapter describes when and how to conduct a particular test based upon the level of measurement of the dependent and independent variables. Chapter 10 covers various t-tests and when to use them when the dependent variable is measured at the interval level and the independent variable is measured at the nominal level. Chapter 11 is a short chapter on Analysis of Variance (ANOVA), a test used when the dependent variable is at the interval level and the independent variable is nominal or ordinal. For hypotheses dealing with nominal dependent and independent variables, students will use Chapter 12, which covers contingency tables and the chi-square test. Finally, Chapter 13 departs from traditional textbooks by including a short discussion of the Wilcoxon rank-sum test for use with ordinal dependent variables.

Part 4 focuses on regression models. Regression is a powerful tool to help establish causality between a dependent variable and independent variable of interest that cannot be attained with the hypothesis tests covered in Part 3 absent certain restrictions and assumptions. Therefore, students of public administration should have a working understanding of regression modeling. Chapter 14 is a thorough and extensive chapter explaining the logic of regression through the bivariate case with one dependent variable and one independent variable. The relationship between the two variables through measures of correlation, graphically through scatterplots, and mathematically through the bivariate regression equation and calculation of a beta coefficient will present the introductory information necessary to conduct more rigorous regression models. These models are the theme of Chapter 15, covering multivariate regression with multiple independent variables measured at the interval and nominal levels. Chapters 16–18 present information regarding regression models that may or may not be covered in MPA statistics courses due to time in the semester, but are important nonetheless. Some instructors may not have enough time to incorporate Chapters 16–18 in their syllabi, but others may find these chapters imperative in their instruction of statistics for public administrators. Chapter 16 discusses the assumptions of the linear regression models detailed in Chapters 14–15, including linearity, multicollinearity, and heteroscedasticity. Chapter 17 introduces students to the concept of interactive relationships and interaction terms in linear regression models. The focus is on when/why to include interaction terms and how to interpret them in regression output. Chapter 18's coverage of logistic regression is included due to the amount of research questions with dependent variables measured dichotomously (e.g. voted or not; success v. failure; yes v. no). Undergraduate statistics courses will likely cover various chapters throughout Parts 1–4, and most MPA statistics courses adopting the text will get through Chapter 15.

Pedagogical Features

MPA programs differ in how they structure their research methods and statistics courses. Some programs combine methods and statistics into one, semester-long course. Other programs separate the courses into a two-course sequence with students taking a research design/methods course followed by a statistics course. The organizational and pedagogical features of this textbook allow it to be adopted in either type of MPA program. The first chapters focus on research design, with Chapter 2 providing an extensive review for students that have already taken a stand-alone research methods course. However, in this chapter, I also assume no prior knowledge regarding research design among students. Therefore, it presents the most common research designs and research design issues and instruction necessary for students to continue on with the book into the statistics chapters.

The chapters containing statistics and mathematical equations include step-by-step instruction on how to solve problems by hand. It is assumed that students already know how to add, subtract, multiply, divide, take a square root, and use an exponent. Knowledge beyond that is not assumed, and students are walked through how to solve equations so that even the most math-phobic students can be successful in learning and applying the concepts in each chapter.

The most unique feature is the extensive use of R Commander software screenshots with step-by-step instructions on how to use the R Commander. Every step of each test is explained and illustrated with a screenshot. This feature allows students to access the dataset used from the Companion Site (www.cambridge.org/scheller) and follow along with the book instructions, to ensure they are engaging in each step correctly.

Real-world public administration examples and datasets are used to complement hypothetical examples. Additionally, several chapters include discussion of published research studies in academic journals. Students are able to see how research methods and statistics can be used in both applied and academic settings.

Most chapters of this textbook have end-of-chapter practice problems for students. Practice problems are divided into different types of problems to help students master concepts. Conceptual problems require students to think theoretically about statistics and research design concepts. Other practice problems require students to conduct statistical tests by hand to help them understand the mathematical components of each chapter's lessons. Finally, computer problems have students use datasets from the Companion Site to answer questions using the R Commander software. Datasets come from original research by the author, data collected from publicly available data sources, and theoretical data.

Online Resources

The following resources are included on the textbook's Companion Site (www.cambridge.org/scheller):

- **Datasets:** All datasets used throughout the textbook for software illustration and instruction are included on the Companion Site. Additionally, all datasets to complete end-of-chapter practice problems are located on the Companion Site.
- **Online Appendices:** Instruction of in-text software examples using STATA and SPSS are included on the Companion Site for students and instructors to use if they prefer STATA or SPSS over the R Commander. Instructors who prefer to use STATA or SPSS can still use this textbook in their courses since each chapter with software instruction has an online appendix with STATA and SPSS

instruction. Examples using SPSS include screenshots of the SPSS interface. Step-by-step instructions on how to use the SPSS dropdown menus to run statistical tests are provided. STATA instruction uses do-files and code. Step-by-step instructions with screenshots of STATA code with explanation are included.

- **Instructor Manual:** Answers to end-of-chapter practice problems are included in the instructor resource page on the Companion Site.
- **Image Files:** Original images/figures in the textbook are available to students and instructors on the Companion Site.

Acknowledgments

I would first like to thank Cambridge University Press for giving me the opportunity to publish this textbook. In particular, I owe a great deal of gratitude to Valerie Appleby, Helen Shannon, Lucy Edwards, Amala Gobiraman, and Rowan Groat for guiding me through this process with support and patience during the writing and production of the book. I also thank the anonymous reviewers who provided feedback on the proposal and chapters of this textbook. Your comments have made this textbook stronger. Other friends and colleagues graciously provided feedback on various chapters. I am indebted to Greg Goelzhauser and Danbee Lee for their comments on chapters. I thank students in my Spring 2023 PA 8320: Public Policy Evaluation course at the University of Nebraska at Omaha, who provided excellent feedback from a pedagogical perspective on various chapters.

To my wife, Joanna Martinez, who was there with me from the inception of the idea to write a textbook on public administration statistics to the submission of the final draft – thank you for your support and for listening to me and helping me craft ideas for examples for the textbook. I hope you see your influence in this book. I could not have completed it without your loving support and encouragement. To my father, thanks for encouraging me to take math courses and making me solve story problems in middle and high school. To my mom, thank you for always being so loving and supportive. Mom and dad: every personal and professional success I've had is because of your hard work and dedication to me. To my son, Fernando, I hope this book makes you proud.

The final acknowledgment goes to the rescue fur baby that was by my side during much of the writing of this textbook, often next to my desk or cuddled next to me on the couch as I typed on my laptop. Sherlock Bones, you were a true outlier of a dog! You are missed.

To the Student

Enrolling in a public administration statistics course may seem daunting. There are new terms, symbols, and mathematical equations you may have never seen. It may seem foreign to you, and as such, you can think of the process of learning statistics as similar to learning a new language, because it is! It takes learning of rules, memorization, and practice. You may need to read the chapters in this textbook more than once, maybe 3–4 times to fully learn the concepts. If so, do not be deterred. As a graduate student learning statistical methods for social science, I had to read, re-read, and then re-read again chapters in assigned statistics textbooks along with practicing with datasets and statistics software. As a PhD student after passing all of my coursework, I sometimes sat in on a professor's statistics lectures for me to "review" the material. Even as an Assistant Professor with a PhD, I attended seminars in statistics to refresh my training and to learn new techniques. With social science statistics as with a foreign language, it really is true that "if you don't use it, you will lose it." It is necessary to continually engage the material, retrain yourself, and learn new techniques. All of this is to say that learning statistics takes time, practice, and patience. I hope that this textbook not only helps you in your required coursework, but may become a permanent piece of your library that you can use in your career as a reference book or a manual for conducting your own research. I still have the original textbook from my first statistics course, taken in 2002 as an undergraduate student at Hanover College. Though very much worn, I still occasionally refer back to it when working with a method I have not used in years. I also have kept most research design and statistics books from my graduate studies at Florida State University, where I credit professors like Bill Berry, Matthew Golder, Charles Barrilleaux, and the late Tom Carsey for their coursework and/or mentorship in my studies.

PART 1

1

Introduction

1.1 Introduction

Research begins with questions needing answers. What is the relationship between police reforms and citizen complaints? What was the effect of a new four-day workweek policy on state government employee job satisfaction? Did a new training for public employees increase their work performance? Did tax incentives increase economic development in a city? What communication strategies led to greater monetary donations from a nonprofit organization's donor list? These are all empirical questions that can be answered or studied using research methods and statistics. They may be the exact questions or similar to questions you have already been tasked with answering in your job, or you anticipate having to answer in your career. Some of these questions have been asked in public administration research in both applied and academic settings, often with researchers needing to collect original data or needing to find data and then analyzing it with statistics or statistical tests.

Learning basic statistics is similar to learning the basics of a new language. In fact, statistics is often its own language. Who really uses the terms "median," "standard deviation," "null hypothesis," "95% confidence interval," "Z-score," or "beta coefficient" in their daily language among friends/coworkers, or even as a public administration student? However, if you are interested in or required to conduct research with quantitative data, you will most likely need to understand these and other terms to help answer research questions and then translate your findings into language interpretable by various constituencies and stakeholders. Even if you will not be conducting original research or engaging in data analysis in your public administration career, no doubt you will be presented with data in presentations and/or will be reading reports containing data and statistical analysis.

This chapter serves as an introduction to research and statistics in public administration. Its goal is to orient you with contemporary research in public administration, with findings from studies addressing social and public issues that have been in national news and/or are major issues facing public administrators. Some of the terms may be unfamiliar, but you will be using them in short time, as they are covered throughout this textbook. This chapter also seeks to begin your statistical training by educating you to be careful and astute observers of statistical findings and helping you understand how statistics can be used for deception, also known as "lying with statistics." Real and fictional data will illustrate common deceptive practices that can be used to manipulate data and its visualization. The final section of the chapter discusses data and research ethics and some best practices for conducting research in social settings with human subjects.

1.2 Contemporary Issues and Research in Public Administration

In 2019, the National Academy of Public Administration (NAPA) released their report identifying "12 grand challenges for public administration" (National Academy of Public Administration, n.d.). Many of the issues faced by public administration practitioners and researched by public administration scholars center on these themes. They also paint a picture of what future research topics will define the field of public administration and be of interest to public administration practitioners. While impossible to cover recent quantitative and statistical research related to all twelve topics (that could be an entire book or anthology), below are some highlights of recent research that used statistical methods to help you acquaint and orient yourself to quantitative research in public administration and public policy. While many of these studies have been published in academic journals, they study research questions of interest to public administrators and practitioners in a variety of settings, and represent research questions in which you may be interested, or for which you may eventually be tasked with studying in your public or nonprofit careers. Even in the short-term you may be required to write a basic research design/analysis paper in your public administration courses.

1.2.1 Natural Resources, Water Issues, and Climate Change

Two of NAPA's grand challenges revolve around contemporary problems, issues, and solutions to natural resources and climate change. Specifically one challenge is to Steward Natural Resources & Address Climate Change, and the other challenge is to Create Modern Water Systems for Safe & Sustainable Use. Concerns with climate change are compelling public administrators and government officials at all levels to engage in strategic planning in the event that the Earth's temperature keeps rising. Coastal cities are particularly concerned about rising sea levels from snow and glacier melts. Other regions are concerned about lack of water and changing meteorological patterns leading to less rainfall for already arid regions. Still other communities are faced with providing clean water to residents despite aging infrastructure.

One crisis that brought greater attention to aging infrastructure across the U.S. and its effects on citizens was the Flint Water Crisis. Flint is a city in Michigan, approximately sixty miles northwest of Detroit, Michigan. In 2014, government officials made the decision to switch Flint's water source from Detroit (via Lake Huron) to the Flint River until the city could build its own pipeline to Lake Huron (Carmody, 2016; Grossman & Slusky, 2019; Zahran et al., 2017). Without getting into chemistry, treatment of the already heavily polluted Flint River water caused lead from the old water pipes to leach into the city's water system. Media coverage showed citizens throughout the world the quality of water for residents in Flint. Tap water poured a yellowish-brown color, and residents complained of rancid smelling water. Chemical analyses revealed high levels of lead in the drinking water. Lead exposure and consumption is related to a number of health complications, and lead can be passed from an expectant mother to her fetus *in utero*, leading to birth complications, poorer fetal health, and even fetal death (Clay et al., 2014; Edwards, 2014; Troesken, 2006).

To understand the effect of the policy decision to move Flint's water from the Detroit source to the Flint River on birth outcomes and fertility rates, Grossman and Slusky (2019) collect birth data across cities in Michigan. Why not just examine Flint? The researchers want to compare Flint, a city that changed its water source, to other cities that did not. This method essentially adds a level of "control" (a topic we will cover in this text), allowing the researchers to look at trends in Flint (which had a policy change – new water source) compared to birth and fertility trends in other cities (that did not change their water source). Their data and analysis reveal a 12% decrease in fertility rates for residents in Flint and a 5.4% decrease in birth weight. They report that this result is statistically significant (another concept we will cover). The researchers also do an admirable job in discussing the "substantive significance" (yet another topic covered in this text) of their finding by noting this 12% fertility rate decrease is equivalent to "7.5 fewer infants per 1,000 women aged 15–49 [in Flint] compared with control cities" (Grossman & Slusky, 2019, p. 2015). This description of the findings helps to better convey the decrease in fertility. For every 1,000 child-bearing age women, we can expect, on average, 7.5 fewer live births if the woman is from Flint. It is important for public administration researchers to present their findings in language that is accessible to many potential readers. Good data and statistical analyses mean nothing if the findings cannot be interpreted by policymakers and administrators!

Moving from the issue of dirty water to an issue of no water, states in the Southwest of the U.S. are facing a major crisis regarding water availability, and struggling to come up with policy solutions to curb declining water supplies for a growing region. Due at least somewhat to changing climate patterns (O'Brien, 2021; Osborne, 2022), the Southwest region is currently facing a major drought, forcing governments and administrators to come up with solutions to mitigate the water crisis in a sustainable manner.

The Colorado River brings snowmelts and rainwater downstream to communities in the desert Southwest, and is dammed by the reservoirs of Lake Mead and Lake Powell. Millions of residents in the states of Arizona, Nevada, and California rely upon these reservoirs for water. As of this writing, Lake Mead stands at the lowest levels of water in its history, necessitating the federal government to scale back the amount of water released from Lake Mead to communities downstream like Las Vegas, Nevada (Osborne, 2022). One policy tool in effect since the late 1990s to combat excessive water use is the Cash-for-Grass subsidy that provides residents of Las Vegas monetary benefits for converting their traditional lawns to a less water-reliant style of landscaping, incorporating the use of xeriscaping and the planting of flora common in deserts that require less irrigation. Baker (2021) evaluates this policy tool using data from twenty-five years of single-family residential water use in Las Vegas. He finds that the Cash-for-Grass program resulted in approximately a 19–21% decrease in water use for Cash-for-Grass households.

Water crises, climate change, and responses to natural disasters are just a few of the issues that may compel cities, counties, and states to include sustainability topics in their strategic plans. Zeemering (2018) makes a call/plea for local governments to include sustainability in their strategic plans. Certainly, some cities have moved to the forefront in creating strategic plans that address sustainability. What are the characteristics of these cities in terms of bureaucratic capacity that may enable them to do so? Hawkins et al. (2023) survey local governments across the U.S., measuring city staff levels of support for sustainability initiatives in strategic plans and note whether or not a city has a sustainability office. They find an interactive effect between staff support and the presence of a dedicated sustainability office – "the presence of a sustainability office amplifies the influence of perceived staff support on the incorporation of sustainability into city strategic plans" (Hawkins et al., 2023, p. 892). Their results highlight the potential importance of cities establishing sustainability offices/officers if they are intent on addressing sustainability issues in strategic planning. This, combined with supportive street-level bureaucrats, promotes the inclusion of sustainability in future planning for cities. This study has important implications for cities, counties, and states as they plan for challenges related to climate change.

1.2.2 Public Service Motivation

Why do people work in public service? Is it for the money or the vocation? Another grand challenge NAPA identifies is to Connect Individuals to Meaningful Work, noting that "humans have an innate quest for meaning. Our jobs and our work are a principal means for fulfilling that need ..." (National Academy of Public Administration, n.d., n.p.). Public service motivation is defined as "an individual's predisposition to respond to motives grounded primarily or uniquely in public institutions and organizations" (Perry & Wise, 1990, p. 368). It is no secret that many individuals identify themselves by their career and devote much of their time and passion to it. Public sector employees, particularly in certain public sector jobs may exhibit higher levels of motivation to serve, or public service motivation (PSM). Higher PSM in employees is thought to contribute to increased employee performance (Kim, 2006; Leisink & Steijn, 2009; Naff & Crum, 1999;

Park & Rainey, 2007, 2008; Perry & Wise, 1990; Vandenabeele, 2009; van Loon, 2016).

Houston (2011) notes that certain individuals in careers/positions that interact with the general population, notably in public health and safety sectors, have higher levels of PSM and indicate they are motivated to serve. Fire personnel have been found to have high levels of PSM (Battaglio & French, 2016; Vandenabeele & van Loon, 2015). How are high level PSM employees motivated to improve performance? To what types of management strategies do they respond? How are they motivated to improve performance even if they already have high levels of PSM? One of the datasets you will use throughout this textbook was developed to answer this research question. You will be able to see how the data are set up in terms of the variables collected and formatting. The author and a coauthor test whether or not training for improved performance versus employee discipline/sanctions promote performance in a fire department (Scheller & Reglen, 2021). Specifically, they try to determine how the time from being alerted to an emergency to the personnel leaving for the emergency (known as turnout time) is affected by training versus sanctions. Surprisingly, they find that fire personnel seem to respond more to sanctions, a more heavy-handed approach to management. Does this approach to employees apply to all public sector employees? Probably not. However, PSM continues to be a "hot topic" in public administration research as academics and practitioners seek to understand what motivates public employees.

1.2.3 Social Equity and Modernization of Public Service

NAPA also focuses on improvements to social equity in public administration in their challenges for public administration. In their description of social equity, they state, "we continue to struggle with ensuring the equitable design and implementation of public policies and programs that reduce or eliminate disparities, discrimination, and marginalization" (National Academy of Public Administration, n.d., n.p). Seemingly combined with social equity is their other challenge to modernize and reinvigorate public service. This could include equitable distribution of public services, especially in policing, education, health, and housing, among others.

Citizen–police interactions continue to be a major issue facing communities in the United States, stemming from high-profile cases of citizens dying from police officer actions, most egregiously with African American citizens. The murder of George Floyd at the hands of Minneapolis police officers was a major focusing event for police reform and social mobilization for improved citizen–police interactions in marginalized communities. In the aftermath of Floyd's murder, national polls showed a majority of Americans sympathetic with massive protests and indicated that they believe police officers treat White suspects differently than Black suspects, including in the use of force (Skelley, 2020).

A recent criminology study involved researchers collecting data on police-involved shootings across four states in the U.S. With the data, the researchers engaged in correlation analysis and logistic regression analysis, quantifying the odds and probabilities of suspects being shot by police and dying by police shooting. Black suspects were over three times more likely to be shot by police, but 12% less likely to die from police gunshots than white suspects (Nix & Shjarback, 2021).

One policy that is particularly popular among not only police officers (66%) but also the general public (93%) is the use of body-worn cameras for police officers (Morin et al., 2017). Do they work? Fortunately, there is a plethora of data available to public administration and criminology researchers. Unfortunately, the results are mixed. A study in the *American Review of Public Administration* revealed a minor decline in misdemeanor arrests by officers wearing body-worn cameras, but no significant decline in the Black–White ratio of arrests (Pyo, 2021). In terms of citizen complaints and police use of force, researchers at the Urban Institute collected panel data from Milwaukee, Wisconsin, on citizen complaints, finding that body-worn cameras lead to a general decrease in citizen complaints (approximately 6% for each month worn by officers), but have no effect on the number of use-of-force incidents (Peterson & Lawrence, 2021).

Political representation may matter. One interesting study by multiple researchers used ordinary least squares regression to measure the effect of minority representation on city councils on police searches conducted during traffic stops, finding that in cities with majority-Black councilmembers, searches decline for both Black and White drivers but there is an especially pronounced decline for Black drivers (Christiani et al., 2021). Other researchers use a different dataset and ordinary least squares regression finding more nuanced results. Police searches of minorities decline when there is both an increase in minority councilmembers *and* an increase in minority police officers (Choi & Hong, 2021). Essentially, there is an interactive relationship between minority council members and minority police officers. The effect of having minorities on the city council on a decline in searches is conditioned upon or interactive with having more minority policy officers.

To be sure, more research will occur regarding police reforms and interactions with the general population and marginalized communities. As of this writing, there have only been four years since George Floyd's murder. A time lag exists between the adoption and implementation of public policies that affect policing; therefore, policy evaluations are likely to be published in the next few years examining the impacts of reform policies, most likely utilizing research methods and statistics covered in this textbook. The statistics topics mentioned in this section on social equity – ordinary least squares regression, logistic regression, and interactive effects – are all their own chapters in this textbook.

1.2.4 Covid-19

Perhaps no other event in recent history has affected public administrators – from public health workers to elected officials – more than the Covid-19 pandemic that began in 2019 and continued through this first edition textbook. Frontline public health workers faced the initial brunt of challenges brought on by the pandemic, and public health directors, often appointed public servants, were faced with an onslaught of data and other information requiring them to make drastic public health decisions affecting citizens. As the pandemic became a "new normal," elected officials and sometimes appointed public administrators were tasked with developing and implementing public health measures like lockdowns, public school alternative learning environments, mask mandates, and other mitigation strategies. Remember the term "7-day moving average," a common metric through which public health officials measured the growth/decline of Covid-19 cases and deaths? This seemingly arcane term, rooted in data analysis and statistics (one which the author of this textbook did not learn until graduate school), became common parlance in news reports and conversations. It was often used to make policy decisions regarding public health measures.

The controversial mask mandates – national, state, and local government requirements for citizens to wear masks in public – were not only hotly debated in public meetings, but became a topic of public health and public administration study. Fortunately, governments, organizations, and researchers began collecting quantitative data from the onset of the pandemic, including daily counts of new infections and deaths. One researcher developed an entire dataset on government responses to Covid across the world, collecting data on mitigation strategies imposed by governments like lockdowns and mask mandates (Porcher, 2020). Using this data, An et al. (2021) published a study in the *Public Administration Review* analyzing the short-term and long-term effects of mitigation strategies on Covid-19 infections and deaths. They find that adoptions of mask mandates had the most impact on decreasing infections and deaths as a short term response to the pandemic. Early pandemic adoption of mask mandates also had an impact on decreasing infections and deaths in the long-term.

While the efficacy of masks as a public health measure appears to have supportive evidence in the literature, policymakers are not always keen to adopt them, often based upon political and ideological considerations. Even when adopted, it is up to public administrators, especially law enforcement officials, to implement and enforce policies. Policymakers, especially elected officials, often respond to public sentiment. By definition, in a republic like the United States, elected officials are chosen by majority vote to govern for the population, and naturally are more likely to try to enact policy in line with what is most politically expedient for them. As such, we saw wide variation in the adoption of mask mandates and enforcement mechanisms across states and localities. Lyons and Fowler (2021), in an article in *State and Local Government Review*, used survey methodology in the conservative state of Idaho in the U.S., to measure support for mask mandates and support for fines for citizens violating mask mandates. A sample of 1,000 respondents indicated that 58% of respondents supported a mask mandate (without a fine), but support for a mask mandate with a monetary fine dropped to 51%. They calculated their margin of error to be +/− 3.1%. Margins of error are widely used in polling data (as you may become familiar or have seen in media coverage of elections). If you add or subtract 3.1% from the percentages of support, the range for support of a mask mandate (without a fine) was [54.9%–61.1%], and we can conclude there was general support for a mask mandate since the margin of error range is above 50%. However, applying the +/− 3.1% to the 51% statistic of citizens supporting a mask mandate with a fine, the range of support was [47.9%–54.1%]. The researchers correctly concluded that they cannot be confident that a mask mandate with a monetary fine is supported, stating, "a clear majority supports a mask mandate, but with a fine, a majority may or may not support it" (Lyons & Fowler, 2021, p. 115). These topics and language of interpretation of findings will be a common theme throughout this text, and this is an example of a best practice for presenting/explaining statistical findings.

In some cities, streets previously open to automobiles became pedestrian walkways to promote exercise and/or became added outdoor space for seating for businesses and restaurants attempting to remain financially solvent. San Francisco, California, closed off some previously used parking spaces to allow businesses to expand their outdoor seating into these "parklets," and other cities like Oakland, California, Houston, Texas, and Milan, Italy, engaged in slow-street types of programs, closing automobile lanes to traffic to allow cyclists and pedestrians to have access to outdoor recreational and exercise space (Bereitschaft & Scheller, 2020). One city hit particularly hard in the tourist sector was Las Vegas, Nevada, a hub city for gaming, culinary diversity, and music entertainment. At one point, all casinos were shut down to the public. A group of researchers examined how tourists to the region changed their recreational habits during the pandemic. The Las Vegas Airport not only services tourists to the densely populated city for gaming/entertainment, but also allows tourist to fly in and drive to a number of national parks within 250 miles, like Lake Mead, Death Valley, and the Zion and Joshua Tree National Parks. Using regression, they find that as gaming revenues declined during the pandemic (a proxy measure for casino activity/demand), attendance at national parks close to Las Vegas increased (Lim et al., 2022). They conclude with observing how the tourism industry can use the findings to think about promoting more outdoor tourism during times of health crises, especially for cities that often rely upon densely populated tourist economic activities like gaming and entertainment.

The previous study highlights an important aspect of applied research – recommendations for practitioners. While most of the aforementioned research has been published in academic journals, the need for research that reaches practitioners in an accessible language is important in a field like public administration. If you are an undergraduate student or MPA student using this textbook in a course, most likely you have interest in using the skills learned in applied settings – answering questions you may be tasked with in your job – that requires you to take complex data and make sense of it for your supervisor, stakeholders, or constituents.

One particular arena in which recommendations are needed for practitioners, especially for election officials, is in ensuring fair elections that allow all eligible citizens to express their opinion at the ballot box. One of NAPA's twelve grand challenges is to Protect Electoral Integrity and Enhance Voter Participation. Nowhere was this seen as a more apparent need than in elections conducted during the Covid pandemic, most notably in the U.S. Election officials in many states and communities in the U.S. and across the world adapted to new forms of voter registration and voting. Early voting and mail-in voting options became widely adopted policies requiring officials to adapt their voting systems and ballot access options. Despite some politicians criticizing methods like vote-by-mail (VBM), the Covid-19 pandemic brought many states into practice with VBM for the 2020 election to ensure citizens were able to exercise their right to vote. In a study of VBM in the state of Florida for elections in 2016, 2018, and 2020, researchers found that voters inexperienced with VBM were more likely to have their VBM ballots rejected, usually due to being late, an improper signature on the ballot, or other forms of voter error (Cottrell et al., 2021). This pattern was even more pronounced for minority voters. Given this finding and the likelihood of VBM becoming more popular as a form of voting, what can election officials and/or voting participation nonprofit organizations like the League of Women Voters do? Can they make VBM easier for voters across various demographics with easier instructions on filling out ballots or promoting informational campaigns as elections approach? These are contemporary issues for public and nonprofit administrators to solve.

As previously mentioned, one cannot summarize all contemporary public administration research into a section of a chapter or a full chapter. To be sure, the remaining grand challenges from NAPA are being investigated by applied and academic researchers. Other challenges are likely to emerge and certainly have emerged since the 2019 NAPA document with the Covid-19 pandemic and social justice issues that continue to challenge policymakers and public administrators.

1.3 "Lying" with Statistics

Over twenty years ago during the 2000 Presidential debates between then-Vice President Al Gore and Texas Governor (and future U.S. President) George W. Bush, the candidates occasionally would give statistics or numbers regarding status quo situations in the U.S., proposed policies, and their own policy plans. After listening to Gore present some figures in regards to Medicare and prescription drugs, Bush famously stated, "Look, this is a man who has great numbers. He talks about numbers. I'm beginning to think not only did he invent the Internet, but he invented the calculator. It's fuzzy math" (Commission on Presidential Debates, 2000). And from there, a new phrase was entered into the political lexicon, and greater scrutiny on numbers and statistics would be placed on claims made by politicians. During election season, media outlets like CNN now have fact checkers that rate statements made by candidates during debates, rallies, and other public events as being true, false, or somewhere in-between like misleading. Whether or not Gore's numbers were correct, incorrect, or misleading is beyond the scope of this discussion, but it highlights a concept known as "lying" with statistics.

The word "lying" has been placed in quotations to note that it is not always such a clear-cut case of whether numbers and statistics are completely true, false, or misleading. For example, somebody that wants to make an argument that incomes in the U.S. are high and that poverty is not an issue may choose to report certain statistics over others. They could feasibly state, "In 2020, according to the U.S. Census Bureau, the average household income was $97,026." This individual would not be lying; $97,206 was the average household income in the U.S. for 2020 (U.S. Census Bureau, 2021). However, where things may get misleading or "fuzzy" is usually when normative statements are made based upon statistics. Suppose the individual that reported the average income in the U.S. uses this number to indicate that the typical household is earning nearly six figures in income and that there should be little to no concern about poverty. Indicating that $97,206 is the typical income of households is misleading. You could counter their statement by saying, "Yes. The average household income was $97,206, but the *median* household income was $67,521, which means that 50% of households in the U.S. earned more than $67,521, but 50% of households earned less than $67,521." This statement is also correct per data released by the U.S. Census Bureau (2021). Who is right – you or the other person? Technically, both figures are correct, but the other person is being a bit misleading, "lying" with statistics. Averages are susceptible to outliers (topics covered in later chapters), or extreme values. Think about how many multi-billionaires like Bill Gates and Warren Buffet exist in the U.S. Even though they constitute just a fraction of the population, their enormous incomes (or the incomes of other extremely wealthy) individuals, if included in Census income data, skew the data in a positive or higher direction. Because of this, nearly every wealth indicator is reported as a median, which is not susceptible to these outliers or extreme values. This is why values like household income, house prices, rents, and wages are usually reported as medians. Otherwise, one may not have a clear picture of the typical value for a particular statistic measuring a concept in the world.

Statistical tests can also be used to "lie" or mislead with information through omission of relevant information. Suppose Mr. Bulleemann, director of social workers at a state health and human services department, is collecting data on the number of visits his social workers make for their respective clients in a month. He is concerned about one particular new employee in his probationary period, Javier, who completed 104 visits to clients. According to Mr. Bulleemann, only one other employee had fewer visits (103) than Javier, so Mr. Bulleemann decides to discipline Javier with a formal write-up and proceeds with Javier's termination. Javier knows that his number of visits is fairly typical of the number of visits other social workers complete in his agency, and that those records are public and kept on file in the agency. He requests the previous month's data of all ten employees. It is true that only one other person visited fewer clients at 103, but the average number of visits was 105.5 with a standard deviation of 1.27 visits. With this information, Javier decides to file a complaint with his human resources department. While Javier does have fewer client visits, he is close to the mean number of visits and the standard deviation is low – he likely will win his appeal. Why? These topics appear in later chapters on central tendency/dispersion and standard deviation.

What about when two phenomena are related/correlated? Can we automatically conclude that one phenomenon caused the other? Suppose a young epidemiologist stumbles upon some health data and business data for the city of Cleveland. The epidemiologist notices a strong pattern in the data regarding influenza cases in the city and the number of winter coats sold in local department stores. They beg their county health director to send out a public alert telling citizens to throw out their winter coats. Does wearing winter coats cause people to catch the flu? Obviously not. The data are simply showing that as the temperature cools, people are more likely to purchase winter coats *and* are more likely to catch the flu. Colder temperatures clearly compel people to wear winter coats. Maybe less obvious is that cooler temperatures compel people to remain indoors, in close proximity to others, thereby making influenza transmission easier.

The previous example is somewhat comical in that few people would actually think winter coats cause influenza, but it illustrates an important concept discussed later and should alert you to ask yourself if correlations make sense – do you "buy" the results? Take a real-world example. The Centers for Disease Control (CDC) publishes data on life expectancy at birth by state (Centers for Disease Control and Prevention, 2022). Data from 2019 reveal that the correlation between states in the U.S. South and life expectancy is −0.63, a moderate relationship, suggesting that individuals born in the South do not live as long as people born in other regions of the U.S. What if somebody were to claim that a child born in the South is doomed to live fewer years than a child born in another region. Should expectant mothers flock to hospitals in the Midwest, West, or Northeast? Not necessarily. The data can be misleading. It is unlikely that the physical location of a birth for a U.S. region affects life expectancy – there are medical standards and regulations by which facilities must abide. An astute student of statistics would ask, "What is it about the South that causes lower life expectancy?" It cannot simply be the longitude and latitude. The "South" variable could be capturing or be a proxy for other phenomena like the percentage of the population insured, levels of education, income, diet/exercise, etc.

1.4 Data Manipulation

Data can be manipulated, "massaged," and adjusted to tell a particular story or to create a favorable situation which the analyst wants. Public polls are often conducted to gauge support for a particular public policy or government action. Let's assume the mayor of a city wants to spend some of the budget on increasing funding for the city police department. She hires a consulting firm to survey residents on their support for increasing spending for the police department for extra weapons, vehicles, and officer pay. The consulting firm reports that data from the survey indicate that 8% of the citizens strongly agree to increasing police funding, 13% agree, 35% are neutral (neither agree or disagree), 2% disagree, and 42% strongly disagree. With this data, the mayor makes a public statement where she notes that only 44% disagree to any police funding increase. She states that based upon majority opinion, she will ask the city council to increase police funding. How has she strategically manipulated data and data findings to support her position? She omitted the fact that 35% of the population was neutral and that only 21% agreed or strongly agreed to supporting an increase in police funding. This example would be a clear case of data manipulation/massaging by not reporting what question was asked of respondents and their potential options to answer.

Another example of data manipulation is running a statistical analysis, in particular, a regression analysis, and then changing the variables in the analysis to obtain statistically significant results. Suppose a researcher hypothesizes that the county percent of voters voting for the Democratic Presidential candidate is a function primarily of the county's unemployment rate, believing that as the county's unemployment rate increases, the more likely the county will vote for the Democratic candidate. The researcher collects county level voter percentages for the Democratic candidate across the U.S., along with county unemployment rates, and controls for education, income, age, and gender by collecting county percentages of county citizens with a bachelor's degree, county median household income, county median voter age, and county percentage of females. Running the statistical analysis reveals that county unemployment rate is not related to Democratic voting when including education, income, age, and gender. However, if the researcher eliminates income from the analysis, the unemployment rate variable becomes statistically significant. What is the researcher to do? One can add/eliminate data/variables to try to come up with statistically significant findings. This is known as data massaging or "p-hacking" to get statistically significant results. Later chapters will discuss p-values and how they relate to statistical significance, so by p-hacking, a researcher essentially "beats" the data into submission to show the results/relationship they want. This idea connects to issues of data ethics that are discussed in Section 1.6.

1.5 Visual/Graphing Manipulation

Visual images are used to convey messages, whether that be in visual arts like film or in data science with graphing. Ever notice how movie superheroes (like Batman) or villains (like Darth Vader) are filmed from low camera angles? This camera angle makes the character appear taller, in charge, or dominant to the viewer. It conveys a message of strength. Data visualization is an important aspect of statistics – taking

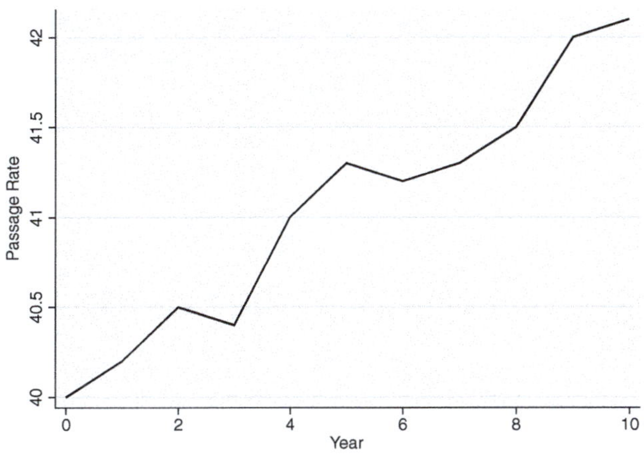

Figure 1.1 Passage rate trend for sophomores (Bragg's graph)

hundreds, thousands, or millions of datapoints and converting them into a readable graph or figure that can help researchers visualize data, making it more understandable for consumers of the data. However, data visualization can also be used to manipulate what the data report with graphing "tricks" that alter the perceptions of unaware viewers.

Here is a fictional, but relevant situation. School superintendent Ms. Bragg has been in charge of her district for the past ten years. When she was hired as the superintendent, she was tasked with bringing the school district's sophomore standardized state testing scores up from a dismal 40% pass rate. After ten years, the school board has asked her to make a presentation of how test scores have changed during her tenure as the school superintendent. The school board is considering not renewing Ms. Bragg's contract if test scores have not improved. Ms. Bragg presents her graph (Figure 1.1) to the school board, excitedly noting the sharp upward trend in the line graph. Year 0 is the district's state passage rate as she entered her position, and then she tracks the scores across each of her ten years as superintendent. She says that during her time as superintendent, there has been a steady and dramatic upward movement in passage rates.

A few school board members that only took a quick glance at the graph laud Ms. Bragg for a job well done. They are super impressed with the steep climb in the trend line. However, another school board member states that the graph is misleading. They note that the y-axis (Passage Rate) only ranges from about 40% to 43%, and that this makes the trend line deceptively steeper. This school board member has the district's raw data and presents a different graph of the passage rate trend, where the y-axis can range from all possible passage values (0% to 100%). Figure 1.2 displays the questioning school board member's graph.

The skeptical school board member highlights the relatively flat trend line now that the graph's scaling has been changed. While passing rates have increased over ten years, they have increased by small amounts. Was Ms. Bragg purposely

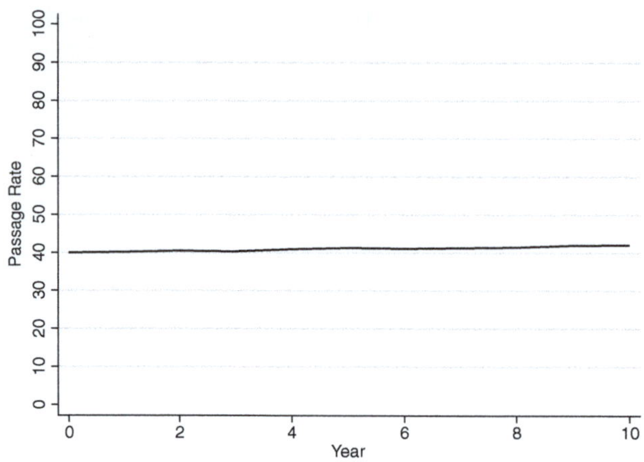

Figure 1.2 Passage rate trend for sophomores (school board member's graph)

manipulating her graph to make herself look better, or was it an honest mistake? Only Ms. Bragg knows, but this situation illustrates how students, researchers, and practitioners should always be looking at all components of data visuals to make sure they are accurately reporting what the data show and are not being deceived by fancy graph work.

1.6 Data and Research Ethics

Suppose researchers at a federal health agency want to study the effects of a potentially deadly disease going untreated in a population. They recruit subjects, identify those with the disease, do not tell them they have a potentially deadly (but treatable) disease (just that they are being treated for a potential wide range of ailments), and then let the disease run its course on those subjects? At the end of the study, subjects are not debriefed on what really occurred during the experiment nor the findings of the experiment. For the researchers, a great deal of scientific and biological information is obtained. Is this study ethical? Absolutely not. Most people would recognize the level of deception, omission of information, and general lack of empathy and care for human subjects. Unfortunately, such a similar research situation occurred with public health researchers in the Tuskegee Experiments. Poor African Americans in Alabama were recruited to participate in a study of untreated Syphillis.

Not all research may have such blatant ethical violations. Suppose a local fire department wants to train all of its personnel across more than twenty different stations in the city on how to improve their response time to emergencies. The chief of the fire department partners with researchers at a local university to study the effects of added training sessions on emergency response times. The researchers randomly assign ten fire stations to receive the initial training sessions, and the remainder to receive the trainings at a later date after data from the ten trained stations have been collected and analyzed. The researchers measure average response times from the ten trained fire departments and compare them to the remaining untrained fire departments. Data indicate that the training dramatically reduces fire department response times. Is this study ethical in its design and implementation?

At first glance, it may appear to be ethical in its design – ten stations were randomly selected to receive the training without any bias to station location, funding, personnel quality, etc. However, is it fair that the constituents living under the jurisdiction of those ten stations were able to benefit from the training, while the citizens in the other jurisdictions did not? The effects of fire and medical emergencies and adequate response to prevent loss of life and property come down to minutes and seconds for adequate emergency response. Maybe an individual suffering from a heart attack is saved by fire personnel who received the training, while another person suffering a heart attack in the untrained jurisdiction is now severely disabled or deceased. This research represents an experimental design, and even though experiments do exist in public administration applied and academic research, they must be carefully constructed so as to not benefit or harm one group compared to others. This is one reason true experiments are not widely used in public administration, especially if the researchers are studying services that may give benefits to a particular group of individuals, even if randomly chosen.

Though you may not be conducting health-related studies or engaging in a typical experimental research design, you must be aware of the effects of your study on human subjects, even if you are using relatively innocuous methods like surveys. The nature of your research and the types of questions you may ask respondents could induce severe mental trauma on some subjects. Sending a survey to elected officials on their positions across a wide range of potential public policies is fairly tame; they are elected officials, used to making public statements and facing tough questions, and research ethics boards are unlikely to place much scrutiny on a proposed survey to elected officials on policy positions. But what about a researcher sending a survey to military veterans on their combat experiences? Or a public health researcher sending a survey to sexual assault survivors on various coping mechanisms? For both of these groups, reliving traumatic experiences could have mental repercussions and cause stress. There would be serious ethical issues with sending these surveys. As researchers, we are obligated to do no harm – physical, mental, emotional, etc. – and to protect our human subjects.

Partly in response to the Tuskegee Syphillis experiments, the U.S. Department of Health, Education, and Welfare released the *Belmont Report* (National Commission for the Protection of Human Subjects of Biomedical and Behavioral Research, 1978) providing principles to follow when conducting research involving human subjects. Public universities increasingly established and utilized institutional review boards (IRBs) to review research proposals and protocols to ensure the protection of human subjects. Even to this day, researchers at universities undergo human subjects research training and are required to read the *Belmont Report* and engage in training modules based upon its principles for human subjects research.

Typically, researchers, especially students and academic faculty at colleges and universities, take human subjects training through the Collaborative Institutional Training Initiative (CITI) Program. Most academic institutions have partnered with this organization to allow their affiliated researchers (students and faculty) to take CITI's human subjects online training. In fact, any researcher wishing to publish or present their research is required to undergo this training and pass the quizzes to obtain their CITI certification in order to proceed with their human subjects research. Training information is available at www.citiprogram.org.

You can click the Register option with your college/university credentials to enroll and complete Human Subjects training. Most likely, the Group 3: Social/Behavioral Course will suffice for most students using this text. It focuses on human subjects for researchers conducting non-medical research focused on the social and behavioral sciences. If you are a student of public administration, political science, sociology, economics, or urban studies, this is likely the course for you. While the remainder of this chapter covers some of the ethical fundamentals of human subjects research, it cannot, nor should, substitute for the full CITI training. As part of your coursework, you may be asked to engage in some form of human subjects research. If this research is part of coursework and will not be presented or published, it is most likely exempt from needing IRB consideration. However, this exemption should not preclude you from treating your research and interactions with human subjects in accordance with IRB expectations and following the principles of the *Belmont Report*. As such, this final section of the chapter will introduce you to these principles and some practices in conducting ethical human subjects research.

The three basic principles outlined in the *Belmont Report* are Respect for Persons, Beneficence, and Justice. They are briefly defined below, and then their applications are considered for best practices in ethical research.

1.6.1 Respect for Persons

The principle of Respect for Persons emphasizes that individuals have agency and can/should be free to make their own decisions. Stated alternatively, as in the *Belmont Report*, individuals have autonomy, "capable of deliberation about personal goals and of acting under the direction of such deliberation" (National Commission for the Protection of Human Subjects of Biomedical and Behavioral Research, 1978, p. 4). Individuals should be able to make their own decisions as to whether or not they participate in a study and be provided information regarding the study and their participation in it (some research can involve deception if information regarding the study may affect the outcome of the results; however, these studies undergo greater IRB scrutiny and must adhere to more stringent requirements for debriefing of subjects after the study is finished).

Certain populations are considered protected/vulnerable given that they have less autonomy and/or mental capacity to voluntarily participate and engage in decision making. Most applicable to social science researchers are children (minors), mentally disabled individuals, and prisoners. Given their tender age, research involving minors usually receives greater IRB attention, and at a minimum, parental permission is required for their child's participation. For prisoners, confined and under the care/supervision of local, state, or federal institutions, particular care in regards to confidentiality and the perceived risks (negative reprisals for participation like greater likelihood of punishment) and benefits of participation (like prisoners receiving compensation or preferential treatment for participation), and the potential cognitive understanding of the risks, benefits, and other parameters of the research should be anticipated to the best extent possible by the researchers. Considerations for cognitive abilities to understand the risks and benefits of participation in the research is also an ethical consideration for the inclusion of mentally disabled individuals in research, especially in terms of obtaining their permission to participate, known as informed consent. Greater attention is needed to ensure some populations are able to fully understand the risks and benefits of their participation and to ensure they understand their participation is their decision, completely voluntary.

1.6.2 Beneficence

Summarized into a few simple, but powerful words, beneficence means to "do no harm." Preventing physical harm is a pretty obvious criterion. In the 1984 Hollywood blockbuster *Ghostbusters*, one of the opening scenes involves parapsychologist Dr. Peter Venkman holding up an enlarged playing card to subjects with the image on one side of the card only visible Dr. Venkman. He asks the subjects to guess the image. The subjects are attached to electrodes. If they incorrectly guess the image on the card, they receive an electric shock, which increases in intensity for each additional negative guess of new cards. His stated goal is to understand extrasensory perception (ESP) and how these shocks affect ESP ability. Under today's standards and guidelines, Dr. Venkman's research would never pass IRB review. It causes harm (physical) and is simply unethical.

This scene is a result of the directors being motivated by Stanley Milgram's obedience experiments involving shock punishments (that actually were not real shocks being administered) (Ramis, 2005). There were two groups of subjects – one group was the learners, or individuals answering cognitive questions. They were in on the fix, or known as confederates, instructed by the study designers to incorrectly answer questions. The other group of subjects were the evaluators, responsible for implementing a negative reinforcement method to the learners for incorrectly answering a question – an electric shock – one that increased in intensity for each subsequent incorrect answer from the learner. Learners and evaluators were positioned in two separate rooms. Each time the learner answered a question incorrectly, the evaluator was instructed to administer an electric shock to the learner. No actual electric shocks were used, but the evaluators believed they actually were administering increasing voltages to the learners. Evaluators listened to fake (but realistic) screams from the learners as they administered the shocks. The study designers simply stated that the experiment must continue, even when the evaluators displayed some ambivalence to administering the perceived physical shocks. Some participants continued to administer shocks when directed despite nonresponsive learners to high voltages (essentially administering shocks to the point of deeming the learner unconscious or deceased). Even those evaluators showing ambivalence to continuing the experiment were told by the administrators that the experiment must continue.

Certainly a great deal of psychological knowledge regarding obedience was learned from this experiment. The experiment administrators represented authority figures and instructed evaluators to continue administering shocks to learners despite clear concerns among the evaluators. It revealed a great deal of scientific knowledge about authority and obedience that can likely explain many historical atrocities. However, in its original design, Milgram's experiment would likely have not been approved by an IRB or it would have been required to be severely altered. Subjects, especially the evaluators, were not explicitly given information regarding their voluntary participation. They could have felt compelled to complete the study's tasks despite real reservations and concerns. Second, post-traumatic stress or mental anxiety could have occurred with subject participants administering the shocks, albeit fake ones. The perceived belief of causing physical harm on another individual up to killing them could cause short- or long-term mental stress for the participants.

Though it is highly unlikely public administration researchers are going to engage in similar types of research or research deception, the Milgram experiment illustrates the concept of "do no harm." In the opening paragraph to this section, it was noted that one could cause emotional or mental distress/harm from certain types of survey questions, notably surveys asking respondents about traumatic experiences. Researchers studying topics like veteran PTSD or coping mechanisms for sexual assault survivors must be ever more cognizant of their research designs to prevent such harm, and IRBs will certainly engage in greater scrutiny to ensure the research does not harm subjects.

1.6.3 Justice

The third principle advocated by the *Belmont Report* is justice. The report states, "An injustice occurs when some benefit to which a person is entitled is denied without good reason or when some burden is imposed unduly" (National Commission for the Protection of Human Subjects of Biomedical and Behavioral Research, 1978, p. 5). In regards to human subjects research, participants should be treated equally and not systematically denied the benefits of the study or systematically face the risks of a study compared to others. Refer back to the fire department response time at the beginning of this section. Had the researchers engaged in a true experimental design whereby a random sample of fire departments received training to improve response times and the other stations did not, one could clearly critique that design on justice grounds – one group benefits disproportionately compared to another group – constituents receiving service from the trained units may experience better response times, which can positively affect survival rates in medical emergencies and decrease property damage in fire emergencies.

1.6.4 Best Practices for Human Subjects Research

IRB-approved research requires that researchers obtain *informed consent* from subjects regarding their agreement to participate in the research study. Obtaining informed consent is one method to help ensure that the principles of Respect for Persons, Beneficence, and Justice are upheld. Common practice is for researchers to have an approved informed consent letter that subjects (or their guardians) read, understand, agree to, and sign. If research is being conducted through non-physical presence means (like telephone, video conferencing, etc.) researchers still must obtain verbal informed consent. An example informed consent letter is located on the Companion Site (www.cambridge.org/scheller) for interested students.

Informed consent letters typically contain all relevant information regarding the study and the subjects' rights, along with any anticipated risks and/or benefits from their participation in the study. Researchers are not necessarily required to explain in full detail their hypotheses or research expectations in the informed consent letter, but should provide some basic information for the subjects. A study using a survey to understand citizen's policy preferences may have a statement like, "You have been selected to participate in a survey on voter policy preferences. You will be presented with some policy options for common issues faced by local, state, and the national governments and asked how much you would support such policies. Other demographic information regarding you and your household will also be asked like your age, gender, education level, etc." Such a statement provides a brief overview of what the study is about and the types of questions asked. It is also good practice to then indicate the amount of time required for their participation.

Another best practice and requirement of informed consent is to indicate that their participation is completely voluntary and that they may withdraw from the study at any time without penalty. For example, if subjects are being recruited to participate in a focus group and paid $20 for showing up, and an individual about halfway through the focus group decides they want/need to leave, they must be allowed to do so and still receive their show-up payment of $20. If they were promised $20 for showing up, but have to leave, they should not be punished.

Subjects should be aware of the anticipated risks and benefits from their participation in the study. These may not appear to be obvious in non-medical studies, but as mentioned previously, conducting research on vulnerable populations can sometimes elicit mental or emotional stress. In the sexual assault coping mechanism example, the informed consent letter would likely require the researchers to have language indicating the types of questions that will be asked and indicating that for some individuals, answering questions about previous traumatic experiences may induce mental and emotional stress. Such sensitive research topics require more explicit and descriptive language in the informed consent letters so that subjects are aware of what they may be getting into in regards to sensitive and emotionally triggering questions/topics.

While informed consent letters may appear to be legal documents (in many respects, they are legal documents to protect human subjects and also universities), they should be written in a comprehensible manner so that the average person can understand what they are reading and fully understand their rights during the study and any associated risks/benefits. It is difficult to give informed consent if one does not fully understand what one is reading. Another good practice is to inform subjects to take as much time as needed when reading the informed consent letter and to encourage them to ask any questions if they do not understand and/or have concerns. Finally, if the study is being conducted in-person, subjects should sign the informed consent letter. For electronic surveys, subjects can electronically sign a document, or more likely, the researcher can embed a response item in the survey software asking subjects if they have read and understand the consent letter and to indicate that they consent to proceeding.

1.7 Summary

The description of the topics covered in this first chapter only grazes the surface of current and historical issues in public administration research. Entire books and courses can, and are, devoted to issues like research ethics, data manipulation, and contemporary issues/trends in public administration. The purpose here is to not only introduce you to ideas and issues in public administration, but to orient your thinking towards that of a public administration researcher, aware of ongoing research design issues like data manipulation and the ethical conduct of research. This chapter hopefully piqued your interest in public administration research and statistics, compelling you to think in terms of questions to be answered with data analysis. Many of the vignettes and their themes/controversies will be revisited throughout this textbook. Some of the terms may appear foreign to you or like academic and mathematical jargon, like regression, interactive relationships, median, etc. However, they are all covered in this textbook and should become less intimidating and more widely used terms for you as a public administration student.

Some of the journals cited in the text and in the references section may also be new to you. Studies published in academic journals usually undergo strict review standards before they are accepted for publication. Upon completion of a research manuscript, authors send their manuscript to a journal. The manuscript is then sent to three or four external reviewers in the field of study to review and critique. Reviewers do not know the identity of the authors, nor do the authors know the identity of the reviewers (process known as blind peer-review). Nearly every manuscript receives either an invitation to revise/resubmit or a rejection. Very few manuscripts are accepted outright. With a revise/resubmit decision, authors make changes to their manuscript and may even need to go back to collect more data. It is then sent back to the reviewers for consideration again. Some of the most prestigious journals have final acceptance rates as low as 10%. All of this is to highlight the rigor used to evaluate academic studies in journals. Applied studies conducted by think tanks, nonprofit organizations, government departments, etc. all have merit. You may even rely on them for your own research. However, they likely undergo less scrutiny before being published, and thus the emphasis in this textbook on published research in journals.

The next two chapters focus on the basics of research design. Some public administration programs have students enroll in an entire semester-length course in research design; other programs combine research design and statistics into a single course. Even though the emphasis of this textbook is on public administration statistics, its information could be less accessible to students in programs that do not have a stand-alone research design course. So, Chapters 2 and 3 present information on how to design research, from developing research questions and hypotheses to operationalizing these into measurable variables that can be analyzed with statistics software. For students that have had a stand-alone research design course, these chapters should be review material. For those students in courses that combine research design and statistics into one course, Chapters 2 and 3 should provide enough information on research design so that you can conduct your own research and understand the language used in subsequent chapters.

PRACTICE PROBLEMS

1. Visit the National Academy of Public Administration's webpage listing and description of the twelve grand challenges: https://napawash.org/grand-challenges/the-12-grand-challenges. Review some of the grand challenges not covered in this chapter. For one of the grand challenges not covered in this chapter:
   a. Identify the grand challenge and then explain the grand challenge in your own words.
   b. Why is this a grand challenge of importance for public administration practitioners?
   c. Using a news source from your local community or community for which you are familiar, find a relevant public administration or public policy issue being faced by the community as it applies to your chosen grand challenge.
      i. Explain the issue and how it applies to the grand challenge.
      ii. What are some proposed solutions to the challenge, or if solutions are not identified, what solutions can you come up with and why?
2. Pick any of the twelve grand challenges identified by NAPA and find an academic journal article that addresses some aspect of that grand challenge using statistics (preferably not an article cited in this chapter).

   a. Provide the article citation and then briefly explain what the researchers study and how they go about studying it.
      i. What is their research question if you can identify it?
      ii. What is their source of data?
      iii. What statistical test do they use?
   b. What are the main findings of the study?
   c. How can the research findings be of use to public administrators working in the field/applied settings?

3. Come up with three different research questions that you would like to study as part of a paper for your course. List them below. (Caveat: There are obviously no right or wrong answers to this question, and you may have trouble coming up with questions; however, give it a try.)

4. In the scenarios below, suppose researchers have found correlations between the phenomena listed and have made some bold conclusions. What other factors may be relevant or causing the observed correlations/relationships?
   a. Researchers notice a relationship between the rise in new voter registrations for U.S. presidential elections and leaves falling from trees. Conclusion: Leaves dying and falling cause people to be motivated to register to vote.
   b. State education officials notice that test scores across the country for ten year olds have declined from a high in 2019 to much lower levels in 2020 and 2021, with a slight uptick in 2022. Conclusion: Children born in 2010 and 2011 are systematically less intelligent than children born before and after 2010 and 2011.
   c. The virus that caused Covid-19 tended to spread more effectively in areas with greater number of elected town/city officials identifying as Democrats. Conclusion: Liberal town/city public health policies increased cases of Covid-19.

5. The following data come from the U.S. Bureau of Labor Statistics (BLS), available at the following website: www.bls.gov/charts/employment-situation/civilian-unemployment-rate.htm. It contains nine months of unemployment rate data. It has been put into a table below.
   a. Assume you are a special advisor to the Secretary of Labor who has been asked by the President to present data on unemployment rates over the past nine months. The Secretary of Labor entrusts you to come up with a graph of the unemployment rates. They bring you into their office and say the President is hoping to present data on unemployment rates to show their economic plan has been providing jobs and decreasing the unemployment rate. The Secretary says, "Make it look good and reflective of the White House's message that unemployment rates are drastically declining." Using paper and pen or a computer if you are so inclined, construct a line graph with month on the horizontal axis and unemployment rate on the vertical axis.

b. Assume you are communications director for Senate Minority Leader, Republican Mitch McConnell. Senator McConnell wants to counter the President's claim that unemployment rates are drastically declining. He has tasked you with taking the data below and presenting it in a line graph to convey the Republican Party's message that while unemployment rates have decreased, they have only slowly decreased and not by large margins. Using paper and pen or a computer if you are so inclined, construct such a line graph with month on the horizontal axis and unemployment rate on the vertical axis.

c. Assume you are a data analyst for a non-partisan think tank that tracks economic data and provides briefs on the state of the economy. The mission of the think tank is to provide policy makers and analysts with unbiased information and analysis of data. You have been tasked to present nine-month unemployment rate data and trends in a line graph. Using paper and pen or a computer if you are so inclined, construct such a line graph with month on the horizontal axis and unemployment rate on the vertical axis.

d. You have produced three different graphs. Explain how and why you chose to construct the graphs for each scenario.

Unemployment Rates

Month	Unemployment Rate
Sept. 2021	4.7
Oct. 2021	4.6
Nov. 2021	4.2
Dec. 2021	3.9
Jan. 2022	4.0
Feb. 2022	3.8
Mar. 2022	3.6
Apr. 2022	3.6
May 2022	3.6

6. For many years, city employees worked five eight-hour workdays during the week. Recently, the city manager piloted a new program by having employees work four ten-hour workdays in the hopes that employees would be more satisfied with three-day weekends and productivity would increase. At the end of the pilot program, the city manager sent a survey to city employees measuring their opinions on the four ten-hour workdays compared to their experiences with the traditional five eight-hour workdays. The main survey question of interest for the city manager is: "I prefer the four ten-hour workdays model to the five eight-hour workdays model. Please indicate how much you agree with this statement by selecting ‘Strongly agree, Agree, Neutral, Disagree, or Strongly disagree.’ The city manager collects the responses and finds the following:

Strongly agree: 5 %
Agree: 46%
Neutral: 10%
Disagree: 20%
Strongly disagree: 19%

a. Suppose the city manager is adamantly opposed to the four-day workweek. How can they “lie with statistics” to present information against the four-day workweek?
b. Suppose the city manager is adamantly for the four-day workweek. How can they “lie with statistics” to present information supporting the four-day workweek?

7. Each of the following scenarios presents ethical issues in the conduct of research. For each, explain what the ethical issue is, how it may violate a principle in the *Belmont Report*, and provide a design improvement that is more ethical.

a. Suppose researchers invite citizens from the community to come to the local public university to participate in a focus group where individuals will engage in discussion about various policies to improve life in the city. Once all participants arrive, the researchers tell them that the focus group session will last two hours and that everybody is required to stay the entire two hours. Sixty minutes into the focus group session, an individual receives a phone call and they state they must leave due to an emergency. The researchers strongly implore (quite angrily) the participant to remain for the entirety of the session and pressure them to remain.
b. A researcher wants to understand how small grants may affect community development activities in a city. Their city is extremely diverse across all categories of economics and demographics (race, income, education, etc.). The researcher has received $100,000 in research funds to conduct their research. As part of their research protocol, they indicate that they will give five, $20,000 awards to neighborhoods for their use to promote community development. These five neighborhoods will serve as “treatment groups,” or neighborhoods that receive the funds. All other neighborhoods will not receive any money. The researcher will track the types of community development activities occurring in each of the treatment and control neighborhoods, measuring the number of activities engaged for each neighborhood. The researcher decides to distribute the funds to five predominantly Asian neighborhoods, believing they have been most underrepresented in receiving development funds.

c. A researcher wants to understand the effects of bullying on public school children's (Kindergarten–12th grade) self-esteem. The researcher connects with school counselors to identify students that have the most experiences being bullied. Throughout the school year, the researcher interviews each of the identified students during recess asking them to recount their experiences with bullying and how it made them feel. The researcher hopes to publish their findings in the top journal in public education.

2

Basic Research Design

2.1 Introduction

Conducting research is not simply just finding data and running analyses. Any type of data can be collected/entered into a spreadsheet, loaded into software like the R Commander, a few buttons "pushed" or clicked, and output will result. Does it mean that the output actually tells us anything about the social or public administration world? Not necessarily. Researchers must be meticulous in how they design their research studies – how they collect and analyze data – or else they may come to false or biased conclusions. Statistics software will "spit out" results/output no matter how poorly or adequately collected the data or designed the research. Even though the focus of this textbook is on how and when to run specific types of statistical tests, the front-end of research – the design phase – is of the utmost importance for researchers to conduct rigorous scientific research and to make conclusions and recommendations from their data analysis. This is why entire courses are devoted solely to different types of research design. In some MPA and PhD in public administration programs, students are required to pass a research design course before they can take a data analysis or statistics course. When it comes to research design, think of the phrase "garbage in, garbage out." A garbage research design will likely yield garbage data, garbage data analysis, garbage data conclusions, and garbage policy/program recommendations.

It should be noted that while this chapter covers some of the most common research designs in public administration along with instruction on how to engage in research design, it should not replace an entire semester course devoted to research design. For students in programs where there is a separate research design course from a statistics/data analysis course, this chapter should be used as a review chapter, or a refresher on the main topics of research design in the social sciences and public administration. For students in programs that combine research design and statistics into one course, this chapter should suffice to present the most important concepts to be able to conduct individual research to engage in data analysis. While it does not cover every possible research scenario, it should provide enough instruction to complete research for a capstone or thesis project. As such, the bulk of this chapter focuses on the research design process, from the development of a research question and hypotheses to reporting results. Different types of designs (experimental versus non-experimental) are discussed. Given the growth of surveys in public administration and student interest, the final portion of the chapter describes survey design and implementation.

2.2 Philosophy of Science

Most published public administration research is scientific in nature, as it should be. Even though it may be difficult to imagine public administration studies and research as "science," well-conducted research is conducted scientifically. One may think that scientific research is only conducted in the hard sciences like biology, chemistry, medicine, physics, etc. To be sure, public administration researchers are not using chemicals, petri dishes, test vials, and models of machines; however, much like researchers in the hard sciences, public administration researchers engage in systematic processes and methods in their research. It is these systematic and rigorous processes/rules/procedures/methods that put the science in the social sciences (Frankfort-Nachmias and Nachmias, 2008; Singleton & Straits, 2005). Like the fields of political science, sociology, and economics, where academics and other researchers engage in scientific research, the goal is the same in public administration research – to contribute to knowledge, explain patterns and relationships (Frankfort-Nachmias and Nachmias, 2008), and/or to reveal causes of phenomena (Meier et al., 2015) in an unbiased manner. Then, how does a researcher go about engaging in unbiased, rigorous research? Much like the scientific method you may have learned in middle or high school, the processes are similar, but have greater complexity.

At this point, you may be thinking that your goal in research, or more specifically, what you may be tasked to do in your job, is not to "produce knowledge" in the same manner as public administration scholars and academics that publish their research in books and journals. Maybe you have been asked to determine if your organization's employees have higher levels of satisfaction after the organization switches to a new insurance contract. Or maybe you work for a nonprofit organization promoting alternative modes of transportation and your boss needs you to collect data on the effects of a recent local policy putting bicycle lanes on a busy street – level of usage, number of accidents, and number of cyclist traffic violations with the new lanes – all for the purpose of giving your boss information that they can use to lobby local government for more bicycle lanes and/or changes to the current lanes. If you were the researcher in each of these cases or similar situations in your own job, you are unlikely to be publishing your results in academic journals. However, the end goal is still the same – the pursuit of knowledge. If you engage in systematic and rigorous processes/rules/procedures/methods in the pursuit of this knowledge, you can be more confident that your "knowledge" is accurate and reflects the phenomena under study. That you are not publishing the results does not make it any less scientific – the science is in the systematic and rigorous research methods.

The focus of scientific research is the production of knowledge. The generation of this knowledge should be unbiased and not based upon a researcher's opinions, desires, or political ideology. Certainly, a supervisor may want you to present research in line with the organization's goals or mission and you may be compelled to "spin" findings in a favorable direction or to "lie with statistics." Doing so would take the science out of the knowledge if the research methods and/or conclusions were manipulated in a biased manner. Scientific research is also non-normative (Singleton & Straits, 2005) or does not involve the pursuit or declaration of what "should" be done. Normative considerations, or what should be done, are based upon opinion, and while scientific research may be used by policymakers to make certain decisions, it is not up to the scientific researcher to conclude what should be done regarding a situation in the social sciences. For example, suppose a public administration researcher finds that an after-school sports program improves student achievement and classroom behavior, but only for middle-class male students. There is no effect on the program for females and no effect of the program for poor and wealthy male students. Should the researcher conclude that the program should be ended, expanded, amended? For a scientific researcher, that is of no importance – their goal is to present unbiased findings in the pursuit of information provision and the development of knowledge. Other decision makers must use this information accordingly in making their decisions.

2.3 Dependent and Independent Variables

Does one thing cause another – increased education to more income? Type of city government and citizen satisfaction with city services? Percent of population vaccinated against a disease and deaths from disease? All of these questions present potential relationships between two variables, an independent variable and a dependent variable. Does one variable affect or cause another variable? Does increased education lead to more income? Does the type of city government affect levels of citizen satisfaction? Do increased vaccinations against a disease lead to fewer deaths from the disease? All of these questions implicitly reveal empirical, testable questions about the relationship between two variables. Before delving into research design, understanding the difference between dependent and independent variables is an important step in being able to design and implement a rigorous research project.

Much of social science and public administration research seeks to determine the relationship between variables and to determine any causal relationship between such variables. Such relationships are usually described as an independent variable affecting, causing, or being related to a dependent variable. The types of statistics researchers are able to report and the specific statistical test are completely dependent upon identifying/stipulating a dependent variable and independent variable(s). Additionally, the level of measurement (nominal, ordinal, or interval/continuous) of both the dependent and independent variable dictate what statistics can be reported and statistical tests run that test the relationship between these variables. One of the most important definitions to differentiate and understand is that of a dependent variable versus an independent variable.

A dependent variable depends upon independent variable(s). It is affected by, or a function of, the independent variable(s). In each of, the empirical questions/statements above, the dependent variables are: income, citizen satisfaction with city services, and deaths from a disease. The dependent variable is the concept or phenomenon which we seek to explain. It "depends" upon other variables or "things." In the above statements, the independent variables are education, type of city government, and percent of population vaccinated against a disease. Each of these variables does the affecting of the dependent variable, or the dependent variable is dependent upon them. The next section discusses research design. In the relationships described in the upcoming sections, think about which concepts or variables represent the dependent variable and which concepts or variables represent the independent variables.

2.4 Research Design Process

How does one come up with a research topic or idea? There are no hard and fast rules for picking a research topic and research question (King et al., 1994; Popper, 1968). What may be of interest to you may not be of interest to others. You may think that studying Theory X and Theory Y styles of management (McGregor, 1957) and their effects on worker productivity in the Department of Agriculture are interesting, while a classmate or other scholar thinks studying the effects of red-light cameras at stoplights on drivers running red lights is at the forefront of scientific importance. King et al. (1994) suggest picking a topic of significance in real-world settings and a topic that can add to the extant findings in the literature. These suggestions are definitely sage advice for researchers in academia and/or for researchers looking to advance scientific knowledge through publishing in a journal. However, in the real-world, public administration practitioners may not be seeking to advance this knowledge for publication. Maybe their topic has been given to them, like their boss asking them to conduct a survey of the organization and report the findings, or them being asked to determine if a pilot program achieved its intended results. While the results will not be published publicly, the results are still important for the practitioner and the end-goal is still the same – to understand and/or explain. While the findings may not have implications for academic research, they certainly have an effect for the practitioner's organization that will use the results for further decision making. Therefore, the principles of rigorous scientific research design that somebody conducting a study to publish in the leading public administration journal uses should also be used by the practitioner or public administrator conducting small-scale applied research in their work setting.

Conducting research either for academic or for practitioner purposes requires the systematic use of scientific processes to ensure confidence in the design and ultimately the results. De Vaus (2001, p. 9) states that "The function of a research design is to ensure that the evidence obtained enables us to answer the initial question as unambiguously as possible." A bevy of textbooks in the social sciences and their subfields, including some in public administration, typically present the same basic steps in the research design process. Some present the five main steps, and others are more in-depth, with a seven-step approach, sometimes using different terms, but all generally reflecting the same process. For the purposes of this textbook, the seven-step approach is used, adapted from Nishishiba et al. (2014) and Frankfort-Nachmias and Nachmias (2008). The steps are: *Problem Identification, Generation of a Research Question, Hypothesis Development, Research Design, Data Collection, Data Analysis, Reporting and Conclusions.*

2.4.1 Problem Identification

The first two steps in the research design process (Problem Identification and Generation of Research Question) may or may not work in lock-step motion. Public administration researchers may first identify a problem that is intriguing to them. Problems could be evident and clear to the researcher or they could be perceived problems that need additional observations. This step is also often referred to as the Research Objective or Problem Definition stage. Below are some potential "problems" that researchers may initially observe that compel them to engage in research:

a. A manager notices that younger workers are less motivated by monetary incentives for performance compared to older workers.
b. A federal agency report indicates that fentanyl overdoses are increasing in rural areas of the U.S.
c. A fire department wants to improve emergency response times and is considering the use of certain training modules to help emergency responders.

2.4.2 Generation of a Research Question

Researchers may not have a specific problem identified, but begin their process with a research question that they want to test. Several examples across public administration and policy may be:

a. Do rent controls lead to more or less affordable rental units in a city?
b. Do sexual harassment trainings lead to fewer sexual harassment incidents in the workplace?
c. Why do some cities adopt climate change action plans compared to other cities?
d. What is the effect of a new budgeting system on cost savings?

e. What is the effect of the free/reduced school lunch program on student achievement?

Each of these research questions is stated in a manner that is testable, whereby data can be collected and analyzed.

In Section 2.4.1, the researcher identified a problem first. If this is the case, then the natural next step is to produce a research question from the problem identification. Plausible research questions for the three scenarios in Section 2.4.1 could be:

a. A manager notices that younger workers are less motivated by monetary incentives for performance compared to older workers.

   Research Question 1: Are younger workers less motivated by monetary incentives than older workers?
   Research Question 2: Are the effects of monetary incentives for performance motivation smaller as the age of the employee decreases?

In this situation, the research problem is easily turned into a research question simply by phrasing it as a question. The researcher likely would then need to define younger versus older workers and how to measure motivation, but these are later steps in the research process. Two research questions are presented to show how both are legitimate questions, but Research Question 2 is more specific and defined with an anticipated direction of the relationship, which can be more readily formulated into a *directional hypothesis*. This concept of directional hypotheses as a means to promote increased testability of research questions is discussed below in section 2.4.3.

b. A federal agency report indicates that fentanyl overdoses are increasing in rural areas of the U.S.

   Research Question: Are per capita fentanyl overdoses higher in rural areas compared to urban areas?

This problem needs more specificity given the nature of rural versus urban. One could feasibly collect data on overdoses in rural versus urban areas, with the absolute number of overdoses naturally higher in urban areas since they have larger populations. Therefore, the research question takes into consideration size of area by using a per capita, or per person, measure.

c. A fire department wants to improve emergency response times and is considering the use of certain training modules to help emergency responders.

   Research Question: Does the new training module decrease emergency response times?

This example is fairly straightforward. A department wants to know if their policy/program (a training module) is effective.

Whether or not the researcher has a research question in mind immediately or if they identify a problem and then must generate a research question, a few best practices for generating research questions are evident.

1) The research questions are specific and narrow. De Vaus (2001) notes that the research question moves beyond the statement of a general topic into a specific question of interest that the researcher wants to answer.

2) It may be necessary to further narrow the research question for testing. In the age of worker and monetary incentive example, the initial problem was that the researcher anecdotally noticed that younger workers are less motivated by monetary incentives than older workers. Research Question 1 asked, *"Are younger workers less motivated by monetary incentives than older workers?"* As noted above, the researcher would need to do some additional work defining young versus old. Additionally, the point of the research in the first place is to determine what motivates workers to perform. The problem identified was that it seemed that younger workers were not as motivated to perform from monetary incentives compared to older workers. Research Question 2 gets into more specifics, stating that as the age of the worker increases, monetary incentives are less likely to motivate them to perform. This question is much more specific with easily measurable components. Age is easier to define and quantify than "young" or "old." A researcher could feasibly conduct a survey asking employees if they received a raise versus extra vacation days and if they would be more motivated to perform and then compare responses across ages.

At this stage of the research process, it is also common for researchers, if they have not done so already, to begin the literature review portion of the report/paper. It is first important to determine if the specific research question has already been addressed by other researchers and what they find. As a student, you likely have already done a literature review or a paper similar to a literature review in other classes. Conducting a literature review typically involves searching for journal articles, books, applied studies, etc. that either address your research question or larger topic area. Synthesizing and summarizing the nature of the current literature for your research topic/question is an important step in the research process to not only explain to the reader what previous studies have found, but to also help you develop hypotheses from your research question. Maybe there are nuances to your specific question/topic that make your study unique or the potential findings innovative. Conducting a literature review can also inform you on how other researchers engaged in their research process and analysis that may help you determine what specific data to collect and statistical tests to conduct.

2.4.3 Hypothesis Development

A hypothesis is an informed guess stemming from the research question regarding the concepts, phenomena, or variables of interest. It may also seek to explain a causal relationship between concepts, phenomena, or variables of interest (Leedy & Ormrod, 2010; Nishishiba et al., 2014). A hypothesis can be defined as the expected relationship between an independent and a dependent variable. All of these descriptions and definitions of a hypothesis are valid and show the range of what can be considered a hypothesis. It may also be considered a statement of expectation, based upon theory, observations, the extant literature, or logic that can be empirically tested.

For academic researchers, hypotheses may stem from gaps in the literature or basic observations in the field. Practitioners operating in the public sector may develop hypotheses from their interactions and observations in the workplace (Nishishiba et al., 2014). Whatever setting one may be required to conduct research, suggestions for developing testable hypotheses are still the same. Meier et al. (2015) offer two main suggestions for the generation of hypotheses. First, they argue that hypotheses need to contain elements that are measurable. If a hypothesis includes the concept of wealth, it must be measurable, which naturally is likely measured by income. A more difficult concept to measure is something like satisfaction. The researcher would need to ensure that they can measure satisfaction – probably through a survey with a question or series of questions asking how satisfied the respondent is in a given situation. A much more difficult, if not impossible concept to measure is morality. Attempting to create a measure of whether or not a policy, institution, or individual is moral is probably not measurable. Not only is morality subjective, but what would be used to measure levels of morality?

Second, Meier et al. (2015) argue that the hypothesis should provide the expected relationship, stated concisely. Basically, it is better to have a directional hypothesis (when applicable) that explains the predicted pattern among the concepts hypothesized. As an example of a hypothesis that is measurable and directional, take the fire department research question: *Does the new training module decrease emergency response times?* Response times are obviously measurable if they are collected by the fire department. The use of a training module (yes/no or before training/after training) is measurable as it can be observed whether or not the unit engaged in the training. A hypothesis of "Training matters," would be concise, but would not express a direction of the expected relationship. A measurable, concise, and directional hypothesis would be: "The training module decreased response times."

A more difficult research question to generate a hypothesis is the generational motivation question: *Are the effects of monetary incentives for performance motivation smaller as the age of the employee decreases?* A plausible hypothesis could be: "As the age of an employee increases, they are less motivated by monetary incentives for performance." Age of employee is relatively easy to measure. How would motivation from monetary incentives be measured? A researcher could simply survey employees, asking them a battery of questions about different incentive programs, asking which programs they think would motivate them to be more productive. The questions could involve monetary incentives like raises or bonuses. Comparative questions could ask about non-monetary incentives like extra vacation days or employee awards. Other designs surely exist, but the key point is that the concepts must be measurable, and when applicable, the hypothesis should specify a predicted direction.

The hypotheses we have been developing are known as research or alternative hypotheses. They are usually represented by an upper-case H with a numerical subscript identifying which number hypothesis it is in the research (assuming that the researcher has multiple hypotheses). So, for the fire training hypothesis, it could be labeled:

H_1: The training module decreases emergency response times.

The null hypothesis is a statement of no effect. Given that a research hypothesis indicates a relationship between two variables or a causal direction between them, the null hypothesis states there is no relationship between variables. The null hypothesis is usually represented by an upper-case H with a 0 subscript. Applied to the employee motivation research hypothesis, a null hypothesis would be:

H_0: The training module has no effect on emergency response times.

The null hypothesis depicts no relationship or no effect, thus its name as the null hypothesis. What is the point of a null hypothesis? In research, the goal is to test empirically based hypotheses. The answer lies in the philosophy of science and the acceptance of the fact that our hypotheses could be wrong. Hypotheses should thus be falsifiable (Popper, 1968) and stated in such a manner. We must be willing to acknowledge that they can be nullified. In the case of the emergency response training modules, we must accept the idea that the training may not work and that it has no effect. Berman and Wang (2018) describe the importance of the null hypothesis in terms of the percent chance of being incorrect with the goal of rejecting the null hypothesis (and thus accepting the research hypothesis). When we engage in hypothesis testing, we allow for a certain level of error, usually 5%. If we are able to reject the null hypothesis of no difference/no effect, we can reject that there is greater than 5% chance of error in our estimates. With this threshold, as we will see in future chapters on hypothesis testing, we can claim support for our research hypothesis.

2.4.4 Research Design

Once a researcher has established their research question and hypothesis, the next step is developing a plan to test the hypothesis, or a plan of action, so to speak. The research question dictates what type of design to use. While the focus of this text is on quantitative research designs using data collection methods and quantitative statistical analyses of such data, the research question may dictate the use of a qualitative design. For example, if a researcher wants to understand the thought processes and decision-making criteria of public managers on a daily basis, it is probably best to interview them. Such "data" and information needed by the researcher are unlikely to be adequately collected through an existing database or even through surveys. Such in-depth information is likely only obtained through interviews, and entire courses exist dedicated to the rigorous design and implementation of qualitative methods.

Research questions dictating the use of a quantitative design usually fall into one of three categories: experimental, non-experimental, or quasi-experimental. Each of these specific designs is considered in the next sections. Nevertheless, it is within this stage of the research process that the researcher needs to know the type of design they will be using and the specifics of the design. They may only need to collect secondary data that is already available through public sources. A researcher studying state budget deficits over time will likely be visiting state financial websites and pulling the data or using other online entities that collect this information and that make it publicly available. Likewise, a researcher wanting to determine if a new stoplight at an intersection decreases the number of accidents will solicit accident data from the police department or public works department, comparing daily accidents before and after the installation of the stoplight. Or a researcher may use the Census Bureau's American Community Survey to understand the relationship between urbanism and access to the Internet, believing that citizens in rural areas are less likely to have access to it.

Unfortunately, not all data may be available to researchers. One may have to simply generate the data itself. This, of course, is the most likely scenario if one is a practitioner charged with studying a particular aspect of their organization. A survey of job satisfaction in the auditing unit of the Alaska Department of Economic Development is unlikely to exist. If you are the analyst in that unit charged with understanding changes in job satisfaction in the unit, you are likely creating that data through a survey. It probably does not exist unless somebody beat you to the task and already conducted a survey. Or if you are in charge of studying if changing the operation hours of the local library increases daily traffic, you will likely be collecting data by having a staff member count the number of visitors or actually viewing security footage and counting the number of visitors before and after the change in hours.

It is during this stage of the research design process that you will need to identify how you will measure the concepts or the variables you wish to study. Covered in more detail in Chapter 3, this process is known as operationalization. Such is the term regarding the movement from concepts to variables to study. Variables must be measured with observable data, otherwise known as the operational definition of a concept. One question to ask as you move from concepts to their operationalization is "How do you measure that?" For example, suppose a researcher hypothesizes that rural citizens have less access to high speed internet than urban citizens. The main concepts of this hypothesis are that of rural v. urban and access to high speed internet. The concept of access to high speed internet can be fairly easily operationalized into whether or not the household has access to internet that meets a certain mb/second download/upload speed. This would likely be achieved through survey methods. The concept of rural may be defined by the researcher as an area falling below a certain population density level (population per square mile), or they may use an established designation like the Census-defined rural areas, noting whether or not the location is in a Census-designated rural area.

It is also in the research design section of the process where it is necessary to identify your unit of analysis, or the entity for which you will be collecting information. It can also be thought of as what each particular data point represents in your data spreadsheet. If conducting a survey of public sector workers, the unit of analysis would be the individual, more specifically, individual public sector workers. Each row of the spreadsheet would correspond to a unique respondent to the survey. John Doe would be a row if John responded. Then, if Jane Doe responded, she would have a row. If you are collecting budget data from state agencies, the unit of analysis is state agency. Each row would be a different agency. A little bit more complex is if you are collecting agency budgetary data over time, say for the past ten years. Then, you are collecting agency data by year and thus the unit of analysis is agency-year. Each row would be a particular agency year.

Identifying the unit of analysis will also help to establish the sample from which you will obtain the data or from whom/what you will collect the data. Even though a survey of individuals may be the desired tool of choice, the specific pool of individuals must be known. The population is all possible subjects from where you could obtain data. If the survey was directed towards public sector workers, then the population would be all public sector workers. If your population is smaller, like if you were interested in surveying the Florida Department of Education employees, then the population would be all of the employees in the Florida Department of Education. In either case, it is not likely you could survey the entire population. Therefore, a sample would be needed, and in your research design, you would identify that you would be taking a sample of public sector workers or a sample of Florida Department of Education employees. You would need to identify the ideal number or percentage of respondents from the population you seek to survey.

Other samples may come from non-human entities. If interested in state budgetary data, your sample selection would be which agencies you want to collect information from. If you wanted budgetary data from all of California's state agencies for one year, then the population would be all of the state agencies, and you could feasibly obtain that data. Your sample would then be the population – all California state agencies. However, if you wanted to conduct a budgetary analysis of every county's agencies in the U.S., the population would be every county department for all 3,243 counties. While technically possible to obtain this information, it would likely take too long to collect. Therefore, you could take a sample of counties in the U.S. and collect data on their agencies. Chapter 9 focuses in more detail on sampling and how/why we can make conclusions from samples to the larger population. However, for the purposes of this chapter and the steps in the research design process, the important skill is to be able to identify the sample from which data will be collected.

2.4.5 Data Collection

The data collection stage is when the researcher obtains the data in the most appropriate manner. If using secondary data from various sources, this stage would involve compiling the data into one spreadsheet for analysis. If the data are already in a single spreadsheet and ready for analysis, then the researcher is in luck and can immediately move on to analysis. Though an ideal situation, this is rarely the case, because even if all of the desired variables and data are in a single spreadsheet, there may need to be some data cleaning to get the data ready for analysis. This is a topic covered in Chapter 4.

If using a survey, this is the time when the researcher sends the survey and incorporates the responses into a data spreadsheet. If the researcher is in the field making observations, this is the time when they engage in this process and record their observations. As may be evident, the data collection stage varies widely in the time needed, depending upon data availability and ease of obtaining. Creating a single dataset from multiple sources and even conducting surveys can take months to accomplish, so it is always better to prepare for a worst-case scenario and to plan for any access obstacles by allocating extra time for this stage of the process.

2.4.6 Data Analysis

The bulk of this text is focused on the final two steps in the research design process: Data Analysis and then Reporting and Conclusions. Once all data have been entered in a spreadsheet, it is now time to analyze it using rigorous, scientific tools of analysis. The focus of this text is on quantitative or statistical analyses of data. Data analysis usually begins with some basic descriptive statistics as covered in Chapters 6–8. Running descriptive statistics gives the researcher a diagnostic view of the data, where they can see if there are any odd patterns in the data. Sometimes, you may only need to present descriptive statistics like means and medians for your report, and maybe a few visual graphs. If you are interested or tasked with more advanced analyses, then your analysis would likely extend into conducting the appropriate statistical test based upon your research question and data collected. From Chapter 10 onwards, each chapter presents a different statistical test to analyze data based upon the data collected. More often than not, if you are interested in actual statistical analyses beyond descriptive statistics, you will be using one of the tests covered in Chapters 10–20.

2.4.7 Reporting and Conclusions

Once you have run your data analyses, it is then time to interpret the findings into a report. Statistical software used during the data analysis stage will certainly "spit out" a wealth of numbers and other information, but it is essential to be able to interpret the output correctly, and then put it into the appropriate language for your audience so that they can understand the findings and implications. In the

Reporting and Conclusions stage, you present findings from the analysis, often in table-form, with written explanation of the numbers in the table. In addition to this, you may also present visual results (as covered in Chapter 8) to help illustrate your findings. Numbers in tables and their explanations are not always easily understood by all audiences. However, if research findings can be supported with visual aids like scatterplots or bar graphs, they can be a useful tool for comprehension.

All research should also have a Conclusion. If you are writing a paper or a report, you should conclude with what you found, and for many public administrators, you may be tasked with providing overarching suggestions for your conclusion. For example, if you find that a million-dollar training program did not achieve its intended results from your data analysis, it may be appropriate in the Conclusion to recommend altering the training or completely scrapping it from future use. If writing a more academic paper, Conclusions will likely focus on what your study found and whether or not it comports with previous findings. You may also discuss next steps in the research agenda based upon your findings.

2.4.8 A Note on Theory

Absent in the discussion of the research process has been theory. Practitioners likely are not using theory when conducting their research for reports. A data analyst for a public works department charged with determining if switching to a new and supposedly improved asphalt for the city streets decreased the amount of money and time spent on repairing them is unlikely to be invoking theory. If there is such a theory of asphalt quality/durability, it is probably rooted in the hard sciences like engineering or chemistry, something a public administration data analyst is unlikely to know or care about. Nevertheless, for academic studies, theory is often a key component of the research process, and may be the starting point in the process for which the researcher begins a study. For example, a theory on public sector worker motivation may state that public sector workers are less productive in top-down management styles (a la McGregor's [1957] Theory X v. Theory Y). A research question could emerge like, "How do public sector workers respond to top-down management styles?" Plausible hypotheses could include:

H_1 Public sector workers in top-down management style departments are less productive compared to public sector workers in more balanced management style departments.

The researcher would then need to define "top-down management style" v. "balanced management style," along with productivity, and ensure they could be empirically observed with data. They could then collect and analyze the data to test their hypothesis and ultimately the theory. This process refers to deductive reasoning and is an important component of many academic studies. As stated previously, as a practitioner, you are unlikely to be dealing with theory, but it is important to understand where it fits in the research process as studies you read while conducting a literature review may discuss and test theory.

2.5 Experimental, Quasi-Experimental, and Non-Experimental Designs

Research designs generally fall into one of two categories – experimental or non-experimental. The differences between the two designs lie in the amount of control the researcher has over the assignment of the unit of analysis to manipulations for study. Most public administration research by academics and practitioners will fall within the non-experimental category. However, some experiments do exist, and understanding experimental design can help students and researchers in public administration understand the necessity of using control variables in a regression, for example, if the data were not collected through an experimental design.

2.5.1 Experimental Design

Though most public administration researchers are not using test tubes and studying chemicals, medicines, or manipulations to biological agents, experimental design in the manner of what you may have learned about in science courses does exist, minus the chemicals, biological agents, and medicine. To better understand experiments in public administration, it is important to think back to the main design elements and concepts of hard science experiments that are included in biology, chemistry, and medical courses. Let us assume a medical study example, whereby scientists want to know if a new, experimental cancer drug reduces colon cancer tumor growth in patients receiving chemotherapy. They hypothesize that if patients receive both chemotherapy and the new, experimental drug, then tumor growth will decrease, effectively shrinking the tumors. Researchers at the hospital obtain a list of volunteers (colon cancer patients about to undergo chemotherapy) willing to participate in the study. A total of 100 people volunteer for the study. Each individuals' tumors are measured in millimeters. The researchers randomly assign fifty individuals to a treatment group, where all fifty individuals will receive the same chemotherapy regimen along with the new, experimental drug. The other fifty individuals are in the control group, receiving the same chemotherapy treatment as the treatment group individuals, but minus the new, experimental drug. They take a placebo or sugar pill. At the end of the trial, researchers measure each individual's tumor in millimeters. Changes in tumor sizes for members of the treatment group are compared to changes in tumor sizes for the control group.

In this medical, hard science example, what are the main elements of experimental research design? First, individuals are *randomly assigned* to treatment and control groups. There is no rhyme or reason as to why/how an individual was put into the treatment group v. the control group. Men were not more or less likely to be in the treatment group than women. Neither were older individuals. Neither were members of an underrepresented minority group. Assignment was totally at random. Essentially, names were drawn out of a hat to determine who was in the treatment group versus the control group. In reality, the more likely mechanism was that each of the 100 patients were assigned a number, and fifty numbers were drawn at random to be in the treatment group. The remaining fifty naturally would comprise the control group.

Random assignment to the treatment and control group ensures that everybody has an equal opportunity to be in the treatment group. Therefore, the probability that a fifty-year-old, white male smoker with a family history of colon cancer is in the treatment group is the same as the probability of a seventy-year old African American female non-smoker with no family history of colon cancer being in the treatment group. Thus, if the sample sizes are sufficiently large and random assignment to treatment and control groups has been used, there are no systematic differences between the treatment and control group. At the aggregate, the treatment group and the control group will look the same in all respects – age, race, gender, income, education, medical history, etc. The only difference will be that the treatment group receives the treatment, while the control group does not. In a diagram, this experimental design can be represented as:

Treatment Group:	RA	0	X	0
Control Group:	RA	0		0

RA refers to random assignment to the treatment and control groups. Each 0 represents a period of data collection or observation. X refers to the treatment, exogenous shock, or manipulation that the treatment group receives, which is absent from the Control Group. The final 0 refers to another round of observation or data collection. As described, the only difference between the treatment and the control group is that the treatment group receives the treatment or manipulation (represented by the X). Therefore, if using random assignment, and if the sample sizes are large enough, we can be reasonably confident that the only difference between the treatment and control groups is the treatment.

Applied to a public administration hypothetical situation, suppose a city's public works department and police department want to run a pilot program regarding red-light cameras. Their hope is that the installation of red-light cameras will deter drivers from running red lights. The city already has cameras at all major and intermediate intersections in the city to monitor traffic, but they are not used to catch traffic violators. Let us assume that there are 250 intersections with normal cameras. These intersections vary in terms of daily traffic, number of lanes, location in the city, and speed limits. With 100 red-light cameras available for a pilot program, the city officials **randomly** select 100 intersections to place red-light cameras. The remaining 150 intersections with regular cameras do not receive any red-light cameras. For thirty days prior to the installation of the red-light cameras, city officials count the daily number of vehicles running red lights using their normal cameras. This is done for all 250 intersections. These are the pre-policy observations. For transparency purposes, the city officials release a statement on their website, on social media, and in the news outlets informing the citizenry of the red-light cameras installed at the specific 100 intersections. The red-light cameras are installed, and then the city collects data on the number of vehicles running red-lights each day for thirty days. The data collected are organized so as to make a comparison of the number of vehicles running red-lights before and after the inclusion of red-light cameras, with the data coded if a red-light camera was installed at the intersection or not.

The easiest and most straightforward test of differences would be to make the unit of analysis the intersection and sum the number of violations in the first thirty days and then sum the number of violations in the last thirty days, coding each intersection as whether or not it had a red-light camera. Then, changes in violations before and after the installation of the red-light cameras could be compared using the intersections with the red-light cameras to the intersections without the red-light cameras.

2.5.2 Quasi-Experimental Design

Some studies and designs contain some elements of experiments, but lack key characteristics that define experimental designs, usually a lack of random assignment to treatment and control groups. In the above red-light camera example, suppose out of the 250 intersections in the city, officials with the city decide to place the red-light cameras in intersections of their choosing, twenty-five in each quadrant of the city (NE, SE, NW, and SW). This is not random assignment and is therefore not a true experiment. They track the number of violations in the thirty days before the installation of the red-light cameras and the thirty days after installation of the red-light cameras. They track this data for the 100 intersections with red-light cameras, and the other 150 intersections in the city without red-light cameras. They look at before-and-after data to make their conclusions. If they notice a change in the number of violations in red-light camera intersections, does it mean that they work? Not necessarily. There has not been random assignment to treatment and control groups. Random assignment would help to ensure that the treatment and control groups look the same on various aspects (traffic volume, speed limits, type of intersection, etc.) except for the actual treatment. Therefore, they need to control for any biases that may exist between the red-light camera intersections and the non-red-light camera intersections. Variables they should take into account for each intersection include traffic volume, speed limits, number of lanes at intersection, location in the city, residential v. commercial area, etc. All of these variables may affect the number of violations. Only when controlling for these factors can the researcher then make more definitive conclusions about the effects of the red-light cameras.

In the previous scenario of quasi-experimental design, the general diagram of the design can be depicted as:

"Treatment Group":	0	X	0
"Control Group":	0		0

This particular design is known as a nonequivalent control group design. While there is no traditional treatment or control group (hence the treatment and control group words being in quotation marks), some entities receive the manipulation, policy, or program, while others do not. In the schematic representation of the design, the "RA" for random assignment has been removed since the researchers did not randomly assign the red-light cameras to intersections. Observations, represented by "O," were still taken before and after the installation of the red-light cameras. This step is represented by the X for the 100 intersections with the red-light cameras installed in the "treatment group." This X is absent from the "control group" and represents the remaining 150 intersections without red-light cameras. The "treatment" and "control" groups are nonequivalent, meaning that they could differ in some important respects that could bias results if not taken into consideration. Particular to this example would be if there are commonalities between the intersections selected for treatment and those not treated. As stated previously in this section, researchers would need to account for/control for other factors to help isolate the independent effect of the red-light camera on violations. Variables like traffic volume, speed limits, number of lanes at intersection, location in the city, residential v. commercial area, etc. for each of the intersections need to be collected and included in analyses, because all of these variables may affect the number of violations. Where possible, the researcher should choose control groups that closely match the treatment group characteristics. Matching techniques have become more common in social science research, where researchers use statistical software to match treatment group cases to control group cases on a variety of characteristics. However, this is not always possible to do, especially if a policy or program implemented on a "treatment" group does not have any near-equivalent control group matches.

Other common quasi-experimental designs in public administration involve making observations over time – making observations before a policy/program is implemented and then after implementation. When examining one case or entity, this method is known as an interrupted time series design, and can be diagrammed as:

O1 O2 O3 O4 O5 X O6 O7 O8 O9 O10

All of the O's before the X represent a period of pre-policy/pre-program observations. They can range from virtually any number. The X represents the intervention or shock. All of the O's after the X represent the post-policy/post-program observations.

One popular urban policy in the 1990s was city-county consolidation, where city and county departments and government are merged into one entity with the idea that consolidation may decrease spending and promote economic development. In 2000, the city of Louisville, Kentucky, consolidated its city and county governments. To determine the effect of consolidation on economic development, one could use an interrupted time series design. Suppose economic development is defined as the total number of new firms (manufacturing and commercial). A researcher could collect firm data for Louisville for twenty years prior to consolidation (prior to 2000) and then collect the same data for twenty years post-consolidation. The unit of analysis would be year, the dependent variable would be total number of firms, and the independent variable would be whether or not the city-county government was consolidated for the particular year. The researcher could use specific statistical analyses to examine how the number of firms changed pre- and post-consolidation.

Carr and Feiock (1999) excellently conduct this type of design in their widely cited *Urban Affairs Review* article where they test the effects of city-county consolidation on economic development (defined as the number of manufacturing and non-manufacturing firms) for nine different consolidated city-counties. They use a specific time series analysis known as the Box–Tiao method (Box & Tiao, 1965) and create autoregressive integrated moving average (ARIMA) models to determine that city-county consolidation did not have an impact on economic development. ARIMA models are an advanced statistical procedure common in time series analyses not covered in this text, but the Carr and Feiock (1999) study serves as a textbook example of setting up an interrupted time series design. Students interested in pursuing a more in-depth and mathematically incorporated treatment of time series analyses can find rigorous and valuable instruction in Box-Steffensmeier et al. (2014) and Pickup (2015).

One potential weakness with interrupted time series is that it is often an analysis of one entity and no other variables are collected. Even if the researchers were to find that the number of firms increased after consolidation, they cannot be sure that it was consolidation that caused the increase. Applied to the Louisville, Kentucky, consolidation, maybe other city, county, state, or national factors really affected economic development. It could be possible that consolidation occurred at the same time as a general economic boom in the state of Kentucky, or maybe a city policy like greater tax incentives for new firms was instituted that compelled companies to locate to Louisville. As currently designed, the research methods would not be able to make such determinations.

An improvement to the interrupted time series design that can help to overcome (but not eliminate) some of the causal concerns is the multiple time series design. It is essentially the interrupted time series design with a comparison group. Applied to the Louisville example, a researcher could attempt to find a city similar to Louisville in nearly all aspects (population, racial demographics, income dispersion, economy, etc.) with the difference that this comparison city did not consolidate its city and county governments. Diagrammed, the multiple time series design looks like:

"Treatment Group":	O1 O2 O3 O4 O5 X O6 O7 O8 O9 O10
"Control (Comparison) Group":	O1 O2 O3 O4 O5 O6 O7 O8 O9 O10

Louisville would be the "treatment group" city as in the interrupted time series design. The "control/comparison group" city would be a city that looked very similar to Louisville in nearly every respect (population, race, economy, region, etc.) except that the control/comparison city would would not be consolidated. Twenty years of economic data before and after 2000 (the year Louisville consolidated with Jefferson County) would be collected for Louisville and its comparison city. No similar cities to Louisville really exist in Kentucky, so the researcher would likely have to pick a city within the same region with similar demographics. Cincinnati, Ohio, could be one possible control/comparison city since it is a similar river city like Louisville, in the region, and with similar demographics.

Carr and Feiock (1999) did not include comparison cities, but for their cities analyzed, there are likely few comparison cities. Is there really a comparison city for the consolidated city-county of Anchorage, Alaska, or Indianapolis, Indiana? Anchorage is a unique city in Alaska, and it is not clear that other cities like Juneau or Fairbanks could serve as comparison cities. The same applies to Indianapolis, the largest city in Indiana. If remaining in the state, Fort Wayne is likely the closest city that compares to Indianapolis, and that is a stretch given that Fort Wayne is much smaller and is a racially and economically different city compared to Indianapolis. Therefore, sometimes researchers must simply use the most-applicable design given data and study setting restrictions and limitations. As such, this discussion on multiple time series is not a critique of the Carr and Feiock (1999) study; it is well-designed and likely the best method given the uniqueness of city-county consolidation and its relative rarity as a policy.

Faulk and Schansberg (2009) attempt to incorporate a form of multiple time series design in their update to the Carr and Feiock (1999) study. As it was mentioned that finding comparison cities/counties is difficult, Faulk and Schansberg (2009) only examine three of the nine consolidations from the Carr and Feiock (1999) study. For each of the three selected consolidations, they select a number of similar counties in the respective state as comparison groups, comparing the consolidated city-county with multiple comparison counties in the respective state. They include the number of firms and employment figures as the dependent variables and find the same results as Carr and Feiock (1999) – consolidation had little to no effect on economic development.

2.5.3 Non-Experimental Design

Non-experimental designs naturally do not have random assignment to treatment and control groups. Unlike even quasi-experimental designs that often use comparison groups that closely resemble "treatment groups," non-experimental designs usually do not have analogous comparison groups. Non-experimental designs rely heavily on statistical controls introduced in the Quasi-Experimental Designs Section 2.5.2 to help account or control for other variables that affect the relationship between a dependent variable and its independent variable(s). As such, even with these controls, the lack of random assignment to treatment and control groups, lack of comparison groups, and lack of time series data create increased difficulties in making causal claims. Therefore, most non-experimental studies are more descriptive, or describe relationships/correlations among variables. Non-experimental designs are no less important, and they certainly contribute to scientific knowledge, but the limitations must be noted when considering them as a research design and in making conclusions from their findings. Most survey research is conducted in this manner if the survey is a one-time survey with no follow-up.

The most common type of non-experimental design in the social sciences is a cross-sectional design (Frankfort-Nachmias and Nachmias, 2008), and most survey research studies that are conducted at a single point in time are considered cross-sectional. Like a medical cross-section of an organ is a cut through or slice of the organ and not the entire organ, a cross-sectional study in the social sciences is a sample or cut of the population and unit of analysis at a particular point in time. If using a sample, a cross-sectional study does not represent the entire organ or population, but a sample of it. It is essentially a slice of society at one point in time that can be studied to make descriptive or correlational inferences.

One of the main datasets used in examples and as practice problems in this book is from a survey of neighborhood and homeowners associations. Neighborhood and homeowners associations represent neighborhood governance structures that govern the neighborhood. Homeowners associations are more formalized than neighborhood associations, having residents bound by the governing documents that require paid membership with the dues providing amenities and services like swimming pools, tennis courts, street-lighting, commons areas, etc. Neighborhood associations tend to be more informal, with voluntary membership/membership dues, and their activities tend to focus on neighborhood social activities and neighborhood appearance maintenance. The survey asks association presidents to answer questions related to their activities and concerns. This survey was conducted at one point in time, and the research stemming from it focused on understanding the differences in activities and concerns between neighborhood and homeowners associations in a city (Scheller, 2016). For example, one of the questions in the survey asked whether or not the association has representatives that attend city government meetings. Analysis indicated that neighborhood associations are more likely than the more formal homeowners associations to have a representative attend a city government meeting (Scheller, 2016).

Finally, a short note is in order regarding case studies. Case studies usually do not include advanced statistics – but instead usually basic descriptive statistics like percentages, averages, and frequencies (if any) – and are thus not a core focus of this text. However, as a public administration student, you may run into them as part of readings for other courses. They are no less rigorous than quantitative designs that use statistical tests; they are just a different type of research method that may be necessary depending upon the research question at hand.

A case study is usually an in-depth examination of one unit of analysis or phenomenon – a public policy, event, organization, department, judicial case, city, state, etc. Hence, the sample size is usually one, the unit of analysis or phenomena under study. In case study research, the researcher delves deeply into the specific unit of analysis or phenomenon, gathering multiple forms of information "for exploratory, descriptive, or explanatory purposes" (Johnson & Reynolds, 2012, p. 196). The focus is on the case at hand, seeking to provide rich information or explanations. If more than one case is being considered, then the method is known as a comparative case study design. In case study research, researchers may use different methods to describe or explain the phenomenon. Interviews, document analyses, focus groups, or simply watching/observing are common means to collect information for the case study. Political scientist Richard Fenno was famous for the "soak and poke" method of following and observing members of Congress in their multiple work settings, soaking/immersing himself in the setting to obtain information (see Fenno, 1978 for his seminal book).

A case study example in public administration and policy, building off the work of Carr and Feiock's (1999) city-county consolidation study, is work by Durning and Sanford in their chapter from a larger volume on city-county consolidation (Durning & Sanford, 2010; Leland & Thurmaier, 2010). They study the effects of city-county consolidation for one county. Given their interest is in describing and understanding the effects of city-county consolidation for a single county, a case study approach is warranted. As in typical case study design, they collect numerous pieces of information from government departments to collect information on the county's population, operating expenditures, personal income, employment, and crime before and after consolidation to present any patterns and to make conclusions regarding consolidation's effect in Clarke County. From their in-depth case study analysis, they find an increase in government efficiency post-consolidation but no change in economic development. Their economic development finding comports with Carr and Feiock (1999). Thus, two very different methods of research (one quantitative and one with a case study) have contributed to scientific knowledge regarding city-county consolidation, both leading to better understanding of this particular policy.

2.6 Experimental Research Design Examples from Public Administration

Within public administration, most research falls into the category of non-experimental. This does not mean that experimental designs do not exist. In the general social sciences, laboratory experiments are common in psychology and economics, with political science having some research and studies focusing on understanding political phenomena within a highly controlled laboratory setting. Such studies are much less common in public administration. Scheller (2015) conducted a laboratory experiment to study the effects of participating in a homeowners association meeting on cooperative behavior. The study took place in a computer laboratory using university students due to the inability to conduct the study in real neighborhoods. Students participating in the study were randomly assigned to a treatment group where they participated in a mock homeowners association meeting and then made donation decisions to a community public good using fake money on a computer program. Other students were randomly assigned to the control group condition where they only made donation decisions to a community public good using the computer software program. They did not engage in a mock homeowners association meeting. Donation amounts for individuals in the treatment group were compared to donation amounts for individuals in the control group with the hypothesis that participation in the mock homeowners association meeting would increase donations.

The previous study is an example of a basic laboratory experiment. The researcher engaged in random assignment to treatment and control groups, with the treatment group receiving the "treatment" or policy or program or intervention. Members of both groups engaged in the donation component so that the researcher can observe their behavior, with the only difference between the groups being the treatment in the treatment group. In theory, the random assignment ensures that the treatment and control groups are identical on all aspects except for the treatment group receiving the treatment. In practice, it is usually necessary to run additional descriptive tests to ensure the groups truly are identical on important aspects like age, gender, income, and race distributions, among others. Because we do not operate in 100 percent ideal settings where *everybody* is a potential research subject, it is good practice to make sure the random assignment has resulted in truly similar treatment and control groups.

In the general social sciences, field experiments are common in political science and sociology, and are growing in use in public administration. Within public administration, field experiments are the most often used type of experimentation. Non-experimental designs predominate, but field experiments have grown in importance as researchers find unique ways to study important concepts, theories, and relationships in public administration. Bellé (2013) published a unique field experiment study in the *Public Administration Review* examining public service motivation (PSM) in nurses in an Italian hospital. PSM is "an individual's predisposition to respond to motives grounded primarily or uniquely in public institutions and organizations" (Perry & Wise, 1990, p. 368). Individuals with high levels of PSM have a tendency to be motivated in their jobs from more intrinsic rewards like serving the public than more extrinsic rewards like salary – they have a strong desire to serve their community and the public good, broadly defined. The research setting for Bellé's (2013) study is an Italian hospital that is involved in producing medical kits for various organizations working in areas suffering from war and other conflicts. Hospital staff like nurses are able to volunteer time to help put together these kits outside of normal working hours.

In the study, Bellé (2013) randomly assigned ninety nurses into three equal groups – a control group, Condition A, and Condition B. All nurses were given a survey that measured their levels of PSM using a battery of five questions. All nurses were also given information about the medical kit project and how to participate. For those assigned to the control group, this was the only information provided. Those nurses in Condition A were subjected to a treatment whereby they met with the beneficiaries of the medical kits. The hypothesis was that contact with beneficiaries would induce nurses, especially those with high levels of PSM, to be more likely to volunteer time to produce the medical kits. Nurses in Condition B did not meet beneficiaries, but were asked to engage in a reflection activity where they were asked to write about the perceived impacts of the project, with the hypothesis that these individuals would also be more likely to volunteer, especially if they have high levels of PSM. Bellé (2013) then observed various performance measures of the nurses in the control group, Condition A, and Condition B, one of which was minutes volunteered. She found that each treatment had a positive effect, increasing the number of minutes volunteered compared to the control group, especially for individuals with high levels of PSM.

Bellé's (2013) study illustrates a typical example of a field experiment in public administration. Hansen and Tummers (2020) provide an excellent review of field experiments in public administration, finding zero examples of their use in public administration research prior to 2010, and they note the growth in field experiments in public administration. One can find more examples of field experiments by searching Google Scholar with the simple search terms of "Field experiment – public administration."

2.7 External and Internal Validity

A few concepts to understand that are important considerations when evaluating research designs and study findings are *external validity* and *internal validty*. External validity refers to how much the study's findings extend beyond the particular research setting of the study. It is often also described as the generalizability of the study and its findings. Essentially, one can ask, how generalizable are the results? Or, how extensive/applicable are the results to other situations? For example, a researcher studying management practices and their effects on employee turnover in one veterans' affairs nonprofit may face questions regarding external validity. Specifically, do the findings apply to all veterans' affairs nonprofits? Maybe there is something unique about this particular veterans' affairs nonprofit organization that separates it from all others in its management practices. If it is truly unique, it may essentially bias the results and generalizability of the findings. It does not mean that the results are not important, just that they may be unique to that particular organization. Additionally, can the findings be generalized to the general population of all nonprofits, regardless of specialty? Compare, for example, a researcher that randomly samples various nonprofit organization directors across a city, state, or country on their management strategies and collects data on their level of employee turnover. This research study probably has more applicability to all nonprofits and thus greater external validity.

Another consideration with external validity deals with the topic of sampling, a topic covered in Chapter 9. The purpose of sampling is to obtain a representative group or sample of data from a population under study. If a sample is biased and not representative of the larger population (for example, a survey sample that is overrepresented by one race), then it becomes more difficult to make conclusions about the larger population. Thus, results from a biased sample are less externally valid than a true, representative sample.

Internal validity refers to how well we can be certain of the findings/conclusions/explanations drawn from the research design. How robust are our causal claims? As a rudimentary test of internal validity, a researcher or somebody critiquing research findings should ask themselves if there are other plausible explanations for the findings of the study. A study on the effects of an organization's new insurance policy where employee satisfaction is measured before and after the implementation of a new insurance policy may reveal a high correlation between the new policy and employee satisfaction. However, there may be other factors that are driving an increase in satisfaction instead of, or to a greater extent than, the new insurance policy. One should ask if there were any other variables or conditions that occurred during the study period that could increase employee satisfaction – raises, new management, better physical working conditions, a major accomplishment in the organization, etc. may all be alternative explanations. Thus, such a limited analysis would have low internal validity unless other factors are controlled/taken into consideration in the study.

2.8 Causality Conditions

While understanding relationships between variables is of descriptive importance, researchers may also want to try to determine a causal relationship. It is one thing to say that an independent variable (X) is related to or correlated with a dependent variable (Y), but sometimes we may want to claim or even test if X causes Y. While it is virtually impossible to make concrete, 100% causal claims in the social sciences, it can be established with a high degree of probability that a causal relationship likely exists between X and Y, pending meeting certain assumptions.

Time Order: One assumption to establish a causal relationship is that of time order, or that one concept or event precedes another concept or event. For X to cause Y, it must necessarily be the case that X occurs before Y. Stated alternatively, any change in Y that can be attributed to a change in X must occur after the change in X (Nishishiba et al., 2014). This concept may appear obvious – observe a phenomenon and then its effect like an HR department increasing the number of job posting sites it lists for employee recruitment and an increase in the number of diverse applicants. However, other situations and relationships are harder to establish a temporal order in a similar manner to the proverbial chicken and egg problem – which came first? The chicken or the egg? For example, we might think that raises affect productivity. Raises could serve as an incentive to produce more. We could likely collect data on worker productivity and raises, but it could be the case that worker productivity affects raises in the sense that raises serve as a reward. Do raises cause productivity or does productivity lead to raises? Maybe they occur simultaneously? Or take satisfaction with government and civic involvement. Does increasing satisfaction with government increase the likelihood of a citizen becoming civically involved, or does increased civic involvement increase citizen satisfaction with government? The causal arrow between these two concepts could go in either direction.

Covariation: Two variables must covary or correlate with each other for there to be a causal relationship. Another way to think about covariation is that a change in one variable leads to a change in another variable. For example, if Y changes in response to a change in X, then there is covariation. If Y increases as X increases or Y decreases as X decreases, this is known as a positive correlation. The two variables change in the same direction. If the variables change in opposite directions, the relationship is known as a negative correlation. If Y increases as X decreases or if Y decreases as X increases, a negative relationship/correlation exists between the two variables. Correlation does not necessarily mean causation, and thus covariation is a necessary, but not sufficient condition to establish causality. This truism is reflected in the next criteria of nonspuriousness.

Nonspuriousness: Suppose that a researcher has established that X precedes Y in time order and that they covary. Meeting these criteria is still not enough to establish causality. Eliminating a third, lurking variable (Z) that affects both X and Y must also be established. If Z causes both X and Y, but is not accounted for, then we will incorrectly attribute changes in Y to be caused by X. The reality is that Z is responsible for the observed changes in both X and Y. An often used example in research design textbooks is the relationship between ice cream sales and shark bites. One could feasibly collect data on both, observing an increase in shark bites immediately following spikes in ice cream sales. Logically, we know that ice cream consumption does not induce sharks to bite more, even if human swimmers may taste sweeter after consuming all of that sugar and cream! The third, lurking (Z) variable is temperature or even the season. When temperatures rise, people cool off – some by eating ice cream, some by swimming in the ocean (and thus being more likely to be attacked by a shark), and some by engaging in both activities. Nevertheless, the correlation between increasing ice cream sales and increasing shark bites is simply a function of warming temperatures.

A more policy- and urban-related example of a spurious relationship may be the relationship between homes in walkable areas having higher values. An initial causal claim could be that walkability increases house prices. Other research indicates that maybe this relationship is spurious, a function of development or the level of development of an area in terms of amenities like commercial and recreational entities

(Boyle et al., 2014). This development likely leads to increased home values as demand to live near these amenities increases. Additionally, this development likely increases an area's walkability as many developed areas have increased walking infrastructure like sidewalks and are also inherently more walkable as people use the various entities.

2.9 Survey Methods

Sometimes data necessary for researchers to answer questions are not readily available, and the researcher needs to create the data. Common in public administration research is the use of surveys to obtain needed information and data from research subjects. Forty, thirty and even twenty years ago, researchers most often utilized telephone and mail survey methods. They are certainly still used today, but the growth and ease of use of online survey websites and software like SurveyMonkey and Qualtrics have made conducting surveys through email or other online means much easier. These sites and software allow the researcher to craft their survey questions and response items on the computer and then produce a link and/or QR code that can then be distributed through email or other electronic communication systems. Your organization may have used a software like Qualtrics to take quick, internal surveys, even for mundane issues like when to schedule a meeting or to take a vote on a policy. No matter the medium through which surveys are distributed, some of the best practices for designing and administering surveys are the same. Though not a substitute for an entire class or chapter on survey design, this section should highlight some common considerations and suggestions for designing and administering surveys to ensure accurate data collection that can be used for analyses.

2.9.1 Best Practices in Survey Question Wording

You are likely very familiar with surveys, often as part of consumer satisfaction studies when you purchase goods from a store. Or you may have been asked to fill out a survey as a citizen, solicited by a government body. Additionally, you may have received a survey as part of an academic study. Surveys are a common tool to better understand public opinion or to gain data from individuals. As with any other research method, scrutiny must be placed on the minutiae of the research elements. For surveys, the questions are naturally the element needing the most scrutiny. Remember the phrase "Garbage in, garbage out." Garbage survey questions will result in garbage responses/data and garbage conclusions. Of the utmost importance is ensuring that the questions measure the concept you want to capture. Question wording should be crafted to ensure accurate representations of the concept being measured. Given that most surveys involve obtaining information from the general population, keeping the survey simple elicits the best and most accurate responses. Some tips to consider follow:

Mutually Exclusive and Exhaustive Response Categories One best practice in developing survey questions is to create exhaustive and mutually exclusive categories for questions. Exhaustive categories mean that the researcher includes all possible/relevant (within reason) options for the survey question/item. If individuals are being surveyed about their preferences for a city's budget priorities, it would be impossible to cover every possible line item; however, the researcher could list what they think are the most commonly preferred items and then have a "catch-all" option with an "other" category. They could also include an option to enter the specific category under the "Other" option or they can create a follow-up question that states something like, "If you selected Other for the previous question, please write-in your preferred option below." A better way to create options for this question, while retaining the criteria of being exhaustive, would be to display the categories as:

a. Roads
b. Parks
c. Crime/Public Safety
d. Economic Development
e. Affordable Housing
f. Climate Change
g. Other

Another element of good survey question wording and options is to make sure the categories are mutually exclusive. In the survey question above regarding city budgetary spending, the categories are mutually exclusive, meaning that each category represents one item or concept. We know that road spending is different from parks spending which is different from economic development. None of the categories could fit into the other. Categories that would not be mutually exclusive would be if "parks" were a category followed by "greenspaces." Both could represent separate items, but could also represent the same thing, as most parks contain greenspaces. It is important to make sure there is no cross-over among categories.

Language Complexity, Jargon, and Acronyms Survey questions should also be composed of commonly used, simple words, especially if surveying the general population. Not everybody has an extensive vocabulary or dictionary handy to decipher survey wording. For example, consider a question stating, "What is your biggest trepidation about the upcoming flu season?"

a. Vaccine availability
b. Severity of the flu
c. Interactions with other viruses like Covid-19
d. Potential time off work
e. Other

Sure, context clues can likely allow most people to figure out what the question means. However, that may not be the case for everybody. A better way to ask the question is to remove "trepidation" and replace it with a more commonly used word like "concern." Additionally, avoid the use of jargon and acronyms that only specialized populations or individuals familiar with those terms will be able to correctly understand. A question asking how strongly the respondent approves/disapproves to the following statement is likely to not be understood by many people: "A recent MOA between the city and county was signed stating that the city would provide street winterizing/mitigation efforts in unincorporated areas. How strongly do you approve of this new policy?" This question has a lot of information that most individuals unfamiliar with the acronym and jargon will not understand. The question ultimately seeks to determine how much the respondent agrees with a new agreement between the city and county for the city to provide winter road treatment (snow/ice removal and prevention) in areas outside of the city limits. Most people probably also do not know what an MOA is or references. It is a memorandum of agreement, but can simply be referred to as an agreement. Therefore, the survey question could be rephrased to: "A recent agreement between the city and county was reached stating that the city could provide snow/ice prevention and removal on roads outside the city limits in the county. How strongly do you approve of this policy?"

Vague Quantifiers Other suggestions provided by Dillman (2000) are to avoid using vague quantifiers when it is reasonable for the respondent to answer with an exact number or range of numbers provided to them. "How often do you read the newspaper in a week?" is a possible survey question. However, if the response categories are "Never, sometimes, or a lot," the responses may not be consistent for everybody answering the question. People may differ in their definitions of "sometimes" and "a lot." It is more reasonable to have the range of categories, something like:

a. 0 days
b. 1–2 days
c. 3–4 days
d. 5–6 days
e. 7 days

Additionally, one could simply ask the respondent, "Typically, how many days of the week do you read the newspaper," allowing the respondent to enter a value of 0 to 7 on their own.

Leading Questions and Differing Positive/Negative Responses Though it may seem obvious, it is also important to not use leading questions (Robinson & Leonard, 2019) or questions with disparate numbers of positive and negative categories (Dillman, 2000). Comedian Stephen Colbert, on his television show *The Colbert Report*, would sometimes asks guests, "President George Bush – great president or greatest president?" This comical bit highlights the elements of leading questions with dissimilar numbers of negative responses. There are no responses for a negative evaluation of the president. Though good researchers do not engage in this behavior, it is not uncommon for political campaigns to send along surveys to their constituents. Options to the question, "Please evaluate Congresswoman Jane Doe on her performance this year," may include "Fair, good, very good, excellent." An unbiased researcher conducting a poll on Congresswoman Jane Doe's performance would likely rephrase the question's options to:

a. Very Good
b. Good
c. Neither good/poor
d. Poor
e. Very Poor

2.9.2 Survey Design

Outlined so far have been best practices for writing survey questions. Other important considerations include the length of the survey along with the response types for the questions. A survey that is too long and/or complicated may deter individuals from participating in the survey or they may be likely to stop in the middle of the survey, also known as survey or respondent fatigue (Lavrakas, 2008; Robinson & Leonard, 2019). Such fatigue could thus affect the number of responses and data the researcher obtains, which could also introduce bias, known as response bias (Lipka, 2011; Robinson & Leonard, 2019) if there are any systematic differences between individuals that are more likely to fill out the entire survey versus those that only answer a certain portion of the questions. While some survey organizations publish survey results with hundreds of questions that likely take 30–45 minutes to complete via the telephone, internet, or mail, response rates likely will increase if the survey is designed to be completed in 15 minutes or less. It is therefore important to focus on crafting the survey in order to obtain the most pertinent data in the shortest time possible. One way to do this is to steer clear of open-ended questions where the respondent is asked to provide their answers in written or short-answer responses.

Personal questions regarding age, income, race, and gender are often best placed towards the end of the survey. Placing them at the start of the survey may deter individuals from further filling out the survey. Sometimes, individuals regard these questions as too personal, and thus may be inclined to stop filling out answers. If placed at the end of the survey (with options for them to select "choose not to answer"), the respondent is more likely to provide this information.

Responsible researchers also provide information at the beginning of the survey explaining why the respondent has been selected along with a general description of the nature of the research and how the responses will be utilized. Information regarding anonymity and confidentiality of the respondent's identifying information and their answers should also be highlighted and discussed in depth. The end of the survey should contain a brief thank you and provide contact information of the researcher(s) so that individuals may direct any questions or concerns to them.

2.9.3 Sending Out Surveys

With increased survey software and internet technology, there are a number of mediums through which to distribute surveys beyond the traditional telephone and mail surveys that predominated before the turn of the twenty-first century. During the era of mail surveys, a few techniques were used to increase the legitimacy of the surveys along with increasing response rates. Even though mail surveys have declined in use, many of these best practices and suggestions can be modified for use in soliciting responses to web-based and email surveys. Dillman's (2000) seminal manual on mail and internet surveys still serves as a gold standard textbook in survey methodology.

With mail surveys, Dillman (2000) recommends sending a pre-notice letter, essentially a "heads-up" to the potential respondent that a survey will be in their mailbox in the coming days/week. In this pre-notice, it is advised to personalize the letter where possible, explain the general research and survey, indicate the importance of their participation, and your appreciation of their time. A more detailed cover letter can be included when you send the actual survey. If sending through mail, it is extremely important to include a personalized cover letter and self-addressed stamped envelope (SASE) for them to return the survey (Dillman, 1991). It should not cost respondents more than their time to provide important information for your research, and response rates will likely dramatically increase with the inclusion of a SASE. If you have the funds to do so, including a small token of appreciation, like money; even as little as $2–3 can increase response rates. Other times, researchers will inform respondents that they will be entered in a raffle to receive a gift card.

With mail surveys, it is customary to wait a few weeks, before sending a reminder to non-respondents. Often, a postcard with a short message stating that you had sent a survey a few weeks ago and hope that they participate by filling it out. Language thanking them for participating if they have already filled it out and it is in transit in the mail can be included. You can also include contact information in case they need another survey in the event that it did not arrive to them or they lost it. An additional two-week wait will typically generate some responses. After this waiting-period, Dillman (2000) recommends sending a final round of surveys (replacements) to the non-respondents with a similar cover letter and new copy of the survey. This represents the final attempt to make contact with the respondent. You may find that additional responses come in. Continued attempts to reach these potential respondents will likely have high marginal costs per returned survey and/or increase the likelihood of annoying the individual. At the end of the study, it is also customary and good form to send a thank-you note to all of those individuals that responded to the survey.

When conducting surveys via email, usually by providing potential respondents with a link to an online survey, the same previous steps and best practices can be utilized, just simply adapted to the email medium. It is important to ensure the survey link is included in the email and the web survey has a generalized welcome screen with information about the study like the general topic, anticipated time to complete the study, IRB information, and contact information for the researchers. An instruction screen also can help individuals understand how to fill out the survey. At the end of the survey, it is also good to have a thank-you screen, information for them to obtain their participation fee (if applicable), and contact information for the research team.

2.10 Summary

This chapter has been presented as a quick review or presentation of critical information needed to conduct research and how to design research to answer questions and test hypotheses. It is not a substitute for a formal research methods course in public administration, but should serve as a refresher chapter for those students previously enrolled in a research design course or as a guide for new researchers to conduct applied public administration studies.

The research design/methods dictate the statistical test to be used, based upon the dependent and independent variable(s). One can correctly run a statistical test in the R Commander software used in this textbook (or any statistical software), and results will be generated. However, unbiased interpretation and conclusions are not possible if the research was poorly designed and the data collected/generated in a nonscientific and rigorous manner. The next chapter continues the design focus of research with measurement of concepts into variables that can be represented with quantitative data.

PRACTICE PROBLEMS

1. A number of public administration studies use a field experiment design. Access the articles listed below (see References section for full citation) from an article database and answer the associated questions for each study.
   a. Access the Bellé (2013) study.
      i. Explain each of the specific hypotheses that she tests in her study. Which hypotheses were supported?
      ii. What is the unit of analysis in her study?
   b. Access the Hock et al. (2012) study.
      i. What is the population considered for the study?
      ii. Was random assignment to treatment and control groups used? How?

iii. Explain the treatment and how it was implemented.
iv. What was the dependent variable of the study?
v. Explain the findings from the research.

c. Access the Elbel et al. (2013) article.
i. What are the initial expectations of the authors for their research?
ii. Was random assignment to treatment and control group used? How?
iii. Explain the treatment and how it was implemented.
iv. What was the dependent variable of the study?
v. Explain the findings from the research.
vi. What limitations to the research do the authors describe? What other limitations can you identify?

2. For each of the following statements, identify the dependent variable and the independent variable(s):

a. Building basketball arenas has been shown not to increase economic development.
b. In a research study, researchers identify several factors that increase voter turnout. Some of them are levels of education, income, and employment status.
c. Donations to nonprofit organizations are a function of the unemployment rate and inflation.
d. One scientist hypothesized that vaccinating children may lead to higher incidences of autism.
e. A researcher hypothesizes that grocery stores are less likely to exist in neighborhoods that are greater than 50% underrepresented minority.
f. Public hospitals and health providers that provide access to tele-health options are hypothesized to have more positive health outcomes.

3. For each of the following scenarios, indicate whether or not principles of rigorous, scientific research are being followed. If not, explain why.

a. A researcher randomly selects 1,000 individuals to survey their opinion on upcoming elections and who they plan to vote for. The researcher obtains a list of registered voters, publicly available from the state's secretary of state office.
b. The state ombudsman's office wants to know if the number of ethics complaints against state employees and offices declined after instituting a new, more streamlined reporting process and website. The office policy director asks their policy analyst to collect data before and after creation of the new process and website to determine any statistical differences.
c. A policy researcher for a liberal think tank conducts a program evaluation of a federal policy finding that the program did not achieve the intended goals in the same manner as the program was criticized by conservative politicians. In their report, the researcher states that the policy would achieve the intended results if more funding was allocated to it.

d. After conducting a study that finds that lower-income housing options have decreased in the past ten years, a researcher writes an article for a newspaper arguing that local governments should institute a 0.5% increase in local sales tax to increase funds to build lower-income housing.
e. To measure citizen preference for parks/recreation improvements, the city parks director asks their staff to survey people participating in softball leagues on Wednesday evenings. Results from these surveys will be used to determine spending priorities for the next fiscal year.

4. Engage in a plan for a research project using the research design process.
a. Identify a "problem" or issue in public administration, public policy, or management.
b. Generate a research question from this problem or issue.
c. Generate a directional hypothesis (if applicable) to your research question.
d. Generate a null hypothesis for your research question.
e. Explain the type of data you would collect to test your hypothesis and where you might locate this data or how you might create the data.
f. Is your design experimental, quasi-experimental, or non-experimental. Explain why.

5. Turn each of the following relational hypotheses into directional hypotheses. Explain the logic behind the direction you chose.
a. There is a relationship between education and income.
b. There is a relationship between council-manager type of government and citizen satisfaction with city services.
c. There is a relationship between the percent of population vaccinated against the flu and the number of deaths from the flu.
d. There is a relationship between conservative ideology and support for immigration policy.
e. There is a relationship between diversity in public organizations and citizen contact with public organizations.
f. There is a relationship between time of day a public meeting is held and attendance at the meeting.
g. There is a relationship between Theory X management style and worker productivity.

6. For each of the scenarios in Problem #5, briefly explain what data/method you would use to test the hypotheses. Then, identify the unit of analysis for each design.

7. For each of the following pairs of variables, describe a potential causal relationship by hypothesizing a directional relationship between them. Identify the dependent variable and the independent variable. If you think the causal relationship could go in both directions, explain why.
a. Income and education.
b. Number of TSA agents and number of baggage violations identified.

c. Implementation of Obamacare and the number of uninsured individuals.
d. Amount of pesticides used and rates of cancer.

8. Identify the unit of analysis for each scenario:

a. A researcher uses a survey of neighborhood association presidents and asks them questions about the activities of the association this month.
b. Data on graduation rates for each school in the district for this year are collected.
c. Data are collected measuring the budget deficits for fifty cities for the previous fiscal year.
d. Data are collected measuring the budget deficits for fifty cities for the previous twenty years.

9. Create survey questions that are exhaustive and mutually exclusive for the following scenarios:

a. A researcher wants to create a survey question asking an individual's political party identification.
b. You want to ask residents of your city to indicate which park they use the most.
c. Your boss wants you to generate a survey question asking employees how satisfied they are with their work-life balance.
d. You need to create a survey question that includes gender identity.

3

Measurement

3.1 Introduction

Measurement – that of concepts into variables for study – is one of the most crucial aspects of research design and statistics. How a variable is measured, especially the dependent variable, determines what kind of information researchers can report on the variable and dictates the correct statistical test to use to analyze relationships between variables and to conduct hypothesis testing. This chapter covers how to turn concepts we want to study into observable, measurable variables. Much attention is given to the differences between nominal, ordinal, and interval variables: their characteristics and common uses. The connection between levels of measurement and statistical tests is also introduced to provide a preview of important concepts to come in later chapters.

3.2 Measuring Concepts (Operationalization)

Researchers conducting studies often want to understand the relationship between concepts. Sometimes, concepts are very easy to measure and are self-explanatory. For example, if a researcher asks, "What is the effect of park entrance fees on number of visitors?," the concept of cost (entrance fees) is obvious and measurable in dollars for admission, and the concept of usage (number of visitors) is measured in persons using the park. However, research questions may not be so specific as the park example, and researchers may have research questions regarding concepts that are not easily as measurable simply by their name. Think of the following viable research questions. What is the relationship between education and wealth or health insurance and health outcomes? What is the relationship between employee morale and employee productivity? Education, wealth, health insurance, health outcomes, employee morale, and employee productivity are all concepts that can be measured, but how are they defined?

The process by which concepts are turned into observable, measurable data is called "operationalization." It is commonly stated that concepts are operationalized into measurable variables. Refer back to the research question, "What is the relationship between education and wealth?" How can we operationalize the concept of education into an observable measure? Likewise, how can we operationalize the concept of "wealth" into an observable measure? To answer these questions, what is a workable definition of education? Is it the number of degrees? Well, what if somebody does not even have a high school degree – do they receive a value of 0? Is education defined as a score on a standardized reading test? Probably not. Such a measure likely depicts intelligence, reading comprehension only, or simply test-taking ability. Education is usually operationalized as number of years in school. If a researcher operationalizes education as the number of years in school, and collects information from individuals regarding the number of years of school completed, they have created a variable. Twelve years indicates an individual graduating high school. Fourteen years, a person with some college experience. Sixteen years a college graduate. Greater than 16, likely a postgraduate degree. Less than twelve years, no completion of high school. Likewise, wealth is often operationalized as income, most typically measured through an income variable or how much an individual earns in salary in a year.

Other concepts may be more difficult to operationalize and turn into variables. For the question, "What is the relationship between health insurance and health outcomes?," it certainly is easy to measure whether or not somebody has health insurance – either through a survey or through aggregate level community data from a health department or other public health organization. But what are "health outcomes?" Is it life expectancy or years lived? Is it percent of the population with diabetes? Heart disease? Terminal cancer? Any or all of these pieces of information could be considered a health outcome. It is up to the researcher to define and operationalize concepts. Shortly, types of variables – nominal, ordinal, and interval – will be introduced. However, it is important to first understand some common best practices when operationalizing variables to ensure that they fully and adequately capture/measure the desired concept. In the next example, these best practices are applied to a nominal variable, mode of transportation, a non-numeric categorical variable.

3.2.1 Best Practices in Creating Variables

Regardless of how a concept is operationalized into a variable, categories or indicators of the variable should be both *exhaustive* and *mutually exclusive* (Frankfort-Nachmias and Nachmias, 2008). For a variable to be exhaustive means that all possible options (within reason) of categories are included. Suppose a transportation director is interested in citizens' mode of transportation to work to determine if they should push for more funding for the city's bus system in a post-Covid world where people may be altering their work patterns. They send a survey to a random sample of citizens. If one is surveying individuals on the type of transportation they typically use to go to work, they may ask the respondent a question like:

"Which of the following forms of transportation do you most often use to get to work?"

a. Car
b. Bus
c. Subway
d. Bicycle
e. Walking
f. Multiple (e.g. park and ride)
g. Other
h. Not Employed
i. Work from Home

In this example, the typical modes of transportation like car, bus, bicycle, subway are all included. It is not always practical to include every single option. In this operationalization of the variable "mode of transportation to work," train, motorcycle, skateboard, etc. are all not included. So as to keep with the principle of being exhaustive, but not to overwhelm individuals with so many options, the "Other" category/indicator is used as a type of "catch-all" so that individuals who use the train, or motorcycle, or skateboard, have an option to select. Often the use of the "Other" category will be used to capture less common categories or categories for which the researcher is less interested in studying. Additionally, for the particular example, "Multiple" can be included for people that use more than one form of transportation to get to work. One example as listed is park and ride, where somebody drives their car to a public transportation terminal like a light-rail, bus, or subway station.

The "Not Employed" and "Work from Home" categories also highlight the need to be exhaustive with the categories/indicators and for the researcher to really plan ahead to think of all types of different contingencies/unique scenarios – in this case, some people may not use any form of transportation to get to work. They may not be employed (retired, unemployed, ineligible to work) or they may work from home (and thus not need any transportation). Without these exhaustive options, individuals that are not employed or work from home may either simply not answer the question (thus, the researcher loses out on gaining important data), or they may feel compelled to mark some answer, even if not accurate.

A measurement of a variable is considered *mutually exclusive* if the categories/indicators do not overlap. A city's human resources director may be interested in collecting data on city employees going up for promotion for the past year, and whether or not they were promoted and if they are a member of an underrepresented minority group. There are two variables in the previous statement: promotion (operationally categorized as promoted or not promoted) and minority (operationally categorized as underrepresented minority or not underrepresented minority). The categories/indicators of the promotion variable are mutually exclusive. One cannot be both promoted and not promoted. Additionally, for the minority variable, one cannot be a member of an underrepresented minority group and at the same time not be a member of an underrepresented minority group. This case may appear to be an obvious example of mutually exclusive categories.

Mutual exclusivity may become trickier if respondents or the unit of analysis can fall into multiple categories. Consider a previous example of modes of transportation to work with the categories/indicators of:

a. Car
b. Bus
c. Subway
d. Bicycle
e. Walking
f. Multiple (e.g. park and ride)
g. Other
h. Not Employed
i. Work from Home

What if somebody sometimes uses their car, and other times, walks to work? This would make sense, especially if somebody usually walks to work, but relies on their car on rainy days. Has mutual exclusivity been violated? Not necessarily. Recall the phrasing of the question which was, "Which of the following forms of transportation do you most often use to get to work?" The key phrase in the question is "most often use." This is where meticulous scrutiny to question wording and coding is necessary for researchers. The survey question implicitly acknowledges that people may use multiple forms of transportation depending upon particular circumstances. However, if the researcher is really trying to gauge typical transportation use, they can craft their question to eliminate any confusion in the respondent. "Most often use" is the phrase in this example that keeps the measurement of the mode of transportation variable in line with the principle of mutual exclusivity.

3.3 Nominal Variables

As previously mentioned, in research and statistics, we use variables to measure concepts. We describe, analyze, and compare variables. To do so correctly requires knowledge of levels of measurement – nominal, ordinal, and interval. Table 3.1 provides a quick reference guide to the main differences between nominal, ordinal, and interval variables based upon the criterion discussed in greater detail in this section along with Sections 3.4 and 3.5.

Nominal variables are often also referred to as categorical variables. Values of nominal variables are categories. Variables like gender, ethnicity, form of government, political party identification, job title, attended/did not attend workshop, and passed/failed inspection are all considered nominal variables. The "values" for each of these variables are categories. An individual or other unit of analysis falls into

Table 3.1 Levels of measurement

Level	Rank order?	Measurable distance between categories?	Examples
Nominal	No	No	Gender, job title, ethnicity, party identification, form of government, management style (Theory X v. Theory Y), policy adopted or not, dichotomous variables coded 0/1 (e.g. Yes/No)
Ordinal	Yes	No	Likert scale questions measuring degrees of satisfaction, happiness, confidence, agreement, etc.; variables showing various levels and labels of more than/less than.
Interval	Yes	Yes	Count variables (# of employees, demerits, visitors, etc.); percentages; response times; test scores; salary; budget surplus amount

a particular category for each of these variables. Take form of government, for example. It is common for public administration and urban studies researchers to examine the effect of a city's form of government on a variety of potential dependent variables like budget spending, citizen satisfaction with services, and likelihood of certain policy adoptions. In the U.S. the most common forms of local government are strong mayor, council-manager, and weak mayor. As such, when collecting information on city form of government, a researcher will include categories of "strong mayor," "council-manager," "weak mayor," and usually "other" for the small number of municipalities that do not fall within the main categories. A city can only be one of these category items. A city cannot have both a strong mayor and a weak mayor form of government. The city represents one, and only one, category. As another example, if a public administrator is collecting data on restaurant inspections, restaurants either passed or failed inspection. Each restaurant in the dataset either passed or did not. And there is no level of "more passing" or "more failing."

Each of these examples exhibits key characteristics of nominal variables: a) there is no quantitative, measurable difference among the categories, and b) there is no rank-order (greater than/less than or higher/lower) in the categories – categories cannot be ordered. For the city form of government variable, there is no measurable, quantifiable distance between the categories. What measurable distance exists between a strong mayor system and a weak mayor system? None. Additionally, can the categories of the form of government variable be rank ordered from higher to lower? No, there is nothing measurable that separates the categories. For restaurant inspections, even with the dummy variable of passed inspection/failed inspection, there are no measurable distances between passing and failing as the variable is described. A restaurant either passed or failed. A restaurant may have failed inspection with five violations, while another failed with fifteen violations. Unless the variable is measured as number of violations, there is no measurable distance between passing and failing. Additionally, without a count of violations, there is no real way to rank order passing or failing or to determine a level of passing or failing. There are no categories for high pass, pass, low pass, low fail, fail, high fail. Such a coding scheme for restaurant inspections would be considered an ordinal level of measurement, the topic of the next section.

3.4 Ordinal Variables

Ordinal variables differ from nominal variables in that their categories can be rank-ordered from high to low or greater than to less than. In the previous restaurant inspection example, if the inspection variable is coded simply as passed/failed, it is considered nominal. However, if there is a degree of passing/failure with the categories high pass, pass, low pass, low fail, fail, high fail, then the inspection variable would be measured at the ordinal level. While such categories can be rank-ordered, there still is no measurable distance between the categories. As coded, there is no measurable distance between a high pass and a pass, and there is no guarantee that the difference between a high pass to a pass is the same distance/difference between a pass and a low pass.

To think of this another way, take one of the most common types of ordinal measures used in the social sciences, the Likert scale. A popular measure is approval ratings. For example, citizens are often polled on how much they approve of a political figure or institution. People may be asked, "How much do you approve of the Supreme Court overturning *Roe v. Wade*?" Typical options include Strongly Approve, Approve, Neither Approve/Disapprove, Disapprove, Strongly Disapprove. Obviously, a response of Strongly Approve can be rank-ordered higher than Approve, indicating more approval, but the difference or level of approval increase moving from Approve to Strongly Approve is unknown (and likely varies by individual in their personal decision criteria for how they determine if they approve versus strongly approve of the Supreme Court's decision).

Ordinal level variables are widely used in public administration research, especially the Likert scale. Surveys of stakeholders or of the general population often use Likert scale measures to help public and nonprofit managers and officials gauge feelings towards a variety of items like proposed projects, satisfaction with services, effects of policies, etc. Take for example satisfaction with city services. With greater attention being paid to environmental and climate change issues, cities are attempting to engage in more sustainable practices. As an example, some cities have reinvigorated their recycling programs, providing citizens with bigger, sturdier recycling containers to promote recycling and to deter citizens from tossing recyclables into their general trash containers. Suppose a city was under contract with a waste management company that provided citizens with two sixteen-gallon recycling containers. Once that contract expired, the city decided to contract with another company that provided one large ninety-six-gallon recycling container. The mayor, public works director, and waste management director all want to know the effects of the new recycling containers on citizens' recycling behavior and satisfaction with the new bins. They could feasibly send a random sample of citizens a survey asking a variety of questions to gauge use and satisfaction with the new recycling containers. One probable question measuring use could be:

"Tell us how much you agree with the following statement: I now recycle more with the new recycling containers."

a. Strongly Agree
b. Agree
c. Neither Agree nor Disagree
d. Disagree
e. Strongly Disagree

For satisfaction, they could ask:

"Compared to the old recycling containers, how satisfied are you with the new, larger recycling containers?"

a. Much More Satisfied
b. More Satisfied
c. About the Same
d. Less Satisfied
e. Much Less Satisfied

The key thing to remember with ordinal variables is to make sure to include all relevant categories and gradations. The previous examples had five categories and that is a good number. Suppose the previous question regarding satisfaction with the larger recycling containers had only three categories:

a. More Satisfied
b. About the Same
c. Less Satisfied

This option could work, but it limits levels of intensity of preference that the five-category option had. It completely eliminates those respondents that are strongly or much more satisfied/dissatisfied. On the other hand the questions regarding satisfaction with the larger recycling bins could have even more options:

a. Much More Satisfied
b. Somewhat More Satisfied
c. A Little More Satisfied
d. About the Same
e. Somewhat Less Satisfied
f. Less Satisfied
g. Much Less Satisfied

This option may present respondents with uncertainty or cognitive overload. Too many categories may become tedious for respondents, and it becomes difficult to delineate differences among categories. What is the difference between "A Little More Satisfied" and "Somewhat More Satisfied?" These categories may be difficult for respondents to understand and clearly articulate in the survey. There exist no definitive rules on how many categories to include, and researchers should use best judgment on how many categories to include.

3.5 Interval Variables

Interval variables have categories/indicators that can be both rank-ordered and the difference between indicators is measurable and the same across the various categories/indicators. If a state auditing agency is evaluating state agencies' end of fiscal year budget balance in dollars, the variable created can be considered an interval level variable. A balance of $1,000,000 is obviously greater than a balance of $999,999. Additionally, a balance of $1,000,000 is exactly $1 more than a balance of $999,999, which is exactly $1 more than a balance of $999,998, *ad infinitum.* Likewise, a balance of −$555,555 (deficit) is $1 less of a balance than −$555,554, which is $1 less of a balance than −$555,553. In reality, the budget end of year balance variable can take on any value from negative infinity to positive infinity.

As another example from public administration, suppose the Department of Housing and Urban Development (HUD) is interested in collecting the number of affordable housing units in a particular state over time. This variable is interval level. If a state has 12,752 affordable housing units, that is one housing unit more than 12,751 and one housing unit less than 12,753. The distance/difference is the same, exactly one unit. Unlike budget surplus, however, number of housing units cannot take on values from negative infinity to positive infinity. No state or entity can have a negative housing unit. Therefore, number of affordable housing units has a definite and substantive zero value – it cannot fall below zero. There is no such thing as a negative housing unit, and a value of zero affordable housing units has a substantive meaning of no existence of affordable housing units. Variables with a definite zero value are defined as ratio variables. In the grand scheme of things, the difference between interval and ratio variables is based upon this definite zero value and really semantic for statistical purposes. For clarity, they can, and will, be referred to throughout this text as interval variables.

Interval level variables are usually considered the highest level, or most specific level of variable measurement. They provide the most information. What does this mean? A commonly used ordinal measure of income used in surveys provides ranges of incomes for respondents to choose, something like:

$0–$24,999
$25,000–$49,999
$50,000–$74,999
$75,000–$99,999
$100,000–$124,999
$125,000+

Compare this measure to an interval level version of income, where respondents are asked to provide their exact income. Under the interval level form of the income variable a respondent who earns $85,000 a year would write or enter $85,000 in the survey. With the ordinal level version of the income variable, they would select the option for $75,000 to $99,999. The interval level variable provides more specific information given that respondents are asked to indicate their exact income instead of a range. If so desired, one can transform interval level variables down to an ordinal level (for example, if the researcher decided to recode all of the exact incomes into an ordinal range), or even nominal (transforming the exact incomes to "low" or "high" based upon some defined criterion). However, it is impossible to transform up to higher levels. There is no way to transform a nominal or ordinal level up to an interval level, because that information is not possible to ascertain. As such, it is usually recommended to use interval level variables where possible. Obviously, for variables like gender, party identification, ethnicity, etc. there exists no way to turn them into interval level variables.

3.6 Index Variables

Sometimes researchers may want to aggregate responses to create a general measure, known as an index variable. Suppose a researcher wants to measure citizen trust in government. They could ask citizens a question like the Gallup organization,

"How much trust do you have in your city council?"

a. Great Deal
b. Fair Amount
c. Not Very Much
d. Not At All

Other questions could be asked to better measure general trust in government, like:

"How much trust do you have in your mayor?"
"How much trust do you have in your state legislature?"

"How much trust do you have in your governor?"
"How much trust do you have in Congress?"
"How much trust do you have in the President?"

If each of the questions offers the same categories/indicators, an aggregate or index measure can be created. Numeric values can be assigned to the categories/indicators according to:

a. Great Deal (+2)
b. Fair Amount (+1)
c. Not Very Much (−1)
d. Not At All (−2)

A researcher could then create an aggregate or additive measure if the same coding scheme is used for all of the trust in government questions. In the example above, there are six separate trust in government questions. A researcher could then calculate an additive measure by adding the response values for each respondent's answers to the six questions. Therefore, the range in values for the trust in government variable could range from −12 to +12. A value of −12 would indicate that a respondent answered "Not At All" for all six questions (6×-2). A value of +12 would indicate that a respondent answered "Great Deal" for all six questions ($6 \times +2$). Index variables are usually treated as interval level measures, especially if they are constructed of multiple questions. They allow researchers to generate aggregate or composite measures of concepts that cannot be captured by a single question.

3.7 Reliability and Validity in Measurement

Since measurement is one of the most important topics to master to know what statistics researchers can report and what type of statistical tests can be utilized based upon the level of measurement, it naturally makes sense that the measures should be dependable and "good measures" of the concepts that we wish to operationalize. Common sense dictates that we would not use an individual's amount they can bench press as a measure of their work experience. Likewise, in studying a person's vital signs, a nurse would not use a faulty blood pressure machine that is inconsistent in its readouts. These obvious examples point to important research design and measurement issues that researchers must address – validity and reliability, respectively. This section briefly covers the important topics of reliability and validity in measurement. It is not an exhaustive discussion of these issues, nor can it replace an in depth treatment of these issues usually covered in a research design course. Its purpose is to provide a brief review for students that have had a standalone research design course, and to also provide enough information for students without a course the necessary information to better operationalize variables for research.

Validity refers to the degree that an operational measure actually measures or represents the concept it purports to measure. Obviously, in the previous nonsensical example, nobody would actually use one's bench press maximum as a measure of work experience. The amount a person can bench press is likely only a valid measure of strength, specifically upper body strength. It is an invalid measure of work experience. Years worked is a valid measure of work experience. Or if a hiring committee is trying to gauge work experience within their respective sector, say in budgeting, then a candidate's years worked in budgeting/finance positions would be a valid measure. This example points to one manner in which to gauge a measure's validity – *face validity*. If we think to ourselves, "on the face of it, does years worked in a budgeting/finance position represent budgeting/finance work experience?" Most likely so. Examining the face value of an operational measure's ability to measure a concept is a great initial check for measurement validity.

Other examples may not be so clear regarding measurement validity. Suppose a city council member bases their vote for a policy on the number of communications they receive from constituents telling them to vote "yay" for a proposed policy versus "nay" for a proposed policy. Is this a valid measure of constituent support – the number of yays to nays? On the face of it, maybe, but thinking more critically, it probably is not a valid measure of citizen support for a policy. It likely fails in the realm of *construct validity*, or the ability of a measure to fully represent the concept it purports to measure and not other concepts. This case may appear tricky. What else could the number of positive (yay vote) communications to negative (nay vote) communications represent? Most likely, the measure adopted by the member of city council is measuring *intensity* of preference for a policy. Those citizens that feel the strongest for/against a policy are probably the most likely to express their opinions in communication. While many other citizens in the member's district likely have an opinion, it may not be as salient or important of an issue for them compared to those that communicate their opinions. Additionally, the measure could be capturing an interaction between intensity of preference and resources to communicate with the council member. Even if some citizens feel strongly about a proposed policy, maybe they simply do not have enough time to communicate their opinion and/or they do not have access to a computer to email the council member or to get contact information for the council member. A more valid measure with greater construct validity would likely involve the council member randomly surveying (through various mediums – door-to-door surveying, phone banking, and internet surveys) their district to gauge the level of support for the proposed policy.

Measurement validity often is heavily scrutinized for aptitude tests and skills assessments (IQ tests, reading comprehension tests, standardized tests). These often high-stakes evaluations for school admissions, passing to another grade, awarding of scholarships, etc. are widely used in educational settings. Students with test-taking anxiety may systematically perform lower on standardized tests, thus inaccurately reflecting their mastery of concepts and skills or their potential for academic success. If a measure systematically errs or biases the results in a particular direction of the likes of

a. students with test-taking anxiety systematically scoring lower on a statewide exam;
b. a police radar gun systematically erring by +5 miles per hour; or
c. a job satisfaction survey asking respondents only if they like their boss,

there is likely bias in that:

a. the test is biased against students with test-taking anxiety, making it a less valid measure of college preparation;
b. the radar gun does not measure actual vehicle speed, but actual vehicle speed *plus* 5 miles an hour; and
c. the survey only measures how much an employee likes their boss instead of job satisfaction, which may be a function of how much they like their boss *along with* other indicators like how much they enjoy their job tasks, how fulfilled they are in their position, etc.

Reliability of a measurement refers to the consistency of the measure's reflection of the concept. Stated another way, a reliable measure consistently gives the same values across different iterations or uses of it. In the beginning of this section, there was a description of an inconsistent blood pressure machine. Suppose it initially reported a patient's blood pressure as 190/120, then immediately after 120/80, and then 70/30. It is clearly unreliable as it provides inconsistent results.

Applied to public administration, some states contain high levels of radon, an odorless gas that seeps up from the ground into homes that can cause lung cancer. As such, some of these states offer free or reduced price home testing kits so citizens can test their home and install a mitigation system if so desired. Suppose a state solicits bids from companies that produce the tests, and Company Radon't wins the bid with their new, patented radon tests. The first batch of tests go out to homes, and each home receives two kits, containing two tests (total of four) that are short-term, ten-day tests. With these tests, residents put a vial containing activated charcoal in the lowest level of their home. Tests are sent off and results usually returned within a few days. A concerned citizen uses one test and gets a reading of 10 pCi/L, a very high level of radon. Before spending money on a mitigation system, the citizen then places all three tests in the same location. Results then return 1.2 pCi/L (a very low level), 7.2 pCi/L, and 3.8 pCi/L (a moderate level). Even though radon levels fluctuate, they should not fluctuate to this degree and suggest that Radon't's test kits are not very reliable. This is an example of the citizen engaging in the *test-retest* method to gauge a measure's reliability.

Suppose a researcher is trying to determine the effect of citizens' comments during the public comment period of a city council meeting on a policy to grant tax incentives to real estate developers to revitalize a neighborhood in the city. The researcher listens to each speaker's testimony and codes the testimony as being very pro-development, pro-development, neutral, anti-development, or very anti-development. Instead of relying on their own opinions of the testimony, the researcher also asks two other members of their team to listen to the testimonies and code them accordingly on the same scale. The researcher then examines the consistency of the three different ratings of testimonies. This method is common practice in coding documents and the process of content analysis to ensure that a measure consistently measures a concept in the same way, and is known as *inter-coder reliability.*

These examples and discussions of validity and reliability illustrate the importance of ensuring the use of valid and reliable operational measures of concepts. We can report all types of statistics and can be running the correct statistical tests based upon the level of measurement. However, if the measure is unreliable and/or invalid, our results may very well be meaningless, and we cannot be confident in our results. It is best if our measures are both reliable and valid.

Many texts ask students to think about a bullseye as a target. If a measure is reliable, but invalid, the measure will return similar results over time, but will be off the mark – all hits on the target will be clustered together, but away from the bullseye. If a measure is unreliable, but valid, hits will be all over the bullseye in no pattern, but averaged out, the hits close to the bullseye and far from the bullseye would cancel each other out. The measure ultimately captures its concept. The best case scenario is a reliable and valid measure, with hits all clustered at the center-point – the bullseye. Therefore, correct research design and attention to measurement issues are important first steps in conducting empirical analyses with quantitative data.

3.8 Importance of Levels of Measurement for Statistical Tests and Summary

Knowing the level of measurement of variables is of the utmost importance for researchers. This chapter focused on turning concepts into variables and how to measure concepts with observable data. It also covered the differences between nominal, ordinal, and interval measures. The level of measurement dictates what types of statistics can be reported for a particular variable along with the types of statistical tests that can be used to understand the relationship between a dependent variable and an independent variable. Future chapters will cover how to describe variables based upon their level of measurement, including how to report the typical value of variables. Mean, median, and mode are all measures of the typical value of a variable, but the level of measurement dictates which to report.

This is a topic explored in Chapter 6. Additionally, statistical tests measuring the relationship between a dependent variable and an independent variable are based upon the level of measurement of both the dependent and independent variables. T-tests, chi-square, ANOVA, and regression tests all have assumptions that must be met, predicated on levels of measurement. While these topics may be foreign right now, they will become important in later chapters. It is thus imperative to master an understanding of research design and variable measurement in order to conduct the correct statistical tests, report correct findings, and make well-informed recommendations.

PRACTICE PROBLEMS

1. For each of the following concepts, offer an operational measure/variable with categories/indicators (where applicable). Explain your logic.
   a. Organizational efficiency
   b. Government corruption
   c. Budget deficit
   d. Gender
   e. Socioeconomic status of individual
   f. Job satisfaction
   g. Healthy lifestyle
   h. Ethnic diversity in workplace
   i. Support for paid maternity leave policy among population
   j. Blighted neighborhood
   k. Organizational effectiveness
   l. Speed of service delivery for postal service
2. For each of the operational measures/variables you used in Problem 1, indicate what level of measurement you used and why it is considered that particular level of measurement.
3. For each of the following variables, determine if they are measured at the nominal, ordinal, or interval level of measurement:
   a. Ranking (Poor, Fair, Excellent)
   b. Gross Domestic Product in Dollars
   c. Went to college (Yes/No)
   d. Approval rating (Disapprove, Neutral, Approve)
   e. Animal caught by animal control (dog, cat, snake, other)
   f. Fire department response time in seconds
   g. Expected benefits of project in lives saved
   h. Type of traffic violation (speeding, seat belt, failure to stop, driving under the influence)

i. Voted (Yes/No)
j. Number of times voted
k. Likelihood of voting in next election (Very Likely, Likely, Not Sure, Unlikely, Very Unlikely)

4. Explain how the following measures are problematic and provide a better method of measurement.
a. A measure of gender includes the categories of Male and Female.
b. A researcher asks respondents how much they like President Biden with the options of "Very Much Like" and "Like."
c. A researcher measures support for a policy in the population by reading op-eds in the local newspaper.
d. A researcher uses a measure of income as a dummy variable, coded 1 if the individual has an income greater than $10,000 and 0 if the individual has an income less than $10,000.
e. A researcher codes respondents to a survey as conservative only if they answer that they are pro-life.

5. Is it possible for a measure to be reliable but not valid? Why/why not?
a. Provide an example of your own and describe why it is reliable, but not valid.
b. Provide an example of your own measure of a variable in public administration that is valid and reliable.

6. Suppose a department director is seeking to measure performance effectiveness of their policy program. The director is in charge of a state agriculture department that implemented a grant program to provide needy families with farm fresh fruits and vegetables in various communities in the state, with a fruit/vegetable kit, with the goal of encouraging more healthy eating habits in the population. The director wants to know the effectiveness of the program and tells their data analysts that they think effectiveness is measured by the number of kits delivered. As one of the department's analysts, it is up to you to evaluate effectiveness. Do you agree with the director's measure of effectiveness? Why/why not? Is it a reliable measure? Is it a valid measure? How can it be improved if so?

7. Explain how you would create an index variable of conservative ideology to be used in a citizen survey. What questions would you include and why?

8. City traffic engineers are attempting to measure traffic flow at a major intersection to determine whether or not to recommend adding additional turn lanes. They use the city's traffic cameras at the intersection to count the number of vehicles turning at the intersection for each hour of the day between 5AM and 9PM for three months. A problem is that the cameras sometimes randomly get disconnected and the engineers lose the camera feed. Sometimes, the camera goes down for 15 minutes in rush hour; another day, it goes down for 45 minutes during rush hour; another day it goes down at 5AM for 30 minutes. Is this measure of traffic reliable? Why/why not? Suppose a data analyst tells the engineers to not worry – as long as the outages are random, and a large number of days are observed, the measure will still be valid. Is this possible? Why/why not?

4

Good Data Collection

4.1 Introduction

The phrase "Garbage in, garbage out" has been mentioned a few times in previous chapters. It applies to data setup – the collecting and entering of data in spreadsheets. Poor data setup (garbage in) into spreadsheets will likely result in incorrect output when running analyses with statistics software (garbage out). In reality, poorly inputted and/or formatted data may not even lead to garbage output – there may actually be no output except for a confusing error message from the statistics software. Many public administration students have devised testable research questions with publicly available and downloadable data only to import it into a statistics software and receive an intimidating error message when trying to obtain even some descriptive statistics like means and medians for variables. The culprits are often data incorrectly formatted for importing into software, string (word) coding for variables needing numeric coding, extraneous information/cells in the spreadsheet that is unreadable (and unnecessary), or improper organization of the data into the rows and columns of the spreadsheet.

This chapter focuses primarily on how to collect and organize your own data into a spreadsheet. Best practices for coding and recording variables based upon level of measurement (nominal, ordinal, or interval) are discussed. These principles may not be followed by all individuals or entities that collect and make data available. Therefore, attention is devoted to what to pay attention to if using data from secondary sources. Recoding or reorganizing secondary data may be necessary, and the steps to do so are presented in the next chapter. Different types of data formats based upon sample and timing (i.e. cross-section versus time series) are shown, as is how to correctly input the data into spreadsheets for immediate analysis. Finally, the construction and use of codebooks is illustrated so that researchers can organize their variables for ease of interpretation from statistical tests and also to allow for sharing of data and replicability of research methods/findings.

4.2 Data Entry and Spreadsheets

Probably the most common spreadsheet for data entry is Microsoft Excel. It is a program often utilized in public sector organizations, is relatively easy to use, and can easily be uploaded to organization websites for researchers to download. It is the focus of this textbook for data entry as it is widely used among public administration practitioners, is easily downloaded without a lot of computational memory, and is widely readable by statistics software like R, SPSS, and STATA.

Despite the widespread use of Excel for data collection/entry, it is not always utilized in the best manner for data entry and uploading into software for analysis. Many students will develop a research question with testable hypotheses and find data from a public source that uses Excel. They will be excited that the data exists and is free, but then that excitement turns to frustration when they attempt to upload the data into a statistics software only to receive a confusing error message upon upload or when attempting to conduct a statistical analysis. Unfortunately, there is no universal standard by which public organizations and researchers collect, enter, and store their data despite the fact that the formatting of the spreadsheet is of the utmost importance for researchers to be able to use the data and conduct analyses. The best method to use with data entry is the KISS method – Keep It Simple, Sam! Columns in Excel should be for variables while the rows are for the unit of analysis or individual observations. The first row of an Excel document should contain the variable names.

Often, you may find that datasets provided by organizations and websites do not follow this rule. Sometimes organizations that make their data publicly available have extraneous information in their Excel spreadsheets and/or include multiple sheets in their Excel file. Others may not even use Excel, relying on a different file type, which needs to be identified so that the software program can read it correctly. This is not necessarily a critique on how the data are organized by the department or organization – just an observation that it is not always common to obtain data from the Internet or organizations that can be automatically uploaded into a statistics software for analysis. The need to make some adjustments to the data files and data organization in the spreadsheet is often referred to as "cleaning" the data. Cleaning data may involve deleting extraneous information and reorganizing the data into a more readable format for software. It may also include recoding data so that variables can be read and analyzed by the particular software program. Though mundane, cleaning may involve removing commas, dollar signs, or percentages from observations. It may also involve recoding variable observations including words (e.g. Yes/No; Approve/Disapprove; Male/Female/Other; etc.) into numeric values depending upon the software used or vice versa (turning numeric observations into words/string variable). One may also need to take data collected in multiple Excel sheets and store them in separate Excel files and then merge the data back into one common spreadsheet.

The principles and best practices discussed in this chapter do not cover every scenario of data collection issues. It really becomes a "learn by doing" or "learning by experience" for most researchers. However, some of the most common data collection issues/troubleshooting needs are covered here. Additionally, upcoming sections of this chapter provide information on how to input your own data that can be easily read by most software or set up in a format where variables can be easily transformed/recoded to be read by software.

First, a few examples of problematic data collection/organization are depicted – likely scenarios you may encounter when obtaining data from secondary sources (not initially collected/created by you) – and how to adjust the data for ease of analysis.

The U.S. Census Bureau is an absolutely integral and reliable resource for data. One can obtain national, state, and local levels of data across numerous variables. It is a well-respected institution, and many studies utilize its datasets. However, it is unlikely that if you download data from the Census Bureau it will be automatically ready to be uploaded into a statistics software program for analysis. This is not an indictment of the Census Bureau, because the data are organized well for downloading and viewing, but often the dataset needs some adjustments to run analyses and present data visuals and test results.

Let's take a fairly mundane dataset to examine, a data link providing an Excel spreadsheet of the percent of population identifying as White alone by state. The link is: www.census.gov/acs/www/data/data-tables-and-tools/ranking-tables/. You may download the data on your own and open it, but a screenshot (Figure 4.1) appears below of the Excel spreadsheet.

Let's assume we are interested in collecting and analyzing data on the percent of population identifying as White for each state and want to organize the data with the state as the unit of analysis. The initial data setup would not be conducive to running descriptive statistics and analyses in software. Figure 4.1 has arrows pointing to two specific problems in the data setup. Problem #1 has arrows corresponding to the areas between rows 1 and 8. All of the information in these rows is unnecessary

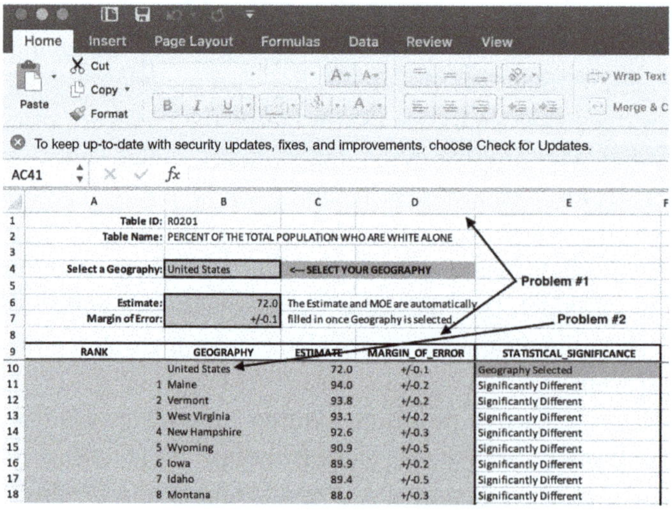

Figure 4.1 Census data cleaning issues, part 1

for data analysis and is simply FYI for the researcher. They can be deleted since the software will not be able to understand this information and will treat each row as an observation.

If one were to upload this Excel sheet into the R Commander, no analyses or statistics could be computed. Row 9 of the data should actually be Row 1, corresponding to the variable names of the data. If we are only interested in the data showing the state's name and its corresponding percent of population identifying as White, we could then delete all columns except for the "Geography" and "Estimate" columns. The "Rank," "Margin of Error," and "Statistical Significance" columns are of no importance and can thus be deleted.

Problem #2 is less of a setup problem and more of a research design problem. If we are interested in the percent of the population who are White by state, the row with information on the entire United States is not needed. It is essentially a "Total" column, compiling all of the state information into the nation's values. If we uploaded this dataset into the R Commander, that row would be treated as an observation and would be included in any descriptive statistics or statistical analyses. The United States would be considered its own state by the software! Therefore, its row can/should be deleted from this particular analysis.

Additional problems with the data spreadsheet are presented in Figure 4.2, specifically with arrows pointing to Problems #3 and #4.

Problem #3 has arrows pointing to the District of Columbia and Puerto Rico. Neither entities are states. So, if you are interested in analyzing state-level data, you would want to delete these rows/observations from the Excel spreadsheet. While this example may appear minute, it illustrates the importance of knowing your data and your observations, ensuring the data in the spreadsheet contain the observations necessary for answering your research questions/hypotheses.

The arrows corresponding to Problem #4 in Figure 4.2 are very similar to Problem #1. There is extraneous information that is not needed for analysis and will not be correctly read by statistical software. These rows should be deleted. All

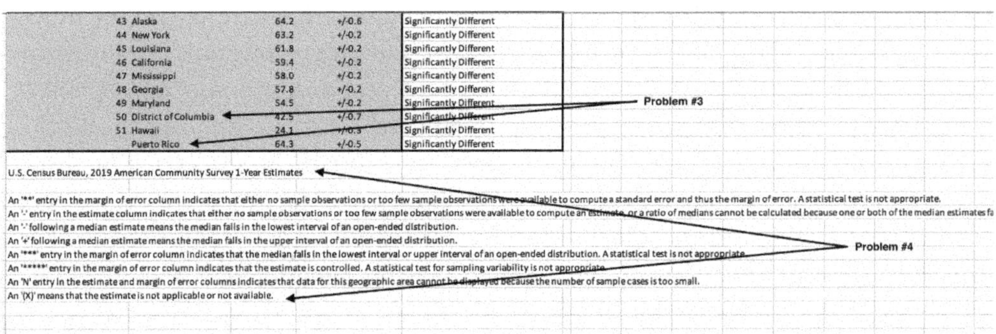

43	Alaska	64.2	+/-0.6	Significantly Different
44	New York	63.2	+/-0.2	Significantly Different
45	Louisiana	61.8	+/-0.2	Significantly Different
46	California	59.4	+/-0.2	Significantly Different
47	Mississippi	58.0	+/-0.2	Significantly Different
48	Georgia	57.8	+/-0.2	Significantly Different
49	Maryland	54.5	+/-0.2	Significantly Different
50	District of Columbia	42.5	+/-0.7	Significantly Different
51	Hawaii	24.1	+/-0.3	Significantly Different
	Puerto Rico	64.3	+/-0.5	Significantly Different

U.S. Census Bureau, 2019 American Community Survey 1-Year Estimates

An '**' entry in the margin of error column indicates that either no sample observations or too few sample observations were available to compute a standard error and thus the margin of error. A statistical test is not appropriate.
An '-' entry in the estimate column indicates that either no sample observations or too few sample observations were available to compute an estimate, or a ratio of medians cannot be calculated because one or both of the median estimates fa
An '-' following a median estimate means the median falls in the lowest interval of an open-ended distribution.
An '+' following a median estimate means the median falls in the upper interval of an open-ended distribution.
An '***' entry in the margin of error column indicates that the median falls in the lowest interval or upper interval of an open-ended distribution. A statistical test is not appropriate.
An '*****' entry in the margin of error column indicates that the estimate is controlled. A statistical test for sampling variability is not appropriate.
An 'N' entry in the estimate and margin of error columns indicates that data for this geographic area cannot be displayed because the number of sample cases is too small.
An '(X)' means that the estimate is not applicable or not available.

Figure 4.2 Census data cleaning issues, part 2

	A	B	C
1	GEOGRAPHY	ESTIMATE	
2	Maine	94.0	
3	Vermont	93.8	
4	West Virgini	93.1	
5	New Hampsl	92.6	
6	Wyoming	90.9	
7	Iowa	89.9	
8	Idaho	89.4	
9	Montana	88.0	
10	Utah	87.3	
11	Kentucky	86.7	
12	Nebraska	86.2	
13	North Dakota	85.8	
14	Wisconsin	85.2	
15	South Dakota	84.1	
16	Colorado	83.7	
17	Kansas	83.6	
18	Oregon	83.5	
19	Indiana	82.8	
20	Minnesota	82.1	
21	Missouri	81.8	
22	Ohio	80.9	
23	Pennsylvania	79.6	
24	Rhode Island	78.7	
25	Arizona	78.3	

Figure 4.3 Cleaned Census data

of these deletions are known as "cleaning" the data, readying it for use in statistical software. Properly cleaned, the Excel spreadsheet should look like Figure 4.3.

Based upon the KISS principle, there are only two columns – a column for the state name and a column for the percent of the population identifying as White. This is the information needed for the situation. The extraneous information is not useful.

4.3 Best Practices for Data Entry

If you are collecting your own data or recoding existing data into a more readable format, there are some good practices to use to ensure your data can be easily imported into statistics software and recorded and stored for ease of use for other researchers. Replicability is a principle of good social science research. Ideally, data should be readily available for any researcher to access and use not only for their own research, but to test/ensure previous findings are robust. Another researcher should be able to access your data to replicate your statistical analysis. This principle is not only important for the pursuit of knowledge and ensuring our results are correct, but is important for research ethics. It provides additional evidence that our results are not a function of malfeasance or data manipulation. The next subsections explore some common practices for entry of data based upon their level of measurement. Data entry using Microsoft Excel is the assumed spreadsheet for entry.

	A	B	C	D
1	state	census	region1	region2
2	Alabama	South	3	2
3	Alaska	West	1	4
4	Arizona	West	1	4
5	Arkansas	South	3	2
6	California	West	1	4
7	Colorado	West	1	4
8	Connecticut	Northeast	4	1
9	Delaware	South	3	2
10	Florida	South	3	2
11	Georgia	South	3	2
12	Indiana	Midwest	2	3
13	Iowa	Midwest	2	3
14	Kansas	Midwest	2	3
15	Kentucky	South	3	2
16	Louisiana	South	3	2
17	Maine	Northeast	4	1
18	Maryland	Northeast	4	1

Figure 4.4 Nominal variable coding

4.3.1 Nominal Variables

Recall that nominal variables are categorical. Categories of the nominal variable cannot be ranked from high to low, and there is no measurable difference/distance among the categories, so variables like gender, political party affiliation, job description, sexual orientation, type of municipal government, etc. cannot be rank-ordered nor is there a measurable difference/distance among the respective categories of these variables. It may seem counterintuitive to use numbers to represent various categories of nominal variables, but it is common practice, and in fact, may be a best practice for data collection for readability across various statistics software.

Let's take an example of collecting state data and a researcher wanting to code for the region of the state. Suppose the researcher wants to code regions as West, Midwest, South, and Northeast like the Census Bureau does for each state. In the Excel spreadsheet, the researcher enters a 1 for each state in the West, a 2 for each state in the Midwest, a 3 for each state in the South, and a 4 for each state in the Northeast. This scheme is depicted in the "region1" column in Figure 4.4. Even though numbers are used for region, there is still no ranking. The numbers are simply placeholders for each respective category of the variable. As such, the researcher could change the coding so that a 1 represents a state in the Northeast, a 2 represents a state in the South, a 3 represents a state in the Midwest, and a 4 represents a state in the West as shown in the "region2" column of Figure 4.4. As long as the researcher is aware of the coding scheme, it does not matter what numbers are used to represent nominal variable categories. They could use either the "region1" scheme or the "region2" scheme from Figure 4.4.

Another common nominal variable included in analyses is the dummy variable. If a variable's categories include a Yes or No, then it should be coded as a nominal variable with two categories, or a dummy variable. Common practice is for a Yes response to be coded as a 1 and a No response to be coded as a 0. The 1/0 coding is the common way to code dummy variables. For example, Figure 4.5 depicts a dataset asking respondents if they voted in the previous election, with a 1 indicating a Yes and a 0 indicating a No.

	A	B
1	respondent	voted
2	1	1
3	2	1
4	3	1
5	4	0
6	5	1
7	6	0
8	7	1
9	8	0
10	9	0
11	10	0
12	11	0
13	12	1
14	13	1
15	14	1
16	15	0
17	16	0
18	17	0

Figure 4.5 Dummy variable coding

4.3.2 Ordinal Variables

Ordinal variables have a rank order of categories that can be ranked from lower to higher or less than to greater than. However, it is not possible to know the difference/distance between the categories. With an approval rating variable ranging from Strongly Approve to Strongly Disapprove with the categories Strongly Approve, Approve, Neutral, Disapprove, and Strongly Disapprove, we can code the responses from low to high or high to low using numeric placeholders. As a best practice, numbers should be used to represent categories of the ordinal variable with the caveat that order matters for the coding, and they should have equal distances between them (even though the distances for the actual categories are unknown).

Using the categories Strongly Approve, Approve, Neutral, Disapprove, and Strongly Disapprove for a variable, one coding scheme could be:

1 = Strongly Approve
2 = Approve
3 = Neutral
4 = Disapprove
5 = Strongly Disapprove

With this coding, higher numbers indicate greater disapproval. The researcher should make a mental note of this coding order and meaning for proper interpretation of statistical tests/results. Alternatively, one could code the approval variable as:

1 = Strongly Disapprove
2 = Disapprove
3 = Neutral
4 = Approve
5 = Strongly Approve

This coding indicates that higher values connote more approval. Yet another common way to code approval is the following:

−2 = Strongly Disapprove
−1 = Disapprove
0 = Neutral
1 = Approve
2 = Strongly Approve

Using this system, negative numbers indicate disapproval while positive numbers indicate approval. When running more advanced statistical analyses like regression, results will not change based upon coding, only the interpretation based upon the coding. The researcher should know what higher/lower and/or positive/negative values correspond with in terms of variable observations for correct interpretation. If the data are coded using the first coding pattern where higher values indicated greater levels of disapproval, but the researcher/analyst thinks the second coding mechanism where higher values indicate greater approval is being used, incorrect

	A	B	C	D	E
1	respondent	approval	coding1	coding2	coding3
2	1	Strongly Approve	1	5	2
3	2	Strongly Disapprove	5	1	-2
4	3	Approve	2	4	1
5	4	Approve	2	4	1
6	5	Neutral	3	3	0
7	6	Approve	2	4	1
8	7	Disapprove	4	2	-1
9	8	Neutral	3	3	0
10	9	Strongly Approve	1	5	2

Figure 4.6 Ordinal variable coding

conclusions may be made. In fact, if the results of a statistical test are significant in this scenario, the researcher would make conclusions completely opposite to what the data reveal! This illustrates the importance of knowing how data are coded and the importance of recording data coding in a codebook, discussed shortly in Section 4.4.

The Excel screenshot in Figure 4.6 depicts different ways to code the same ordinal variable. The first column has the respondent ID. The second column lists the string coding of the respective respondent's approval rating of a policy. Then, the subsequent columns ("coding1," "coding2," and "coding3") show various ways to code the approval variable. Any of them will suffice, but as noted, the researcher should know the numeric coding for correct interpretation of statistical results.

4.3.3 Interval Variables

Probably the easiest types of variables to input are interval variables. Counts of observations, percentages, monetary figures, test scores, etc. are all examples of interval variables. The key for data entry for these types of variables is to abide by the KISS principle and to omit any special characters like dollar signs, percentages, and commas. If entering percentages, omit the % sign – simply enter the number and note in your notes or the codebook (discussed in the next section) that the variable is a percent.

For monetary figures, eliminate any dollar signs or other currency symbols and do not include commas. The only symbol that should be used for monetary figures is the decimal point to indicate cents (if using dollars) that denote fractions of the currency unit. One may wonder the specific reason to omit symbols like dollar signs, percentages, and commas. Some statistics software do not readily read these symbols, and it thus makes it difficult to run analyses. As long as the researcher has correctly input the data and provided a codebook for the variables in the dataset,

	A	B	C
1	state	pupil	percent
2	A	19211	12.1
3	B	18433	11.3
4	C	21761	18.2
5	D	22379	16.7

Figure 4.7 Interval variable coding

they and any others seeking to use the dataset should be able to understand how the data are coded, and subsequently, be able to correctly interpret any statistics output.

Figure 4.7 depicts the data setup for a hypothetical state level dataset on education spending. The unit of analysis is the state, represented by the "state" column. The "pupil" column represents the state per pupil spending in dollars (total education spending divided by number of students). All dollar signs have been eliminated. The "percent" column shows the percent of the state budget allocated to education. All percentage signs have been eliminated. This basic setup is the best manner to input data for various software to successfully read/upload the data.

4.4 Creating Codebooks

Good record-keeping is important for nearly any industry. It is especially crucial when collecting and coding your own data. Recording how variables are coded is not only important for you to remember what your spreadsheet depicts, but is crucial for proper interpretation of statistical tests. Additionally, the recording of variable coding and making it publicly available and understandable promotes the principle of replicability if somebody else would like to use your data to run their own analyses and/or replicate your study.

In creating your codebook, one common way to organize the document is to list each variable in your dataset/spreadsheet. Given that columns in spreadsheets represent unique variables, it makes sense to list each of the columns of your spreadsheet in your codebook and then what each value represents. If using a survey, it is also important to list the exact survey question for each variable. In the Companion Site (www.cambridge.org/scheller), there is a dataset titled *associations_survey* with a corresponding codebook titled "Associations_Codebook." They represent a survey of neighborhood and homeowners association presidents. It may be helpful to open both documents and view them to see how the codebook translates into the Excel dataset. Figures 4.8 and 4.9 depict both the *associations_survey* dataset and its associated codebook, respectively.

	A	B	C	D	E	F	G	
1	id	form	houses	career	profmgr	requests	ownonly	e
2	1	2	6	0	0	1	1	
3	2	2	110	0	0	1	0	
4	3	2	22.5	0	0	1	0	
5	4							
6	5	2	350	0	0	2	0	
7	6	1	120	0	0	1	1	
8	7	2	250			1	0	
9	8							
10	9	2	14	0	0	1	0	
11	10	2	30	0	0	1	1	
12	11	2	30	0		1	1	
13	12	4	0	0	0	1	0	

Figure 4.8 Neighborhood and homeowners association dataset

Codebook

(id) Unique association identifier

1. (form) Circle the item that best describes your association.

   1 = Formed by developer
   2 = Formed by community following establishment of neighborhood
   3 = Formed by city or county government
   4 = Other ____________________

2. (houses) Approximate number of households in your association:

3. (career) Do you consider association management your primary profession?

   0 = No
   1 = Yes

4. (profmgr) Does your association have a professional manager?

   0 = No
   1 = Yes

Figure 4.9 Neighborhood and homeowners associations dataset codebook

Take a look at the data entered to ensure the data entered into the spreadsheet match with the codebook explanation. Publicly accessible datasets should have their codebooks readily available so that researchers understand the coding scheme and can make adjustments as necessary. The association codebook and corresponding data depict how data may be organized according to the coding scheme outlined in the codebook.

4.5 Types of Data

Data need to be organized correctly for accurate statistical analysis and data visualization. One rule of thumb is to organize data in spreadsheets according to the unit of analysis. The unit of analysis is the organizing feature of the data and determines how to set up the data in a spreadsheet like Excel. In public administration and social science research, data are most often organized in a cross-sectional, panel, or time series format. These formats affect how one can run analyses; therefore, it is of the utmost importance to either know how the data are organized in the spreadsheet or to be able to "clean" the data into the proper format for the software to read.

4.5.1 Cross-Sectional Data

Cross-sectional data can be thought of as taking a cross-section or a cut of the particular unit of analysis at one point in time. The associations survey in the previous section is an example of cross-sectional data. The unit of analysis is neighborhood organization, or neighborhood association president, to be more exact, since association presidents are answering questions about their respective associations. The survey is taken once, and only once – a survey for each president at one point in time. Follow-up surveys are not collected, nor are data collected over time. Even if questions exist like, "Thinking back over the past five years, how have your association's activities changed," they do not make the data longitudinal or time series in nature. Even this specific question asks respondents at one particular time their opinion. It is not tracked over time. Most surveys are cross-sectional in nature in that they ask a sample of individuals their opinions once.

Instead of only considering individuals, cross-sectional designs can have other entities as the unit of analysis. A researcher sampling the budgets of 100 cities for fiscal year 2021–2022, collecting data on revenues and expenditures for each city across police, parks, and roads would be conducting a cross-sectional study. If this is the only fiscal year the researcher uses in analysis, the data collected would be cross-sectional in nature and setup. Figure 4.10 shows how such budgetary cross-sectional data can begin to be set up.

As before, each column represents a variable, with variable names in the first row of the Excel spreadsheet. The unit of analysis is city, which is the first column. Then, dollar figures for spending for each category of police, parks, and roads are listed. City B, for example, spent \$890,000 on police, \$96,358 on parks, and \$1,000,000 on roads in fiscal year 2021–2022.

The associations survey seen in Figure 4.8 shows a similar setup. The unit of analysis is the neighborhood association (or association's representative, the president), represented by the "id" variable to denote each neighborhood. Columns again

	A	B	C	D
1	city	police	parks	roads
2	A	1250000	110569	10569832
3	B	890000	96358	1000000
4	C	3567000	1000219	6589574
5	D	235498	16987	568963
6	E	999004	63527	105638941
7				

Figure 4.10 Cross-sectional data setup

represent the various variables or questions in the survey. Each association's response for each question is recorded in its respective row. There are several blank cells in the full dataset. These represent no response for that particular variable or question item from the association's president. Leaving the cells blank or using a period (.) to indicate a non-response or missing data is common practice for data entry/organization.

Cross-sectional data are widely used in public administration research, especially for descriptive studies and any studies focused on one particular time period and the relationships among variables at one particular point in time. They do have some limitations that researchers must be cognizant of to ensure they can make strong conclusions from their data.

Because most cross-sectional studies are non-experimental, researchers do not randomly select their units of analysis to treatment and control groups. For example, across the various survey questions in the associations survey, like questions asking if the organization lobbies local government (a possible dependent variable) and whether or not the organization is a neighborhood or homeowner association (a possible independent variable), researchers are unable to randomly select neighborhoods to be governed by a homeowners association and others to be governed by a neighborhood association. They obviously do not have that level of control.

Researchers also cannot absolutely ensure that non-respondents to cross-sectional surveys are completely random. Ideally, non-response is random, and there are no systematic patterns or biases in whom or what respond to surveys. If rich neighborhoods and homeowners associations are more likely to respond than poorer associations, the data are biased in that particular direction. Such issues are less likely to be problematic when collecting secondary data like the budget example – most cities are statutorily required to post or make publicly available their budgets.

Despite these issues, cross-sectional designs and data are important for public administration research and often the main types of data used in studies due to time

	A	B
1	date	price
2	6/6/21	105.31
3	6/7/21	108.87
4	6/8/21	106.32
5	6/9/21	109.98
6	6/10/21	110.21
7	6/13/21	109.65
8	6/14/21	110.28
9	6/15/21	110.58
10	6/16/21	111.02
11	6/17/21	111.59
12		

Figure 4.11 Time series data setup, example 1

and resource constraints or the fact that longitudinal data collected over time are simply not available.

4.5.2 Time Series Data

This data is perfectly described in its name – data collected over time. The most basic forms of time series data involve collecting observations/data for a particular variable of interest over a predetermined time period of interest/need for the researcher. One common type of time series data that individuals often use without really realizing what it is, are the prices of a stock. At the close of the trading day, a stock has a closing price. Take the daily price of a hypothetical stock over two trading weeks (ten days). The data are presented in the Excel spreadsheet of Figure 4.11.

The data are quite simply organized. Given the data are time series in nature, one column is the time period of interest. In the case of stocks, the daily price dictates that the date variable is entered as the day/month/year. The second column shows the variable of interest – the price of the stock, corresponding to each respective day's closing price.

Applied to a public administration example, a public works director may be interested in tracking the number of pothole repair requests in the city by month and year as a means of tracking asphalt usage and demand based upon the season. The previous two years' data are listed in their spreadsheet (Figure 4.12).

In this setup, the first column is the month, the second column is the year, and the third column is the amount of asphalt (in pounds) needed to repair the city's potholes. One can easily see the data indicate increased demand in the winter and

	A	B	C
1	month	year	pounds
2	January	2020	1000
3	February	2020	1249
4	March	2020	2500
5	April	2020	1985
6	May	2020	810
7	June	2020	600
8	July	2020	402
9	August	2020	225
10	September	2020	107
11	October	2020	142
12	November	2020	201
13	December	2020	625
14	January	2021	1205
15	February	2021	1400
16	March	2021	2687
17	April	2021	2991
18	May	2021	750
19	June	2021	301
20	July	2021	116
21	August	2021	98
22	September	2021	62
23	October	2021	210
24	November	2021	589
25	December	2021	710

Figure 4.12 Time series data setup, example 2

spring months. Winter brings snow and ice that lead to potholes, which need to be fixed, but also increased repairs in the spring as the city catches up on winter freezing/thawing effects on roads. Predictably, summer months have less demand with asphalt usage likely needed for routine repairs from normal wear and tear. Nevertheless, this setup easily allows the director and other analysts to view the data and then use it to produce graphs and run descriptive statistics and time series analyses.

4.5.3 Panel Data

Panel data combines the elements of both cross-sectional and time series data. It can be thought of as collecting data on the particular unit of analysis (using the same entities/individuals) over time. Whereas cross-sectional data's unit of analysis is the individual or entity being observed at one point in time, and the unit of analysis in time series data is the unit of time (e.g. day in the stock market example and month in the pothole example), panel data combines both (same individuals/entities over time). Because of the limitations of cross-sectional data only being observed at one time-point, and thus being unable to meet the time-order principle for determining causality, panel designs aid the researcher in being more confident in their results if time is important in the research design or crucial for understanding the relationship between variables (Frankfort-Nachmias and Nachmias, 2008).

Let's take a hypothetical public administration example to see what we mean by panel data. In the U.S., it is often common to joke about the department of motor vehicles (DMV). This department is where citizens go to obtain their driver's license, renew their license, and/or register a new vehicle, among several other services. Lines are often long, the paperwork is frequently complex, and the customer service is not always of the highest quality, or at least such is the stereotype of the DMV and its employees. Famous comedians Steve Harvey and Tony Baker, along with the sitcom *Big Bang Theory* all have comedic bits about the DMV.

Suppose a local DMV office manager is tired of their DMV having a bad reputation and wants to improve customer service and decrease complaints. Beginning the first week of the new year, the manager collects data on each employee at the local office and their weekly number of complaints against them for the week. At the beginning of the fifth week of the year, the manager announces to the employees that they would like to see improvements in customer service and trains them on new methods for customer service. Their hope is this new training helps to decrease each employee's number of complaints. The office manager is an astute research designer and collector of data and sets up their data spreadsheet according to Figure 4.13.

The dataset contains four columns. The first column lists the respective employee ID. The second column lists the week of the data collection period. The third column lists the employee's number of complaints for that particular week. The final column, "trained," is a dummy variable coded 1 if the week was Week 5 or later (employee had received the training). With this panel setup, the unit of analysis is the employee-week, and each employee-week is an observation. Data are being collected for each employee, each week. For employee #1, they began the analysis period with 15 complaints in Week 1 all the way up to 18 complaints in Week 4. After training in Week 5, the employee had 14 complaints, which is similar to the number of complaints they had in Weeks 1–4, but the complaints decline to 7 and then 3 in Week 6 and Week 7, respectively. It appears that the training may have worked in reducing the number of complaints levied against this employee. Other employees, maybe less so, but you will analyze those trends in the Practice Problems section in this chapter.

The important matter to consider is whether or not the data are correctly set up for the manager and any other analyst to read/understand the data and then be able to run analyses in software. In this particular example, the data are correctly inputted so that the analyst can engage in the correct type of panel analysis.

	A	B	C	D	E
1	employee	week	complaints	trained	
2	1	1	15	0	
3	1	2	10	0	
4	1	3	12	0	
5	1	4	18	0	
6	1	5	14	1	
7	1	6	7	1	
8	1	7	3	1	
9	2	1	2	0	
10	2	2	8	0	
11	2	3	4	0	
12	2	4	3	0	
13	2	5	6	1	
14	2	6	4	1	
15	2	7	4	1	
16	3	1	21	0	
17	3	2	20	0	
18	3	3	25	0	
19	3	4	16	0	
20	3	5	21	1	
21	3	6	20	1	
22	3	7	23	1	
23	4	1	12	0	
24	4	2	14	0	
25	4	3	9	0	
26	4	4	6	0	
27	4	5	7	1	
28	4	6	3	1	
29	4	7	15	1	
30	5	1	3	0	
31	5	2	2	0	
32	5	3	4	0	
33	5	4	5	0	
34	5	5	1	1	
35	5	6	0	1	
36	5	7	1	1	
37					

Figure 4.13 Panel data setup

4.6 Sources of Data

If you are engaging in the collection of primary data, you will be the individual collecting the original data. The most common type of primary data generated by public administrators and students and researchers of public administration are the types of data in the previous DMV example through the researcher's own observations/manipulations or through surveys like the association survey. In the DMV example, the office manager decided to track the number of complaints they received per employee and then engaged in their own treatment/manipulation by engaging in training sessions and collecting complaint data after the trainings. The office manager is the source of the data. In the association survey, the researcher designed a survey that was sent to neighborhood and homeowner association presidents with questions chosen by the researcher. Just like the DMV office manager, the association researcher was the principal in charge of creating and collecting the data.

If students, administrators, and researchers are not creating their own data, they are most likely retrieving data collected by other individuals and/or entities for their use. Such data are known as secondary data. For example, a researcher using Census Bureau data is using secondary data. Another example is pulling data from publicly available sources. A researcher may be interested in collecting state economic and political data and may utilize reports and data made available from various sources like the Bureau of Economic Analysis, state departments of commerce and economic development, state legislatures, etc. The resulting dataset would also be considered as using secondary data.

One of the challenges many students and researchers have is finding the data they need to use to answer their research questions and hypotheses. Many interesting and certainly valuable research questions and hypotheses are developed, but in the absence of data, they cannot be tested. Not all desired data exists, and it can be frustrating and time consuming for students to find data or even know where to begin to look. A Google search, while a good starting place, is not always enough to find the desired data. Sometimes it helps to know a few places to visit online first. Below is a short list of some common sources of data. By no means is this list exhaustive.

American National Election Studies (ANES): Conducted every four years among U.S. voters with a variety of demographic, political, and voting data/variables.

Bureau of Economic Analysis (BEA): Provides economic indicators data (GDP, income, inflation, government expenditures, etc.) at national, state, and local levels over time.

Bureau of Labor Statistics (BLS): Resource for national, state, and local unemployment, inflation, and wages data, among other variables over time.

Dataverse: Data repository housed at Harvard University. Researchers can deposit their data on the dataverse, and it contains the data files of many published research studies. Contains a search engine to search for particular datasets, researchers, or topics.

ICPSR (Inter-University Consortium for Political and Social Research): Data repository housed at the University of Michigan. Contains many datasets from the organizations in this list in addition to datasets used in some published academic research studies. The online repository has a search engine to search by topic or even specific variable.

Uniform Crime Reports: Federal Bureau of Investigation (FBI) data on national and state crimes by type and arrests.

U.S. Census Bureau: Chief data collection agency of the United States government. Conducted every ten years, the Census provides comprehensive information from U.S. citizens across numerous socioeconomic and demographic characteristics. Additionally, several common surveys and datasets in public administration research are conducted and/or collected by the U.S. Census Bureau, including (but not limited to):

American Community Survey (ACS): Annual survey sent to a sample of the U.S. population, collecting household socioeconomic demographics like income, housing, education, health, etc., including data across race. Estimates of population characteristics like total population across states and localities are also made available each year through the ACS.

American Housing Survey (AHS): The AHS is a longitudinal survey of a sample of households in the U.S., conducted every odd year. It seeks to obtain information on the quality and type of housing of households in the U.S., demographic data of household members, housing finances, etc.

Census of Governments: Conducted every five years and solicited to the various types of state and local government entities. Size of the government (number of employees), wages, revenues and expenditures (across various taxing and spending categories), and other financial data are collected.

County Business Patterns: Annual county-level data reporting the number of business establishments and size (number of employees) across various industries.

Survey of Income and Program Participation (SIPP): Annual data on citizen enrollment/participation in government programs like welfare, disability, veterans' benefits, and unemployment assistance, among other programs. It also includes socioeconomic and demographic information of participants.

Most national, state, and local government departments collect and make public their data. Going to their respective webpages can usually yield lucrative results in terms of data. If not available online, email or phone requests to the organization's chief data officer, information technology department, or public relations department are other manners by which to obtain data. Sometimes, filing a Freedom of Information Act (FOIA) request is necessary to obtain the data if it is not readily available but still subject to being open to public inspection.

4.7 Summary

While this chapter has covered some of the basic principles and practices of data discovery, collection, and entry, learning-by-doing will yield the most practice and learning experiences with data collection. It is impossible to cover every possible error or provide troubleshooting advice for a wide range of issues and complications that one may encounter in collecting and cleaning data for analysis. As a relatively new student to data collection and analysis, you will likely encounter a situation where you have downloaded data or collected it, uploaded it to software and then receive an intimidating and confusing error message when trying to run statistics. In fact, it is probably certain that you will, at some point, receive an error message and start to be frustrated with the data and software. Do not let this deter you. There is probably a small typo or setup/entry issue that appears mundane, but will prevent analysis. Maybe a letter was accidentally entered instead of a number, or a variable has a character like a $ or % that the software is unable to read.

The purpose of this chapter has been to alert you to some common issues and to present some best practices for data setup and entry to minimize frustration and to make data analysis run more smoothly when you are ready to use the software. The remaining chapters will make use of software – the R Commander. The next chapter is a short tutorial on how to install R, the R Commander itself, and how to call up data into the R Commander. From there, each of the remaining chapters will make use of the R Commander, beginning a hopefully beneficial journey in basic statistics and data analysis.

PRACTICE PROBLEMS

1. Here is a screenshot of data and its codebook for variables as collected by the original researcher. Answer the questions after the screenshot and codebook to help the researcher better improve their dataset.

   Codebook

   -observation = survey respondent ID
   -age = age of respondent:
   < 20
   20–29
   30–39
   40–49
   50–59
   60+

   -income = annual income
   -owner = owns home (Yes or No)
   -gender = gender (Male or Female)
   -housing = self-report of estimated percent of income spent on housing
   -trust = How much do you trust your city council?
   -A lot
   -Somewhat trust
   -Somewhat distrust
   -Distrust a lot
   -trust2 = How much do you trust your city's mayor?
   -A lot = 1
   -Somewhat trust = 0
   -Neither trust or distrust = 0.5
   -Somewhat distrust = 2
   -Distrust a lot = −2

   -meetings = number of public meetings attended in the past year

	A	B	C	D	E	F	G	H	I	J
1	observation	age	income	owner	gender	housing	trust	trust2	meetings	
2	1	20-29	$35,000	Yes	Male	45%	A lot	Somewhat trust	1	
3	2	20-29	$19,000	No	Female	50%	Distrust a lot	Distrust a lot	0	
4	3	60+	$78,000	No	Female	20%	Somewhat distrust	Distrust a lot	0	
5	4	50-59	$125,000	Yes	Female	15%	Somewhat distrust	A lot	5	
6	5	<20	$14,500	No	Male	60%	Somewhat trust	A lot	3	
7	6	40-49	$55,000	No	MISSING	25%	Distrust a lot	Distrust a lot	6	
8	7	60+	$95,000	Yes	REFUSED	30%	A lot	Somewhat trust	2	
9	8	60+	$72,000	Yes	Male	22%	Somewhat trust	Somewhat trust	1	
10	9	30-39	$36,000	No	Male	37%	Somewhat distrust	Somewhat distrust	0	
11	10	40-49	$45,000	No	Female	18%	Somewhat trust	Distrust a lot	0	
12										
13										
14	Data come from a 2022 survey conducted by the researcher using a random sample from a large Midwestern U.S. city.									
15	For questions on the data, call the researcher at 555-555-1234									
16										

a. As entered, and assuming the researcher has saved the data correctly, can it be successfully loaded into the R Commander or other software? Why/why not?

b. For each of the variables/columns in Excel listed below, indicate if the data is set up correctly using best practices for data entry and research design. If not, explain why.

   i. age
   ii. income
   iii. owner
   iv. gender
   v. housing
   vi. trust
   vii. trust2
   viii. meetings

c. For those variables where you have identified as being problematic in terms of their measurement design and/or entry, offer a solution and then redo the codebook to how you would collect and enter the data.

d. With your new codebook, reenter the data for the researcher into Excel and provide a screenshot of your new spreadsheet.

2. Explain how panel data combines elements of both cross-sectional and time series designs.

3. For each of the spreadsheet screenshots, indicate if they reflect cross-sectional, time series, or panel data:

a.

	A	B	C	D
1	organization	year	budget	
2	a	2013	1256987	
3	a	2014	1106978	
4	a	2015	1056324	
5	a	2016	999057	
6	a	2017	1000006	
7	a	2018	1000985	
8	a	2019	1115874	
9	a	2020	1119210	
10	a	2021	1245634	
11	a	2022	1245888	
12				
13				

b.

	A	B	C	D
1	organization	year	budget	
2	a	2013	1256987	
3	a	2014	1106978	
4	a	2015	1056324	
5	a	2016	999057	
6	a	2017	1000006	
7	a	2018	1000985	
8	a	2019	1115874	
9	a	2020	1119210	
10	a	2021	1245634	
11	a	2022	1245888	
12	b	2013	87852	
13	b	2014	89635	
14	b	2015	88921	
15	b	2016	86954	
16	b	2017	91236	
17	b	2018	91002	
18	b	2019	91326	
19	b	2020	92568	
20	b	2021	91524	
21	b	2022	93473	
22				

c.

	A	B	C	D	E
1	organization	year	budget		
2	a	2022	1245888		
3	b	2022	93473		
4	c	2022	859632		
5	d	2022	1635964		
6	e	2022	751647		
7	f	2022	99163		
8					
9					
10					

4. Examine the DMV panel data from Section 4.5.3 in this chapter. What hypothesis can you devise regarding the training and number of complaints. Without using software, eyeball the data and make a tentative conclusion about whether or not the training worked based upon the data and why.
5. Using one of the data sources from Section 4.6 or through your own online search, find a dataset that would need to be cleaned before it could be analyzed. Provide a screenshot(s) of the problems with the dataset and provide solutions to make the dataset readable and able to be analyzed by software.
6. Find a public administration journal article or applied article that uses one of the types of data mentioned in the chapter (panel, time series, cross-sectional, etc.).
   a. Identify the data setup (panel, time series, cross-sectional, etc.). Explain if and how the author(s) explains the setup and type of data used.
   b. Identify the unit of analysis.
   c. State the hypotheses of the study.
   d. Identify the statistical test used.
   e. Briefly summarize the results of the study and if the hypotheses were supported.

5

R Software and the R Commander

5.1 Introduction

The previous four chapters have focused on the principles of robust research design and measurement of variables. By now, as a student, you should have some working knowledge of how to devise research questions and hypotheses, including how to operationalize concepts into observable variables. The purpose of this chapter is to describe the R Commander software and how to access it – how to download it, open the software, upload data into the software, and to make sense of the software for beginners. From there, the focus of the chapter turns to the basics of the R Commander software and how to use it for recoding data.

5.2 Description of R and the R Commander

The R software for statistical computing is an open source software, available for free download from the Internet. Being open source, any computer programmers and statisticians can create their own programs for running statistical tests, known as packages. In fact, the package used in this textbook is the R Commander package (Fox and Bouchet-Valat, 2022), which was created by John Fox and turns the R software interface into a more user-friendly drop-down or Graphical User Interface (GUI) program for students and researchers. When one downloads the R software and opens it on their computer, it is a largely nondescript interface. In fact, to get the R software to make calculations or to conduct statistical tests, R code needs to be entered into the interface. Therefore, it becomes necessary to understand the R coding language to run your analyses in the R interface. With the R Commander package one does not need to code, so running statistics becomes much easier, in the same vein as the popular SPSS software.

5.2.1 Comparing R with Other Software

The most often used software in public administration courses tends to be SPSS. It is seen as the most user-friendly and accessible software. To be sure, SPSS has a fairly intuitive GUI with drop-down menus. Its popularity has led to the publication of many resources and tutorials from books to YouTube videos. Certainly, the benefit of SPSS is its level of intuitive use and availability of tutorial resources. However, it is a fairly expensive software to own and can be pricey to rent. Despite these drawbacks, this textbook recognizes the importance of SPSS in public administration research and its continued use. As such, each chapter with software instruction in this textbook includes the relevant SPSS steps to conduct the statistical tests located in the online appendix. There is no debate regarding the ease of use for many students with SPSS and its popularity in public administration programs and thus the reason for its inclusion in this textbook. The one downside of SPSS is its cost and its lack of use in the public sector. This lack of use increases the importance of free and easily downloadable software like the R Commander.

Another software that is gaining popularity in public administration programs is STATA, especially at the PhD level. While STATA has drop-down GUI options, it is more commonly used as a code-based program, where analysts create do-files of STATA code to run statistical tests. For many, the STATA coding language is much more intuitive than the R interface coding language. However popular STATA may be among some public administration programs, it is still a fairly expensive program to purchase and is not widely used in the public sector compared to other software like Excel. However, given the increasing popularity of STATA in public administration programs, I include STATA instruction alongside SPSS instruction in the online appendix for each relevant chapter. The focus of this STATA instruction is on the use of code in do-files as this is usually the main method of STATA use.

The most commonly used data software in the public sector is Microsoft Excel. Most students and practitioners are at least somewhat familiar with Excel or have used it in some manner in their studies or profession. Excel is certainly a great tool/spreadsheet for data entry. However, beyond basic graphing and descriptive statistics, Excel is quite difficult to use. This textbook utilizes Excel in the manner for which the author sees its strength – data organization/entry. Excel is an excellent and often preferred software for data entry. It can be easily uploaded to nearly every statistics software. Therefore, its use is highlighted in this text as a tool for data entry and organization to be uploaded into the R Commander for analysis.

5.3 Installation of R and R Studio

There are a few ways to download and access the R Commander software program. The general R platform can be downloaded from the Comprehensive R Archive Network (CRAN). It is a code-based platform and can be used to call up the R Commander. However, a more user-friendly platform to call up the R Commander is RStudio. The RStudio is free to download. Follow these steps to easily download RStudio (note that these steps may be slightly altered or different as the RStudio website changes):

1. Go to www.rstudio.com/.

2. There should be a "Products" menu towards the top of the webpage. Hover over "Products" with your cursor. Doing so should reveal more options.
3. Slide your cursor to the words "RStudio IDE" under the "Open Source" column and click.
4. A new page should appear. Scroll down and you will see two versions for downloading RStudio. Click on the box with the words "RStudio Desktop" where the pricing indicates "Free."
5. A new page should emerge. Scroll down a bit. The free Open Source Edition RStudio Desktop is the correct version. Click the blue box that says "DOWNLOAD."
6. A new page will appear stating that R is required for installation of R Studio. It should be listed as "1: Install R." This step is normal since RStudio needs the regular R software to operate. So, click "DOWNLOAD AND INSTALL R."
7. A new tab with the R webpage appears. Download R for your operating system by clicking the relevant link in the top box.
8. A new page should emerge with various versions of R (.pkg files for Mac, .exe for Windows). Download the relevant file for your operating system. Be aware of where your file downloads automatically store on your computer.
9. Find the downloaded file in your downloads folder and double-click on it. Follow the installation instructions.
10. Once R has been installed, go back to the previous tab from the RStudio website. You can now proceed to "2: Install RStudio." Click its blue download box. It should download an installation file.
11. Double-click the installation file and follow the on-screen instructions if asked. Note: for a Mac, move the RStudio icon to a relevant folder (most likely the Applications folder). Note where you have installed RStudio. You may go to that folder and double-click on the RStudio icon to double-check that it has been installed.

5.3.1 For Mac Users – Downloading X Quartz

Mac users need to download an additional piece of software for the R Commander to run and successfully display results and graphics. This software is called X Quartz, and it is also free. To download X Quartz:

1. Go to www.xquartz.org/. The page should have a ".pkg" file to download under "Quick Download."
2. Click on the ".pkg" file, which will be downloaded to your computer.
3. Double-click the downloaded ".pkg" file where download files are stored on your computer, which will open a window containing the XQuartz software file and follow the on-screen instructions to install to your computer.
4. Several approval windows/popups may appear. Allow all approvals, and continue with the installation instructions on the computer. There should be no need to

change any installation location on your computer. Default settings should work. Your computer may ask if you want to send the Installer to the Trash. That is perfectly fine to allow, since the file is simply the installation file and not the actual software. At this point, you can proceed to the next section of accessing and installing the R Commander package.

5.4 Installing and Accessing the R Commander

Once RStudio is installed, simply double-clicking its icon from its stored location on the computer will open the RStudio. Depending upon your computer, a popup security-type box may alert you that the RStudio is an application downloaded from the Internet. If this box appears, simply agree to open the application. The RStudio should open and look like Figure 5.1.

At this point, one could begin using the RStudio as a general R interface if one knows R code to upload and analyze data. Since this is not our purpose in this text, and we want to use a drop-down version of R, called the R Commander, we must install the R Commander package. To install the R Commander package:

1. In the R menu at the top of the screen, click Tools → Install Packages. A popup box should appear like that in Figure 5.2.
2. In the blank "Packages" box, enter "Rcmdr" as shown in Figure 5.2. A list of packages may appear. If so, simply click Rcmdr in the list. It will populate Rcmdr

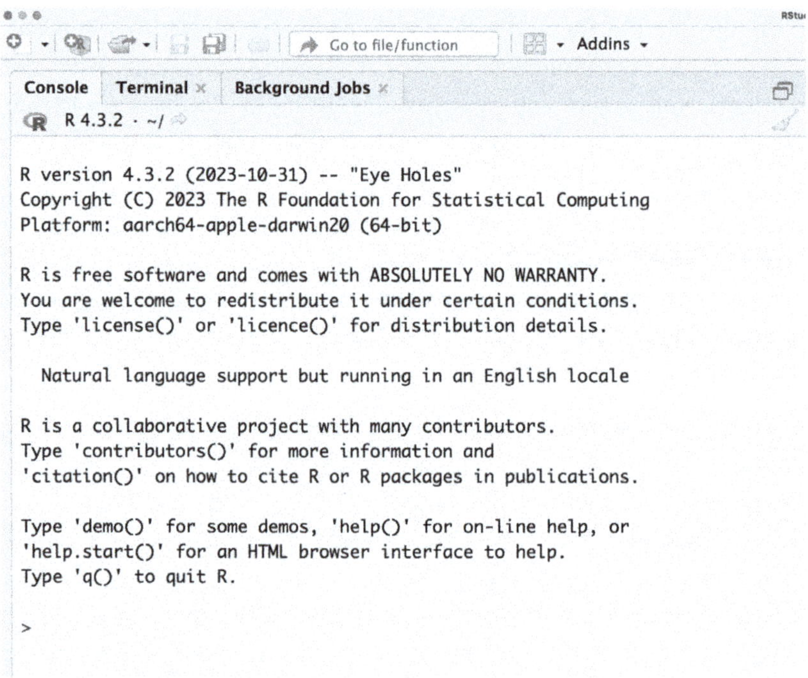

Figure 5.1 RStudio platform

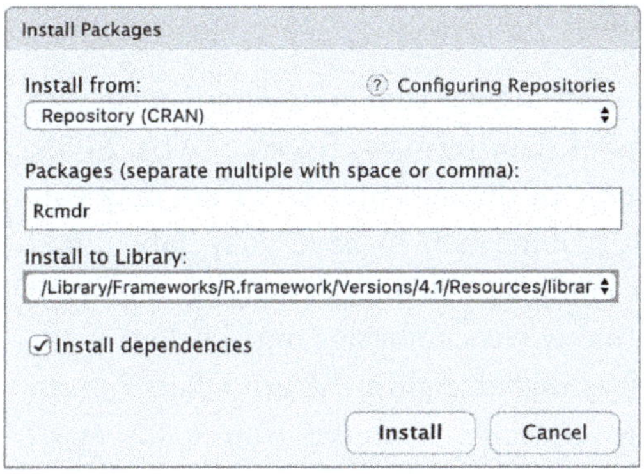

Figure 5.2 Installing packages

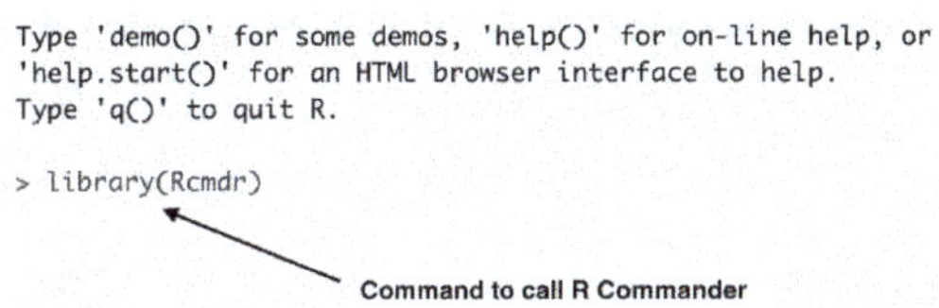

Figure 5.3 Calling/accessing the R Commander

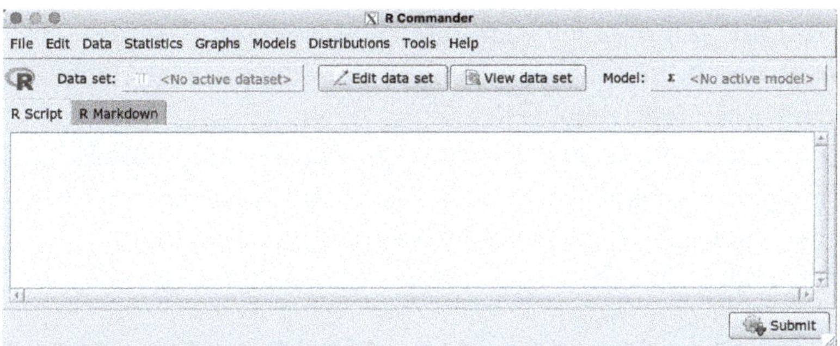

Figure 5.4 R Commander interface

into the blank "Packages" box. There is no need to change the Library where the package is stored. Also, make sure that the "Install dependencies" box is checked. It should be checked by default. Click Install.

3. The installation process should be completed fairly quickly. When the cursor appears again in RStudio, type "library(Rcmdr)" and click Return/Enter. See Figure 5.3 to ensure you have correctly written the code. This is really the only code that you need to know for this text. Once you click Enter or Return, the R Commander should load. Some users may initially see a popup box giving a list of packages that are missing but necessary to be installed. If so, simply click "Yes," and then OK on the box asking where to install packages from. The R Commander should now appear and look like Figure 5.4.

This interface is the main application you will use for all of your data analysis and visualization and will be referred throughout the text as the R Commander or R Commander interface.

5.5 Uploading Data in the R Commander

With the R Commander software open, the next logical step is having it read data from a dataset. It can call up different types of data formats: Excel, STATA, SPSS, SAS, delimited files, etc. As a reminder of some of the best practices from data collection and storage from the last chapter, it is important to have your data stored in a central location, like a folder on your computer, or other easily remembered and accessible location. In the Companion Site (www.cambridge.org/scheller) is located the *associations_survey* Excel file. It was introduced in the last chapter as an example of cross-sectional data. This dataset contains responses from a survey of neighborhood and homeowners associations presidents. We will simply use it as a small dataset to ensure that we have successfully downloaded the R Commander and can call up data. To call up this dataset, in the R Commander menu at the top of the screen, do the following:

1. Click Data → Import data → from Excel file... as seen in Figure 5.5. If your dataset was stored in STATA format, for example, you would obviously use the "from STATA file" option.
2. The next window will ask you to name your dataset. The default "Dataset" and other defaults should work if your data is organized according to the principles discussed in Chapter 4. Therefore, simply click OK.
3. The R Commander will then bring up a window for you to select the file to upload. This is where you have stored your data file. In this particular example, Figure 5.6 depicts the author's screen, where it is stored on the Desktop.
4. Double-clicking this folder should then reveal all files and folders on your Desktop. Find the *associations_survey* file.
5. Double-click the "associations_survey" file icon. This action should upload the data into the R Commander. However, there will be no bells/whistles or confirmation window. Most likely, you will see some complicated-looking code in the R Commander window. Not to worry. Simply click the "View data set" button in the R commander. Figure 5.7 shows what you may see, along with an arrow pointing where to click.
6. When you click the "View data set" button, another window should appear with the dataset. Confirm with Figure 5.8.

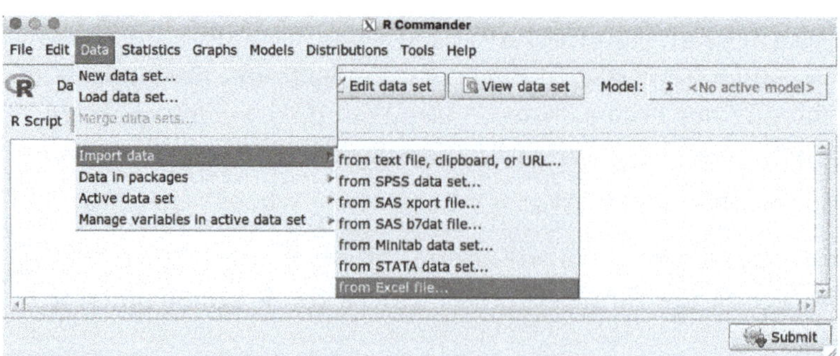

Figure 5.5 Importing data, step 1

Figure 5.6 Importing data, step 2

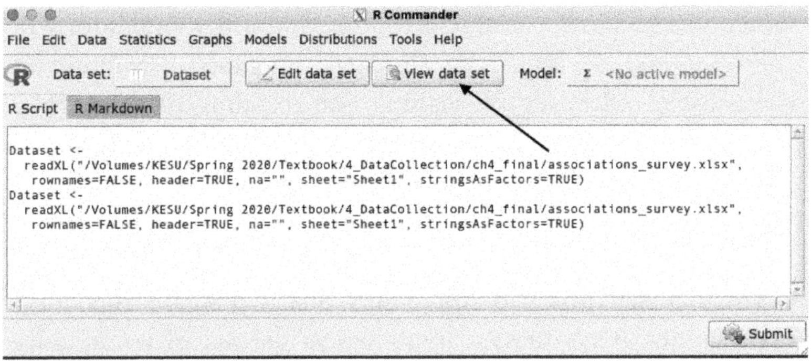

Figure 5.7 View data set option

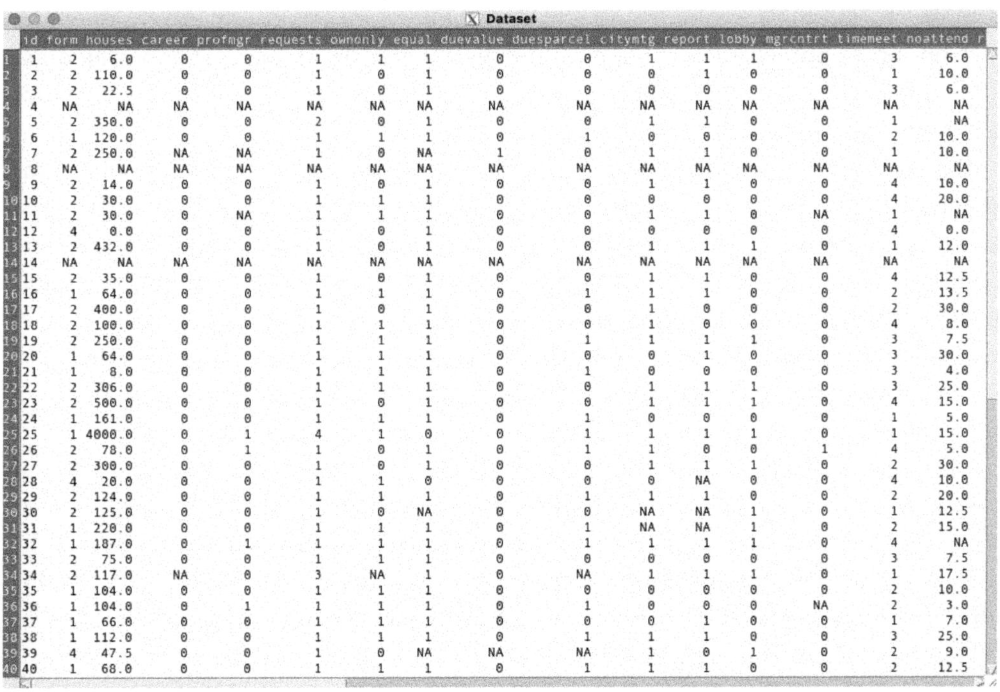

Dataset

	id	form	houses	career	profmgr	requests	ownonly	equal	duevalue	duesparcel	citymtg	report	lobby	mgrcntrt	timemeet	noattend
1	1	2	6.0	0	0	1	1	1	0	0	1	1	1	0	3	6.0
2	2	2	110.0	0	0	1	0	1	0	0	0	1	0	0	1	10.0
3	3	2	22.5	0	0	1	0	1	0	0	0	0	0	0	3	6.0
4	4	NA	NA	NA	NA	NA	NA	NA	NA	NA	NA	NA	NA	NA	NA	NA
5	5	2	350.0	0	0	2	0	1	0	0	1	1	0	0	1	NA
6	6	1	120.0	0	0	1	1	1	0	1	0	0	0	0	2	10.0
7	7	2	250.0	NA	NA	1	0	NA	1	0	1	1	0	0	1	10.0
8	8	NA	NA	NA	NA	NA	NA	NA	NA	NA	NA	NA	NA	NA	NA	NA
9	9	2	14.0	0	0	1	0	1	0	0	1	1	0	0	4	10.0
10	10	2	30.0	0	0	1	1	1	0	0	0	0	0	0	4	20.0
11	11	2	30.0	0	NA	1	1	1	0	0	1	1	0	NA	1	NA
12	12	4	0.0	0	0	1	0	1	0	0	0	0	0	0	4	0.0
13	13	2	432.0	0	0	1	0	1	0	0	1	1	1	0	1	12.0
14	14	NA	NA	NA	NA	NA	NA	NA	NA	NA	NA	NA	NA	NA	NA	NA
15	15	2	35.0	0	0	1	0	1	0	0	1	1	0	0	4	12.5
16	16	1	64.0	0	0	1	1	1	0	1	1	1	0	0	2	13.5
17	17	2	400.0	0	0	1	0	1	0	0	1	0	0	0	2	30.0
18	18	2	100.0	0	0	1	1	1	0	0	1	0	0	0	4	8.0
19	19	2	250.0	0	0	1	1	1	0	1	1	1	1	0	3	7.5
20	20	1	64.0	0	0	1	1	1	0	0	0	1	0	0	3	30.0
21	21	1	8.0	0	0	1	1	1	0	1	0	0	0	0	3	4.0
22	22	2	306.0	0	0	1	1	1	0	0	1	1	1	0	3	25.0
23	23	2	500.0	0	0	1	0	1	0	0	1	1	1	0	4	15.0
24	24	1	161.0	0	0	1	1	1	0	1	0	0	0	0	1	5.0
25	25	1	4000.0	0	1	4	1	0	0	1	1	1	1	0	1	15.0
26	26	2	78.0	0	1	1	0	1	0	1	1	0	0	1	4	5.0
27	27	2	300.0	0	0	1	0	1	0	0	1	1	1	0	2	30.0
28	28	4	20.0	0	0	1	1	0	0	0	0	NA	0	0	4	10.0
29	29	2	124.0	0	0	1	1	1	0	1	1	1	0	0	2	20.0
30	30	2	125.0	0	0	1	0	NA	0	0	NA	NA	1	0	1	12.5
31	31	1	220.0	0	0	1	1	1	0	1	NA	NA	1	0	2	15.0
32	32	1	187.0	0	1	1	1	1	0	1	1	1	1	0	4	NA
33	33	2	75.0	0	0	1	1	1	0	0	0	0	0	0	3	7.5
34	34	2	117.0	NA	0	3	NA	1	0	NA	1	1	1	0	1	17.5
35	35	1	104.0	0	0	1	1	1	0	0	0	0	0	0	2	10.0
36	36	1	104.0	0	1	1	1	1	0	1	0	0	0	NA	2	3.0
37	37	1	66.0	0	0	1	1	1	0	0	0	1	0	0	1	7.0
38	38	1	112.0	0	0	1	1	1	0	1	1	1	0	0	3	25.0
39	39	4	47.5	0	0	1	0	NA	NA	NA	1	0	1	0	2	9.0
40	40	1	68.0	0	0	1	1	1	0	1	1	1	0	0	2	12.5

Figure 5.8 Data view

This nondescript window allows you to check that your dataset is correctly uploaded and allows you you to double-check that it is in a readily analyzable format for data analysis.

5.6 Recoding Data in the R Commander

One necessary skill when cleaning datasets for analysis and visualization is recoding data. Variables in secondary data may not be coded in the manner for which you need to analyze. For example, maybe the variables are in string/factor format with words for categories like Strongly Agree through Strongly Disagree, and you need to recode the variable to a numeric format. Other times, maybe the variable categories are in numeric format and you would like to change them to string/factor. This section will introduce you to basic variable recoding, and other examples will abound throughout the textbook. So, this is to say that the short instruction in this section is not exhaustive of all types of cleaning and recoding that you may need to do in your studies or career. The Recommended Reading section at the end of this chapter contains a few books with much more instruction on different cleaning and recoding scenarios if you are interested in the nuts and bolts of data editing.

For now, load the *grants* dataset from the Companion Site (www.cambridge.org/scheller) into the R Commander. It contains a hypothetical dataset of community grants awarded by a city mayor's office. Often, cities have monies in their budgets to allocate to nonprofit groups to help them in their activities. Some examples are the funds being used to host a community-building event in a neighborhood, a nonprofit purchasing plants and garden supplies for their community garden, an arts nonprofit purchasing art supplies for their youth program, a neighborhood association using funds to purchase an entrance sign and landscaping at the entrance to the neighborhood, etc.

During this year's application cycle, suppose the mayor allocates four $7,000 community grants. The *grants* dataset contains four columns of information. The first column, "application," is the application number. A total of twelve applications were received by the mayor's office. The "minority" column represents if the application is from a minority-run community organization – whether or not the president or chief executive officer is a member of an underrepresented minority group. It is coded 0 if the organization is not minority-run and 1 if the organization is minority-run. Suppose the mayor has their staff rate the application's request for funds in terms of their perceived priority of being funded. The staff rank the application priority tasks "low," "medium," or "high." This variable is labeled "priority." Finally, there is a column labeled "awarded," where a "Y" represents the application receiving the award and an "N" represents an award denial. A social equity researcher with this data is trying to determine whether or not minority-run organizations are more or less likely to receive funding.

Our task at hand is not to analyze this data quite yet. It is to show how to recode variables with the R Commander. The first example of recoding will be from string/factor coding to numeric coding. The "priority" variable is string/factor. It has words representing categories. We may want to change it to numeric coding. Additionally, the "awarded" variable is also a string/factor variable. The second example of recoding will be for the "minority" variable. It is coded as a numeric variable, with numbers as placeholders. If desired, we can recode it to a string/factor variable.

5.6.1 String/Factor Coding to Numeric Coding

Once the dataset has been loaded into the R Commander, we can begin to change a string/factor variable to a numeric variable. The "priority" variable includes labels of "low," "medium," and "high." Suppose we want to recode it where a 1 represents "low," 2 represents "medium," and 3 represents "high." One easy manner to do this is to create a new variable, one which we will call "priority2." Use the following steps in the R Commander:

1. Click Data→Manage variables in active data set→Recode variables (Figure 5.9).
2. Highlight the variable of interest ("priority") in the "Variables to recode" box. In the "New variable name or prefix for multiple recodes" box, give your new variable a name. We said we would call it "priority2." Uncheck the "Make (each) new variable a factor." We want to create a numeric variable, not a factor variable. Finally, you will need to tell the R Commander how to recode the string/factor original variable into the new numeric variable. In the "Enter recode directives" box, we can enter language to do just that based upon the variable's categories. We want "low" to be recoded to a 1, "medium" to a 2, and "high" to a 3. The code in Figure 5.10 does this by putting each string/factor category in quotes,

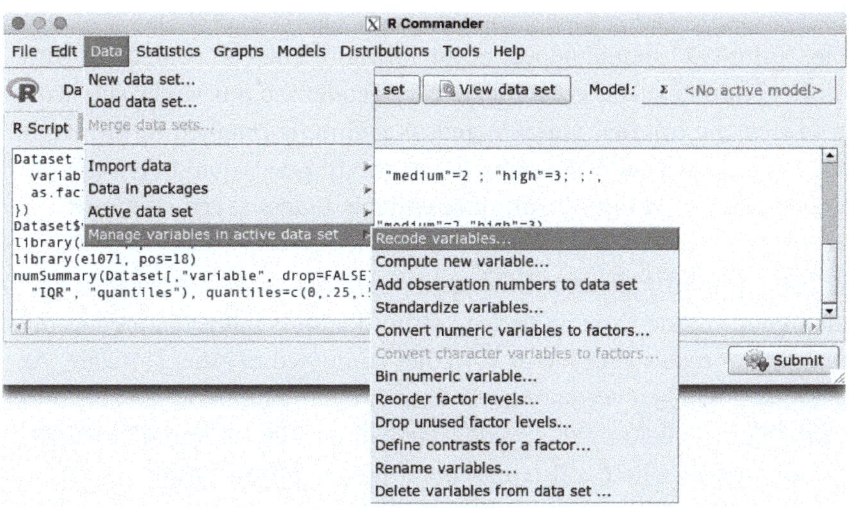

Figure 5.9 String/factor to numeric, step 1

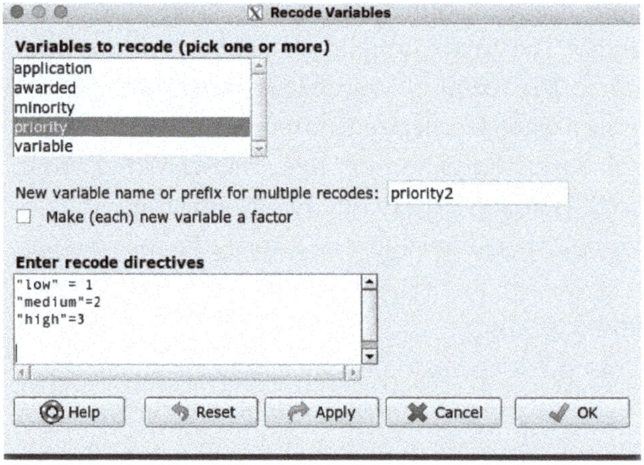

Figure 5.10 String/factor to numeric, step 2

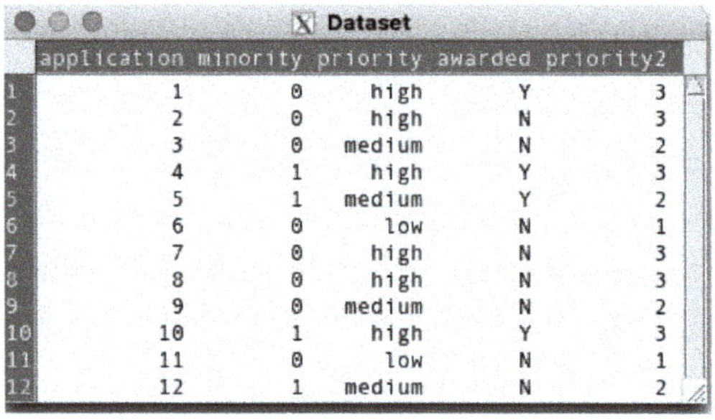

Figure 5.11 String/factor to numeric data view

adding an equals sign, and then inputting the numeric value for each respective category. Each category recoded should be entered on a separate line in the box as depicted in Figure 5.10. Click OK.

3. To determine if the recoding was successful, you can then click the "View data" set button on the R Commander. If successful, your data should look like Figure 5.11.

The new variable, "priority2" should appear at the far right. You can compare it with the original "priority" variable. It is good practice to recode into a new variable with a similar name so that the original variable and its coding is retained in the event of making an error. If recoded into the same name, the recode would overwrite the original coding and you would lose the original variable unless saved elsewhere.

5.6.2 Numeric Coding to String/Factor Coding

With the R Commander, coding from numeric to string/factor is more common as the R Commander can better read string/factor variables compared to other software. As seen in later chapters, it will be necessary at times to convert a numeric variable into a string/factor variable. To illustrate this recode, we will use the "minority" variable, which is numerically coded where a 0 represents a non-minority run organization and a 1 represents a minority-run organization. Let's recode a 0 to show "Non Minority," and a 1 to show "Minority."

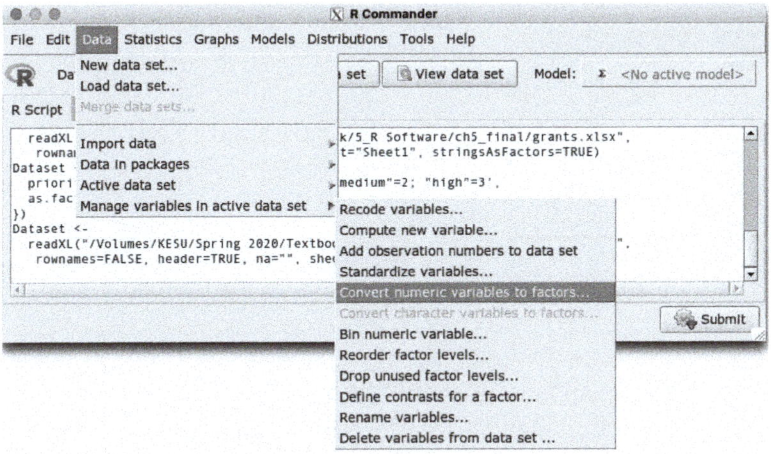

Figure 5.12 Numeric to string/factor, step 1

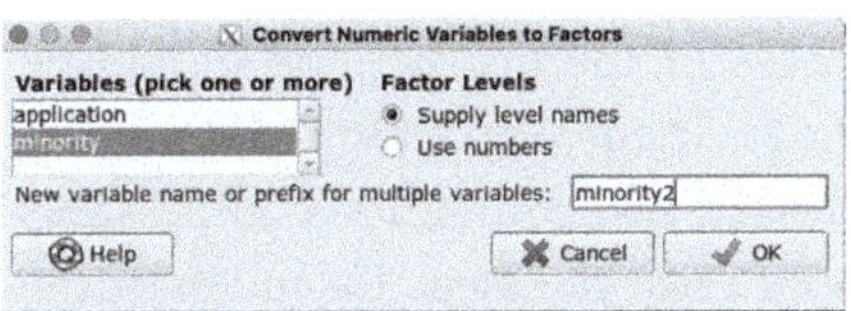

Figure 5.13 Numeric to string/factor, step 2

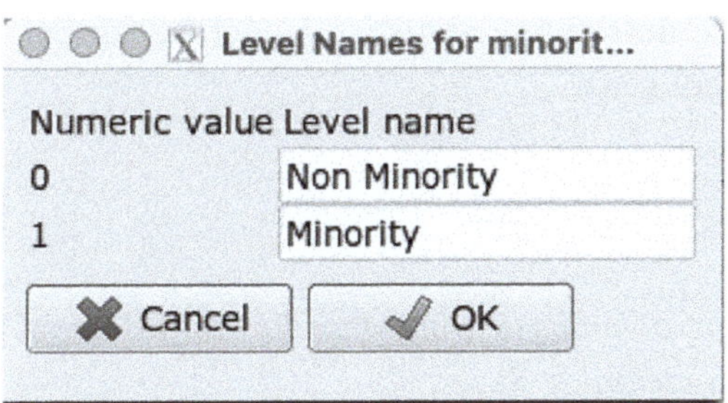

Figure 5.14 Numeric to string/factor, step 3

1. Click Data → Manage variables in active data set → Convert numeric variables to factors (Figure 5.12).
2. Highlight the variable of interest in the "Variables" box. In this case it is the "minority" variable. Go ahead and create a new variable called "minority2" in the "New variable name or prefix for multiple variables" box (Figure 5.13). Ensure that the "Supply level names" box is checked. Click OK.
3. A new box will emerge with the original coding of the variable. As previously stated, we want 0 to represent Non Minority, so we type that into the 0 box. We want 1 to represent Minority, so we type that in the 1 box (Figure 5.14). Then, click OK.

To determine if the coding was successful, click the "View data set" button in the R Commander. The newly recoded variable should appear at the far right and look like Figure 5.15.

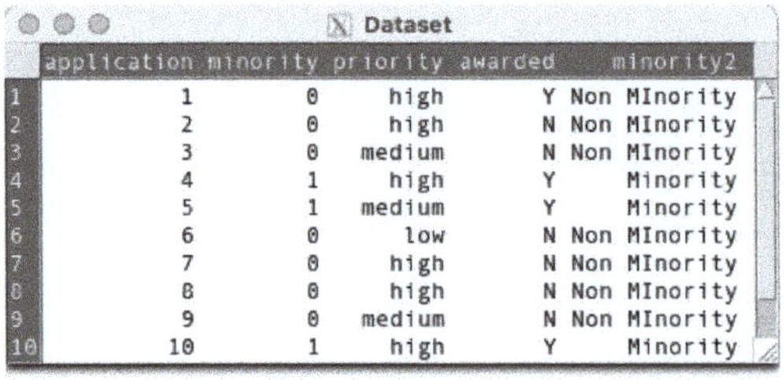

	application	minority	priority	awarded	minority2
1	1	0	high	Y	Non MInority
2	2	0	high	N	Non MInority
3	3	0	medium	N	Non MInority
4	4	1	high	Y	Minority
5	5	1	medium	Y	Minority
6	6	0	low	N	Non MInority
7	7	0	high	N	Non MInority
8	8	0	high	N	Non MInority
9	9	0	medium	N	Non MInority
10	10	1	high	Y	Minority

Figure 5.15 String/factor to numeric data view

5.7 Summary

If you followed along with this chapter, you should have at least successfully been able to install and call up the R Commander interface in RStudio. Instructions are current as of the publication of this chapter. Websites and versions of software often change. If the instructions do not correspond perfectly with what you see online, it is likely a function of R being updated to a newer version or the download websites being slightly altered. Nevertheless, the general steps of the instructions should be very similar. What are less likely to change are the methods of recoding data in the R Commander. The examples from this chapter showed two common recoding steps for string/factor and numeric variables. They should form the basis for much of the recoding necessary in the remaining chapters of this text. Chapters 6–18 will now make use of the R Commander to produce descriptive statistics, generate various data visualization plots, and to run statistical tests.

Recommended Reading

Fox, J. (2017). *Using the R Commander: A point-and-click interface for R.* CRC Press.
Osborne, J.W. (2013). *Best practices in data cleaning.* Sage.

PART 2

6

Central Tendency

6.1 Introduction

The next two chapters present descriptive statistics of data. It is usually a good idea to examine the descriptive statistics of variables in datasets before running analyses. Think of descriptive statistics as diagnostic tests. Just as an automobile mechanic runs diagnostic tests on vehicles to determine the condition of a vehicle or to diagnose potential problems, data analysts do the same, but with the data they want to analyze.

The descriptive statistics covered in this chapter are broadly referred to as measures of central tendency. Specifically, the mode, median, and mean (average) are presented along with their calculation and when it is appropriate to use them. It is often useful to know the central or typical value of a variable and the appropriate statistic to use. For example, if an analyst has obtained Census data, what is the central or typical value of household income? If collecting policy approval data using a Likert scale (ordinal measure), what is the typical or central approval rating/value? Questions like these will be answered in this chapter, with the next chapter covering dispersion, or the spread of data, around a measure of central tendency.

6.2 Measures of Central Tendency

Central tendency is the term used in statistics to describe the typical, central, or middle value of a variable's observations (though middle is often used incorrectly as will be discussed below). Measures of central tendency are widely used/reported not only in statistics and research, but in news reports and everyday language. In the world of baseball, a sport heavily reliant on statistics, a team's batting average is often used to describe how well the offense is performing. Advanced metrics like the exit velocity and launch angle are reported to show how fast and at what angle a ball is hit off a bat to better understand what hits end in home runs, and others just long fly balls that tend to result in outs. As such, average exit velocities and launch angles of the season's home runs are now commonly reported.

Back to the world of public administration, a news report will often discuss how median rents have risen over the past ten years, or the report may also present mean (average) rent. Which one is the better measure to report? The recent repeal of the constitutional right to an abortion in the United States led think thanks and news outlets to report survey results of questions asking citizens whether or not they supported the appeal of *Roe v. Wade* (the previous Supreme Court ruling that had granted abortion rights). Presented with percentages for each category from Strongly Approve to Strongly Disapprove, what is the central or typical value? These questions highlight the need to understand measures of central tendency, when to use them, and when they may be problematic to report based upon the level of measurement of the data. The three measures of central tendency covered in this chapter are the mode, median, and mean.

Each measure of central tendency will be discussed in detail, starting with the mean. We will start with the bare basics of the differences between the mean, median, and mode, with a very small dataset for ease of computation and illustration. After examining this dataset, Section 6.3 provides in-depth description of when it is appropriate to use each measure of central tendency based upon the level of measurement of a variable. This is extremely important since one can always calculate a mean, median, or mode for variables, and most computer software will report them. However, the level of measurement of a variable (nominal, ordinal, or interval) dictates what measure of central tendency is best (and at times, most sensical) to use.

6.2.1 Mean

The mean is also known as the average. These terms are used interchangeably in most research settings. Arithmetically, the mean of a set of values is simply the sum of the values divided by the total number of values. It is usually represented by the Greek symbol mu (μ) or by "X-bar" ($\bar{X}$). Mu is used to represent the mean of a population while X-bar is used to represent the mean of a sample. These terms become important for calculations in later chapters, but can be used interchangeably in a general discussion since the calculation of them is the same equation, represented by:

$$\bar{X} = \frac{\sum X_i}{N}, \qquad (6.1)$$

Or

$$\mu = \frac{\sum X_i}{N}, \qquad (6.1a)$$

Where

μ = mean (population)
$\bar{X}$ = mean (sample)
X_i = each respective value
$\sum$ = Summation or add
N = Total number of cases

For this chapter, we will use $\bar{X}$ to represent the mean since we typically work with samples in public administration. X_i is the mathematical representation of every value in the dataset or every value being used to calculate the mean. The summation symbol ($\sum$) indicates to add all individual values. Then, divide by the total number of individual values (N).

Suppose city engineers and public works officials are curious about the number of accidents at an intersection. They take a random sample of days throughout the year and note the number of accidents at the intersection. Of the eight days randomly sampled, the number of accidents, ordered from lowest to highest, are (2, 3, 4, 5, 5, 5, 6, 6). Using this intersection accident data from the city engineering and public works department, what is the mean?

First, add up all of the values. Therefore $2+3+4+5+5+5+6+6=36$. Then, divide that number (36) by the total number of observations (N), which is 8. This yields 4.5. Therefore, the mean or average number of accidents at the intersection is 4.5. Using Equation 6.1, the mean is depicted as:

$$\bar{X} = \frac{2+3+4+5+5+5+6+6}{8}$$

$$\bar{X} = \frac{36}{8} = 4.5$$

The mean is a very common descriptive statistic reported in research. One note of caution with the mean, however, is that it is susceptible to outliers, or extreme values. Suppose the city engineering and public works departments were working with the following eight values of accidents at the previous intersection: 2, 3, 4, 5, 5, 5, 6, 20. Apparently, one particular day in the dataset had a large number of accidents at the intersection. How has the mean changed? Using Equation 6.1:

$$\bar{X} = \frac{2+3+4+5+5+5+6+20}{8}$$

$$\bar{X} = \frac{50}{8} = 6.25$$

The mean has jumped from 4.5 to 6.25. Besides the outlier of 20, no other day had more than 6 accidents, so the mean of 6.25 is not really a great reflection of the central value or typical value of the data. The outlier day with 20 accidents pulls the mean towards it, or towards the higher value, thus inflating the mean. The same relationship would exist for extremely small outliers. Suppose the number of accidents at the intersection over eight days was 20, 15, 15, 18, 16, 19, 15, 0, and using Equation 6.1:

$$\bar{X} = \frac{20+15+15+18+16+19+15+0}{8}$$

$$\bar{X} = \frac{118}{8} = 14.75$$

The outlier of an odd day where there were no accidents brings the mean closer to it. The mean is 14.75 despite all observations except for the outlier of 0 being above 14.75.

6.2.2 Median

The median is the middle value of a variable's data, or the middle value of a series of datapoints. Fifty percent of the remaining datapoints lie above the median value, and fifty percent of the remaining datapoints lie below the median value. The first, and most crucial step in finding the median of a series of datapoints is to order all observations from small to large. If given the following series of numbers (2, 2, 1, 3, 4), the first step is to reorder it to (1, 2, 2, 3, 4). Eyeballing the data, one can see that the middle value is 2, in the third position. Fifty percent of the remaining cases are below that particular 2 (1 & 2), and fifty percent of the cases are above that particular 2 (3 & 4).

What if there is an even number of observations? Let's take the previous series of numbers and add another datapoint, a 5, to make (1, 2, 2, 3, 4, 5). What is the median? There is no clear, single middle value. By eyeballing the data, the *two* middle values are 2 and 3. These two values delineate the middle where 50% of the remaining datapoints (a 4 and a 5) are above/greater than them, and 50% of the remaining datapoints (a 1 and a 2) are below the two middle values. There cannot be two middle values, so what is the median? In the case of having an even number of observations, the median value is the mean/average of the two middle values. Therefore, the median for this series of numbers is 2.5 (average between 2 and 3). Even though a value of 2.5 does not actually exist in the series of datapoints, it is still considered the median value.

For larger datasets, it may be difficult to find the middle value. Think about reordering and finding the median of a series with 100, 1,000, or 1,000,000 observations. Thankfully, software can tell us the median, but if dealing with this type of situation without software, use the following equation to determine the location of the median value (remembering to order/sort your data from low to high):

$$\frac{N+1}{2} \tag{6.2}$$

N is simply the number of observations in your series of data, or the number of datapoints. For the first series of numbers in this section (1, 2, 2, 3, 4), the equation to determine the location of the median value would be:

$$\frac{5+1}{2} = 3$$

The value of 3 tells us the median is located in the third position. Remember that your datapoints should always first be reordered from lowest to highest! If not, you will likely report the incorrect median. The value in the third position, read from left to right in the datapoints, is the value of 2, which is the median. Now, examine the series with an even number of observations (1, 2, 2, 3, 4, 5). The location of the median is:

$$\frac{6+1}{2} = 3.5$$

There is no 3.5 location. The way to interpret this location is that the value of the median is halfway between the 3rd and the 4th datapoints. In this case, the 3rd value is 2, and the 4th value is 3. What is halfway between 2 and 3? 2.5, which we previously calculated. "Halfway between the 3rd and the 4th datapoints" is simply a fancier way of saying the average between the 3rd and 4th values.

Let's return to the public administration example involving accidents at a particular intersection. When ordered from low to high, the first series was 2, 3, 4, 5, 5, 5, 6, 6. To find the location of the median:

$$\frac{8+1}{2} = 4.5$$

The median is halfway between the values of the 4th and 5th positions. In this case, the 4th value is 5, and so is the 5th value. Therefore, the halfway point between these two values or the mean/average between these two values is 5. Recall that the mean of this series was 4.5. There is a small difference between the mean and the median, but they are relatively close.

Now, find the median of the accident data with the large outlier of 20 accidents. The datapoints are 2, 3, 4, 5, 5, 5, 6, 20. Since there are still eight datapoints, the median is thc mean between the 4th and 5th observations in this case. The 4th value is 5, and the 5th value is 5 (same as in the previous problem). Therefore, the median is 5. Recall that the mean of this series is 6.25. Now, notice what that one outlier of 20 did to the mean versus the median. The mean changed from 4.5 to 6.25 while the median remained the same. Medians are not susceptible to outliers! This fact sometimes makes it more logical to report the median value than the mean value. Stated another way, the median sometimes is a better reflection of the central or typical value in a dataset, especially if there are some outliers. In this case, with a large outlier, the city engineering and public works department should likely report the median as the measure of central tendency or typical value of the datapoints. Another practice would be to simply report both the mean and the median at all times. If the mean is greater than the median, then we know there is some sort of positive skew or positive numbers pulling the mean upwards. If the mean is less than the median, then we can conclude that there are some smaller values pulling the mean towards them, creating a negative skew. A more detailed explanation of outliers and skew is presented in Section 6.4

6.2.3 Mode

The mode is the most-often occurring value in a series of data for a variable. In both of the series of the accident data (2, 3, 4, 5, 5, 5, 6, 6) and (2, 3, 4, 5, 5, 5, 6,

20), the modes are 5. The value of 5 appears three times in the first dataset, so the mode is 5. The value of 5 appears three times in the second dataset, so its mode is also 5. What if the accident dataset looked like (2, 3, 3, 3, 3, 4, 5, 6, 10, 10, 10, 10)? The values of 3 and 10 each appear four times. In this case, there are two modes: 3 and 10. The data in this situation is often described as bimodal, or having two modes. If the accident data looked like (2, 2, 4, 4, 6, 6, 8, 8, 11, 11), there would be no mode. Each value in the dataset appears the same number of times – in this case, two times each.

For reasons listed in the following section, the mode is not often used by researchers unless they are working with nominal variables. For variables with counts (like interval variables) or variables with an order (like ordinal variables), the mode is not a great reflection of the typical or central value, though for ordinal variables, it may be reported alongside the median for informational purposes.

6.3 Levels of Measurement and Central Tendency

If there is one research design concept that is the most crucial to learn and remember, it is the level of measurement of variables – nominal, ordinal, and interval. As stated before, knowing the level of measurement of dependent and independent variables dictates what statistical tests can be used. Likewise, the level of the measurement of the variable of interest dictates what measure of central tendency can be reported. Software will report the mean, median, and mode for all variables, regardless of level of measurement. Therefore, it is up to the researcher to know what statistic/measure of central tendency to correctly report from statistical output. The subsections below cover when it is appropriate to report the mode, median, and mean, respectively.

6.3.1 Measure of Central Tendency – Nominal Variables

The mode is the only measure of central tendency that should be reported for nominal variables. For example, a researcher may be interested in knowing the largest budget item spent among nonprofit organizations. After reviewing budget documents, the researcher decides to create a variable representing each organization's top non-salary budget item in the dataset. The coding scheme is:

1 = Marketing
2 = Insurance
3 = Travel
4 = Operations
5 = Other

The researcher enters the data into Excel, with two columns: one representing the anonymous ID of the organization and the other column representing the respective organization's top budget item. The dataset appears in Figure 6.1.

	A	B
1	org	budget
2	A	1
3	B	1
4	C	3
5	D	4
6	E	3
7	F	5
8	G	5
9	H	2
10	I	2
11	J	1
12	K	1
13	L	1
14	M	2
15	N	4
16	O	1
17		

Figure 6.1 Budget data

The mode is 1, or Marketing, and should be the measure of central tendency reported. In fact, it should be the *only* measure of central tendency reported. You could calculate the mean value of the series or have statistics software report it, but the resulting mean would be nonsensical. A 1 represents Marketing, while a 4 represents Operations. Numerically, 4 is greater than 1, but substantively, how is Operations greater than Marketing? It is not. Nevertheless, the more 4s and 5s in the dataset, the higher the mean, suggesting the typical or central value is higher, which is absolutely incorrect. You could also order the series from low to high and then find the median, or have a software report the median, but it would be nonsensical. It does not make sense for a nominal variable to have 50% of values higher than the median value and 50% of values lower than the median value. What is higher and lower in this case? Only different categories. Therefore, for nominal variables, only report the mode.

6.3.2 Measures of Central Tendency – Ordinal Variables

The principal measure of central tendency to use with ordinal variables is the median, or the middle value. The mode can also be reported, but not the mean. If the quality of a state's bridges are rated on a scale from Poor to Excellent, it is an ordinal level. One coding scheme could be:

	A	B
1	bridge	rating
2	A	3
3	B	1
4	C	1
5	D	2
6	E	1
7	F	1
8	G	0
9	H	3
10	I	2
11	J	0
12		

Figure 6.2 Bridge data

Poor = 0
Average = 1
Good = 2
Excellent = 3

A sample of ten bridges with IDs ranging from A through J are selected for rating, and their ratings appear in the Excel spreadsheet in Figure 6.2.

Follow the steps from earlier in the chapter to calculate the median by hand. So, the first step is to reorder the data/scores from low to high. If done by hand, the reordered data should be:

0, 0, 1, 1, 1, 1, 2, 2, 3, 3

The location of the median is represented by Equation 6.2:

$$\frac{N+1}{2} \tag{6.2}$$

With an N of 10,

$$\frac{10+1}{2} = 5.5$$

The location of the median is between observation #5 and observation #6. The value for the fifth position is 1. The value of the sixth position is 1. Taking the mean of these two values reveals the median, which is 1. The value of 1 represents the median or the best measure of central tendency for ordinal variables, which in this case, is a rating of "Average". The mode can also be reported, which luckily, is also 1. However, this will not always be the case, and it is usually best to present the median when dealing with ordinal variables.

6.3.3 Measures of Central Tendency – Interval Variables

For interval level variables, it is usually acceptable to report the mean and/or median. Unlike ordinal and nominal variables, the mean can be calculated for interval level variables. However, as seen with the accident data in the earlier section, the mean is susceptible to outliers, which dictates reporting the median instead, or reporting both the mean and the median together so that the reader can gauge the presence of any outliers skewing the data in a particular direction.

The mode can be reported, but it is usually not a useful measure of central tendency for interval variables. Multiple modes or no mode may exist. The one situation where the mode may have some use is in identifying if the interval variable is normally distributed, or if the frequency of values for the series of data take on a bell-shaped curve.

Suppose a social work data analyst is trying to determine the level of demand for childhood health services in a neighborhood. The researcher surveys the parents/guardians asking how many times they needed to take their child to the doctor but avoided doing so due to finances. The researcher obtains the data and orders the values from low to high:

0, 1, 1, 2, 2, 2, 3, 3, 4

The data are clearly interval, so what is the mean? Using Equation 6.1a:

$$\frac{0+1+1+2+2+2+3+3+4}{9} = \frac{18}{9} = 2$$

The mean number of avoided doctor visits is 2. What is the median number of avoided doctor visits? Using the location equation (Equation 6.2), we see that the location is value #5:

$$\frac{N+1}{2} \tag{6.2}$$

With an N of 9,

$$\frac{9+1}{2} = 5$$

The fifth value is 2.

Now, what is the mode, or most often occurring value? The mode is 2, which appears three times. Therefore, the mean, median, and mode are all the same at 2. When this occurs, we say that the data are normally distributed. Eyeballing the data, you can see that below the mean/median/mode of 2 are two values of 1, and one value of 0. Above the mean/median/mode of 2 are two values of 3, and one value

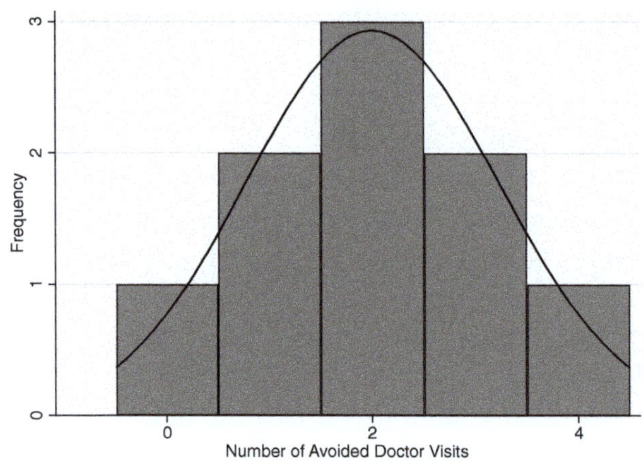

Figure 6.3 Histogram of avoided doctor visits – normal distribution

of 4. This symmetrical pattern makes the data normally distributed or appearing like a perfect bell curve. The data are graphically depicted in Figure 6.3.

Each bar represents a value of the variable for number of avoided doctor visits. Bars include values for 0, 1, 2, 3, and 4. The frequency of observing each value is recorded by the height of the bar according to the frequency on the y-axis. The general appearance of the graph, known as a histogram, is that of a bell-curve, which has been superimposed onto the graph. We will deal more with the normal distribution and bell curves in later chapters.

6.4 Outliers and Skewness

A common theme throughout this chapter has been that the mean is susceptible to outliers, being pulled in the direction of such outliers. If the outliers are large numbers, then the mean will be pulled towards them, making the mean value greater than the median value, also known as a *positive skew*. If the outliers are small numbers, then the mean will be pulled toward them, making the mean value less than the median value, also known as a *negative skew*. The previous section showed a situation where the mean, median, and mode are all equal, giving a perfectly normal distribution of data, or a distribution with *no skew*. Conceptually, it is important to see how skewed data affect data distribution, and graphical representations are one means to better understand this concept, which is one of the topics of Chapter 8.

Consider a scenario in which the mayor's office is trying to determine how often citizens utilize the city's main public library. A random selection of fifteen citizens is conducted, surveying them on the number of times they used the main public library in the last year. To illustrate the difference between a positive skew and a negative skew, consider the data in Figure 6.4.

The first column lists the respondent to the survey. The variables "use1" and "use2" reveal data that are positively and negatively skewed, respectively. The data have

	A	B	C
1	respondent	use1	use2
2	1	1	10
3	2	1	10
4	3	3	11
5	4	2	11
6	5	1	11
7	6	1	12
8	7	3	12
9	8	4	12
10	9	4	13
11	10	5	13
12	11	5	14
13	12	4	12
14	13	3	13
15	14	10	0
16	15	20	1
17			

Figure 6.4 Library data

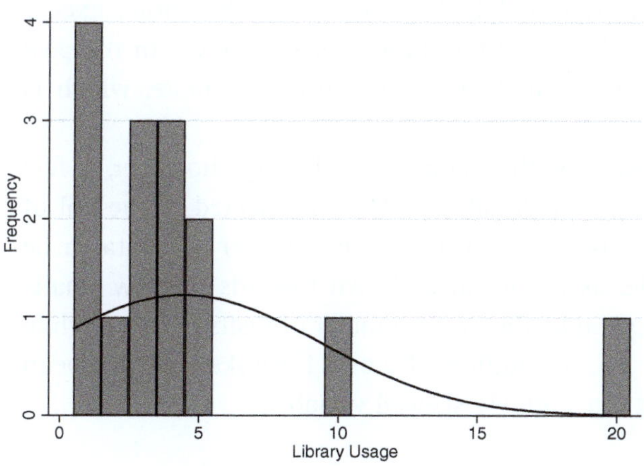

Figure 6.5 Positively skewed data graph

been organized so that the outlier cases are in cells 15 and 16. For the "use1" variable of library usage, there are two obvious outliers of use at 10 and 20, respectively. Figure 6.5 shows a graph of the usage data for the variable "use1." Most of the usage is low in number except for a few respondents who often use the public library. The figure shows a distribution of data that is positively skewed.

In Figure 6.5, the tail of the distribution tends towards the right or towards larger values. Where the tail of the distribution extends describes whether or not the data

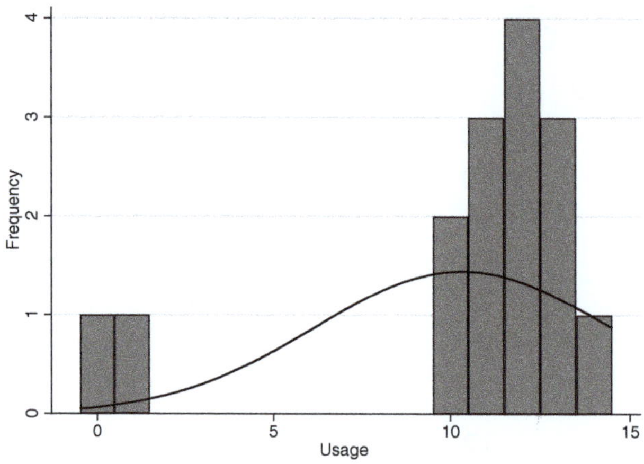

Figure 6.6 Negatively skewed data graph

are positively or negatively skewed. In this case, the data are positively skewed. In this particular example, the mean value is 4.47 while the median is 3. Given that the mean is greater than the median, we know that there is a positive skew; however, if viewing the distribution of the data, we could see the distribution's tail extending towards the larger values, thus suggesting a positive skew.

If the library usage data occurred according to the variable "use2," then a different picture would be painted concerning citizen usage of the main public library. Of the fifteen individuals sampled, all have reported double-digit use of the library except for two individuals indicating that they used the library once or never in the past year. Figure 6.6 shows the distribution of data for the "use2" variable, which is negatively skewed.

Most individuals report high usage of the main public library; however, a few individuals report limited to no usage of the library. This is reflected in the tail of the distribution extending towards the lower values. We consider the data to be negatively skewed in this example, as the mean is drawn towards the few small-valued outliers. In this particular example, the mean number of visits is 10.33, while the median number of visits is 12. So, the outliers of 0 and 1 are skewing the mean towards their values, thus creating a negatively skewed variable.

6.5 Calculating Measures of Central Tendency in the R Commander

6.5.1 Interval Variables – Mean and Median

The R Commander can report all of the measures of central tendency. We will first work with the *baseball* dataset located in the Companion Site (www.cambridge.org/scheller). It contains two years of home game attendance figures for a minor league baseball team. Data are collected for the team from box scores on Minor League Baseball's website (Minor League Baseball, 2023). The *baseball_codebook* contains the labels for the variables, their description, and coding.

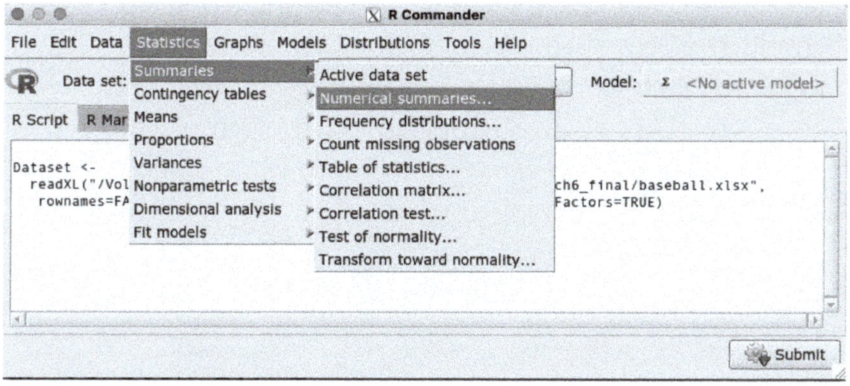

Figure 6.7 Obtaining mean and median, part 1

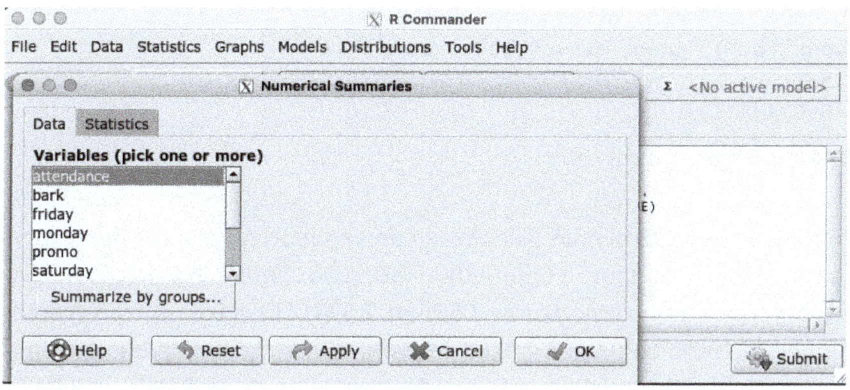

Figure 6.8 Obtaining mean and median, part 2

Team owners/management and likely city officials may be interested in reporting characteristics of home games like typical attendance. Load the dataset into the R Commander. To obtain descriptive statistics related to central tendency, specifically the mean and median of an interval variable like the attendance variable, use the Statistics and Summaries options in the R Commander.

Step 1: As shown in Figure 6.7, click Statistics → Summaries → Numerical summaries.

Step 2: Highlight the variable of interest ("attendance" for this example) (Figure 6.8). Then, click the Statistics tab to see various options of statistics to report.

Step 3: In the next window, the defaults can remain, but if wanting to have less output reported and just wanting the mean and the median, keep the "Mean" box checked and then in the "Quantiles" box, leave only the .5 option, which is the value for the 50th percentile, or median, as shown in Figure 6.9.

Step 4: Click OK. Results are reflected in Figure 6.10.

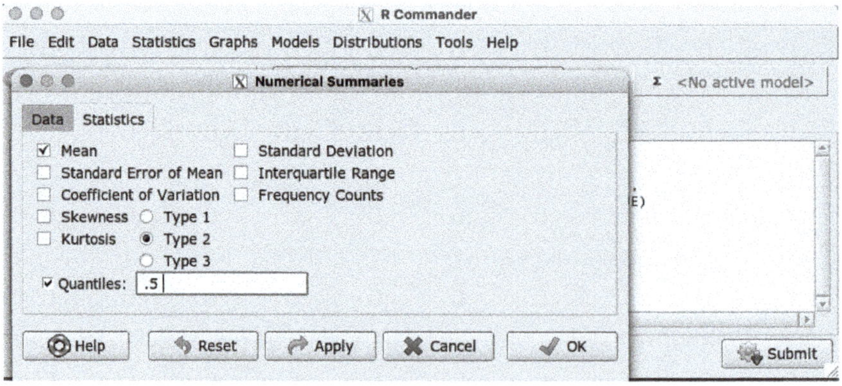

Figure 6.9 Obtaining mean and median, part 3

```
Rcmdr> numSummary(Dataset[,"attendance", drop=FALSE], statistics=c("mean",
Rcmdr+    "quantiles"), quantiles=c(.5))
     mean    50%   n
 7836.413 8046.5 138
```

Figure 6.10 Mean and median output

The mean is 7836.413, or 7,836 people. The mean can be reported as is for the reader to see the exact decimals, or more commonly, since you cannot have 0.413 of a person for attendance, it can be reported as 7,836 or 7,837. The median, represented by the value under the 50% column is 8046.5. Again, given the variable is dealing with physical individuals, the median can be reported as is or as 8,046 or 8,047. Finally, the sample size or number of observations is under the "n" column for 138.

6.5.2 Ordinal Variables – Median and Mode

The *bridges* dataset in the Companion Site has the bridge rating data from earlier in the chapter. You can either enter the data manually into Excel and load into the R Commander or access the data from the Companion Site. Recall that the coding for the bridges was:

Poor = 0
Average = 1
Good = 2
Excellent = 3

The typical measure of central tendency for an ordinal level variable is the median, but we will also have the R Commander report the mode so that the median and mode can be compared. The steps are nearly identical to the previous steps.

Step 1: Click Statistics → Summaries → Numerical summaries.

Step 2: Highlight the variable of interest ("rating" for this example). Then, click the Statistics tab to see various options of statistics to report.

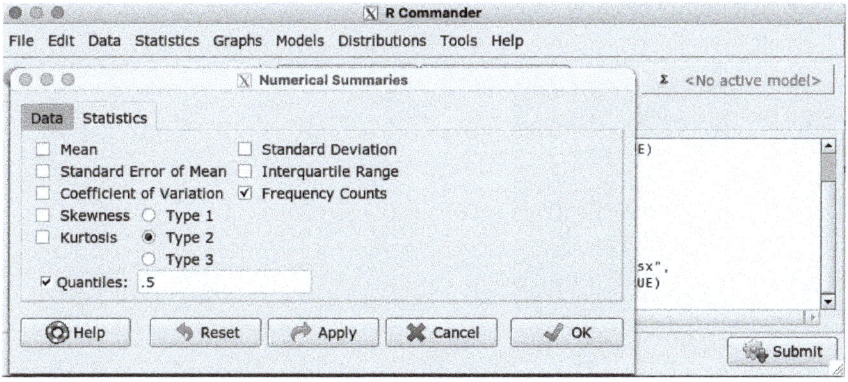

Figure 6.11 Obtaining frequency table and median

```
Rcmdr> numSummary(Dataset[,"rating", drop=FALSE], statistics=c("quantiles"),
Rcmdr+   quantiles=c(.5))
50%
  1

Rcmdr> discreteCounts(Dataset[,"rating", drop=FALSE])
Distribution of rating
      Count Percent
0         2      20
1         4      40
2         2      20
3         2      20
Total    10     100
```

Figure 6.12 Frequency table and median output

Step 3: In the next window, keep .5 in the "Quantiles" box. As before, this will report the median. For the mode, check the "Frequency Counts" box (Figure 6.11). This option will have the R Commander create a frequency table of counts for each category of the variable of interest.

Step 4: Click OK and the R Commander will produce the requested statistics (Figure 6.12).

A value of 1 appears under the 50% column, indicating that the median rating is 1, which corresponds to an Average rating. The next set of output is a frequency table of the variable's values and counts of those values. The left column has each category of the variable. In this case, the options are 0 through 3, reflecting the coding of the bridge rating. The middle column displays the counts for each category. Though the R Commander does not specifically stipulate the modal category, it is simply the category or categories with the most counts. In this case, the mode is a value of 1, corresponding to an Average rating. The mode and the median are the same. The far right column of the frequency table lists each category's percentage count of all observations. The value of 1 accounts for 40% of all the observations

Table 6.1 Frequency distribution of party identification

Party Identification	Count	Percent
Democrat	1210	34.71
Republican	1196	34.31
Independent	872	25.01
Other	208	5.97
Total	3486	100

in the dataset. This should make sense from eyeballing the data in the Excel spreadsheet with 4 out of 10 observations coded as a 1. It is also reflected in the frequency table as the last row shows a Total of 10, referring to the number of observations. The value of 1's count of 4 is 40% of all the observations.

6.5.3 Frequency Distributions

The frequency distribution/table in the previous section is a common table used to present descriptive statistics of nominal and ordinal variables. These tables present counts of a specific variable's categories in a dataset. The first column typically displays the categories of the variable, with the second column listing the frequency or count of observations for each category. If using large datasets, it is also conventional to add a third column, listing the percentage of all observations represented by the category. The last row of the table usually lists the total number of observations for the variable. Table 6.1 is an example of a hypothetical frequency table/distribution of respondents to a survey and their political party identification.

6.6 Summary

The "typical" value for a variable is an important first step in analyzing data. It allows researchers to better understand the central value of a variable and then determine if the data is skewed or contains outliers. Means and medians are typically reported not only in research, but also in news reports and technical reports. They give the audience "a feel" for the typical value of a variable.

The level of measurement (nominal, ordinal, or interval) dictates what statistics of central tendency can be reported. The mode can only be used for nominal variables, the median for ordinal or interval measures, and the mean for interval variables. These facts highlight the importance of knowing the level of measurement for variables, because most statistical software can or will report all central tendency statistics. Knowing the correct statistic to use by variable measurement is a skill required to correctly report statistics and later run more advanced tests covered in this text. The next chapter is another chapter focusing on descriptive statistics of dispersion or the spread of data around a measure of central tendency.

PRACTICE PROBLEMS

Conceptual Problems

1. For an interval level variable, can the mean and median be the same? Can a scenario exist where the mean, median, and mode are identical for an interval level variable? Why/why not?
2. Suppose we code in Excel, gender identity as Man = 2, Woman = 1, and Other = 0. Suppose in our dataset, we have two 0s, seven 1s, and five 2s. What measure of central tendency should we report? Calculate this measure for the gender identity variable as described.
3. In housing studies, the median house price is usually the measure of central tendency reported. Why is the median the measure used?
4. For each of the following variables, which measures of central tendency should be reported based upon their coding and explain why:
   a. Type of animal caught by local animal control (Dog, Cat, Raccoon, Other)
   b. Customer service rating (Excellent, Good, Average, Poor, Very Poor)
   c. Policy approval (Strongly approve, Approve, Neutral, Disapprove, Strongly disapprove)
   d. Number of interviews conducted by job opening
   e. Percentage of forms successfully completed

Problems by Hand

5. Find the mean and median for the following series of weekly incomes:

   555, 200, 890, 750, 84, 55

6. For the series of incomes in problem #5, is there any skew? How do you know?
7. Find the mean, median, and mode of the following number of demerits written for a set of 9 employees this year.

   0, 0, 2, 1, 1, 3, 4, 3, 3

8. For the series of demerits in problem #7, is there any skew? How do you know?
9. For the series of demerits in problem #7, add a 10th observation that would result in a large positive skew to the data. Explain your logic.
10. Suppose a survey of individuals is taken asking them if they agree with increasing the local sales tax by 0.5% to help pay for repairs to city streets. A researcher uses the coding Strongly agree (SA), Agree (A), Neutral (N),

Disagree (D), Strongly disagree (SD) to record the responses. The responses are: D, N, SA, SA, SA, A, D, SD, N, SA, D, SA, A, A, D, D, SD, N, SD, SA, A, N, A, A, D, D, SD, N, SD, D, D, A, A
With this data, create a frequency table.

R Commander Problems

11. Open the *fire_response* dataset from the Companion Site (www.cambridge.org/scheller). The codebook is also in the Companion Site that lists the variables in the dataset, their labels, and their coding. The unit of analysis is the emergency response. Each time the fire department is called out to an emergency, information is collected, so each observation is a unique emergency response.
  a. Use the R Commander to report the mean and median values for the turnout time variable. Is there any skew to the data? Why/why not?
  b. Use the R Commander to report the mean and median values for the response time variable. Is there any skew to the data? Why/why not?
  c. Use the R Commander to report the appropriate measure of central tendency for the apparatus used. Which measure did you report? Why? Interpret the statistic.

12. Open the *mead_level* dataset from the Companion Site into the R Commander. It lists the level of water at Lake Mead for a period of time. Calculate the appropriate measure of central tendency for the water level. Which measure is a better representation of the water level? Why?

13. Open the *associations_survey* dataset from the Companion Site in the R Commander. Also open the codebook for reference. For each of the following variables, calculate/report the appropriate measure of central tendency, interpret it (based upon the variable label's description in the codebook), and produce a frequency table/distribution of the data.
  a. "citymtg"
  b. "report"
  c. "pool"
  d. "pvs"
  e. "ctyattent"
  f. "conduit"
  g. "comm"

7

Dispersion

7.1 Introduction

The previous chapter focused on measures of central tendency, or how to calculate the "typical" or central value of a variable based upon its level of measurement. Another measure that is crucial to calculate is the dispersion of the datapoints of the variable. The term dispersion comes from the word "disperse," so how dispersed or spread out are the data/datapoints of the variable from the mean? This can also be thought of as the amount of variation in the variable, or how much the variable varies from its central or typical value.

A number of different definitions/descriptions of dispersion exist in the social science literature, but they all refer to the same concept. Pollock (2016) defines dispersion as "the variation or spread of cases across its values" (p. 29). Healey (2002) describes dispersion as "the amount of heterogeneity or variety within a distribution of scores" (p. 90). The words "spread" or "variation" are used most often throughout this chapter and textbook when referencing the concept of dispersion and specific measures of dispersion. It should be noted, however, that there is no conventional term to use, as seen in the previous definitions. Each researcher/author may have their own preference.

The major focus of this chapter is on calculating the standard deviation of a variable. It is a measure of the dispersion or spread of the datapoints around the mean of the variable. It is used with interval variables and is a key statistic used in calculations of statistical tests in later chapters, hence the main focus of the chapter. Calculating this statistic by hand is covered in detail, and then R Commander steps are presented for the purposes of calculating the standard deviation for large datasets. For ordinal and nominal variables, the range and interquartile range are also introduced, and steps for obtaining them from the R Commander are also presented. The skewness of data for a variable is also discussed and calculated using the R Commander.

7.2 Measures of Dispersion – Interval Variables

The principal measures of dispersion for interval variables are the variance and the standard deviation, of which the standard deviation is the typical measure used. It is the square root of the variance. Both measures are discussed due to their importance in computations for later statistical tests. Each measure essentially measures the spread of the data from its mean value.

7.2.1 Variance

The variance is known as the "average squared deviation" (Lewis-Beck, 1995, p. 12) of values for a variable. Deviation is defined as the distance from the mean, and the equation for the variance is slightly different if working with the full population compared to a sample. The variance is represented by the symbol s^2 if working with a sample and σ^2 if working with a population. Equations 7.1 and 7.1a, show the respective variance equations.

$$s^2 = \frac{\sum (X_i - \bar{X})^2}{n - 1}, \tag{7.1}$$

where

X_i = each respective value
$\bar{X}$ = sample mean
$n - 1$ = sample size minus 1
$\sum$ = summation

$$\sigma^2 = \frac{\sum (X_i - \mu)^2}{N}, \tag{7.1a}$$

where

X_i = each respective value
μ = population mean
N = population size
$\sum$ = summation

Each equation is fundamentally the same with the exception of the n – 1 denominator used for samples. Because we mostly deal with samples in public administration, the sample variance equation (7.1) will be used to illustrate concepts and calculations moving forward. Ultimately, the results do not change dramatically, especially with large sample sizes.

To illustrate the steps to calculate the variance, recall from Chapter 6 the accident data. The first set of data for an eight day sample of accidents at a particular intersection was (2, 3, 4, 5, 5, 5, 6, 6). Follow these steps to calculate the variance:

Step 1: Calculate the mean ($\bar{X}$) of the data. Remember the equation for the mean is:

$$\bar{X} = \frac{\sum X_i}{N} \tag{6.1}$$

Table 7.1 Completion of step 2

$X_i - \bar{X}$
(2 − 4.5) = −2.5
(3 − 4.5) = −1.5
(4 − 4.5) = −0.5
(5 − 4.5) = 0.5
(5 − 4.5) = 0.5
(5 − 4.5) = 0.5
(6 − 4.5) = 1.5
(6 − 4.5) = 1.5

Table 7.2 Completion of step 3

$X_i - \bar{X}$	$(X_i - \bar{X})^2$
(2 − 4.5) = −2.5	$(-2.5)^2 = 6.25$
(3 − 4.5) = −1.5	$(-1.5)^2 = 2.25$
(4 − 4.5) = −0.5	$(-0.5)^2 = 0.25$
(5 − 4.5) = 0.5	$(0.5)^2 = 0.25$
(5 − 4.5) = 0.5	$(0.5)^2 = 0.25$
(5 − 4.5) = 0.5	$(0.5)^2 = 0.25$
(6 − 4.5) = 1.5	$(1.5)^2 = 2.25$
(6 − 4.5) = 1.5	$(1.5)^2 = 2.25$

Therefore, the mean is

$$\frac{2+3+4+5+5+5+6+6}{8} = \frac{36}{8} = 4.5$$

Step 2: Take each individual observation in the dataset, X_i, and subtract the mean. Table 7.1 depicts this step.

Step 3: Square each difference. Table 7.2 adds a column for the squared differences.

Step 4: Now, sum the squared differences in the second column of Table 7.2. Table 7.3 includes the summation at the bottom of the second column in bold typeface. The sum of 14 is the numerator in the equation.

Table 7.3 Completion of step 3

$X_i - \bar{X}$	$(X_i - \bar{X})^2$
$(2 - 4.5) = -2.5$	$(-2.5)^2 = 6.25$
$(3 - 4.5) = -1.5$	$(-1.5)^2 = 2.25$
$(4 - 4.5) = -0.5$	$(-0.5)^2 = 0.25$
$(5 - 4.5) = 0.5$	$(0.5)^2 = 0.25$
$(5 - 4.5) = 0.5$	$(0.5)^2 = 0.25$
$(5 - 4.5) = 0.5$	$(0.5)^2 = 0.25$
$(6 - 4.5) = 1.5$	$(1.5)^2 = 2.25$
$(6 - 4.5) = 1.5$	$(1.5)^2 = 2.25$
	$\sum = 14$

Step 5: Divide the numerator just calculated by the sample size minus 1 (n − 1). In this case, the sample size is 8, so n − 1 is 7. Therefore,

$$s^2 = \frac{\sum (X_i - \bar{X})^2}{n - 1}$$

$$s^2 = \frac{14}{8 - 1}$$

$$s^2 = \frac{14}{7} = 2$$

The variance for this set of accident data is 2. The variance is not readily interpretable, and is used more for conducting additional statistical tests. However, it does show the level of variation of the datapoints of a variable. Comparing variances can also show some differences in dispersion. For example, let's now calculate the variance of the second set of accident data from Chapter 6 with the outlier. Recall that this sample of data was (2, 3, 4, 5, 5, 5, 6, 20). Going through the same steps to calculate the variance, we can note the differences in dispersion.

Step 1: Calculate the mean ($\bar{X}$) of the data. Remember the equation for the mean is:

$$\bar{X} = \frac{\sum X_i}{N} \tag{6.1}$$

Therefore, the mean is

$$\frac{2 + 3 + 4 + 5 + 5 + 5 + 6 + 20}{8} = \frac{50}{8} = 6.25$$

Step 2: Take each individual observation in the dataset, X_i, and subtract the mean. Table 7.4 depicts this step.

Table 7.4 Completion of step 2

$X_i - \bar{X}$
$(2 - 6.25) = -4.25$
$(3 - 6.25) = -3.25$
$(4 - 6.25) = -2.25$
$(5 - 6.25) = -1.25$
$(5 - 6.25) = -1.25$
$(5 - 6.25) = -1.25$
$(6 - 6.25) = -0.25$
$(20 - 6.25) = 13.75$

Table 7.5 Completion of step 3

$X_i - \bar{X}$	$(X_i - \bar{X})^2$
$(2 - 6.25) = -4.25$	$(-4.25)^2 = 18.06$
$(3 - 6.25) = -3.25$	$(-3.25)^2 = 10.56$
$(4 - 6.25) = -2.25$	$(-2.25)^2 = 5.06$
$(5 - 6.25) = -1.25$	$(-1.25)^2 = 1.56$
$(5 - 6.25) = -1.25$	$(-1.25)^2 = 1.56$
$(5 - 6.25) = -1.25$	$(-1.25)^2 = 1.56$
$(6 - 6.25) = -0.25$	$(-0.25)^2 = 0.06$
$(20 - 6.25) = 13.75$	$(13.75)^2 = 189.06$

Step 3: Square each difference. Table 7.5 adds a column for the squared differences.

Step 4: Now, sum the squared differences in the second column of Table 7.5. Table 7.6 includes the summation at the bottom of the second column in bold typeface.

Step 5: Divide the numerator just calculated by the sample size minus 1 (n − 1). In this case, the sample size is 8, so n − 1 is 7. Therefore,

$$s^2 = \frac{\sum (X_i - \bar{X})^2}{n - 1}$$

$$s^2 = \frac{227.48}{8 - 1}$$

$$s^2 = \frac{227.48}{7} = 32.5$$

Table 7.6 Completion of step 4

$X_i - \bar{X}$	$(X_i - \bar{X})^2$
$(2 - 6.25) = -4.25$	$(-4.25)^2 = 18.06$
$(3 - 6.25) = -3.25$	$(-3.25)^2 = 10.56$
$(4 - 6.25) = -2.25$	$(-2.25)^2 = 5.06$
$(5 - 6.25) = -1.25$	$(-1.25)^2 = 1.56$
$(5 - 6.25) = -1.25$	$(-1.25)^2 = 1.56$
$(5 - 6.25) = -1.25$	$(-1.25)^2 = 1.56$
$(6 - 6.25) = -0.25$	$(-0.25)^2 = 0.06$
$(20 - 6.25) = 13.75$	$(13.75)^2 = 189.06$
	$\sum = \mathbf{227.48}$

The variance increases dramatically in the presence of outliers. The previous variance was 2, but when there was an outlier of 20 accidents in the sample, the variance jumped to 32.50. The next subsection focuses on the standard deviation, the most common statistic reported to express the variance of data.

7.2.2 Standard Deviation

The standard deviation is the most common measure of dispersion used for interval variables and is simply the square root of the variance and represents the average distance of a variable's observations from the variable's mean. Represented by an equation, the standard deviation for a sample is:

$$s = \sqrt{\frac{\sum (X_i - \bar{X})^2}{n - 1}} \tag{7.2}$$

For a population, the standard deviation is represented by σ, and the equation is:

$$\sigma = \sqrt{\frac{\sum (X_i - \mu)^2}{N}} \tag{7.2a}$$

Recall that the variance for the first set of accident data was 2. Therefore, the standard deviation of the data is the square root of 2, which equals 1.41. The second accident dataset with the outlier of 20 accidents had a variance of 32.5. Therefore, the standard deviation is the square root of 32.50, which equals 5.70.

Both the variance and the standard deviation are measures of spread from the mean – the standard deviation is simply the square root of the variance. The standard deviation creates a common measure of dispersion in the variable's units of measure due to the square rooting. For example, if the unit of measure is in years, like for the variable life expectancy, the standard deviation is measured in years. It becomes an important topic for Chapter 9 when it is used to describe the distance from the mean for normally distributed variables. For now, it is good enough to know that the standard deviation is a measure of dispersion and that the greater the standard deviation, the more dispersed the data are around the mean.

7.3 Calculating Dispersion with the R Commander

The R Commander easily reports the standard deviation for variables. The *accidents* dataset in the Companion Site (www.cambridge.org/scheller) is an Excel spreadsheet of the accident data we have been working with in this chapter. Upload this data into the R Commander. To obtain the standard deviation of a variable:

Step 1: Click Statistics → Summaries → Numerical summaries (Figure 7.1).

Step 2: A new box will emerge where you should select the variables for which you want the R Commander to report dispersion statistics. In this case, we want dispersion statistics for the "accidents1" (no outlier) and "accidents2" (with outlier) variables. Using a Mac, you can hold down the "control" button and then click on each variable. If using a Windows computer, hold down the "Ctrl" button and then click on each variable in the box. Figure 7.2 shows the two variables highlighted using a Mac computer.

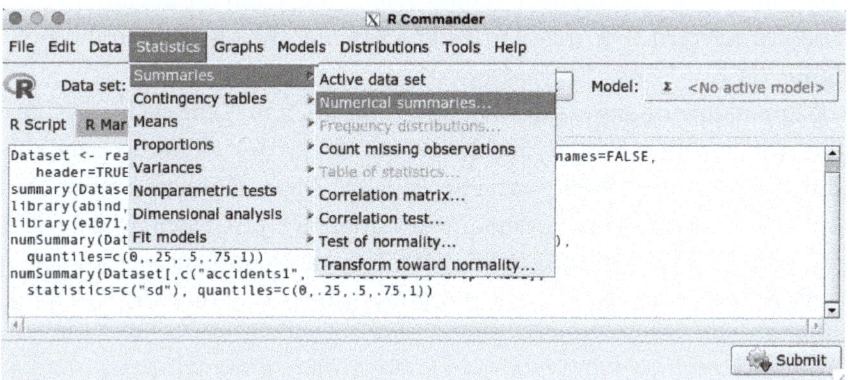

Figure 7.1 Standard deviation in the R Commander, part 1

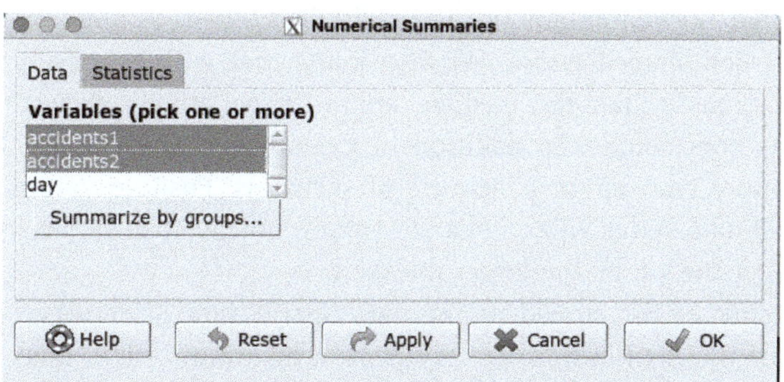

Figure 7.2 Standard deviation in the R Commander, part 2

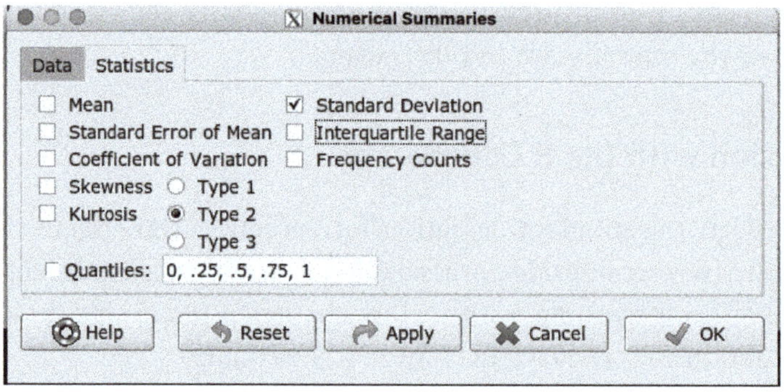

Figure 7.3 Standard deviation in the R Commander, part 3

```
Rcmdr> numSummary(Dataset[,c("accidents1", "accidents2"), drop=FALSE],
Rcmdr+    statistics=c("sd"), quantiles=c(0,.25,.5,.75,1))
                 sd n
accidents1 1.414214 8
accidents2 5.700877 8
```

Figure 7.4 Standard deviation R Commander output

Step 3: Click the "Statistics" tab, which will reveal a new popup window that allows you to tell the R Commander what statistics to report. At a minimum, make sure the "Standard Deviation" box is checked, as in Figure 7.3.

Step 4: Click OK, and the R Commander should report the standard deviations for the variables selected. For this particular example, the output should look like Figure 7.4.

The R Commander reports the standard deviation and N for each variable. The standard deviation for the "accident1" variable is 1.41, and the standard deviation for the "accident2" variable is 5.70. These numbers match the by-hand calculations for the standard deviation we just calculated in the previous section. While the R Commander does not report the variance for each variable, it can easily be calculated by simply squaring the standard deviation.

7.4 Skewness and Kurtosis

We know from Chapter 6 that skewed data is not normally distributed, or does not follow a nice, symmetrical bell-shaped curve. We also know that with positively skewed data, the mean is greater than the median, and with negatively skewed data, the mean is less than the median. In addition to examining the mean and the median, the R Commander can report a measure of skewness. Positive values indicate a positively skewed data series while negative values indicate a negatively skewed data series. The larger the value, the larger the skew.

Kurtosis is another measure of the spread of the data distribution or the level of peakedness or flatness of the distribution. A very peaked distribution is a relatively narrow distribution, with thin tails, also known as a leptokurtic distribution. Flatter distributions are more spread out, with fatter tails. Such distributions are

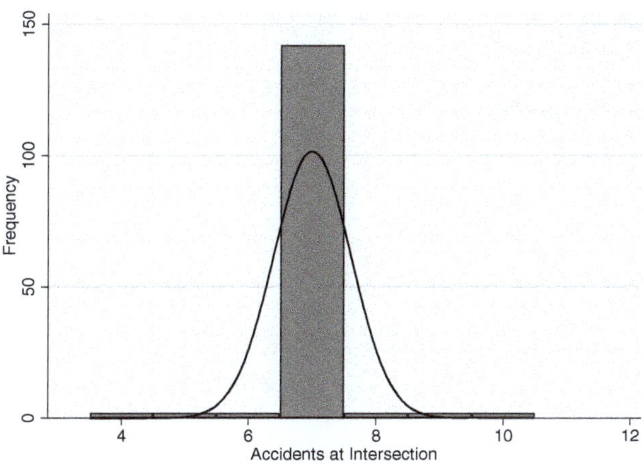

Figure 7.5 Leptokurtic distribution

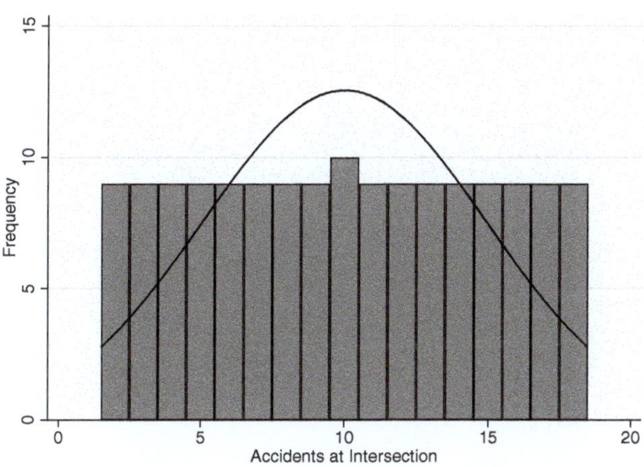

Figure 7.6 Platykurtic distribution

known as platykurtic distributions. One mnemonic to help remember the difference is to remember that "platy" is "flatter." Figures 7.5 and 7.6 show a leptokurtic and platykurtic distribution, respectively, for a different set of hypothetical accident data. The distributions are admittedly quite drastic, but the superimposed normal curves show the difference between a leptokurtic distribution and platykurtic distribution.

A third type of distribution is known as the mesokurtic distribution with a particular value of kurtosis. This distribution is the standard normal distribution that will become important for statistical computations in later chapters. The R Commander can report a kurtosis statistic. A value greater than 3 indicates a leptokurtic, or more peaked distribution. A value less than 3 indicates at platykurtic, or flatter distribution. A kurtosis score of 3 would be a mesokurtic distribution, or the kurtosis value for the standard normal distribution that is the topic of Chapter 9.

7.4.1 Calculating Skewness and Kurtosis in the R Commander

The previous figures were created using the hypothetical accident data from the *kurtosis* dataset in the Companion Site (www.cambridge.org/scheller). It shows a

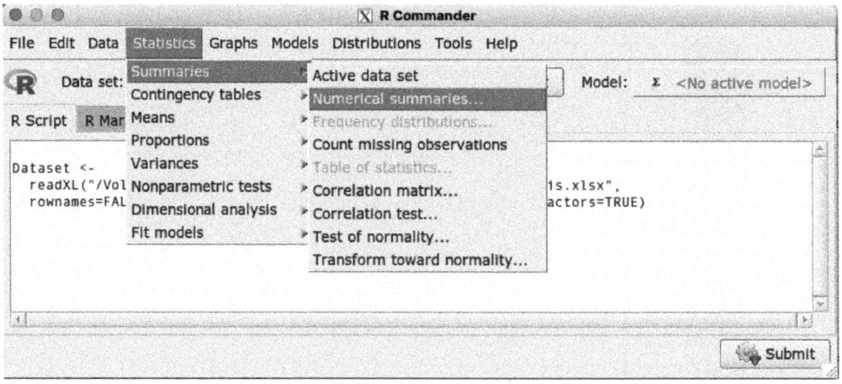

Figure 7.7 Skewness and kurtosis statistics, part 1

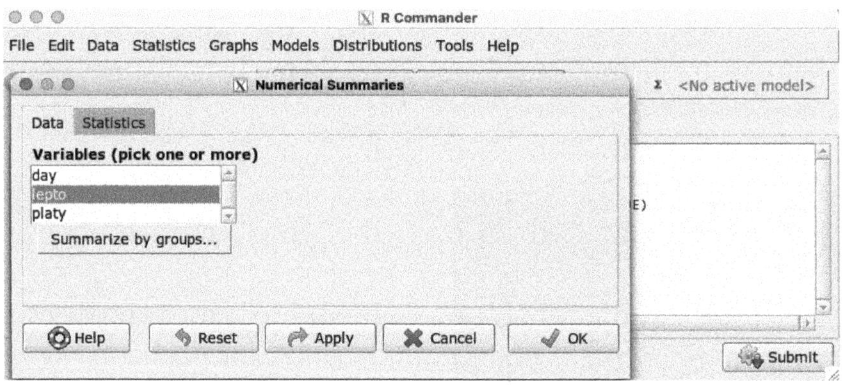

Figure 7.8 Skewness and kurtosis statistics, part 2

different set of hypothetical accident data by day. The first set of accident data in this dataset is in the column "lepto," which was used for the production of Figure 7.5. An analysis of this data should return kurtosis values indicating a leptokurtic distribution. The second set of accident data in this dataset is in the column "platy," which was used for the production of Figure 7.6. An analysis of this data should return kurtosis values indicating a platykurtic distribution.

To have the R Commander return both skewness and kurtosis statistics, use the following steps:

Step 1: Click Statistics → Summaries → Numerical summaries (Figure 7.7).

Step 2: Select the variable for which you want to report statistics. In this case, highlight the "lepto" variable (Figure 7.8).

Step 3: Click the Statistics tab.

Step 4: Check boxes for the following: "Mean," "Skewness," "Kurtosis," and "Quantiles." The default values for the Quantiles should suffice. Simply make sure that .5 is a value. This value will show the median (Figure 7.9)

Step 5: Click OK, and the resulting output should be presented, looking like Figure 7.10.

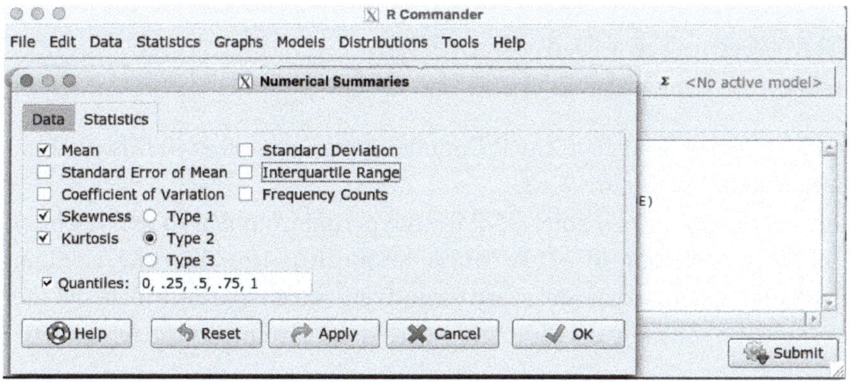

Figure 7.9 Skewness and kurtosis statistics, part 3

```
mean skewness kurtosis 0% 25% 50% 75% 100%   n
   7        0  16.8302  4   7   7   7   10 154
```

Figure 7.10 Skewness and kurtosis statistics output – leptokurtic

```
mean skewness  kurtosis 0% 25% 50% 75% 100%   n
  10        0 -1.196406  2   6  10  14   18 154
```

Figure 7.11 Skewness and kurtosis statistics output – platykurtic

The relevant output is included. The mean number of accidents is 7. The median number of accidents, represented by the value for the 50% quantile is also 7. The skewness statistic is a value of 0, indicating a symmetrical distribution and no skew. The kurtosis value is 16.83, greater than 3, indicating a leptokurtic distribution as we saw in Figure 7.5.

Now, follow the same steps for the "platy" variable to see the statistics reported for a platykurtic distribution. As with the leptokurtic distribution, the skewness has been set to 0 for illustration. The R Commander output for the "platy" variable is displayed in Figure 7.11.

For this hypothetical set of accident data, the mean and median are both 10, and the skewness score is 0, indicating no skew. The kurtosis value is -1.20 if rounding to two decimal places, which is less than 3. This indicates a platykurtic distribution. It is the data generated in Figure 7.6, which we know already to be platykurtic.

In real life, nearly every dataset/data series has a non-zero value for the level of skew. The previous examples were manipulated to have perfectly symmetrical distributions (no skew) and varying levels of kurtosis. Open the *stateGDP* dataset in the Companion Site and load it into the R Commander. It contains data from the Bureau of Economic Analysis of the percent change in state real GDP from the fourth quarter of 2021 to the first quarter of 2022 (Bureau of Economic Analysis, n.d.). Real GDP is the inflation-adjusted gross domestic product of each state, or the amount of economic goods produced by each state under the period of analysis. Run

```
  mean  skewness kurtosis  0%  25%  50%  75% 100%  n
-2.388 -2.215859 6.254884 -13 -2.6 -1.8 -1.1  1.2 50
```

Figure 7.12 Skewness and kurtosis statistics of GDP data

the skewness and kurtosis statistics in the R Commander as presented in this section. Your results should look like Figure 7.12.

The mean percent change in real state GDP for the period (rounded to two decimal places) is −2.39, with a median of −1.8. Since the mean is less than the median, we can initially conclude that the data are negatively skewed, confirmed by the −2.22 skewness statistic. The kurtosis statistic value is 6.25, indicating a leptokurtic distribution.

7.5 Range and Interquartile Range

It is usually not advised to report the variance and standard deviation of ordinal level measures. Software will report the values, but given the limited range of values which ordinal level measures can take, the variance and standard deviation will naturally be lower. For ordinal level variables, Weisberg (1992) recommends reporting the range and the interquartile range. The range is simply the scope of the variable's values from its lowest (minimum) value to its highest (maximum) value and usually defined as the difference between the maximum and the minimum. Conventional reporting of the range in papers and reports is that of the minimum, maximum, and the difference.

The interquartile range (IQR) is the range of values between the value representing the 75th percentile and the 25th percentile, or stated alternatively, the difference between the third and first quartile. These percentiles and quartiles are not only useful for ordinal measures, but also are commonly used for interval variables like test scores to report scores delineating the lower quartile cutoff (25th percentile value) and the upper quartile cutoff (75th percentile value). Visually, a graph known as the boxplot (introduced in the next chapter) is used to show both the range and the IQR. For now, we want to know how to report and interpret these values in the R Commander.

7.5.1 Calculating Range and IQR in the R Commander

Open the *associations_survey* dataset from the Companion Site (www.cambridge.org/scheller). The "appear" variable is a Likert scale measure of responses from association presidents to the statement: "The association helps maintain the neighborhood's appearance." The coding is such that:

Strongly Agree = 2
Agree = 1
Neutral = 0
Disagree = −1
Strongly Disagree = −2

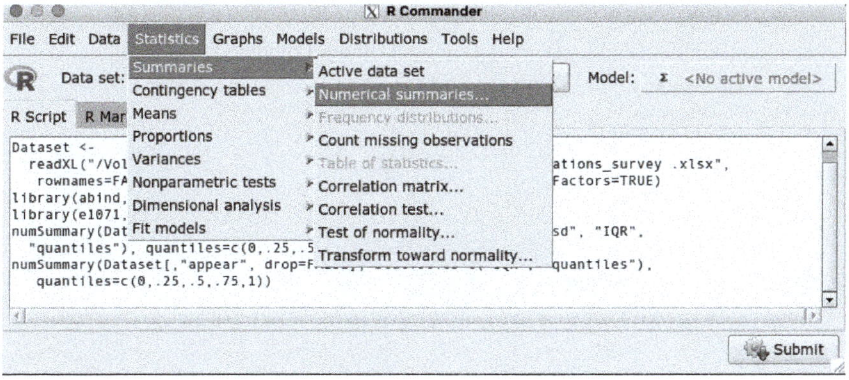

Figure 7.13 Interquartile range in the R Commander, part 1

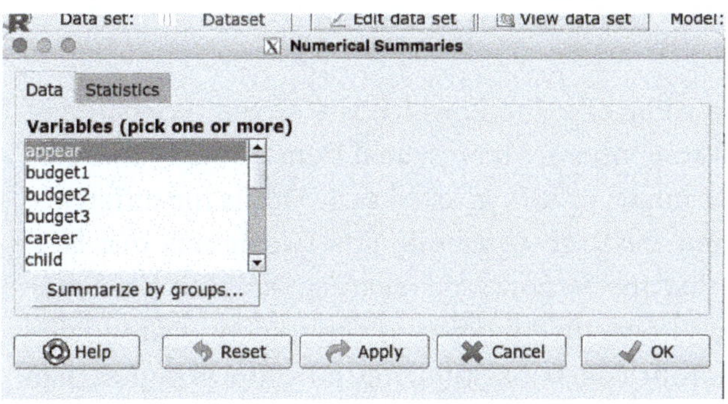

Figure 7.14 Interquartile range in the R Commander, part 2

Use the following steps to have the R Commander report the range and IQR:

Step 1: Click Statistics → Summaries → Numerical summaries (Figure 7.13). A new window will appear asking for additional information.

Step 2: Highlight the variable for which you want the R Commander to report dispersion statistics. In this example, the variable label is "appear" (Figure 7.14).

Step 3: Click the "Statistics" tab to open a window providing various options. Check the "Interquartile Range" box and make sure the "Quantiles" box is also checked. By default, the "Mean" and "Standard Deviation" boxes are checked. Go ahead and uncheck them if you are using an ordinal level variable (Figure 7.15). If using an interval level variable, they can remain checked.

Step 4: Click OK. The R Commander should return the requested information as in Figure 7.16.

A great deal of information is presented, but can be dissected quite easily. The 0% column represents the 0 percentile, or the minimum value, which is −2. The 100% column represents the 100th percentile, or the maximum value, which is 2. The R Commander does not report the range, but with these two pieces of information, we

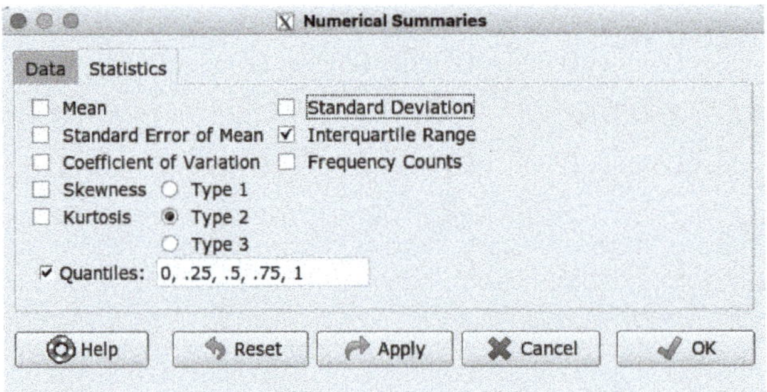

Figure 7.15 Interquartile range in the R Commander, part 3

```
IQR 0% 25% 50% 75% 100%  n NA
  1 -2   1   2   2    2 68  3
```

Figure 7.16 Interquartile range output, example 1

can deduce that the range is from a value of −2 to 2, which is 4. Given the coding of the variable from the codebook, all responses are represented from Strongly Disagree to Strongly Agree. The interquartile range, or IQR, is listed as 1. This is the difference between the 75th percentile (2) and the 25th percentile (1). Two minus one is 1. With this information, we know that the response delineating the 75th percentile is a value of 2 or Strongly Agree. Twenty-five percent of the responses are higher than this value; however, given that the codebook stipulates no value is higher than 2, it simply indicates that the remaining 25% of responses are also a 2, or Strongly Agree. The value delineating the 25th percentile is 1, or a response of Agree. Twenty-five percent of the remaining observations have scores less than 1. So, the scores between the 25th and the 75th percentile are between 1 and 2, or Agree and Strongly Agree. With this information, it seems that very few (less than 25%) of the responses were less than 1, or reflecting a Neutral, Disagree, or Strongly Disagree response. In fact, the median response was a 2. How do we know this? The value of the 50th percentile, or the value in the 50% column, is 2, or Strongly Agree.

For a different spread of data, using the same dataset, have the R Commander return dispersion statistics for the "ctyattent" variable, which codes survey responses to the survey item: "City officials pay attention to the association's opinions." The coding scheme is:

Strongly Agree = 2
Agree = 1
Neutral = 0
Disagree = −1
Strongly Disagree = −2

Following the previous steps, your resulting output from the R Commander should report the same numbers as Figure 7.17.

```
IQR 0% 25% 50% 75% 100%  n NA
  1 -2   0   1   1    2 68  3
```

Figure 7.17 Interquartile range output, example 2

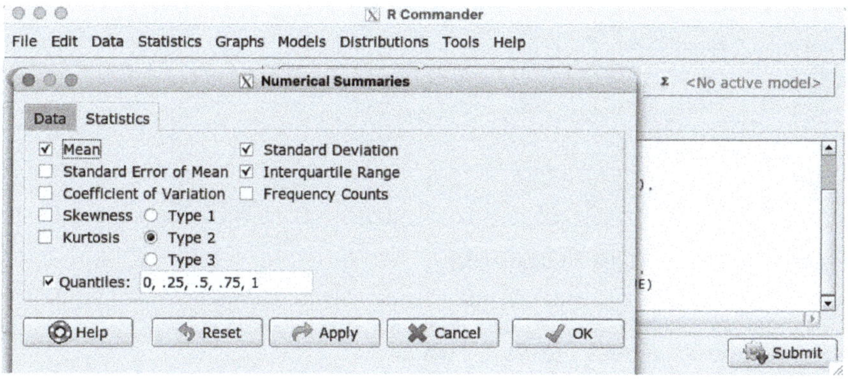

Figure 7.18 Dispersion statistics, example 3

```
    mean       sd   IQR 0%   25%  50% 75% 100%  n
82.43333 12.78923 13.75 49 77.25 83.5  91  100 30
```

Figure 7.19 Dispersion statistics, example 3 output

These results show the same IQR value of 1, with the 75th percentile's value of 1 (Agree) and the 25th percentile's value of 0 (Neutral). So, 25% of the responses are below a 0 value of Neutral, and 25% of the values are above the 75th percentile's value of 1 (Agree). The range is from a −2 (Strongly Disagree) to 2 (Strongly Agree), so there is more variability in the responses to this survey question than to the previous question about the association's role in neighborhood appearance.

The IQR can also be particularly useful when describing interval variables, especially if there is interest in knowing the 25th percentile and 75th percentile values/cutoffs. These cutoffs often become important for those interested in standardized testing or proficiency exams. To see the importance of percentiles for interval variables, open the *testscores* dataset from the Companion Site into the R Commander. It is a hypothetical dataset with student test scores on an exam that can have scores from 0 to 100. Use the R Commander to report dispersion statistics. You can use the same steps as before, clicking Statistics → Summaries → Numerical summaries. For this example, highlight the "score" variable and then click the "Statistics" tab. Since the score is an interval variable, go ahead and make sure the "Mean" and "Standard Deviation" boxes are checked, along with the "Interquartile Range" and "Quantile" boxes. Your window should look like Figure 7.18.

Now, click OK to have the R Commander report the dispersion statistics. Your output should match Figure 7.19.

For this example, the range is less important than the IQR, but it should be reported nonetheless. The minimum value, as represented by the 0% column, is a score of 49,

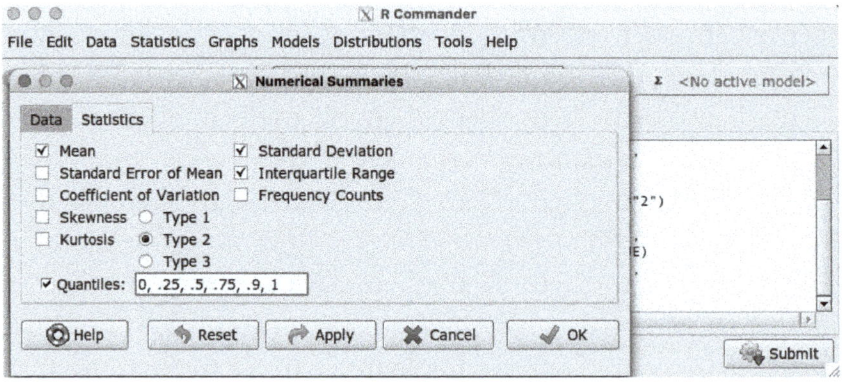

Figure 7.20 Top 10% delineation in the R Commander

```
    mean       sd   IQR 0%   25%  50% 75%  90% 100%  n
82.43333 12.78923 13.75 49 77.25 83.5  91 98.1  100 30
```

Figure 7.21 Top 10% delineation results

while the maximum value, represented by the 100% column, is 100. Therefore, the range for this interval variable is 51. The 75th% and 25% columns show the third quartile and the first quartile, respectively. The third quartile score is 91, indicating that 25% of the observations in the dataset are above 91. The first quartile score is 77.25, indicating that 25% of the observations/scores in the dataset are below 77.25. The mean is 82.43, with a standard deviation of 12.79. The median, as represented by the 50% column is 83.5, indicating a small negative skew to the data.

Why is this information important? For administrators wanting to know who scored relatively well versus relatively poorly on the exam, the percentiles can present information on the scores that identify cutoff percentages of interest to the researcher. What if the researcher was interested in identifying the top 10% of scores, or the test score that delineated the top 10%? All the researcher would have to do is indicate to the R Commander a new threshold in the "Quantiles" box of the "Statistics" tab, the 10% threshold. Figure 7.20 shows that we have added 0.90 to the Quantiles box (the top 10% indicates the 90th percentile, thus 0.90 is entered).

Clicking OK returns the dispersion statistics (Figure 7.21).

The value delineating the top 10% of scores is 98.1. Therefore, we can say that anybody scoring 98.1 or higher on the exam scored within the top 10% of all test-takers.

7.6 Summary

With the information from this chapter on dispersion and the previous chapter on central tendency, you have the necessary tools to have software generate descriptive statistics of variables based upon their level of measurement. Most quantitative academic studies that are published will provide the readers with some review of the data's descriptive statistics for variables of interest. They are usually in the main body of the text or appendix in table format. While measures of central tendency like the mean and median are fairly common in reports and everyday public administration discussions, measures of dispersion like the standard deviation and interquartile range are less common. Yet, these statistics provide important information on the spread of the data and help researchers and consumers of public administration data better understand what the data look like and if there are any unusual patterns. Again, think of these measures of descriptive statistics as diagnostic tests that are run on data like a medical doctor orders diagnostic tests (blood tests) during routine physicals.

Many of the topics covered in this chapter and Chapter 6 will return in Chapter 9 with Z-scores. The next chapter deviates slightly from the extant chapters in that its focus is on data visualization or graphing. The topics of central tendency and dispersion will, however, reemerge, since the graphs and figures constructed in the next chapter use this information, but display them with figures instead of simply numbers.

PRACTICE PROBLEMS

Conceptual Problems

1. Without using mathematics, describe the concept of dispersion as if to somebody not well-versed in research design/statistics. In the same manner, explain what is standard deviation.
2. Suppose two classes, Class A and Class B, take the exact same proficiency exam. Both classes have an average score of 84%. However, Class A's standard deviation is 1.2 and Class B's standard deviation is 10.5. Which class has more As? Which class has more Bs (assume enrollment in both classes is equal)? Explain your logic.
3. What is the difference between a leptokurtic distribution of data and a platykurtic distribution of data? Draw an example of each.

Problems by Hand

4. An HR manager is comparing data between two departments. The manager is concerned that one department's employees have too many write-ups/demerits. Each department has six employees. For each department, calculate the mean writeups and the standard deviation:

   Department A: 0, 0, 2, 1, 1, 4
   Department B: 2, 1, 1, 0, 0, 10

   What can the HR manager conclude?

5. A community survey is conducted by local activists asking residents how affordable they believe housing to be in their community. Possible responses and their coding are: Very affordable (4), Affordable (3), Unaffordable (2), and Very unaffordable (1). Responses from twelve individuals are presented in the table below:

Respondent	Response
1	3
2	1
3	1
4	1
5	2
6	3
7	4
8	1
9	2
10	2
11	2
12	3

a. Calculate the median response.

R Commander Problems

6. Open the *state_politics* dataset from the Companion Site (www.cambridge.org/scheller) in the R Commander and open the State Politics Dataset Codebook for variable definitions/coding. Calculate the mean, median, standard deviation, interquartile range, and skewness and kurtosis statistics for each of the following variables:
   a. unions
   b. tport
   c. debt
7. Using the results from problem #6, interpret the skewness and kurtosis statistics for each variable.
8. Open the *infrastructure* dataset from the Companion Site. It contains hypothetical data on city finances and infrastructure quality. The "infrastructure" variable lists the respective city's quality of infrastructure using the following coding: Excellent (2), Good (1), Average (0), Poor (−1), and Very poor (−2). The "debt" variable lists the city's debt in millions of dollars. Negative values indicate a surplus (lack of debt).

a. Calculate the mean, median, and standard deviation for the "debt" variable.
b. Does there appear to be any skew in the "debt" variable? Why/why not?
c. Calculate the skewness statistic for the "debt" variable. Interpret it. Does it match your reasoning from problem 8b?
d. Calculate the range and interquartile range for the "infrastructure" variable.

9. Calculate the range and IQR for the response data from Problem #5.

8

Data Visualization

8.1 Introduction

Numbers like means, medians, standard deviations, ranges, etc. are helpful statistics for understanding variables, but may not always be intuitive to casual audiences. Putting data into pictures or visualizing data is a growing skillset requested by employers. The ability to turn hundreds, thousands, or even millions of data points into a more comprehensible graph or figure can better help researchers and analysts describe their data to a variety of audiences (Isett & Hicks, 2018). Being able to communicate with data through visualization has been an issue for public administration scholars (Huber, 2016; Isett & Hicks, 2018), making it difficult for public servants to use scholarly findings for real-world policy decisions. Thus, being able to present your data findings visually (when applicable) makes for better presentations and increased likelihood of comprehension by diverse audiences that can result in real policy and programmatic decisions.

A variety of data visualization tools are usually embedded into statistical software, including the R Commander, and can be used depending upon the level of measurement of variables, data setup, and general desires of the researcher on what to present. For example, bar graphs can aid in the visualization of ordinal level data like responses to survey questions measured on a Likert scale so that audiences can visualize the frequencies of respondents answering "Strongly Agree" through "Strongly Disagree." Additionally, it is one thing to say that a pattern has a downward trend over time, but it is more impressive and visually appealing to combine this information with a line graph where the audience can see trends over time, noting any interesting deviations (or "blips") in the data.

Both bar graphs and line graphs are covered in this chapter, along with other graphs for visualizing data like histograms, scatterplots, and boxplots. Attention is paid to when to use these types of graphs based upon a variable's level of measurement, along with the correct data setup for the R Commander. Data must be entered into spreadsheets in a particular manner or rearranged/cleaned to ensure the proper use and output for each particular graphing feature.

8.2 Bar Graphs

Bar graphs are an excellent tool to display the frequency counts of categories for ordinal level variables. You are likely familiar with these graphs already. They are common on news media reports and in applied presentations. The *associations_survey* dataset in the Companion Site (www.cambridge.org/scheller) has responses from neighborhood and homeowners association presidents to a survey. One item that presidents are requested to respond to is "The association helps residents get to know one another." Responses are coded in the "social" variable as:

Strongly Agree (2)
Agree (1)
Neither agree nor Disagree (0)
Disagree (−1)
Strongly Disagree (−2)

To generate a bar graph of all types of responses, the R Commander can produce the graph if the data are set up as a string/factor variable. To change the numeric coding to string or factor variable, for this example:

Step 1: Click Data → Manage variables in active data set → Convert numeric variables to factors (Figure 8.1).

Step 2: A new window will emerge where you should highlight the relevant variable you want to convert ("social" in this case). In the "New variable name ..." box, enter a name for which you may remember the recoded variable. I have used "social2" as the new name, as shown in Figure 8.2.

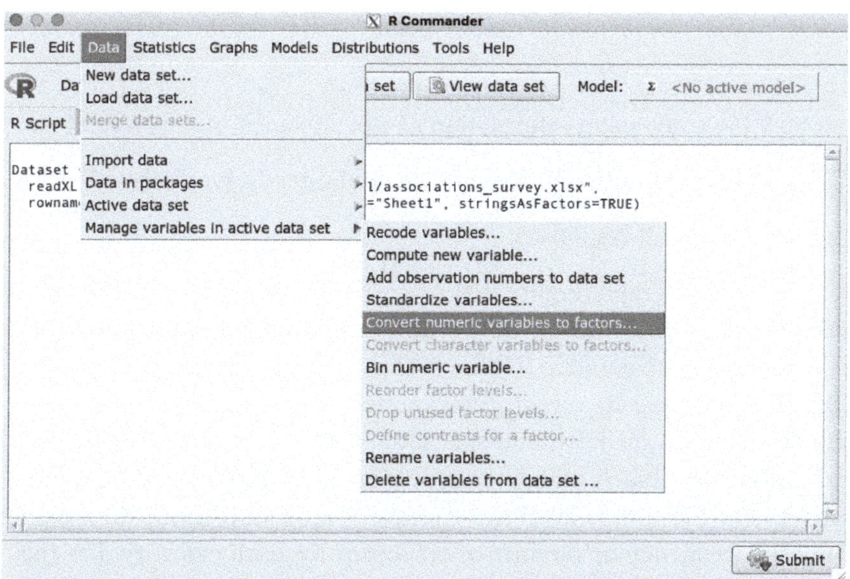

Figure 8.1 Numeric to string, part 1

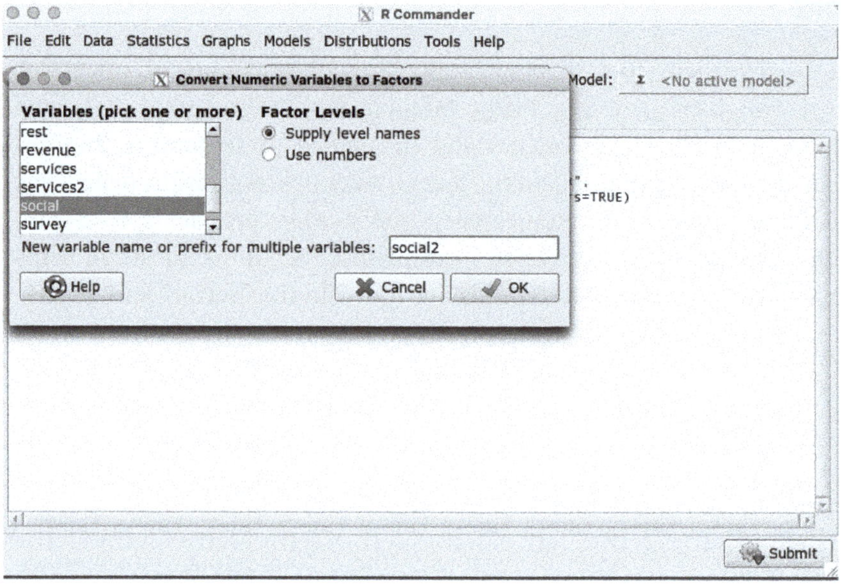

Figure 8.2 Numeric to string, part 2

Step 3: Click OK.

Step 4: A new window will appear asking you to label each numeric category. Always refer back to the codebook if available. In this case, the following should be used to recode from numeric into factor:

−2 = SD
−1 = D
0 = N
1 = A
2 = SA

Figure 8.3 shows how the conversion information can be included in the popup box.

Step 5: Click OK. The new variable should be recoded and ready for analysis.

To generate the bar graph of all responses:

Step 6: Click Graphs → Bar graph (Figure 8.4).

Step 7: Highlight the variable for which you want to produce the bar graph. In this case, it is the "social2" variable (Figure 8.5).

Step 8: Click the "Options" tab to reveal graph preferences, which you can alter. The default values on the left-hand side should suffice. In this window, you can change the axes' labels and graph title. For the x-axis label, we can use "Responses." For the y-axis label, we can use "Frequency," since the graph will show the frequency or number of responses for each category. For the graph title, we can call it "Association Helps Residents Get to Know One Another." See Figure 8.6 for the correct inputs.

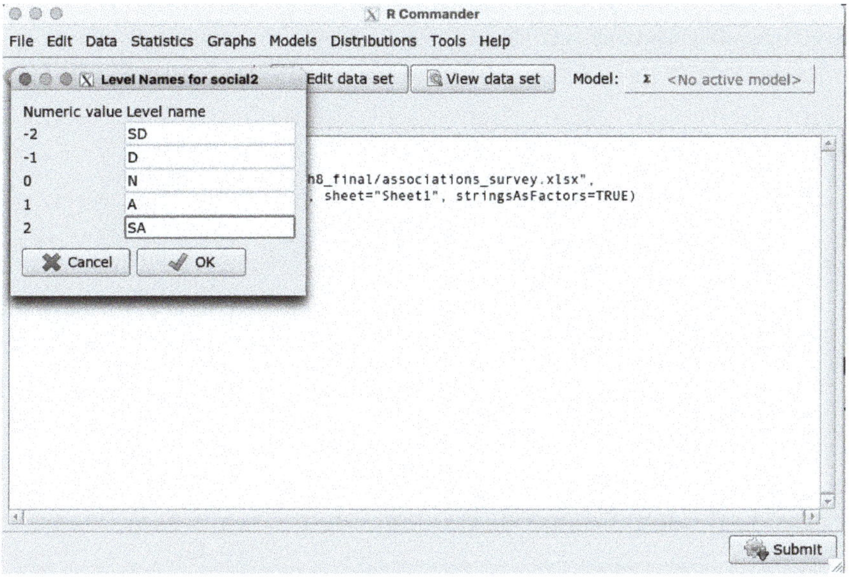

Figure 8.3 Numeric to string, part 3

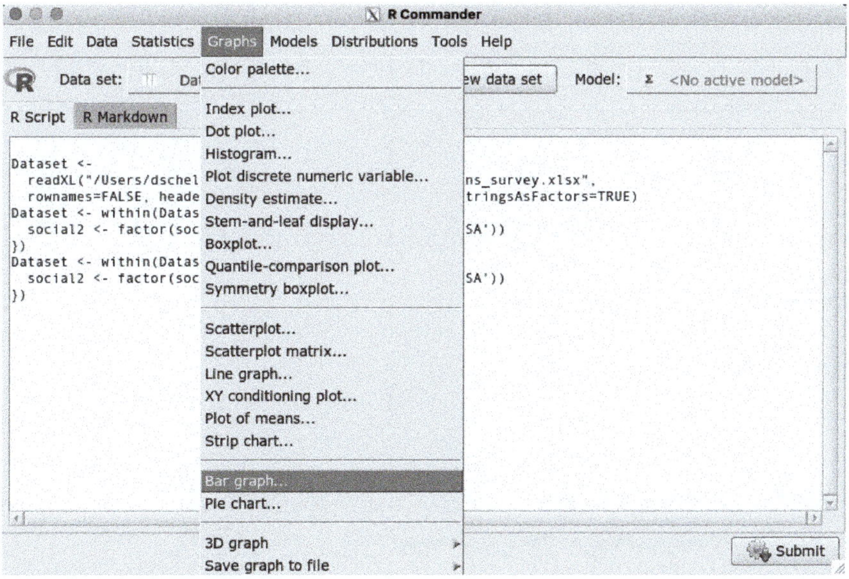

Figure 8.4 Bar graph, part 1

Step 9: Click OK.

The R Commander should generate a bar graph appearing like Figure 8.7.

The numbers in the bars represent the frequency counts for each category of the variable.

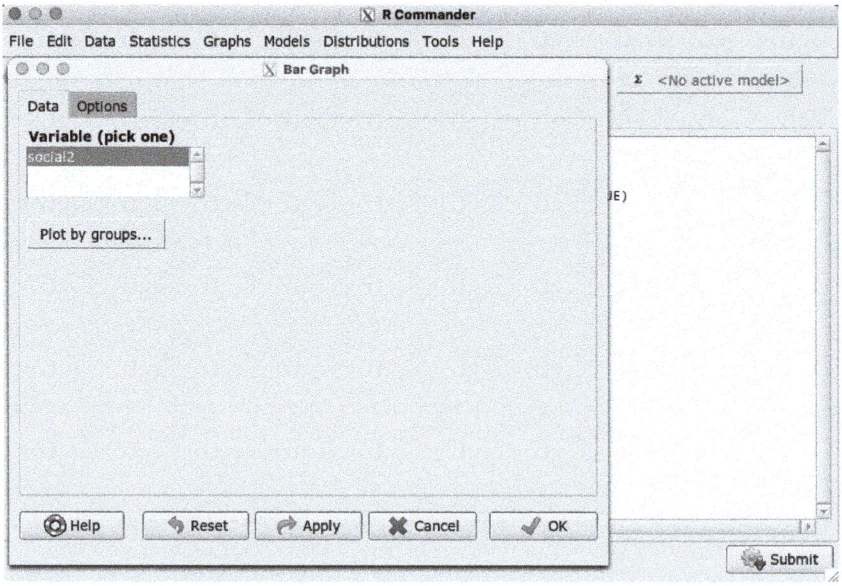

Figure 8.5 Bar graph, part 2

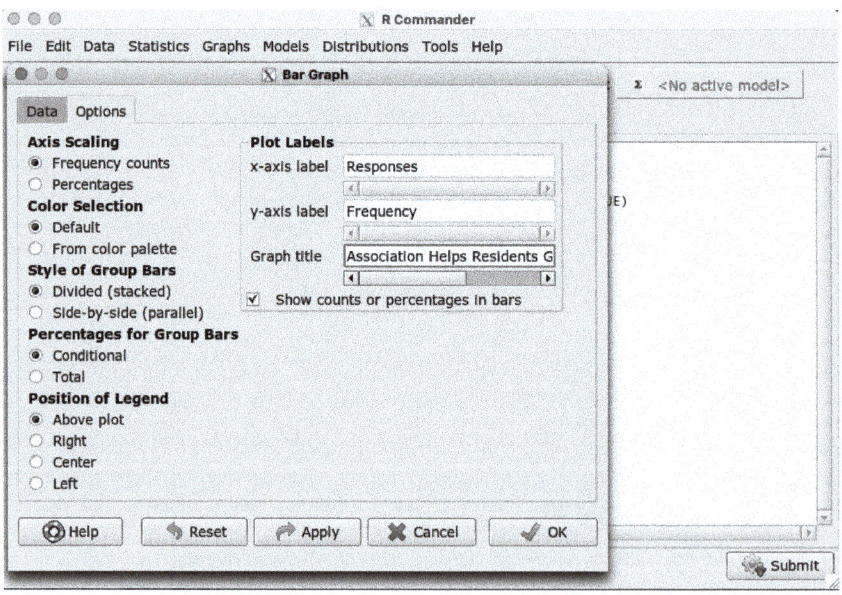

Figure 8.6 Bar graph, part 3

8.2.1 Stacked Bar Graphs

What if we want to plot the responses by type of association? In this case, suppose we want to know the distribution of responses between neighborhood versus homeowners associations. We can do this in a bar graph with a little bit of extra work. The "type" variable lists the type of organization, with a 0 representing a neighborhood association and a 1 representing a homeowners association. Using the steps

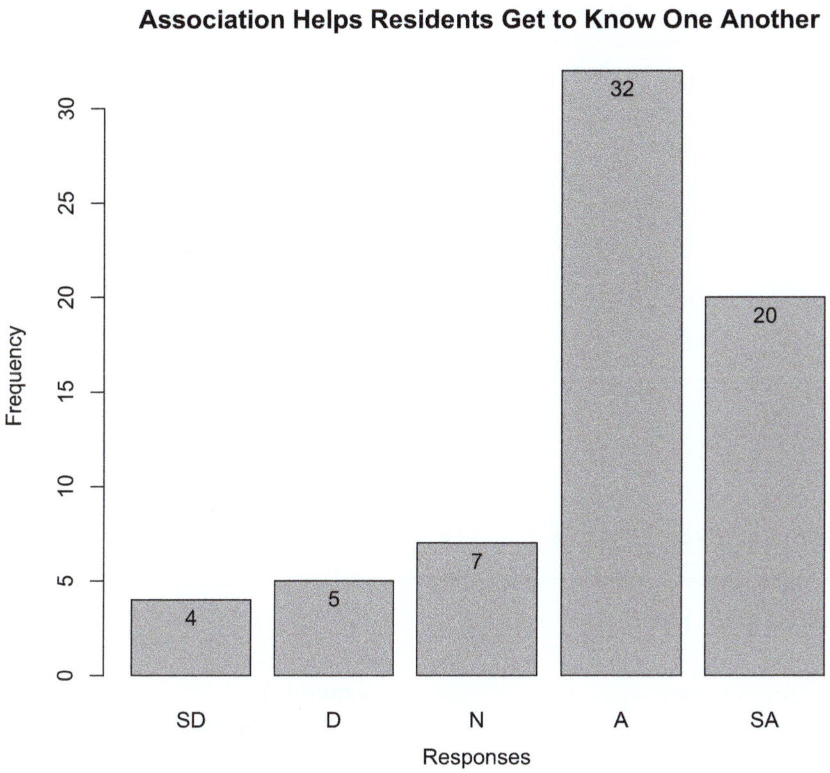

Figure 8.7 Bar graph result

in the previous example, convert the "type" variable to a factor variable, where a 0 is represented by NA and a 1 is represented by HOA. Call this variable "type2". NA is the label for neighborhood association, and HOA is the label for homeowners association. Once you have converted this variable to a factor, you can generate a bar graph of the "social2" variable, separated by type of association – neighborhood or homeowners association.

Step 1: With the previous recoding, click Graphs → Bar graph and then click the "Plot by groups" button.

Step 2: In the Group variable box, highlight the "type2" variable and click OK (Figure 8.8).

Step 3: In the resulting window, highlight the variable of interest, "social2." Then, click the "Options" tab and keep the default "Divided (stacked)" option for the "Style of Group Bars." Labels can also be updated. The y-axis can still be labeled "Frequency." The x-axis can be labeled something like "Responses by Association." Finally, the title of the graph can be labeled "Association Helps Residents Get to Know One Another." These inputs are illustrated in Figure 8.9.

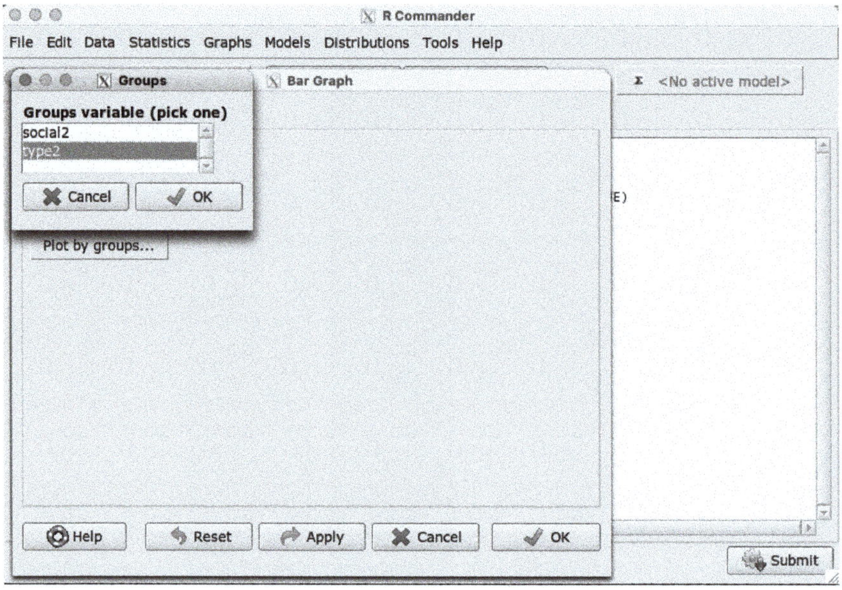

Figure 8.8 Stacked bar graph, part 1

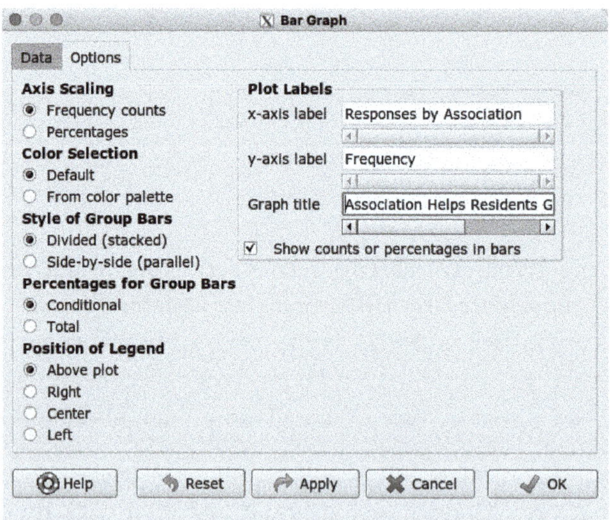

Figure 8.9 Stacked bar graph, part 2

Step 4: Click OK. The R Commander should generate the bar graph that looks like Figure 8.10.

The top part of each bar is the HOA, while the bottom half represents neighborhood associations. A total of 24 HOA presidents either agreed (16) or strongly agreed (8) to the statement that the association helps residents get to know one another. This is in comparison to 28 neighborhood associations presidents agreeing (16) or strongly agreeing (12). The counts for each response are included. You can figure out the

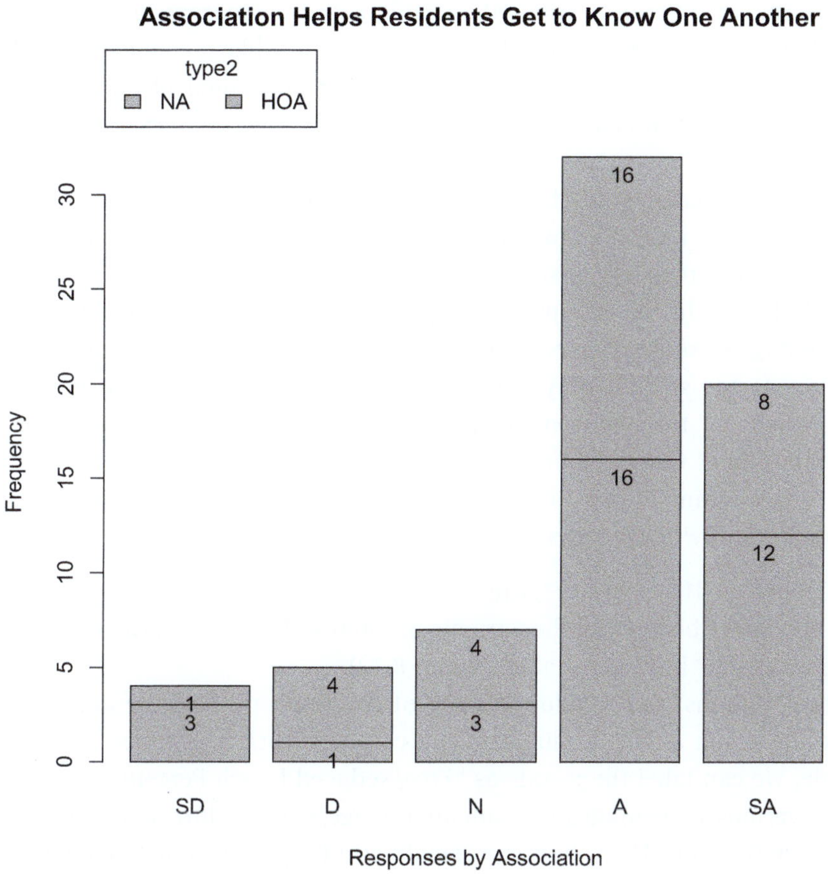

Figure 8.10 Stacked bar graph results

total number of HOA and neighborhood association presidents that responded by summing the numbers for each component of each respective bar. A total of 35 neighborhood association presidents responded to this survey item while 33 HOA presidents responded. This may be helpful if you would like to count the percentage of presidents responding in a certain manner. For example, 12 of 35 neighborhood association presidents responded as Strongly Agree, or just over 34%. A total of 8 of 33 HOA respondents answered Strongly Agree, or just over 24%.

8.3 Histograms

Histograms are a common graph used to visualize the distribution of interval variables, not only to see what values or range of values occurred most often, but to also see how the variable is spread out across values. Histograms are best able to display any skewness in a distribution and help researchers determine if a variable is normally distributed or closely follows a normal distribution (symmetrical bell-curve distribution). As will become evident in later chapters, it is always a good idea to first examine an interval dependent variable with a histogram to check for skewness or odd patterns. Think of it as a basic diagnostic test like a complete blood count or metabolic panel test that a doctor performs for an annual physical. Like these medical tests, a histogram can help to show any concerning patterns or values of a variable.

The state of Nebraska makes available a number of school district data (Nebraska Department of Education, n.d.) via a website (www.education.ne.gov). One measure of school poverty is the percentage of students in the school receiving free or reduced lunch. The *lunch* dataset in the Companion Site (www.cambridge.org/scheller) has data on the percentage of students in each school on the free/reduced lunch program. Data have been redacted so that only a unique identifier for each school and its respective percentage on free/reduced lunch are included in the spreadsheet file. Upload this file into the R Commander.

To generate a histogram of the "lunch" variable (percent of school receiving free/reduced lunch), follow these steps:

Step 1: Click Graphs → Histogram (Figure 8.11)

Step 2: In the "Variable" box, select the variable of interest. In this case, the variable of interest is the "lunch" variable (Figure 8.12).

Step 3: Click the "Options" tab to allow editing of the graph to label the axes and to give the graph a title. From here, you can add labels and titles. For this example, we can label the x-axis as "Free/Reduced Lunch Percentage" as it has the various percentages of students on free/reduced lunch, which can range from 0 to 100. The y-axis can remain as a frequency, and as such, can

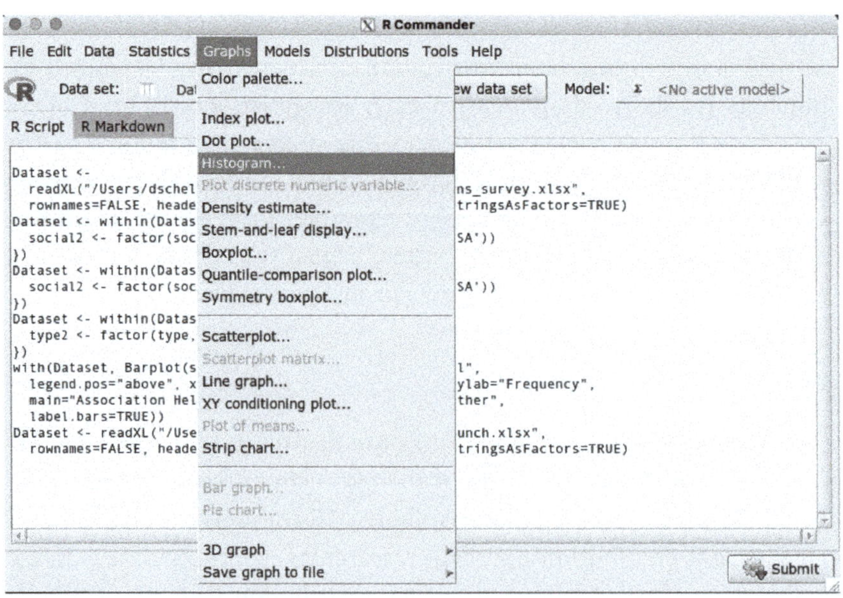

Figure 8.11 Histogram, part 1

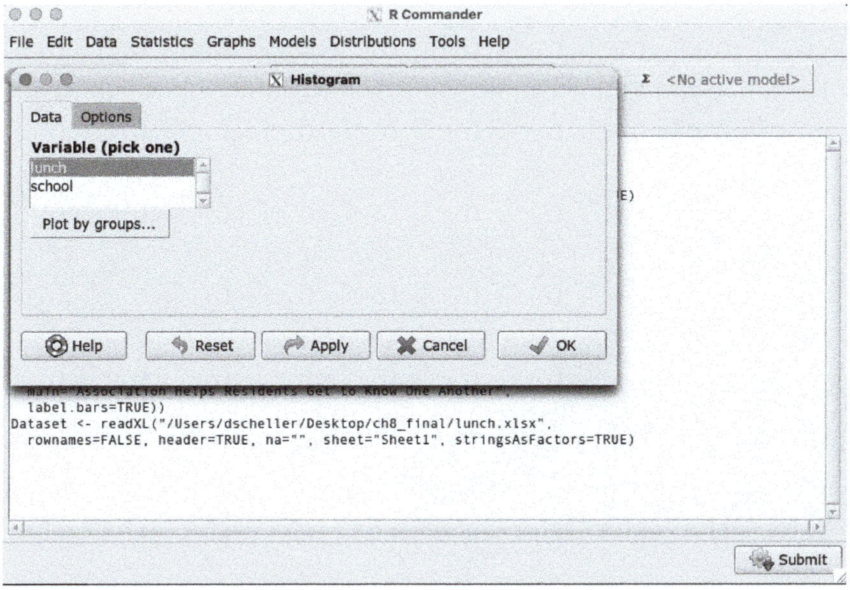

Figure 8.12 Histogram, part 2

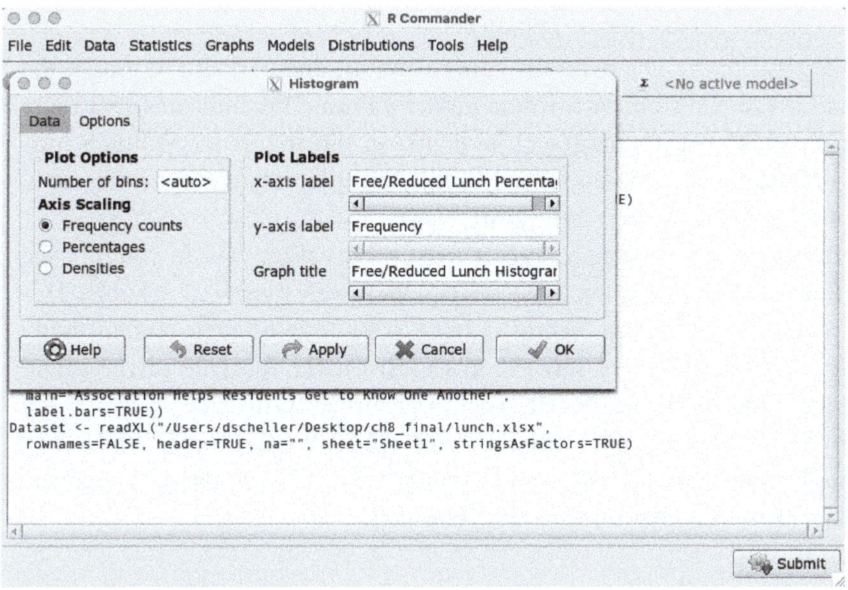

Figure 8.13 Histogram, part 3

be labeled as "Frequency." Finally, we have labeled the title as "Free/Reduced Lunch Histogram." See Figure 8.13 for a visual of the inputs.

Step 4: Click OK.

The R Commander should produce the histogram as seen in Figure 8.14.

From the histogram, it is evident that there are some high values off to the right of the distribution. Mentally attempt to draw a curve around the data to follow its

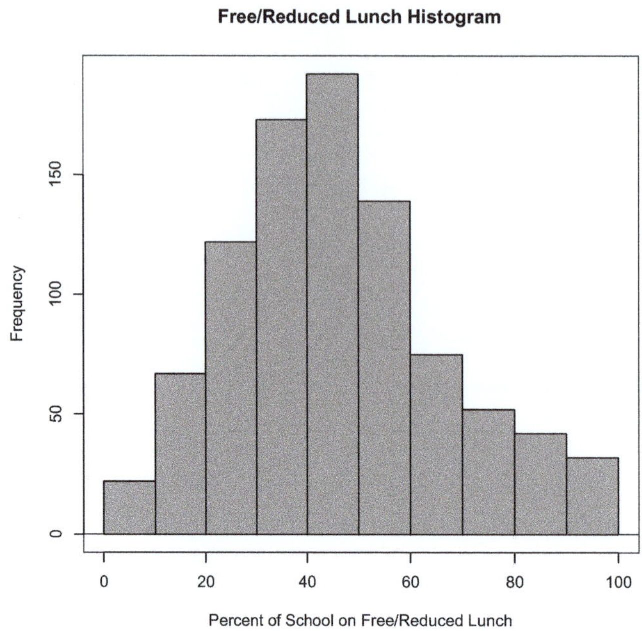

Figure 8.14
Histogram results

pattern. While a great many observations concentrate in one part of the graph, the data tends to tail off to the right or towards higher values. This indicates that there are some outliers of large percentages of students on the free/reduced lunch program. This information can help you to understand that the data are not necessarily normally distributed and that there is a positive skew.

Further interpretation of the graph reveals most observations are in roughly the 40%–50% bin/bar of the histogram, with a frequency well over 150 schools. This indicates that over 150 schools in Nebraska have 40%–50% of their student body receiving free/reduced lunch. Very few schools exist on the left side of the graph where few students are on free/reduced lunch. Off on the right side of the graph contains the frequency of schools with the most students on free/reduced lunch programs. Though under 50 total schools, a small chunk of schools in the dataset have over 90% of their students on free/reduced lunch.

8.4 Line Graphs

A line graph is principally used to show trends over a period of time (seconds, minutes, hours, days, months, years, etc.) for an interval variable. Counts of occurrences, percentages, monetary figures, temperatures, etc. are all examples of variables researchers like to track over time. In producing a line graph it is customary to place the time interval along the x-axis, and the variable of interest on the y-axis in its typical unit (dollars for money, degrees Celsius for temperature, frequency for counts, etc.). With line graphs, researchers can view how the variable changes over time, noting any interesting changes in trends, whether they be long-term or short-term. For example, if somebody has tracked air traffic passengers by year for the last twenty years, they will likely see a general upward trend of people flying, with a precipitous drop in the year 2020, and then a gradual increase back to previous levels. This deviation, or "blip," in the data is obviously the result of the Covid-19 pandemic and people avoiding crowded spaces like airplanes. Other deviations in data may have less obvious explanations, but may be interesting to the analyst to examine in greater depth.

The data setup in a spreadsheet can be particularly cumbersome when dealing with data over time, also known as time series data. Each particular software program has a preference for how the time variable is entered in a spreadsheet. The R Commander has a particularly difficult time handling non-numeric values for the date variable.

For the purposes of this chapter, creating a line graph in R Commander is the focus of this section, ensuring the data are set up correctly, and then producing the graph. First, let's take a look at the data setup of a time series spreadsheet. Open the *mead_level* dataset from the Companion Site (www.cambridge.org/scheller) in Excel and then the R Commander. A screenshot of the data is posted in Figure 8.15. The data come from the U.S. Bureau of Reclamation that includes the water levels (in feet) of Lake Mead at Hoover Dam by month and year (U.S. Bureau of Reclamation, n.d.). Recall from Chapter 1 that the desert Southwest of the U.S. is facing a drought, and much attention is currently being paid to the water levels at lakes from the Colorado River that supply water to residents and farmers in this region.

	A	B	C	D	E	F
1	item	date	month	year	level	
2	1	Jan-20	1	2020	1094.68	
3	2	Feb-20	2	2020	1096.27	
4	3	Mar-20	3	2020	1098.59	
5	4	Apr-20	4	2020	1096.39	
6	5	May-20	5	2020	1091.32	
7	6	Jun-20	6	2020	1087.07	
8	7	Jul-20	7	2020	1084.63	
9	8	Aug-20	8	2020	1084.04	
10	9	Sep-20	9	2020	1083.21	
11	10	Oct-20	10	2020	1081.88	
12	11	Nov-20	11	2020	1081.07	
13	12	Dec-20	12	2020	1083.72	
14	13	Jan-21	1	2021	1085.95	
15	14	Feb-21	2	2021	1087.26	
16	15	Mar-21	3	2021	1084.39	
17	16	Apr-21	4	2021	1079.3	
18	17	May-21	5	2021	1073.5	
19	18	Jun-21	6	2021	1068.77	
20	19	Jul-21	7	2021	1067.65	
21	20	Aug-21	8	2021	1067.96	
22	21	Sep-21	9	2021	1067.68	
23	22	Oct-21	10	2021	1066.77	
24	23	Nov-21	11	2021	1064.97	
25	24	Dec-21	12	2021	1066.39	
26	25	Jan-22	1	2022	1067.09	
27	26	Feb-22	2	2022	1066.78	
28	27	Mar-22	3	2022	1061.49	
29	28	Apr-22	4	2022	1054.69	
30	29	May-22	5	2022	1047.69	
31	30	Jun-22	6	2022	1043.02	
32						

Figure 8.15 Lake Mead water levels

Note that not all data will automatically be set up in this manner; you may have to add information and/or manipulate the data, especially how the time component is recorded. Working from right to left in the spreadsheet, Column E ("level") is the level in feet of Lake Mead at Hoover Dam for the particular month and year in the row. Columns B through D have information on the time component. Columns C and D separate the month and year, respectively, into those columns. One practice when dealing with monthly data is to keep the month as a numerical variable from 1 to 12. Other researchers enter data using a string or letter-based approach like Column B. Unfortunately, the R Commander does not handle the date format in Column B well since it is string in format. It also does not recognize or allow the use of a month/year format in separate columns like C and D. It works best with one numeric value representing the date like Column A. This column has been labeled as "item," or it could be labeled anything of your choosing just so that you know it represents the water level measurement from the first measurement to the last. Therefore, the first level observation is labeled as item #1. This is, unfortunately, one weakness of the R Commander. However, the relationship can still be graphed, and the graph can be saved and edited with other software like Adobe Acrobat.

To have the R Commander produce a line graph, there are two options, but the option covered in this chapter allows the researcher to make the most edits to the graph. With the *mead_level* dataset in the R Commander:

Step 1: Click Graphs → XY conditioning plot (Figure 8.16).

This is technically an XY conditioning plot, but has more "bells and whistles" to edit the graph than the R Commander's Line Graph option in

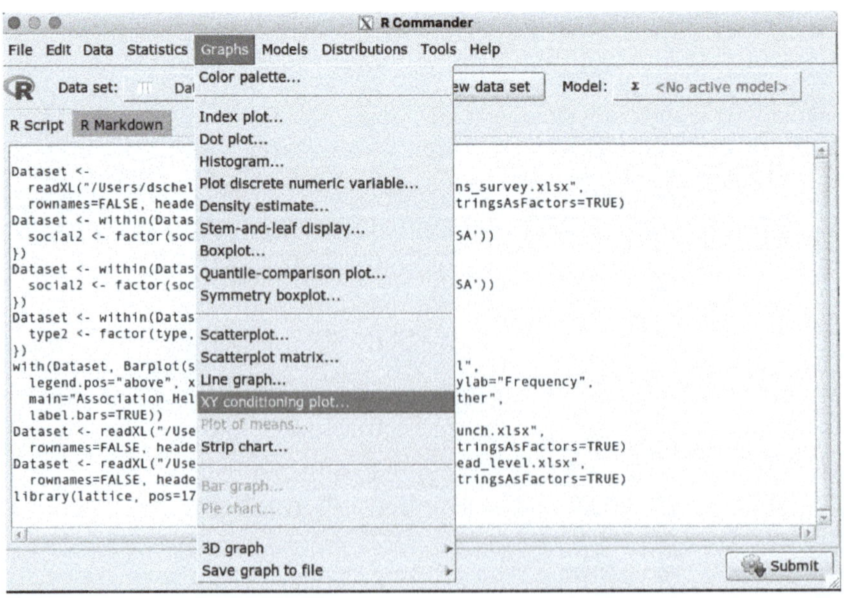

Figure 8.16 Line graph, part 1

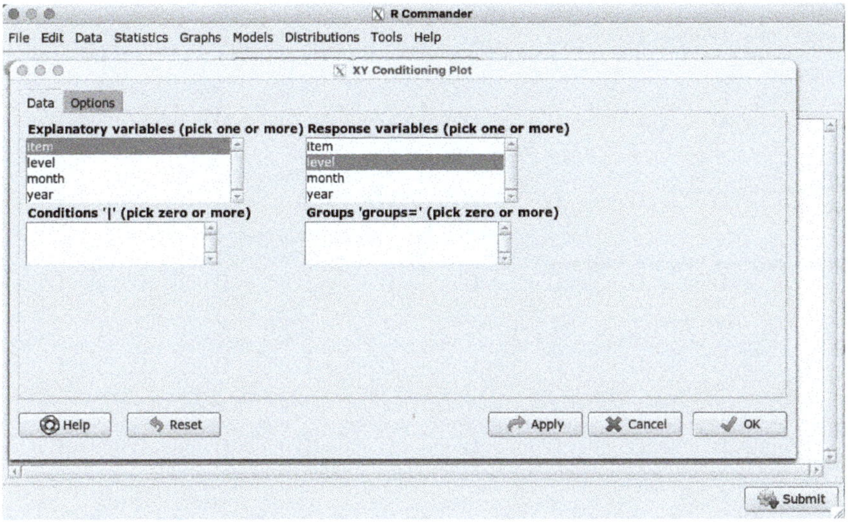

Figure 8.17 Line graph, part 2

the Graphs menu (though you can get the same graph using the Line Graph option).

Step 2: Highlight the time variable in the "Explanatory variables" box. In our example, highlight the "item" variable. Highlight the variable of interest in the "Response variables" box, which will be the y-axis variable. In our particular example, highlight the "level" variable, which measures the water level at Lake Mead. Your screen should look like Figure 8.17.

Step 3: In that same window, click on the "Options" tab to reveal additional options for your graph. For the Plot Options, most of the defaults will suffice. Make sure the "Lines" box under Plot Type is checked. This ensures that the graph becomes a line graph. The "Points" option can be checked or unchecked based upon personal preference. It simply puts a dot for every observation in the line graph. In connecting the dots to make a line graph, it allows you to see every dot, which is every observation in your spreadsheet. This may be a viable option if your observations are fairly low (10–20); however, if you have hundreds or thousands of observations, the dots will likely make the graph very messy. As such, this example has the "Points" option deselected.

Over in the right panel are options for labeling your graph's axes and giving your graph a title. Simply fill in the relevant information. For the x-axis label, we can simply label it "Date." For the y-axis label, we can call it "Water Level (feet)." And for the graph title, we can call it "Lake Mead Water Level (2020–Present)." This is what the data contain – Lake Mead's water levels since 2020. These edits are shown in Figure 8.18.

Step 4: Click OK, and the R Commander should produce your graph like Figure 8.19.

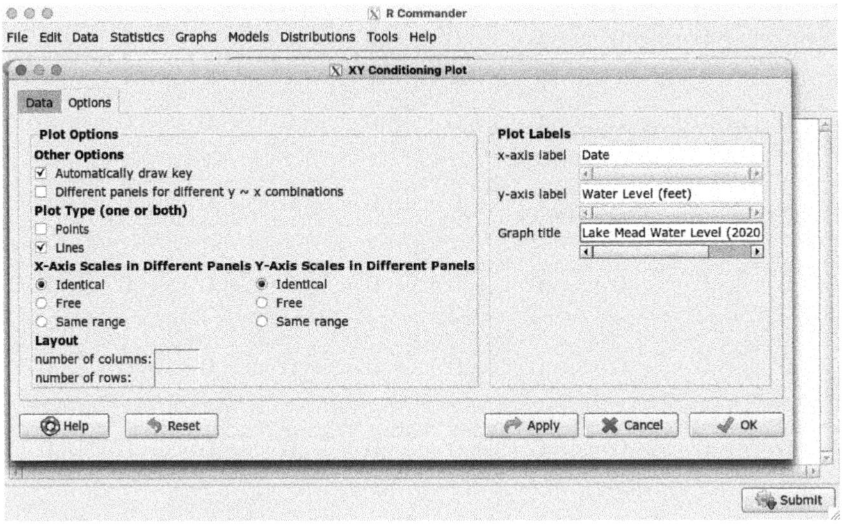

Figure 8.18 Line graph, part 3

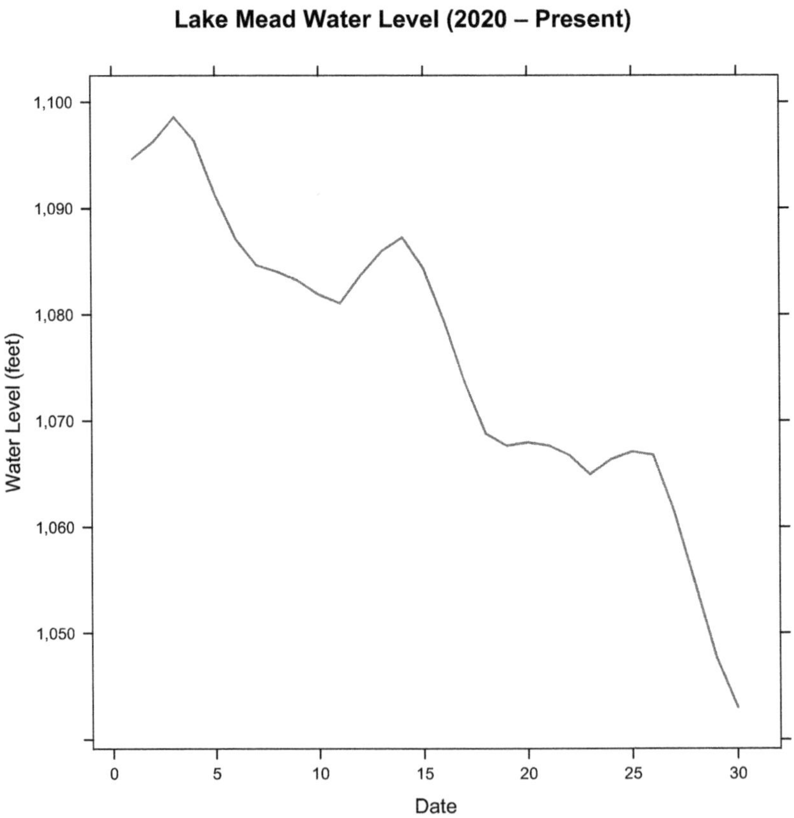

Figure 8.19 Line graph results

The graph shows a general downward trend in Lake Mead's water levels, a potential (and likely) issue of concern for environmentalists and public administrators in the desert Southwest of the U.S. You can see that the x-axis has the date labeled as a number. The number 1 would be the first observation (January 2020 in our example). The R Commander is unable to show the exact date. However, one way to edit the graph is to copy/paste the graph to Microsoft Word and then save it as a PDF. If you have PDF-editing software like Adobe Acrobat, you can edit the labels on the graph to change the numbers to the relevant month/year. Other software like STATA and SPSS do have the advantage of including the relevant date with a little bit of data editing/manipulation. Nevertheless, the graph does show the general pattern over time and presents the most important information. This graph is an example of time series data, an entirely separate subfield of statistics that is often taught in advanced public administration courses and degrees.

8.5 Boxplots

A boxplot is a type of visual that helps to better understand the dispersion of data, especially the range and outliers of the data. Boxplots are most appropriate to use with interval and ordinal variables. Returning to the *lunch* dataset, the histogram is one plot to see the spread of the data across values, but the boxplot is also another excellent plot to see spread and obtain additional information like the range and the median. To create a boxplot in the R Commander use the following steps:

Step 1: Click Graphs → Boxplot (Figure 8.20).

Step 2: Highlight the variable for which you want to produce the boxplot. In this case, it is the "lunch" variable. Then, click OK (Figure 8.21).

The boxplot will be produced and will look like Figure 8.22. Note that labels with arrows have been added to the plot for greater clarity and instruction.

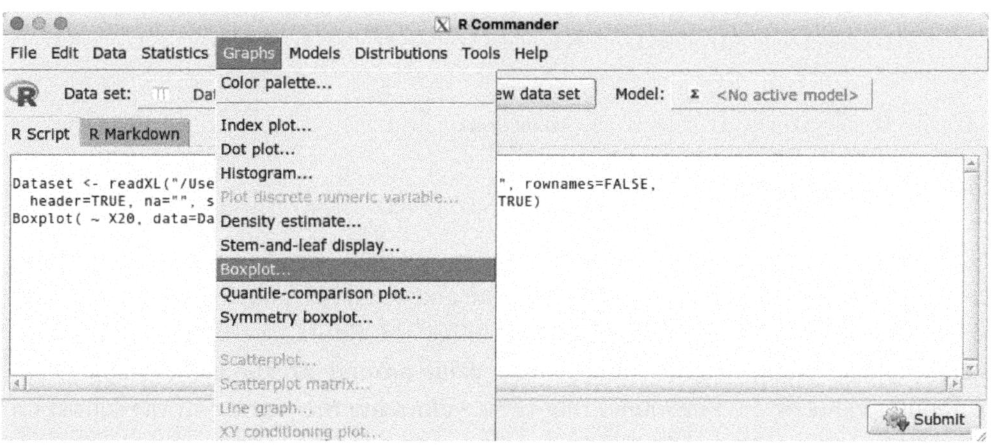

Figure 8.20 Boxplot, part 1

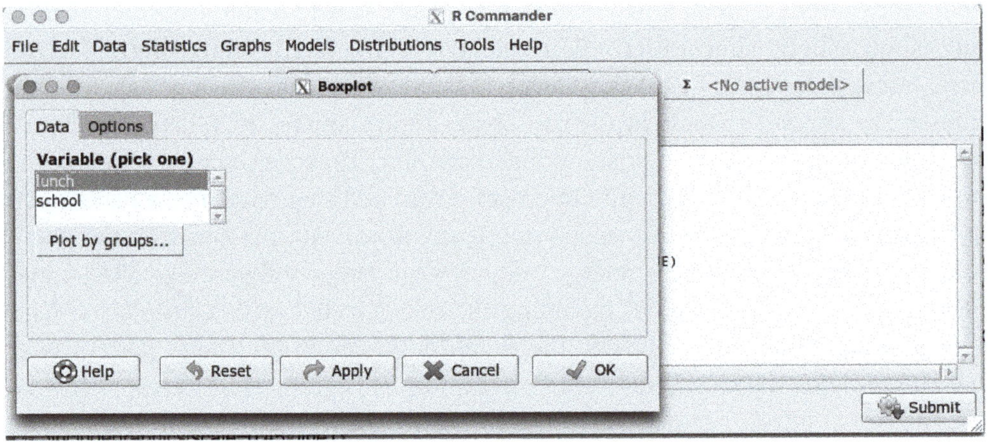

Figure 8.21 Boxplot, part 2

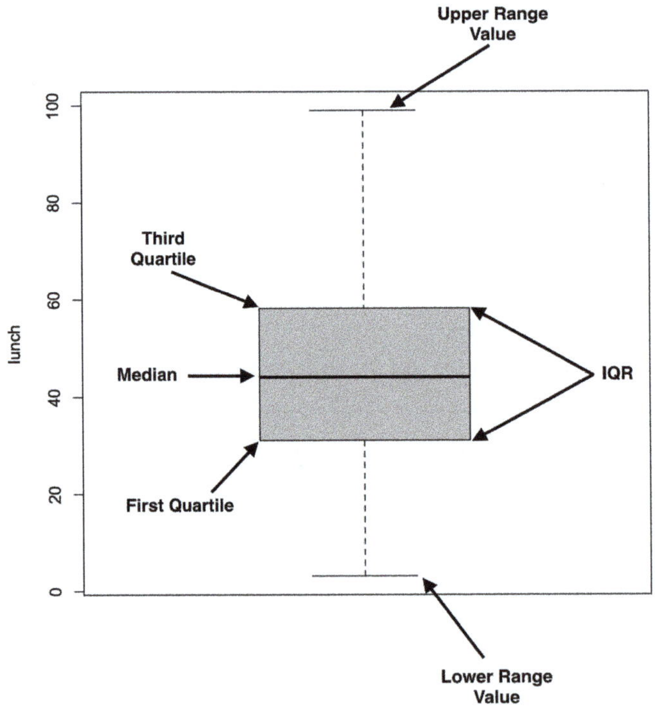

Figure 8.22 Boxplot results

The shaded region shows the interquartile range (IQR), or the range of values between the first quartile (25th percentile) value and the third quartile (75th percentile) value. The median is the bolded line. Eyeballing the figure, the first quartile value is approximately 30, with the third quartile value around 59. The median appears to be about a value of 43. Remember that these values are the percent of the school on free/reduced lunch. The dashed lines fanning out to the top and bottom horizontal lines on the graph represent the range of the data, with a lower range value around

2 and an upper range value of about 99. To know the exact values, simply run the descriptive statistics for the "lunch" variable with the instruction from Chapter 6. Doing so will yield the exact values that could then be edited into the plot if desired. For this variable, the exact values are 31.04 for the first quartile, 58.2375 for the third quartile, 44.105 for the median, with a range of 3.09 to 98.99.

Any outliers in the data would be represented by a circle in the boxplot. An important note is that in the absence of outliers, the range in the boxplot is the true range of the data. If there are outliers, the range in the boxplot will not be the true range of the data. The boxplot will omit any outlier from its range depiction, resorting to showing the range without the outlier and depicting the outlier with a star or circle depending upon the software. Let's take a look at a dataset with an outlier.

Suppose in the "lunch" dataset that I had made a data entry error, accidentally recording the first observation as 212.4 instead of 21.24, indicating that 212.4% of that particular school is on the free/reduced lunch program instead of the correct 21.24%. This error is depicted in the *lunch_error* dataset in the Companion Site (www.cambridge.org/scheller). Load it into the R Commander and then produce a boxplot for the "lunch" variable. It should look like Figure 8.23.

The new boxplot changes to depict the outlier towards the top of the plot with a circle and the number 1 (observation number in the dataset) next to it to call attention to the presence of the outlier. The circle corresponds to the value of 212.4. Why is this important? Producing a boxplot will show any outliers that may have occurred naturally or due to random chance in whatever you are observing. If you sampled from the population over and over an infinite amount of times asking about income, eventually you would sample Bill Gates or Warren Buffett – outliers that could skew the data. Even natural phenomena like measuring daily precipitation may have an outlier day where there was 8 inches of rain (think tropical storm

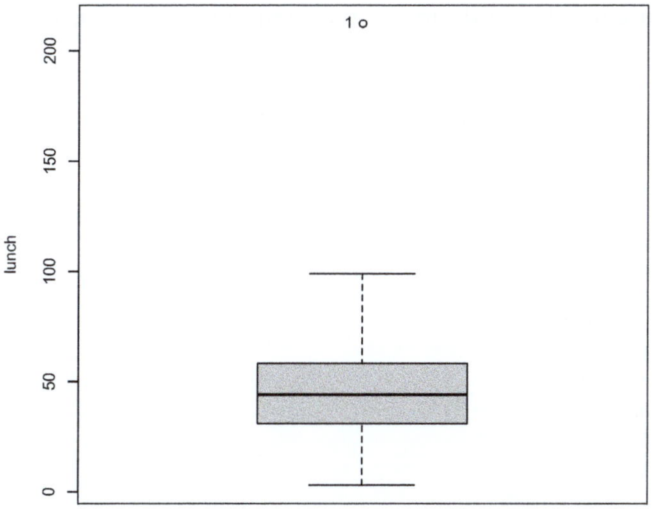

Figure 8.23 Boxplot with outlier

or hurricane) that would skew the data. Additionally, the boxplot that depicts an outlier(s) may show clerical errors in data entry, either by the organization collecting the data or by you if you are entering data into a spreadsheet. These errors happen, and running a diagnostic like a boxplot can help identify and isolate these cases.

8.6 Scatterplots

Sometimes researchers and analysts want to visually display the relationship between two interval variables. The relationship between education and income, campaign spending by candidates and the percent of the vote they receive, daily amount of rainfall and daily park attendance, employees' scores on a public service motivation assessment and years served in the public sector are all relationships that can be depicted using a scatterplot. If a researcher has a hypothesized relationship between the variables, the conventional manner to depict the variables in the scatterplot is to have the dependent variable and its values on the y-axis and the independent variable and its values on the x-axis. A scatterplot will place a dot in a graph that represents each datapoint's respective dependent variable value with its corresponding independent variable value. In the hypothetical dataset below (Figure 8.24), let Y represent the dependent variable and X represent the independent variable for each of the ten observations.

You can enter this same data on your own in Excel or download it from the Companion Site (*scatter* dataset) (www.cambridge.org/scheller). Once the data have been uploaded to the R Commander, a few clicks will generate the scatterplot.

Step 1: Click Graphs → Scatterplot (Figure 8.25).

Step 2: In the next window, select the independent variable in the "x-variable" box. In this case, highlight "X". Select the dependent variable in the "y-variable" box. In this case, highlight the "Y" variable (Figure 8.26).

Step 3: Now, click the "Options" tab to tell the R Commander to add additional information. Here, you can add a title to the plot and label the axes. For

	A	B	C	D
1	observation	Y	X	
2	1	18	2	
3	2	13	5	
4	3	12	6	
5	4	6	9	
6	5	4	10	
7	6	15	3	
8	7	20	1	
9	8	12	7	
10	9	9	8	
11	10	12	4	
12				
13				

Figure 8.24 Scatterplot data

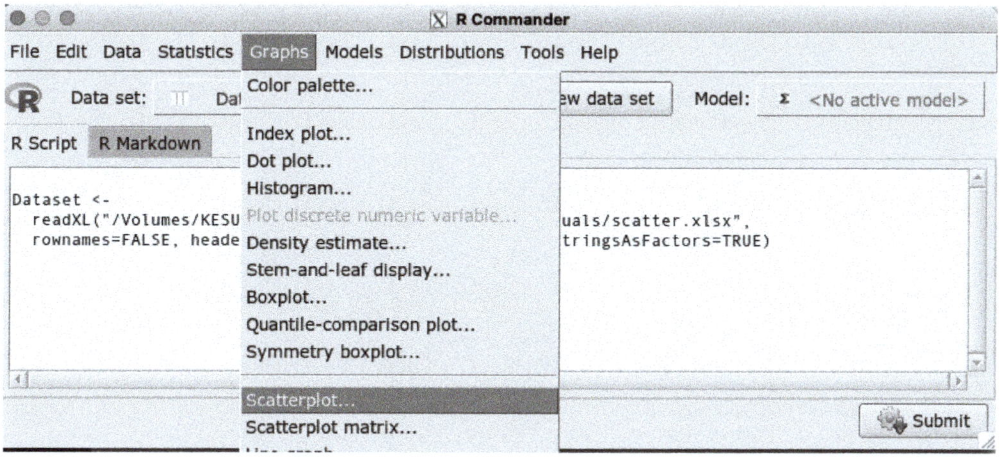

Figure 8.25 Scatterplot, part 1

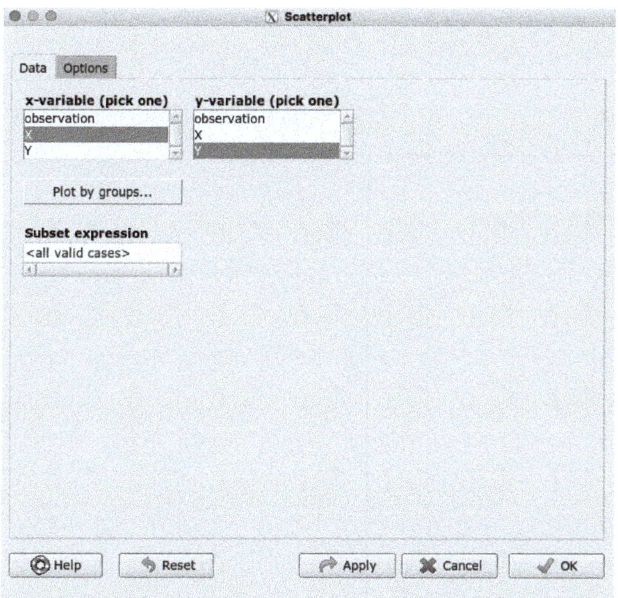

Figure 8.26 Scatterplot, part 2

this basic example, the x-axis label can simply be "X," the y-axis label can be "Y," and the Graph title can be "Scatterplot." This information is shown in Figure 8.27.

Step 4: Click OK. The R Commander will generate the scatterplot like Figure 8.28.

Each circle represents an observation in the dataset. Observation #1 in the dataset has an X value of 2 and a Y value of 18. Where these two values intersect in the scatterplot is a circle. The other circles represent each of the remaining X, Y observations.

The pattern of the observations in the scatterplot suggests a negative relationship between X and Y, or a relationship reflecting the general trend that as X increases,

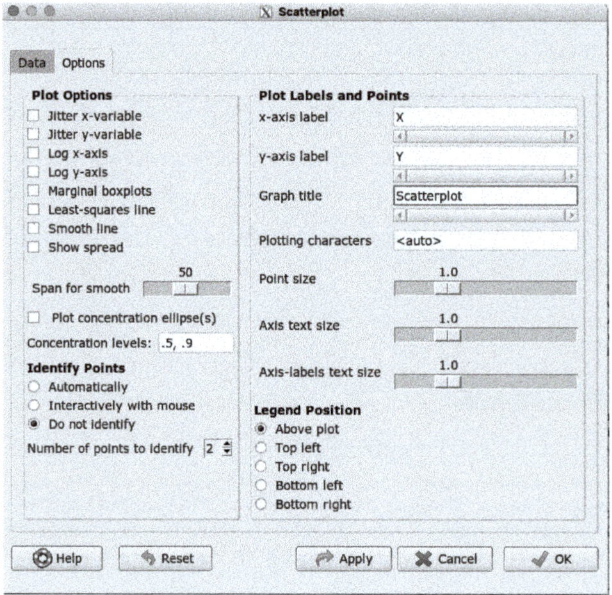

Figure 8.27 Scatterplot, part 3

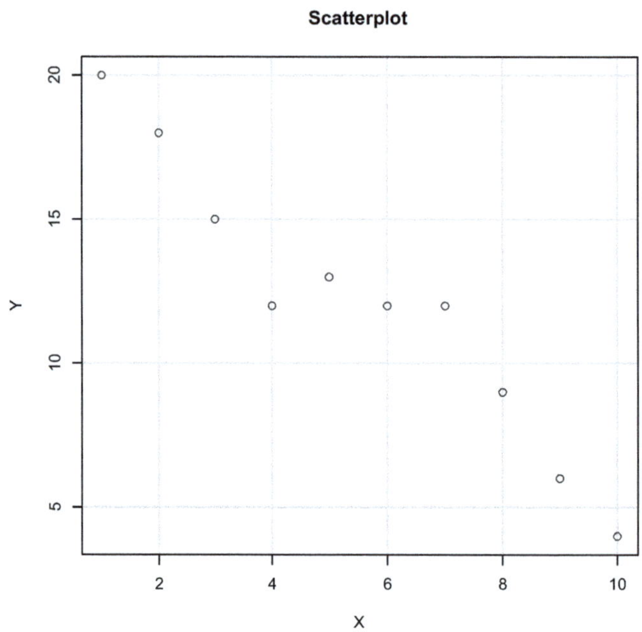

Figure 8.28 Scatterplot results

Y decreases. Imagine drawing a best-fitting line through the data. It would likely slope downward from the upper left region of the plot to the lower right region of the plot.

Now, let's try a more applied example with real-world data. Load the *florida2020* dataset from the Companion Site into the R Commander. This spreadsheet contains county level election and demographic data from the state of Florida. The county is the unit of analysis. For each county, the percent of the vote share for Donald Trump in 2020 is included, based upon data collected from county election office websites. In addition to this information, county percent African American/Black, percent with a bachelor's degree or higher, and population per square mile are included. These demographic data are collected from the Census Bureau Quick Facts (n.d.).

On Election Night in the U.S. as the election results become official, political pundits on national television often discuss a particular candidate's support based upon voter demographics. One general pattern is the general support for conservative candidates in rural counties. Population density, measured as persons per square mile, is a common metric to measure an area's level of urbanism. Higher values generally indicate a more urban area with lower values reflecting a more rural geographical area. With the *florida2020* dataset, let's graph this idea that conservative candidates receive more support from rural areas.

In the 2020 U.S Presidential election, the conservative candidate was Donald Trump. The percent of the county voting for Donald Trump is included in the "trump" column of the dataset, with the county population density listed in the "density" column. We want to create a scatterplot with the "trump" variable as the dependent variable, or the y-axis variable, and the "density" variable as the independent, or x-axis, variable. Following the previous steps to create a scatterplot above, do the same for these variables. The R Commander's output should look like Figure 8.29.

With more observations, the scatterplot is not as neat as the previous example. There appears to be a general negative relationship between county population density and support for Trump, measured as the percent of the population voting for

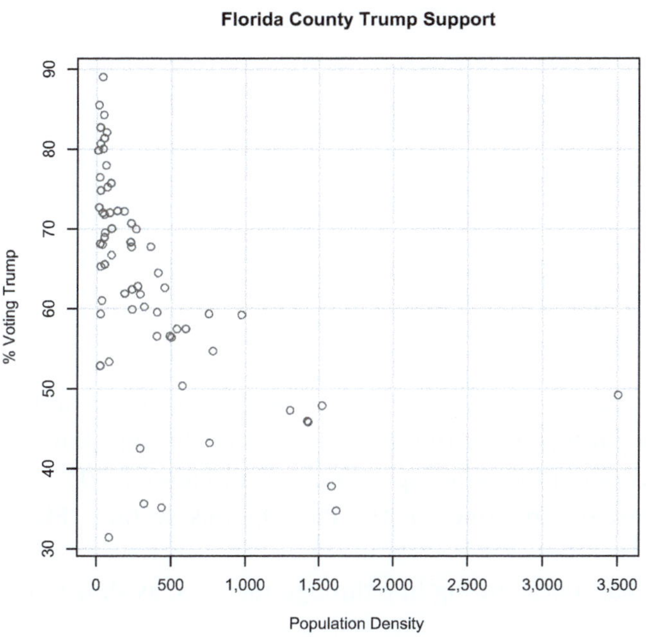

Figure 8.29 Trump support scatterplot

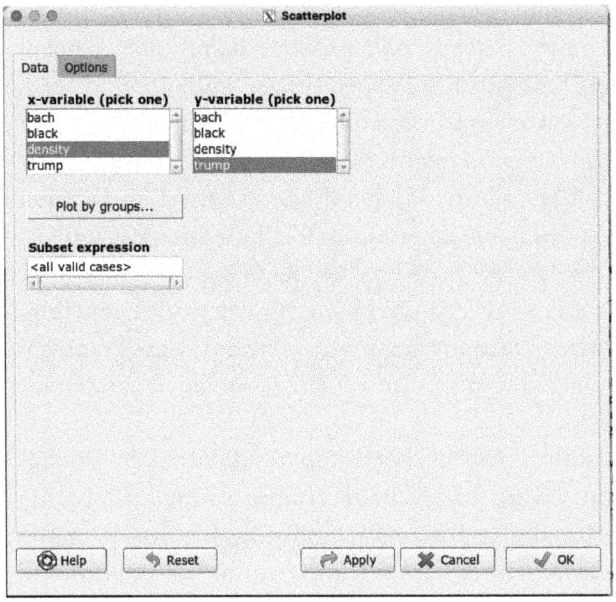

Figure 8.30 Line through scatterplot, part 1

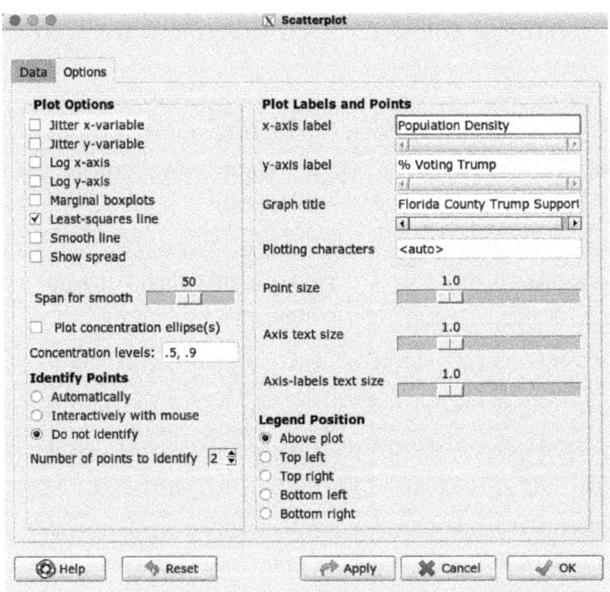

Figure 8.31 Line through scatterplot, part 2

Trump. One additional tool that can be used and added to the scatterplot is a best-fitting line through the data. To put this line through the data, after clicking Graphs → Scatterplot, click the Options tab in the resulting window, as in Figure 8.30.

Make sure to check the "Least-squares line" in the Plot Options section "Figure 8.31".

Then, click OK. The new plot has a best-fitting line through the data, as shown in Figure 8.32.

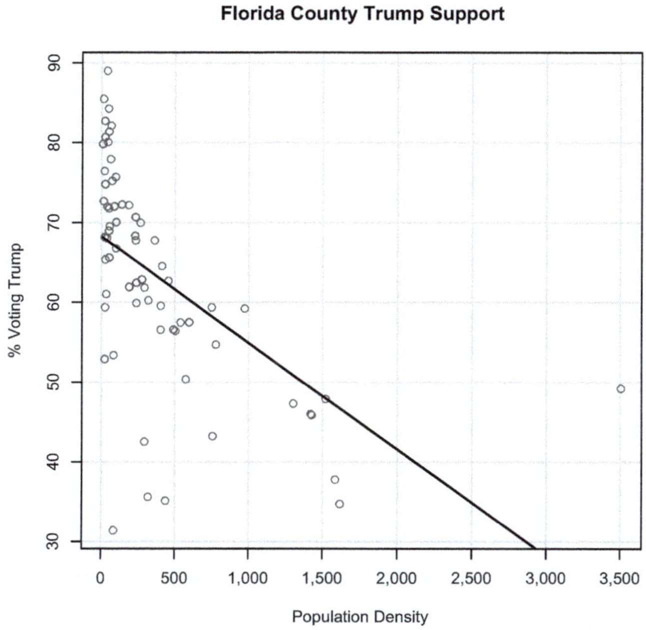

Figure 8.32 Line through Trump support scatterplot

The best-fitting line through the data reflects the negative relationship between population density and percent of the county voting for Trump. It appears that more urban counties, measured by population density, have fewer voters supporting Trump. Whether or not this relationship is statistically significant, however, is a topic for future chapters. However, the scatterplot helps to visualize the general relationship between county population density and county vote percentage for Donald Trump.

8.7 Summary

The data visuals covered in this chapter are just a small representation of the visual tools public administrators and researchers can use to visualize large datasets into comprehensible graphs and figures. The Graphs menu in the R Commander lists more visualization tools and graphs that can be used like 3D graphs, density plots, and index plots. The purpose of this chapter has been to provide some basic instruction on how to produce some of the most common types of graphs used to visualize data in public administration, especially for practitioners and new students to statistics. As a public administration student and future practitioner or researcher, including visuals of data patterns will be a necessary component of many types of reports you will need to write if using quantitative data. If interested in learning about more advanced graphs along with some of the more specific bells and whistles of graph editing, the Fox (2017) citation in the References section is an excellent resource for more advanced graphing capabilities in the R Commander. Additionally, with its growing popularity, more videos are being made by users of the R Commander and posted to various video-hosting sites on the Internet.

PRACTICE PROBLEMS

Use the R Commander for all of the following practice problems to produce the requested visuals.

1. Upload the *associations_survey* dataset from the Companion Site (www.cambridge.org/scheller). Its codebook is also available on the Companion Site. Create a bar graph for the following situations:
   a. For all associations, display responses to the statement "Members are more likely to contact association representatives about neighborhood problems than they are city or county officials."
   b. For the same statement, create a graph that compares the responses for homeowners associations and neighborhood associations in one graph.
   c. For all associations, create a bar graph that displays responses to whether or not the association provides a pool.
   d. For the same statement in 1c, create a graph that compares the responses for homeowners associations and neighborhood associations in one graph.
   e. Interpret the graphs for 1b and 1d. How do homeowners associations differ from neighborhood associations?
2. Open the *grade_scores* website from the Companion Site. It is a hypothetical competency exam for an incoming class of police officers seeking to graduate from the police academy. The "id" variable is simply the unique identifier of the respective cadet. The "grade" variable is a standard academic grading scale from A to F. Let's assume that a D or F is a failing grade. The "degree" variable indicates if the cadet has a four-year college degree, coded "Y" for yes and "N" for no. The academy commandant would like a visual display of the grades for all cadets. Then, the commandant would like for you to disaggregate the graph into one that compares the grades of students with a four-year college degree to those cadets that do not have a degree. Once you have produced both graphs, the commandant would like for you to interpret the results for them in a short memo.
3. Open the *stateGDP* dataset from the Companion Site. It contains the percent change in state gross domestic product (GDP) in a year. Create a histogram of this data. Describe any skew. Within what range are most of the values of GDP change occurring?
4. Open the *response_sample* dataset from the Companion Site. It has over 10,000 observations from a random sample of emergency responses for a city's fire department. Create a histogram from the "response" variable. It is

the amount of time in seconds it took the fire unit to respond to the respective emergency (calculated as the time from when they receive the emergency dispatch until they arrive on the scene of the emergency). Is there any skew to the data? If so, how is it skewed? As a policy analyst for the city, you are tasked with determining if most of the total response times are below ten minutes (600 seconds). What can you conclude?

5. In this chapter, the author proposed a claim that airplane passenger traffic likely declined in 2020 due to the Covid-19 pandemic. The Bureau of Transportation Statistics, a branch of the Department of Transportation, makes available this data via: www.transtats.bts.gov/Data_Elements.aspx?Data=1. Beginning with 2002, enter the yearly passenger data in an Excel spreadsheet. Check that your dataset matches the *passengers* dataset in the Companion Site.
   a. Create a line graph showing airline passengers by year from 2002 to present.
   b. Is the author's claim supported by the graph? Why? What other patterns can you explain in the graph?
   c. Create a boxplot of the data and determine if there are any outliers.
   d. Does the boxplot also provide support for the author's claim of declining passengers in 2020?
6. The Centers for Disease Control and Prevention (CDC) make available a great deal of public health data that can be easily downloaded and analyzed. The Covid Data Tracker contains weekly Covid-19 deaths: https://covid.cdc.gov/covid-data-tracker/#trends_weeklydeaths_select_00. From this dataset, you are interested in analyzing the trend of Covid-19 deaths per week in the year 2020. This dataset is located in the Companion Site and called *covid_deaths*. Upload this dataset and produce a line graph showing the number of deaths per week in 2020. Based upon your knowledge of the Covid-19 pandemic, explain trends in the graph.
7. Using the Covid Data Tracker (Centers for Disease Control and Prevention, n.d.) via the website, https://covid.cdc.gov/covid-data-tracker/#trends_weeklydeaths_select_00, add observations for the year 2021 to the Excel file *covid_deaths*. To do this:
   a. Download the *covid_deaths* dataset to your computer and open it. Notice that the weeks are logically ordered from 1 to 52 and their corresponding days.
   b. Add weekly data for 2021 by starting with week 53, which would correspond to the first week of 2021, and work down the Excel file, entering the respective dates and number of deaths. Note that we start with week 53 to make it easier for the software to read the data and to produce the correct graph.

c. With these new observations, create a line graph of weekly deaths for the 104 weeks in your dataset. Explain any general trends that you see.

8. A city manager is concerned about the number of lawsuits in the city among employees suing the city. The city manager asks you to collect data on the number of lawsuits among city employees since the year 2000. The data are contained in the *lawsuits* dataset in the Companion Site. The city manager would like to know the mean and median number of lawsuits since 2000. Additionally, the manager would like for you to analyze if there are any outlier years. To help the city manager, report the mean and median number of lawsuits and then present this information (including any outliers) in a boxplot. Write a memo to the city manager with your findings.

9. Open the *baseball* dataset from the Companion Site. City leaders are concerned about the effects of weather on attendance for the city's baseball team. Specifically, they are interested in the relationship between temperature and attendance. They want to be able to predict attendance based upon temperature so as to better determine how many staff to have at games to be efficient in wage spending. Create a scatterplot with a best-fitting line to help them understand the relationship between temperature and attendance. What does your graph show?

10. Open the *florida2020* dataset from the Companion Site. Create two scatterplots with the percent of the county voting for Donald Trump as the dependent variable and a.) the percent of the county that is Black/African-American as an independent variable, and then b.) the percent of the county with a bachelor's degree as an independent variable. What patterns do you see?

9

Sampling and Inference

9.1 Introduction

Sampling is the key component in inferential statistics. In the social sciences, researchers want to be able to make claims about the population under study. The population is every case or instance of a group we want to study. A simple example of a population is every resident in the U.S. Other populations that may be of interest to public administration researchers could be every Environmental Protection Agency violation for the last ten years, every state government employee, every emergency response by a fire department for a year, every bill in a state legislature, every city council vote on a zoning item, every county in the U.S., etc. Simply put, the population is every case of the unit of analysis. In a perfect world, a researcher would be able to collect information from the population on whatever characteristics they want to study. If a researcher collects data for the population under study, the statistics obtained are naturally reflective of the population. For example, if the population being studied is every employee in one nonprofit organization, and there are 100 employees, the researcher may be able to collect information on this population. If they wanted to survey the employees asking their number of years in the organization with the goal of knowing the average tenure of employees in the organization, and all 100 employees respond, the researcher can calculate the population's average number of years worked in the organization. If the researcher calculates the average to be 4.2 from these 100 observations, then the true population average is 4.2 – every employee responded.

On the other hand, if the researcher's population was every federal employee (a number like 1,000,000), and wanted to survey them on their number of years of education, it is unlikely the researcher could survey all 1,000,000. Getting information from that many individuals is nearly impossible for a researcher. Additionally, obtaining responses from all 1,000,000 is likely too time-consuming and costly to merit the efforts. Then, how is it that we obtain information about a population without being able to get information for every case?

Surveys of registered voters where an organization reveals results stating that 45% of a state's voters plan to vote for a particular candidate are commonly reported in news outlets. All of the state's voters are not reached or even contacted.

A sample is used, and characteristics of the sample (like percent supporting a candidate, average income, average age) are used to represent the full population. A survey of 5,000 registered voters by a polling organization that reveals 45% of the state's voters support a particular candidate is used to extrapolate that 45% of all the state's voters support a particular candidate. Of course, there is some uncertainty in this estimate since not every individual was sampled, hence why these polls often report a margin of error. Nevertheless, samples as small as 1,000 often accurately reflect the true population from which the sample was created. How can this be?

This chapter covers the basics of sampling and how samples can be used to make inferences about the larger population. It first covers random sampling and the sampling distribution. A discussion of a normal distribution and its implications for making claims for the larger population follows through the Central Limit Theorem. While heavily theoretical, this chapter provides the basis for why we can make statistical claims about a population using the statistical tests covered in the remaining chapters of the book.

9.2 From Sample to Population – Random Sampling

Researchers typically use a random sample of a population. In the case of the 1,000,000 federal employees, suppose the researcher obtains a list of all federal employees. Knowing they cannot survey all 1,000,000, they randomly sample 2,000 to receive the survey. ***Random*** is the key word. Every single individual among the 1,000,000 must have an equal chance of being selected to receive a survey. Researchers will usually use software like Excel, STATA, R, or SPSS to randomly select these individuals. The benefit of random sampling is that there is a high probability that the 2,000 sampled will be representative of the larger 1,000,000 population. Characteristics of the sample should, in theory, match those of the population. The sample's average age, years worked, income, education, percent female, job satisfaction, etc. should reflect the population's averages on these characteristics. Of course, there is some degree of uncertainty since we cannot observe the full population. The larger the sample size, the more reflective it is of the population's characteristics. Sampling 10 individuals from the population of 1,000,000 is unlikely to yield a representative sample. A sample of 100 is better, 1,000 even better, 2,000 better, and so on.

Let's take a hypothetical example of a known population. The *proficiency* dataset in the Companion Site (www.cambridge.org/scheller) contains hypothetical civil service exam scores on a scale from 0–100 for a population of 5,000 test takers. The average test score for this population is 74.64 with a standard deviation of 14.63. This is the known average for the population. Now, let's assume that we cannot observe all 5,000 test scores, and that we need to take a sample. We take samples of size 5, 20, 50, 100, 200, 500, 750, 1,000, and 2,000. See Table 9.1.

Table 9.1 Descriptive statistics from varying sample sizes

Sample Size (n)	Mean ($\bar{X}$)	Standard Deviation (s)
5	83	10.22
20	72.5	15.29
50	78.06	13.03
100	76.09	14.04
200	75.19	15.45
500	75.08	14.56
750	75.30	14.97
1000	74	14.73
2000	74.65	14.61

A very small random sample of n = 5 yielded a mean score of 83 with a standard deviation of 10.22. We know the population mean is 74.64 with a standard deviation of 14.63. The sample of 5 does not yield a very accurate reflection of the population, as can be expected. Only 5 out of 5,000 scores were sampled. In this case, it appears that there were some high scores among the 5 randomly sampled, which yielded a larger sample mean not reflective of the larger population mean. The same can be said about samples of n = 20 and n = 50. Their means (72.5 and 78.06) are somewhat closer to the population mean of 74.64, but still not really reflective of the population mean. As the sample size reaches about 10% of the population, the means consistently begin to hover around the actual population mean. The sample of n = 500 has a mean of 75.08, very close to the true population mean. Ultimately, as the sample size increases, the sample mean converges closer to the true population mean and standard deviation.

So, how large should a sample be? A 10% sample is often used in the social sciences, especially if the population is greater than 1,000. A population of 10,000 thus would have a sample size of 1,000. However, you may wonder why sample sizes for statewide polls often have sample sizes of 1,000 to 5,000, yet a state has over a million citizens. These sample sizes are far less than 10%. As the population size increases, it becomes cost and time prohibitive to sample 10%, especially if the population is something like 5,000,000. Good judgment should be used, and there are plenty of examples of researchers using sample sizes of 2,500 to 5,000 for such large population sizes.

9.3 From Sample to Population – The Sampling Distribution

We have established that random sampling helps to generate a representative sample of the population, and that sufficient sample sizes yield sample statistics (like

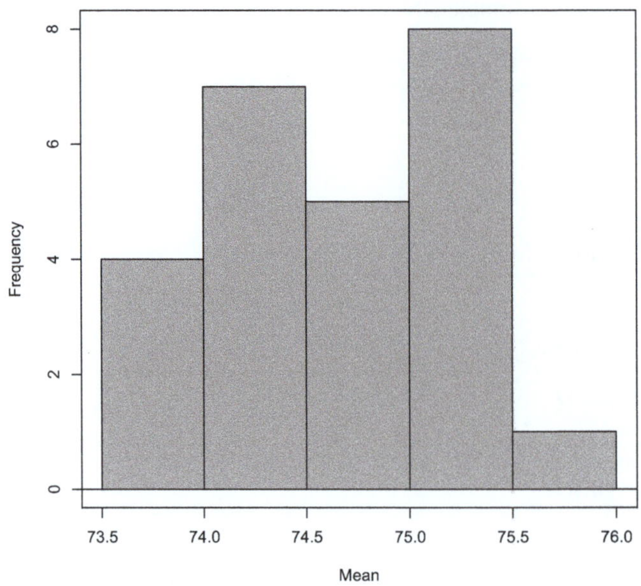

Figure 9.1 Sampling distribution of 25 sample means of n = 500

sample means and standard deviations) that reflect the larger population's statistics. How do we know this? The answer is in statistical theory. Recall the civil service exam scores where the population was 5,000, and we took a random sample of 500 individuals, obtaining the sample mean of 75.08 and the sample standard deviation of 14.56. What if we did this a second time? There would be a new random sample of 500 individuals with a different sample mean and sample standard deviation. What about a third time? There would be a new sample mean and sample standard deviation. One hundred times? One thousand times? One million times? Each new sample would yield a sample mean and sample standard deviation. Some means and standard deviations will be very close to the population mean and standard deviation. Others further away. Run an infinite number of times, the distribution of sample means, known as the sampling distribution, will be normally distributed, or in the shape of a symmetrical bell curve. This logic is captured by the Central Limit Theorem – taking an infinite number of samples of a sample with size greater than n = 30 yields a normally distributed sampling distribution.

To see this, Figures 9.1 and 9.2 depict the sampling distribution of sampling means for 25 samples of n = 500 and 50 samples of n = 500. Figure 9.1 plots the means from 25 random samples of size n = 500 from the civil service proficiency dataset in a histogram. A random sample of 500 was taken and the sample's mean calculated. This was done 25 times. The x-axis depicts the respective means and the y-axis the frequencies. The sampling distribution does not really take on a normal distribution. However, increasing the number of random samples to 50 generates a more normally distributed sampling distribution. Think of what would happen with a histogram of 100 or 1,000 samples. In theory, taking a random sample of size n an infinite number

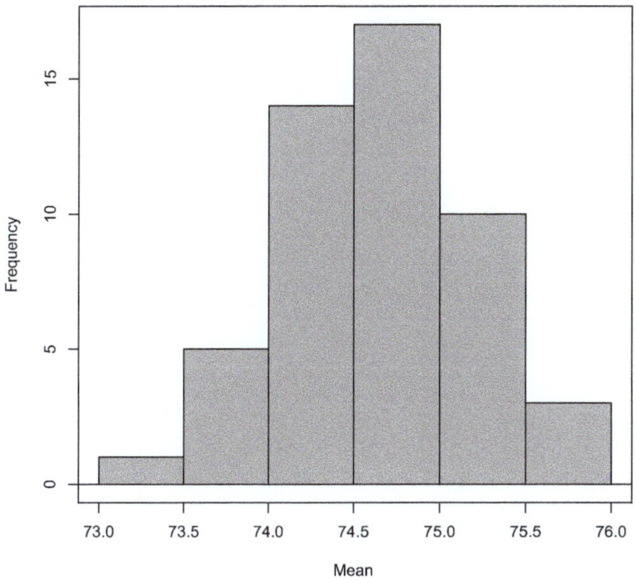

Figure 9.2 Sampling distribution of 50 sample means of n = 500

of times would yield a normally distributed sampling distribution. This would occur even if the characteristic being studied is skewed or not normally distributed in the population (like the population of income or house sales prices).

Because the sampling distribution is normally distributed, we can use it to make inferences from the sample to the larger population based upon probability. The normal curve has statistical properties that allow us to make claims about the larger population from the sample. To see this, we need to understand a bit about probability and the normal curve.

9.4 From Sample to Population – Normal Distribution

To better understand the normality of the sampling distribution, it is important to view a normal distribution. Table 9.2 provides data that are perfectly normally distributed. It provides a hypothetical scenario where a public manager of sixteen employees has collected data on the number of sick leave absences for their employees during the past year.

9.4.1 Normal Curve Basic Form

Normally distributed data take on the shape of a symmetrical bell curve. How can one tell from the table that the data are normally distributed? Most likely not by eye-balling the data. It needs to be graphed to see whether or not the data follow a normal distribution. Figure 9.3 shows a histogram with absences on the x-axis and frequency on the y-axis. The frequency is the raw frequency of observations from Table 9.2. Each bar's height is the number of observations for each respective

Table 9.2 Employee sick absences

Employee	Absences
1	3
2	5
3	5
4	4
5	7
6	6
7	3
8	8
9	2
10	4
11	5
12	7
13	4
14	6
15	5
16	6

number of absences. Double-check that it matches the frequencies from Table 9.2. Look for any curvatures or patterns in the histogram that you drew or produced. In this basic example, the pattern is fairly obvious, but a curve has been added to the figure for visual purposes. The curve looks like a perfectly shaped bell, hence the name bell curve. It has a peak and tails that extend outward in both directions. If the curve is perfectly symmetrical, it is considered to be a normal curve. By symmetrical, what is meant is that one can theoretically place a vertical line through the curve and fold it in half perfectly, with each side matching. Stated another way, split down the middle, each side of the curve is a mirror image of the other.

9.4.2 Assumptions

One of the main assumptions of the normal curve has just been discussed – that it is symmetrical. A first qualifier of this assumption is that the curve is symmetrical about the mean. The peak of the normal curve corresponds to the x-axis value that is the mean of the data. Calculate the mean number of absences from Table 9.2. It is five. Now, examine Figure 9.3. For what x-axis value is the highest bar or the peak of the associated curve drawn in the figure? That value is five.

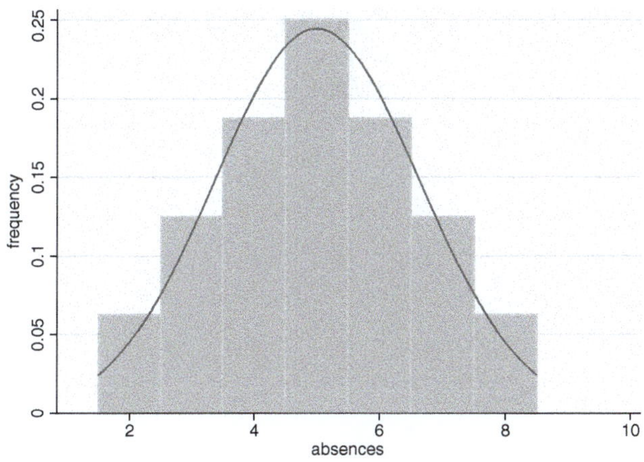

Figure 9.3 Normal distribution

A second qualifier to the symmetry assumption is that the mean and median of the data are the exact same for normally distributed data. Thus, the normal distribution is symmetrical about the median. Calculate the median for the data in Table 9.2. It is five, the same as the mean. Recall that the median is the value of the data for which 50% of the cases/observations/data points are greater than, and for which 50% of the cases/observations/data points are less than. The peak of the normal curve not only corresponds to the mean, but also to the median. If you draw a vertical line down from the peak of the normal distribution in Figure 9.3, it splits the data distribution in half. Four observations from Table 9.2 are a value of 5. How many of the remaining twelve observations are above 5? How many below? The answer is 6 and 6, respectively. The curve is split perfectly in half.

Finally, for a normally distributed dataset, the peak of the curve that depicts the value of the mean and median will also be the mode, or most occurring datapoint. This can also be verified using Table 9.2. The value of 5 occurs the most. Therefore, in a normally distributed dataset, the mean, median, and mode will all be the same value.

9.5 From Sample to Population – Inference with the Normal Distribution

With the basic properties of the normal curve mastered, we can move even further in understanding how it relates to statistical inference. Recall that the mean is at the peak of the normal curve. We can begin to think of the normal curve in terms of standard deviation units. Figures 9.4–9.6 show the normal curve, with areas under it separated by standard deviations. A certain percentage of the area under the normal curve lies within +/−1 standard deviation from the mean. To be exact, 68.26% of the area under the normal curve lies between −1 standard deviation (to the left of the mean) and +1 standard deviation (to the right of the mean) as shown in Figure 9.4. 95.44% of the area under the normal curve lies between −2 standard deviations and

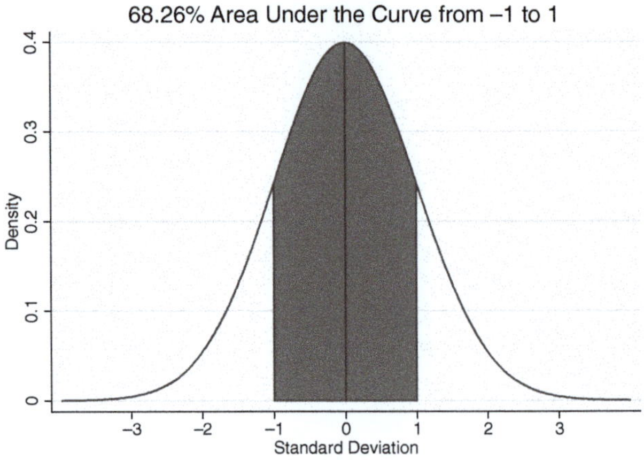

Figure 9.4 Area under curve between −1 and 1 standard deviations

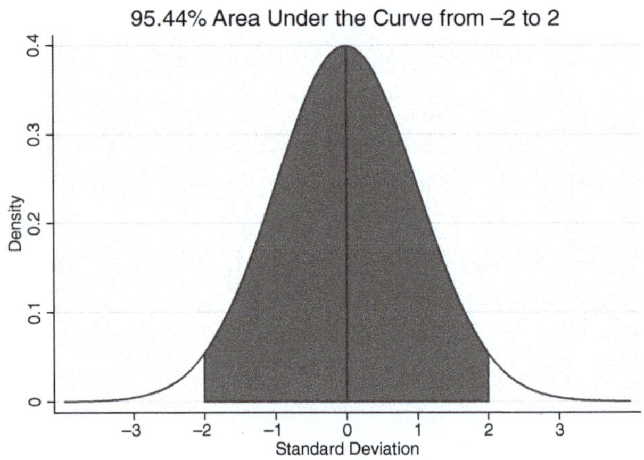

Figure 9.5 Area under curve between −2 and 2 standard deviations

+2 standard deviations from the mean (Figure 9.5). Finally, 99.72% of the area under the normal curve lies between −3 standard deviations and +3 standard deviations from the mean (Figure 9.6).

You will notice in Figures 9.4–9.6 that the mean is represented by 0. This does not mean that the mean of the sampling distribution is 0. It could be −20, 555, or any other number. The 0 simply represents that the mean has been standardized into a standard deviation unit. The mean thus lies 0 standard deviations from itself. The mean is the mean and does not deviate from itself.

9.5.1 Z-Scores

What do these percentages mean for statistical inference and making probabilisitic conclusions about the population from a sample? Let's go back to an example from Chapter 1. Mr. Bulleemann is the director of social workers and wants to write-up an employee, Javier, who is underperforming according to Mr. Bulleemann's standards. Javier completed 104 visits to clients. The average number of visits among the social

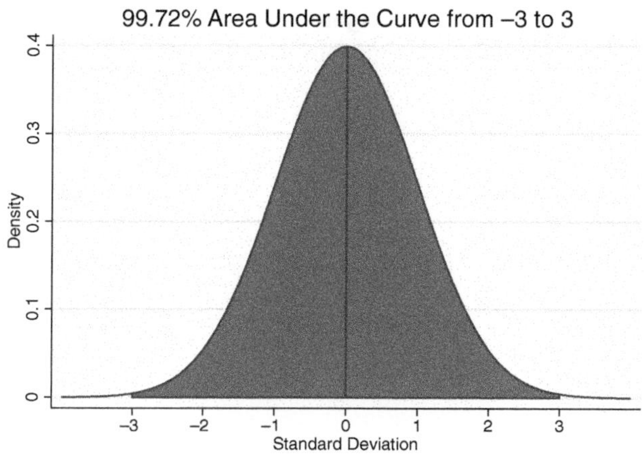

Figure 9.6 Area under curve between −3 and 3 standard deviations

workers is 105.5 with a standard deviation of 1.27 visits. Is Mr. Bulleemann's write-up justified?

Let's assume that visits by social workers is normally distributed. The mean is 105.5 visits with a standard deviation of 1.27. One way to determine if Mr. Bulleemann's write-up is justified is to turn Javier's number of visits to a Z-score, and see where it lies on the normal distribution. The equation to calculate a Z-score is:

$$Z = \frac{X_i - \mu}{\sigma}, \tag{9.1}$$

where X_i is the value of interest, μ is the mean, and σ is the standard deviation.

Entering the information relevant to Javier and Mr. Bulleemann's case:

$X_i = 104$

$\mu = 105.5$

$\sigma = 1.27$

Entering these values into Equation 9.1 yields:

$$Z = \frac{104 - 105.5}{1.27}$$

This reduces to:

$$Z = \frac{-1.5}{1.27}$$

Therefore,

$$Z = -1.18$$

One way to interpret this is that Javier performs 1.18 standard deviations lower than the average employee. Or, stated another way, Javier's 104 completed visits lies 1.18 standard deviations to the left of the mean. Visually, we can apply this to the normal

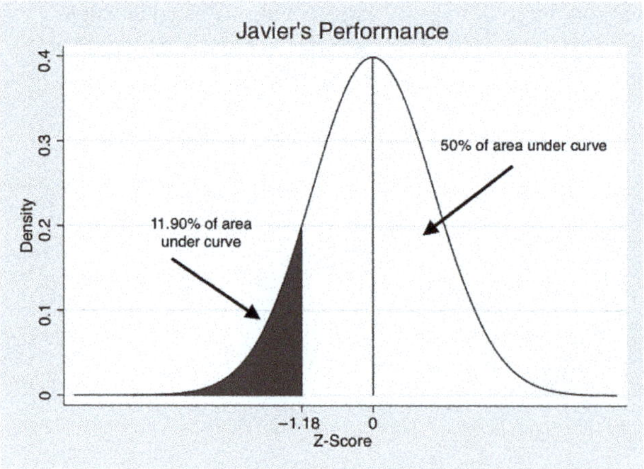

Figure 9.7 Javier's Z-score and performance

curve in Figure 9.7, where the mean of 105.5 has been normalized to 0 and Javier's completed visits of 104 has been turned into a Z-score or standard deviation units of −1.18. The shaded area represents employees that performed worse than Javier. Since the normal distribution is symmetrical, 50% of the area under it is to the right of the mean (represented by 0) and 50% of the area under the curve is to the left of the mean. So, 50% of the employees complete more than the mean number of visits (105.5, or normalized to 0 in the figure), and 50% of the employees complete less than the mean number of visits. Javier does fall to the left of the mean, as represented by the Z-score of −1.18. The shaded region of Figure 9.7 shows the percentage of employees who perform worse than Javier. What percentage is this? We need to go to a Z table. The appendix (Appendix C) of this book contains a Z-table.

The Z-scores in the table show the area under the normal distribution to the *right* of the Z-score. A Z-score of 0 shows 0.5000. Turned into a percentage, this corresponds to 50% of the area under the curve being to the right of a Z-score of 0. This makes sense. Recall that when the Z-score is 0, it is the mean of the distribution, which is at the peak of the normal distribution, and 50% of the area under the curve is to the right of 0 and 50% is to the left. A Z-score of 0 splits the normal curve exactly in half. All of the Z-scores in the table are positive. Therefore, all of these Z-scores lie to the right of the mean. What if, as in the case of Javier, they lie to the left of the mean? This would generate a negative Z-score, like that of Javier's. There are no negative values in the Z-table, but this does not matter. Simply put a negative sign in front of the values in the Z-table, and the table will give you the percent of the area under the normal curve to the *left* of the associated negative Z-score.

So, for Javier, his Z-score is −1.18. To read the Z-table, the first column shows Z-scores to the first decimal. Across the top row of the table are values for the second decimal of the Z-score. Therefore, Javier's Z-score of −1.18 corresponds to an area of 0.1190, or 11.90%. This represents the shaded area in Figure 9.7. We can conclude that 11.90% of workers performed worse than Javier. 88.10% of the workers performed better.

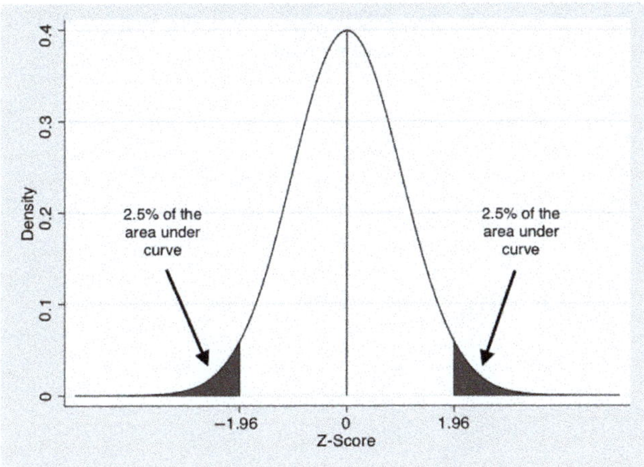

Figure 9.8 Areas of +1.96 and −1.96 Z-scores

With only 11.90% of the workers performing worse than Javier, some may conclude that the write-up is warranted, but maybe not. In the social sciences, we often consider exceptional or rare cases to be approximately two standard deviations away from the mean in either the positive direction or negative direction. Specifically, 1.96 standard deviation units from the mean is often viewed as a significant deviation from the mean. Javier's score does not meet this seemingly arbitrary threshold. But it is not quite so arbitrary. An observation that is 1.96, standard deviations from the mean, or an observation with a Z-score of 1.96, corresponds to 0.0250, or 2.5%, of the area under the normal curve to the right of the observation. An observation that is −1.96 standard deviation units from the mean has a Z-score of −1.96. This corresponds to 0.0250, or 2.5%, of the area under the curve to the left of this observation. These values are depicted in Figure 9.8.

The total shaded area is 5%. If Javier's Z-score were to lie in the shaded area, we would say his performance is exceptional or rare. Or, in statistical terms, we'd say his score is statistically significant at the 95% confidence level. If on the right side of the curve, he would be in the top 2.5% of workers. If on the left side of the curve, the bottom 2.5% of workers. He is neither, so we would say that his performance is not exceptional in either direction. His write-up is probably not justified according to this standard. Even if we were to put the entire 5% of the area under the curve to the left (Figure 9.9), his score would not put him in the bottom 5%. That Z-score would be −1.65 (1.645 to be exact, but the Z-table presented is only to 2 decimal places), and Javier is only at −1.18. This is the logic of a one-tailed test, mentioned in the next chapter; however, most of the focus of this book will consider two-tailed tests, where 2.5% of the area under he curve is in each tail for a total of 5%.

9.5.2 The Sampling Distribution and Statistical Inference

If we assume the sampling distribution of sample means is normally distributed, we can use the properties of the normal curve to determine if an observation is

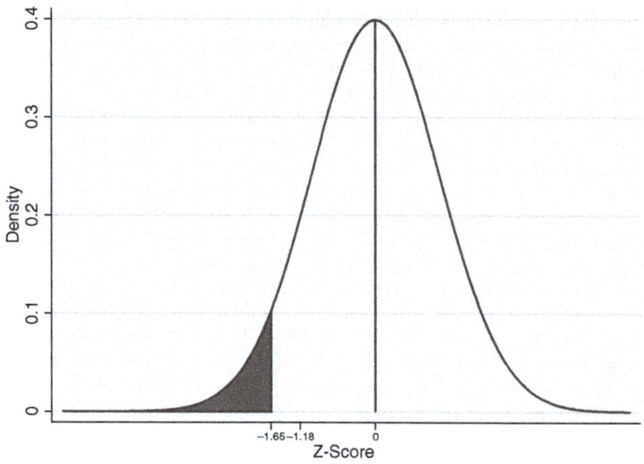

Figure 9.9 Left tail with 5% area under curve

statistically significantly different from the mean. In the social sciences, we talk in terms of confidence levels, specifically the 95% confidence level. We like to say that an observation or relationship is statistically significant at the 95% confidence level. The previous example with Javier assumed that we knew the population, which was feasible in that situation given the manager was looking at their own unit. When we are using samples, we need to account for sample size. We assume the sampling distribution is a normal curve with the sample's mean. The sample standard deviation is divided by the square root of the sample size to obtain the standard deviation of the sampling distribution. This new statistic is known as the standard error of the mean, represented by Equation 9.2.

$$S.E. = \frac{s}{\sqrt{n}} \tag{9.2}$$

The standard error of the mean is used to calculate a 95% confidence interval by Equation 9.3.

$$95\%c.i. = \bar{X} \pm S.E.(1.96) \tag{9.3}$$

where "c.i." stands for confidence interval, $\bar{X}$ is the sample mean, and S.E. is the standard error of the mean. Why do we use +/− 1.96? Recall from Figure 9.8 that the Z-score value of +/− 1.96 puts 2.5% of the area under the normal curve in the right tail and 2.5% of the area under the normal curve in the left tail. We want to generate a confidence interval where 95% of the sample means will fall, leaving 5% of sample means to be exceptional cases. Essentially, we are trying to calculate a confidence interval that captures 95% of the sample means, thus giving us information about the true population's mean. Stated another way, we want to be 95% confident that the true population mean is within this range. From there, we can determine if certain observations, like Javier's work performance, are rare occurrences, outside this range.

To better illustrate, let's alter Javier's scenario and suppose Javier's supervisor is concerned about his performance after Javier only completed 100 visits. Does Javier differ significantly from the population of workers in his unit? But instead of the population, the supervisor, Mr. Bulleemann, takes a sample of 36 employees because there are 250 employees under his supervision. The sample yields a mean of 110 and sample standard deviation of 3 visits. Use Equation 9.2 to calculate the standard error of the mean.

$$S.E. = \frac{3}{\sqrt{36}}$$
$$S.E. = \frac{3}{6} = 0.5$$

Now for the 95% confidence interval using Equation 9.3.

$$95\%c.i. = 110 \pm 0.5.(1.96)$$
$$95\%c.i. = 110 \pm 0.98$$
$$95\%c.i. = 109.02 - 110.98$$

The 95% confidence interval is 109.02 to 110.98. If we took an infinite number of random samples of size 36 from the population of workers, the means of these samples would be between the range of 109.02 to 110.98 a total of 95% of the time. If Javier only completed 100 visits, we would say that he differs significantly from the population of workers. We can say that his 100 visits is statistically significantly different from the population at the 95% confidence level. This is the logic of *statistical significance* and how we can use samples to know about the larger population. It also allows us to use samples to study phenomena in the social sciences and determine if particular observations or relationships are statistically significant in the population with a certain level of probability.

9.6 Summary

The purpose of this heavily theoretical chapter was to ultimately provide you with the logic behind statistical significance. We can infer statistically significant relationships in the population simply by using random samples. Because populations are nearly impossible to observe, we have to rely upon samples in our studies. However, random samples can accurately reflect the larger population and allow us to make these inferences and make claims at the 95% confidence level. The reason for this lies in statistical theory about the shape of the sampling distribution of sample means, which is a normal curve. The properties of the normal curve allow us to calculate 95% confidence intervals and declare statistical significance at the 95% confidence level. This theory and logic permeate the remaining lessons and chapters of this textbook. Tests of differences of means, the topics of the next several chapters, rely upon this statistical theory and logic.

PRACTICE PROBLEMS

1. What is random sampling and why is it the preferred method for conducting research when one cannot observe the entire population?
2. Explain the Central Limit Theorem and its importance for sampling and inference.
3. Provide hypothetical research examples/scenarios where it may be possible for the researcher to observe the entire population. Provide examples/scenarios where it may be impossible or inefficient to observe the entire population.
4. Explain the logic behind the sampling distribution and why it is normally distributed.
5. Assume a normal distribution/curve:
   a. What is the area between the mean and +1 standard deviation?
   b. What is the area between the mean and −1 standard deviation?
   c. What is the area above the mean? Below the mean?
   d. What is the area above a standard deviation of 2.35?
   e. What is the area below a standard deviation of −0.50?
   f. What is the area above a standard deviation of −0.50?
6. Birth weights are often charted, and their distribution is often normally distributed. Assume a population of births at a local hospital has a mean of 6 pounds with a standard deviation of 2 pounds. A baby whose mother participated in a neonatal vitamin program funded by a local nonprofit had a baby born with a weight of 9.5 pounds.
   a. What percentage of babies were born heavier than this baby?
   b. What percentage of babies were born lighter than this baby?
   c. Does this particular baby constitute a rare or exceptional case? Why/why not?
7. In this chapter, you were introduced to Javier, who was faced with getting a write-up for potential poor performance. Let's say that Javier really wants to impress his boss, Mr. Bulleemann, and works extra hard over the next month, completing 120 home visits. He asks his boss for a raise, because he thinks he stands out from his peers. The boss takes a random sample of the 250 employees of sample size 40. The mean of the sample is 104 visits with a standard deviation of 5.3.
   a. Calculate a 95% confidence interval.
   b. Is Javier's request for a raise warranted? Why/why not?
8. Suppose the Department of Transportation is concerned about the number of unruly passengers last December. Christmas may have stressed many people

out, causing them to become belligerent on flights and get arrested. The department has the number of unruly passenger arrests throughout the nation for all months for the past 50 years, which is 600 months. They take a sample of 30 months, finding a mean of 20 arrests with a standard deviation of 6. This last December has 25 arrests. Can we conclude that last December had statistically significantly more arrests than normal? Why/why not?

PART 3

10

T-Tests

10.1 Introduction

The previous chapter introduced in detail the relationship between sampling from a population, collecting data, and making inferences about the larger population based upon the sample's statistics. Are the sample's statistics significantly different after an intervention, or significantly different from an established benchmark or other number of interest? Highlighted here are four different scenarios to help illustrate the topic of this chapter – t-tests.

Scenario 1: The 2020 U.S. Census revealed that the average commute time for Nevada workers was 24.6 minutes.[1] With the competing phenomena of the growth of the Sunbelt region in the U.S. in terms of population, but with more people working remotely due to the Covid-19 pandemic, have mean/average commute times decreased for Nevadans? Suppose a researcher takes a random sample of twenty Nevadans, asking about their work commute. Have there been any statistically significant changes?

Scenario 2: The National Fire Protection Association has set a standard for emergency turnout times at 60 seconds. Turnout time refers to the amount of time that elapses from when fire personnel are alerted of an emergency by 911 dispatch until the time they leave the fire station. It is basically the time that it takes for the personnel to get into the fire engine en route to the emergency. Suppose a large random sample ($n = 10{,}667$) of response turnouts from a local fire department are collected, and the mean turnout time was 74.13 seconds with a standard deviation of 35.27 seconds. Can we conclude that the fire department grossly fails at meeting the national 60 second turnout time standard? What if the department's own standard is slightly more lenient at 90 seconds? Can we conclude that the fire department meets its own standard? Is the mean of 74.13 seconds statistically different from 60 seconds? 90 seconds?

[1] www.census.gov/quickfacts/NV.

Scenario 3: Suppose Scenario 2's fire chief is interested in improving turnout times. The chief implements a new training module that focuses on strategies and best practices for decreasing turnout times. The chief collects turnout time data before and after the training modules have been implemented for all the units under supervision. Results indicate a decrease in the mean turnout time after training. Is this decrease statistically significant? The chief decides to use statistics software to test the hypothesis that the training modules decreased turnout times.

Scenario 4: A public organization's IT supervisor has succumbed to pressure from employees to implement a work-from-home policy. Employees believe they can be just as effective, if not more effective, by having flexibility to work from home. As a pilot program, the supervisor randomly assigns some of the unit's staff to work from home in a remote work setting. The remaining employees are to work from the organization in the traditional, in-person format. The supervisor collects data on the number of unresolved IT cases among remote employees and compares them to the number of unresolved IT cases for in-person employees at the end of the month. The supervisor would like to determine if there are any statistical differences in the number of unresolved IT cases for remote versus in-person employees.

Answering these and similar questions using quantitative data is the focus of this chapter. Since the larger population of data is unlikely to be available or too expensive to acquire, we must rely on a sample of data to infer about the larger population. In the fire department turnout time example (Scenario 2), a sample was taken. Based upon this information, can we conclude that the average turnout time for *all* of the particular fire department's responses is less than/greater than 60 seconds? Sampling allows us to make probabilistic conclusions about the larger population. The focus of this chapter is on conducting statistical tests to help us make these conclusions and to make inferences about the larger population of observations. We do this with a t-test, and this chapter focuses on which type of t-test to use, mainly based off how the data are collected and groups organized. The one-sample t-test, independent samples t-test, and dependent samples t-test are all covered. Understanding when and how to use them is the crux of the instruction in this chapter. As a reference, Scenario 1 and Scenario 2 require the use of a one-sample t-test; Scenario 3 dictates the use of a dependent samples t-test; Scenario 4 calls for an independent samples t-test.

10.2 One-Sample T-Test

The one-sample t-test involves the researcher having one sample of data and using the sample's descriptive statistics in comparison with another value or benchmark. The one-sample t-test allows us to make a conclusion, based upon probability, that the sample's characteristics (usually the mean) are statistically different from a particular value of interest.

10.2.1 Assumptions

Some assumptions must be met when using a t-test, and these assumptions apply to the variable of interest along with some expectations regarding sampling. For the one-sample case, the variable of interest should be measured at the interval level. Additionally, the sample of data is expected to be collected through random sampling, and the sampling distribution of infinite samples from the population on the variable of interest is normally distributed.

This chapter begins with the first type of hypothesis test, the t-test. It is also the first chapter where we create specific research and null hypotheses, collect data, and then conduct the appropriate statistical test. With the one-sample t-test, the research and null hypotheses are relatively straightforward. The null hypothesis indicates no effect or no difference. Returning to the commute time example in the first paragraph of this chapter, the null hypothesis for Nevada workers would be that average commute times have not changed, or the average commute time is 24.6 minutes. The research hypothesis states a difference or change. It may also stipulate a direction. Plausible research hypotheses could be:

H_1 = The average commute time is different than 24.6 minutes.
H_{1a} = The average commute time is less than 24.6 minutes.

Both H_1 and H_{1a} indicate a change, difference, or relationship. H_{1a} is a directional hypothesis, and is usually preferred if the researcher has a reason to believe or a theory that there is a particular greater than or less than situation. The researcher's hypotheses may postulate a change in commute times in the present compared to the past due to the Covid-19 pandemic. Incorporating the specific research into the null hypotheses, the researcher could alternatively state the hypotheses as:

H_2 = Commute times for Nevadans changed since 2020.
H_{2a} = Commute times for Nevadans decreased since 2020.

Any of these formulations are acceptable as research hypotheses. It is important for the researcher to be specific in their explanation and research question description on why they have formulated the specific hypotheses, along with presenting descriptive information like the previous mean commute time.

The null hypothesis expresses no difference, change, or relationship. For this scenario, the researcher could write the null hypothesis in a few different ways:

H_0 = The average commute time has not changed.
H_{0a} = Commute times for Nevadans have not changed since 2020.
H_{0b} = The average commute time is 24.6 minutes.

Any of these depictions of the null hypothesis of no difference will suffice. Preference will dictate how the researcher presents the null hypothesis. The essential component is the expression of no difference.

10.2.2 Conducting One-Sample T-Test by Hand

To conduct the one-sample t-test, we must know the sample's mean, standard deviation, and sample size. Returning to the commute time example in the first paragraph of the introduction, we are told that the mean commute time for Nevadans in 2020 was 24.6 minutes. We also know from the description that a researcher randomly sampled twenty Nevadans in 2022 asking each how long it takes them to get to work. With only this information, we cannot conduct a one-sample t-test. We need more information. So, let's assume that the researcher finds that the mean commute time from the sample is 22.3 minutes with a standard deviation of 8.9 minutes. Can we conclude that commute times are less in 2022 than 2020? The difference is 2.3 minutes less in commute time in 2022, but is this difference statistically significant? Stated alternatively, is this 2.3 minute difference no different than 0, and only due to random chance?

To conduct a t-test, we must calculate a t-score for the sample. The t-score equation is

$$t = \frac{\bar{X} - \mu}{S.E.}, \tag{10.1}$$

where
$\bar{X}$ = sample mean
μ = comparison value
$S.E.$ = standard error of the sample mean

The use of μ as the comparison value may be confusing since it has previously been used to represent a population mean. In the world of the one-sample t-test, we will use μ to represent both. In some instances, you may have the population mean that is being used to make a comparison. If the 24.6 minute commute time from the example was used with Census data that surveyed all citizens, then it is the population mean. If the 24.6 comes from a sample of Nevada commuters in 2020, we can still use μ to represent the comparison value we want to use as a baseline or benchmark to compare our sample mean.

The standard error of the sample mean is the same sample mean referenced in the previous chapter, Equation 9.2:

$$S.E. = \frac{s}{\sqrt{n}} \tag{9.2}$$

To use Equation 10.1, first calculate the standard error ($S.E.$). Using Equation 9.2,

$$S.E. = \frac{8.9}{\sqrt{20}}$$

$$= S.E. = \frac{8.9}{\sqrt{4.47}} = 1.99$$

Now, substitute all the relevant information into Equation 10.1,

$$t = \frac{22.3 - 24.6}{1.99},$$
$$= t = \frac{-2.3}{1.99},$$
$$t = -1.16$$

We have obtained a t-value of −1.16. What does this mean? We need to utilize the t-table (in Appendix B) to help with interpretation. The 95% confidence column is labeled by the 0.025 column (two-tailed test). The critical value in this table indicates the value needed for us to say that there is a 5% chance of obtaining the sample mean (of 22.3) if the true value in the 2022 population is no different than the comparison value (of 24.6). The critical value in the 0.025 column (two-tailed test) is dictated by the degrees of freedom (df) in our sample, which is simply n − 1, or the sample size minus 1. Since the sample size is 20, there are 19 degrees of freedom. For the 95% confidence level, there is not a critical value for 19, just for 15 and 20. More specific tables can be found on the Internet, but for our purposes, either value will suffice. If you want to be particularly conservative in your estimates, use the value for the lower degree of freedom. In this case, we'll use 2.131. Our calculated t-value of −1.16 is not equal to or greater than +/− 2.131. Therefore, there is a greater than 5% chance of obtaining the sample mean of 22.3 if the population from which it is drawn has a mean of 24.6. This does not meet our threshold for statistical significance. We want the chance of obtaining the sample mean of 22.3 if the true population mean is 24.6 to be less than or equal to 5%. Therefore, we cannot conclude that the mean commute time in 2022 for Nevadans is any different from the mean commute time in 2020 of 24.6 minutes. We therefore cannot reject our null hypothesis. Stated differently, we accept the null hypothesis.

10.2.3 One Tail v. Two Tail Tests

You may notice multiple columns in the t-table in Appendix B. This is because researchers can conduct a one-tailed test or a two-tailed test. The default in this book is to use the two-tailed test. A one-tailed test puts all of the error consideration into one side of the t-distribution. To better understand this, think of the Z-distribution from Chapter 9 where the values of +/−1.96 put 2.5% of the error in the left tail and 2.5% of the error in the right tail for a total of 5% error for the 95% confidence level. Assume that we put all 5% of the error in one tail, say the left-hand tail. The Z value that would do this would be −1.645. There would be no error in the right-hand tail. Researchers use a one-tailed test when they have a directional hypothesis. For example, they could study the effect of training on reducing turnout times to emergency responses and assume that it will decrease turnout times. If they think there is no theoretical reason that turnout times would increase after training, they could argue for the use of a one-tailed t-test. Doing so makes it easier to reject the null hypothesis and to find statistical significance. As mentioned, the more conservative method is to not make assumptions and conduct a two-tailed test that accounts for error in either direction –2.5% to the right or 2.5% to the left.

10.2.4 One Sample T-Test in the R Commander

We will use the second example from Section 10.1 to conduct the one sample t-test in the R Commander. The descriptive statistics (mean of 74.13 seconds, standard deviation of 35.27 seconds, and sample size of 10,667) come from the *response_sample* dataset in the Companion Site (www.cambridge.org/scheller). It is a random sample of fire department emergency responses from a large city. The unit of analysis is the response or emergency. The "turnouttime" variable is the time in seconds it took for the fire personnel to leave the fire station to respond to the emergency from when they were alerted by 911 dispatch of the emergency. By definition, this is known as the turnout time, a component of the entire response time. Response time is the turnout time *plus* the travel time, or the time it takes the personnel to reach the emergency from when they leave the fire station.

In Section 10.1, a number of questions were asked in regards to the turnout times: Can we conclude that the fire department grossly fails at meeting the national 60 second turnout time standard? What if the department's own standard is slightly more lenient at 90 seconds? Can we conclude that the fire department meets its own standard? Is the mean of 74.13 seconds statistically different from 60 seconds? 90 seconds? To answer these questions, we need to run a one-sample t-test, comparing the mean of 74.13 to 60 seconds and 90 seconds, respectively. A plausible alternative hypothesis is that the fire department's mean turnout time is greater than the 60 second national standard. The null hypothesis would be that there is no difference between the national 60 second standard and the fire department's mean turnout time. To run the one-sample t-test, load the *response_sample* dataset into the R Commander.

Step 1: Click Statistics → Means → Single-sample t-test (Figure 10.1).

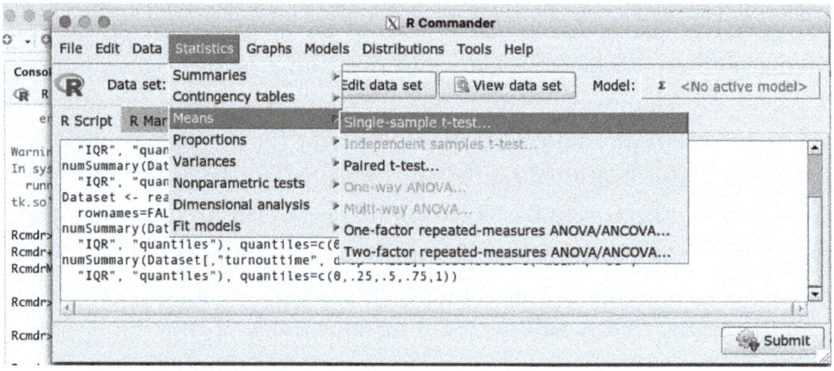

Figure 10.1 Single-sample t-test, part 1

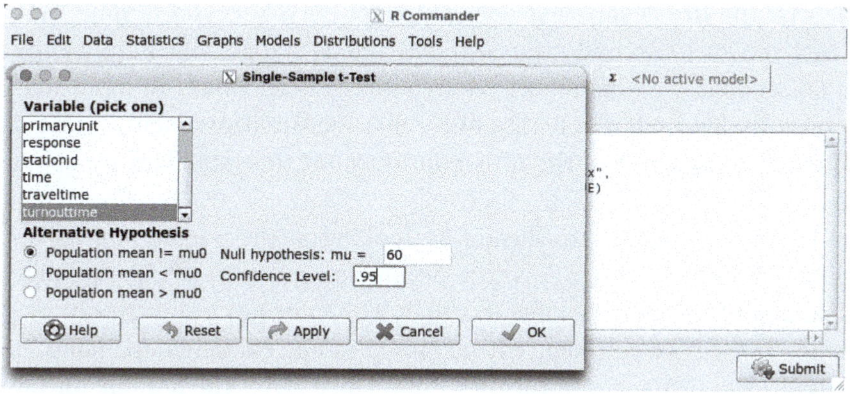

Figure 10.2 Single-sample t-test, part 2

```
        One Sample t-test

data:  turnouttime
t = 41.385, df = 10666, p-value < 2.2e-16
alternative hypothesis: true mean is not equal to 60
95 percent confidence interval:
 73.46363 74.80243
sample estimates:
mean of x
 74.13303
```

Figure 10.3 Single-sample t-test results

Step 2: In the "Variable" box, highlight the variable of interest. For the turnout time example, the respective variable is "turnouttime." In the Alternative Hypothesis section of the box, keep the default option bubbled, which is the "Population mean != mu0" option. However, change the default of "Null hypothesis: mu = 0.0" to the benchmark or figure of interest. For the first test, we want to know if the 74.13 second turnout time is statistically different from the 60 second National Fire Protection Agency standard. Therefore, enter 60 in the box and then click OK (Figure 10.2).

The R Commander output presents several pieces of important information, including the mean of the sample, t-score, confidence interval, and p-value (Figure 10.3).

The mean of x is indicated as 74.13. This is simply the sample mean. In our example, it is the mean of the turnouttime variable. The R Commander nicely includes the alternative hypothesis that the true mean of the population from which the sample was drawn is not equal to 60, or the 60 second standard we are comparing the 74.13 sample mean to. The 95% confidence interval is the range of the true mean of the population from which the sample is drawn if we were to take infinite samples. If we took infinite samples, the true population mean would fall within the confidence interval (73.46 to 74.80 seconds) 95% of the time. This interval naturally allows for 5% error, or a small chance that the confidence interval does not correctly capture the true population mean turnout time. With this information, we can likely conclude that the fire department does not meet the 60 second turnout time standard and that the 74.13 second mean turnout time is statistically significantly different from 60 seconds. So, the alternative hypothesis is accepted. To more substantively interpret the finding, it is highly likely that the fire department's turnout times are significantly higher than the 60 second turnout time standard by about 14.13 seconds.

We can also come to the same conclusion by looking at the t-score and its respective p-value. The t-score is 41.385 with a p-value of 2.2×10^{-16}. The p-value is very, very small, almost 0. Any p-value less than 0.05 indicates a statistically significant difference at the 95% confidence level; any p-value less than 0.01 indicates a statistically significant difference at the 99% confidence level. The p-value for the turnouttime variable is obviously less than 0.01, so we can conclude that the 74.13 second turnout time is statistically different from 60 seconds, or that there is less than 1% of a chance of obtaining a sample mean of 74.13 if the true mean of the population was 60 seconds. As before, we can conclude that the fire department is very unlikely meeting the 60 second time standard and missing it by about 14.13 seconds.

Now, what about the fire department's own 90 second standard? Is it likely that it meets its own standard? Using the same steps for the 60 second test, run the analysis for the 90 second test. You will simply change the mu = 60 to mu = 90 in Step 2. An alternative hypothesis is that the fire department's mean turnout time is less than their 90 second standard. The null hypothesis is that there is no difference between the mean turnout time and the 90 second standard. Again, the null hypothesis states a relationship of no difference. Your new one-sample t-test results should look like Figure 10.4

The sample mean and 95% confidence intervals will remain the same, because we are simply conducting a t-test to determine if 74.13 is statistically different from 90. Again, the confidence interval is 73.46 to 74.80, so from here, we know that there is a statistically significant difference at the 95% confidence level. The sample mean is statistically different from the 90 second standard. We know this from the t-score that is −46.463 with a p-value of 2.2×10^{-16}. The negative sign is of no importance. With this information, we see that the 74.13 value is statistically significant at the

```
        One Sample t-test

data:  turnouttime
t = -46.463, df = 10666, p-value < 2.2e-16
alternative hypothesis: true mean is not equal to 90
95 percent confidence interval:
 73.46363 74.80243
sample estimates:
mean of x
 74.13303
```

Figure 10.4 Single-sample t-test results, second example

99% confidence level and is different from 90. Given that 90 seconds is the standard and the sample mean is 74.13 and statistically significant, we can conclude that the fire department very likely meets the 90 second standard, with an average turnout time of 74.13 seconds, meeting the standard by almost 16 seconds.

10.3 Independent v. Dependent Samples T-Tests

A policy evaluator may be interested in the effects of a program or policy on an outcome. For example, a city administrator may be tasked with determining the effects of real estate developer tax incentives on the number of new housing startups. The administrator could collect information on the number of new housing units for twenty-four months before the tax incentive policy and twenty-four months after implementation of the tax incentive policy. Suppose the administrator notices that the mean number of new monthly units pre-policy is 102. After the policy, the mean monthly units is 110. It certainly *appears* that the policy increased the number of new housing units being built, but can the administrator simply rely on these mean differences? No. They must conduct a statistical analysis to help determine if this difference is potentially due to chance or if the observed difference is significant and less likely due to chance.

All t-tests use an interval level dependent variable. The simple difference between an independent samples versus a dependent samples t-test is in the independent variable or the grouping variable. To determine which test to use, ask yourself if the sample of data are from the same unit of analysis – are the same individuals, organizations, etc. being observed? Are they being tracked over time or in different time periods? As an example, an employer of a large organization may want to track the number of absences of their employees (say the employer has fifty employees) before and after the implementation of a new sick leave policy. The employer collects data on a sample of fifty employees' days of absences before the new policy, and then tracks the same employees' absences after the policy. Since the sampled individuals are the same before and after the policy, or dependent, the employer would run a dependent samples t-test to determine the relationship between the new policy and absences.

Opposite a dependent samples t-test is the independent samples t-test. In this case, the unit of analysis, whether it be individuals or other entities, are not tracked over time or sampled more than once. One example is a national survey of citizens where respondents are asked their political party identification and then asked to rate the current president's performance on a scale from 0 to 100. If, at a later time, a new group of individuals are sampled and asked to rate the current president's performance on a scale from 0 to 100, the samples are considered independent. The individuals in the first sample are not the same individuals in the second sample – they are independent of each other. Another example for use of the independent samples t-tests comes from the first example in this section – the effect of tax incentives on new housing startups. Examining monthly new housing counts for twenty-four months before the policy, then twenty-four months after the policy would use an independent samples t-test. While the city where the data are collected is the same, the months are independent of each other.

Any type of data that are collected at a single point in time is also usually considered as an independent sample. If there are no pre- or post- samples of the same individuals, by definition, the sample is considered independent. One-time surveys are considered independent samples, for example. The preponderance of public administration research will use independent samples because of the difficulty and expense of collecting data over time over the same individuals/entities. Much of the Census data, like the American Community Survey, should be treated as independent samples. Even though the survey is conducted at regular intervals, it is not possible to know if the same individuals are contacted for each year of the survey (most likely, they are not).

10.3.1 Independent Samples T-Test in the R Commander

Independent samples t-tests can be calculated by hand with fairly involved equations and steps. It is much easier to use statistical software. A hypothetical example can help illustrate when to use an independent samples t-test, along with how the data are set up and analyzed in the R Commander. Suppose an IT department for a state government agency is experimenting with having employees work from home. The IT supervisor is interested in determining if there are any differences in employee productivity among the at-home versus in-person IT specialists. The supervisor measures productivity as the number of the employee's cases not resolved at the end of the month. During a trial period, some employees were allowed to work from home for a month, while the other IT employees stayed working in-person at the department. At the end of the month, the supervisor recorded the number of each employee's cases not resolved. The data screenshot contains the setup, including the anonymous employee number, whether or not they worked at home or in person ("work" variable), and the number of their cases not resolved or pending action ("cases" variable).

With this setup, the R Commander can run a t-test, whereby the mean number of unresolved cases for employees working from home is compared to the mean number of unresolved cases for employees working in person. The first step in the analysis is to develop the research and null hypotheses. A plausible research hypothesis could be:

H_1: Employees working from home will have more unresolved cases compared to employees working in-person.

The null hypothesis would be an expression of no difference in the means. Therefore:

H_0: There is no difference in the number of unresolved cases between employees working at-home versus employees working in-person.

	A	B	C
1	employee	work	cases
2	1	athome	15
3	2	inperson	19
4	3	inperson	7
5	4	inperson	2
6	5	athome	0
7	6	athome	0
8	7	athome	3
9	8	inperson	25
10	9	athome	16
11	10	athome	17
12	11	inperson	2

Figure 10.5 IT data

Since we are dealing with samples of data, it is important to remember that we are using the samples to make inferences about the larger population. Since we cannot observe all IT employees in the organization, we took a sample of twenty. With this sample, and by comparing the sample means, we want to conduct a t-test to infer about the larger population of IT workers in the unit. A new step or statistic to consider when running the independent samples t-test is whether or not the variances between the groups on the dependent variables ("cases") is equal. In addition to the assumption that the dependent variable is interval with an independent variable that is dichotomous with two groups, that the two groups are truly independent, and that the dependent variable is normally distributed (Nishishiba, Jones, & Kraner, 2014), the variances are assumed to be equal. See Appendix 10.1 for testing for equal variances.

Given that the employees are independent of each other and the scenario does not involve tracking them over time, the independent samples t-test is appropriate to use. To run the independent samples t-test in the R Commander, load the data from the Companion Site (www.cambridge.org/scheller). In this example, it is the *it_cases* dataset.

Step 1: Click Statistics → Means → Independent samples t-test (Figure 10.6).

Step 2: Highlight the independent variable in the "Groups" box ("work" variable). Highlight the dependent variable in the "Response Variable" box ("cases") (Figure 10.7).

Step 3: If equal variances have been confirmed, click the "Options" box. You will need to change the default to "Yes" for "Assume equal variances" (Figure 10.8). If equal variances have not been confirmed (which is what we will assume), then the default works and you can click OK.

The results should appear like Figure 10.9.

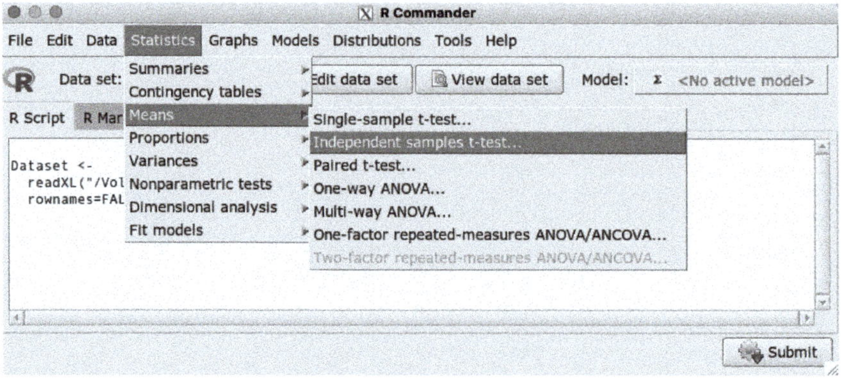

Figure 10.6 Independent samples t-test, part 1

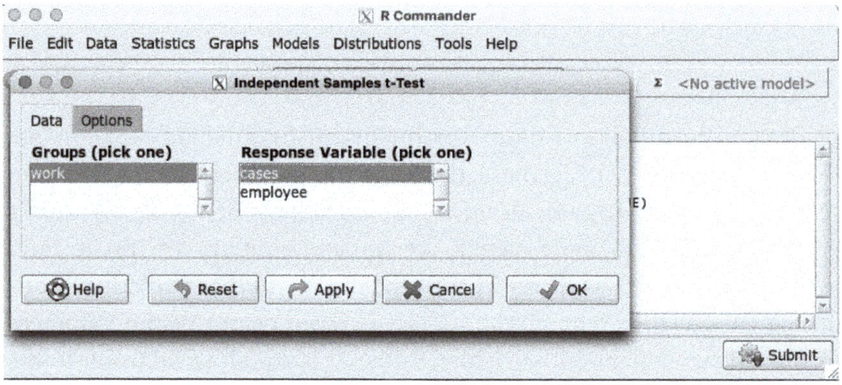

Figure 10.7 Independent samples t-test, part 2

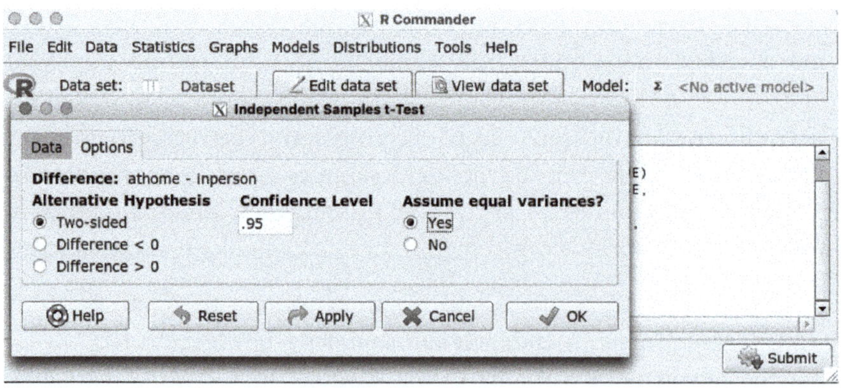

Figure 10.8 Independent samples t-test, part 3

The results indicate that the mean number of unresolved cases for at-home employees is 10.4 while the mean number of unresolved cases for in-person employees is 8.8, for an average difference of 1.6 cases. So, on average, at-home employees have 1.6 more unresolved cases than in-person employees. Is this relationship statistically significant? The t-score is 0.435 with 18 degrees of freedom. If we go to the t-table, the critical value for statistical significance (two-tailed) is not shown,

```
        Two Sample t-test

data:  cases by work
t = 0.43529, df = 18, p-value = 0.6685
alternative hypothesis: true difference in means between group athome and group inperson is not equal to 0
95 percent confidence interval:
 -6.122456  9.322456
sample estimates:
  mean in group athome mean in group inperson
                  10.4                    8.8
```

Figure 10.9 Independent samples t-test results

```
        Welch Two Sample t-test

data:  response by callprocpolicy
t = 3.97, df = 24820, p-value = 0.00007208
alternative hypothesis: true difference in means between group Old and group New is not equal to 0
95 percent confidence interval:
 2.323091 6.853982
sample estimates:
mean in group Old mean in group New
         364.1206          359.5320
```

Figure 10.10 Independent samples t-test, second example

but we can use 2.131 at 15 degrees of freedom for a conservative measure. So, no, the relationship is not statistically significant. There is a greater than 5% chance of observing this difference due to random error, and we cannot conclude that the 1.6 case difference is statistically different from 0. We could also look at the p-value in the output to make this conclusion. It is 0.6685. Therefore, we fail to reject the null hypothesis. We cannot conclude that there is a difference between the at-home and in-person employees. Even though the mean number of unresolved cases is 10.4 and 8.8, statistically, the means are statistically equal.

As a note of caution, this t-test was conducted with a sample size of twenty and was created for ease of illustration. It should be obvious that we need to be cautious of interpreting any results from small sample sizes. When sample sizes become sufficiently large, we can be more confident in the statistical tests. In reality, the data that public administrators and public administration researchers typically use have hundreds and thousands of observations. To see this, open the *response* dataset of fire department emergency responses. The fire chief is interested in learning if a new type of dispatch software for allocating units to emergencies has an impact on response times. Let's assume that one policy (coded 0 in the "callprocpolicy" variable) is the old software. The new software is coded 1 for the "callprocpolicy" variable. Recode the "callprocpolicy" variable using the information from Chapter 5 so that a 0 is now coded as "Old" and a 1 is coded as "New." Remember that this is a process of turning a numerical variable into a factor variable.

The chief hypothesizes that turnout times are smaller under the new call processing policy (new software) than with the old software. The independent samples t-test in the R Commander returns the results shown in Figure 10.10.

The mean response time under the old dispatch policy is 364.12 seconds. The mean response time under the new dispatch policy is 359.53 seconds. The average difference in response times is about 4.5 seconds less under the new policy compared to the old policy. Is this difference statistically significant? The t-score is 3.97 with 24,820 degrees of freedom, indicating that the t-score should meet or exceed a value of 1.96 to be statistically significant at the 95% confidence level. 3.97 obviously exceeds 1.96, so we can accept the chief's research hypothesis. The difference is statistically significant. The p-value is reported as 0.00007, also indicating statistical significance.

In this case, the sample size is very large, over 24,000. As the sample size increases, the likelihood of finding a statistically significant relationship increases. In this manner, we introduce substantive significance. With large sample sizes, mathematical or statistical significance becomes a more likely scenario, but we must be cautious in the realm of substantive significance, or if the mean differences are of importance in the real world. We know that the 4.5 second difference is statistically significant, but is it substantively significant? Stated alternatively, does 4.5 seconds make any difference in the real world. It depends upon the unique scenario as to whether or not a small difference in time makes substantive significance. While we all would like for emergency responders to arrive at our emergencies as fast as possible, 4.5 seconds probably does not make much difference in the grand scheme of things. Therefore, while we can say the new dispatch policy leads to faster response times, it probably has minimal effect.

10.3.2 Dependent Samples T-Test

In contrast to an independent samples t-test, a dependent samples t-test involves observing differences with repeated samples or repeated units of observation. Studying the same group of subjects at two different points in time, for instance, would necessitate the use of a dependent samples t-test. The requirement is that the dependent variable is interval and the independent or grouping variable is dichotomous, composed of the same entities or subjects. For example, suppose a group of medical researchers hypothesize that the Mediterranean diet lowers cholesterol and triglyceride levels in middle-aged men. Fifty men who do not use the Mediterranean diet are randomly selected for the study. Their levels of cholesterol and triglycerides are measured. The group's mean cholesterol level is 235 and triglyceride level is 600. The men are then required to only eat meals and foods from a predetermined list provided by the researchers that follows the Mediterranean diet. They do this for one month. After a month, their levels of cholesterol and triglycerides are measured. The mean cholesterol for the group is 200, and the mean triglyceride level is 430. The researchers run a dependent samples t-test to determine if the pre-diet and post-diet means differ statistically. The reason they use a dependent samples t-test is because the subjects are the same – they are not independent – John Doe was a subject in

	A	B
1	pre	post
2	102	64
3	80	73
4	103	30
5	53	50
6	131	94
7	63	64
8	75	38
9	142	64
10	95	70
11	58	45
12	54	50

Figure 10.11 Training & Turnout Time Data

the pre-diet measurement, and his cholesterol and triglyceride levels were studied after the diet. He has a pre- and a post-observation, thus being dependent.

Applied to a public administration situation, refer back to Scenario 3 in Section 10.1. The fire chief implements a training module to decrease turnout times, a major component of total emergency response times. The chief collects average response time data for 11 randomly selected stations before and after implementation of the training. The data appear in the spreadsheet screenshot in Figure 10.11.

The "pre" column lists the turnout times for responses before the training. The "post" column lists the turnout times after the training. How can the chief evaluate the effectiveness of the training? The next subsection explains how to conduct the dependent samples t-test in the R Commander.

Dependent Samples T-Test in the R Commander

The data for the previous scenario is located in the Companion Site (www.cambridge.org/scheller), labeled *stations*. The chief would like to study the effects of training on response times. To conduct the dependent samples t-test:

Step 1: Click Statistics → Means → Paired t-test (Figure 10.12).

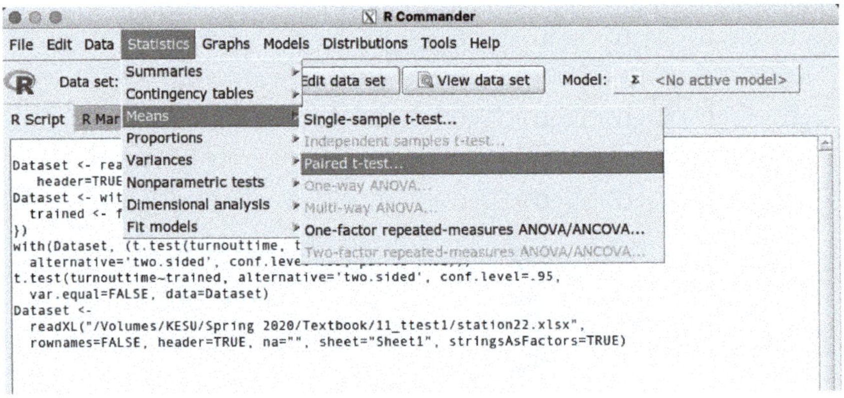

Figure 10.12 Dependent samples t-test, part 1

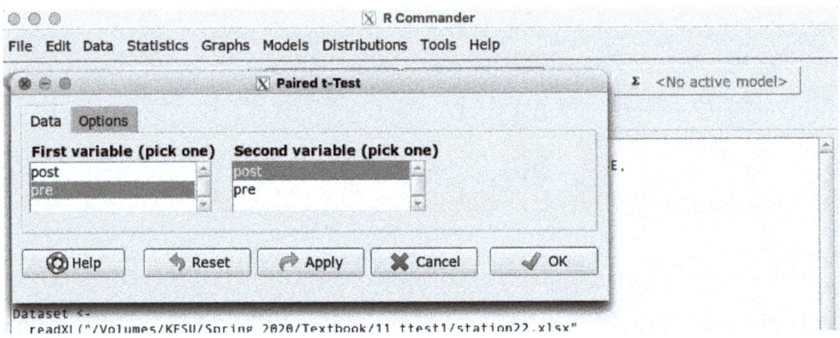

Figure 10.13 Dependent samples t-test, part 2

```
        Paired t-test

data:  pre and post
t = 3.4569, df = 10, p-value = 0.006155
alternative hypothesis: true mean difference is not equal to 0
95 percent confidence interval:
 10.14631 46.94460
sample estimates:
mean difference
       28.54545
```

Figure 10.14 Dependent samples t-test results

Step 2: Highlight the pre variable in the "First variable" box. In this case, highlight the "pre" variable. Then, highlight the post variable in the "Second variable" box. In this case, highlight the "post" variable (Figure 10.13).

Step 3: Click OK, and the results should appear the same as those in Figure 10.14.

```
        mean       sd  n
post 58.36364 18.03481 11
pre  86.90909 30.59560 11
```

Figure 10.15 Post-dependent samples t-test descriptive statistics

The results indicate that the t-score is 3.4569 with a p-value of 0.006. Therefore, there is a statistically significant difference between the turnout times pre- and post-training. The results are statistically significant at greater than the 99% confidence level given that the p-value is less than 0.01. However, did the turnout times increase or decrease after the training? Simply run descriptive statistics for the means (instruction in Chapter 6), and it is easy to see the direction of the effect. We see from the descriptive statistics in Figure 10.15 that the mean turnout time pre-training is 86.91 seconds, while the mean turnout time post-training is 58.36 seconds. Combined with the statistically significant t-test, we can conclude that turnout times were about 28 seconds less after the training compared to before the training.

10.4 Summary

This chapter has given several scenarios on when it is appropriate to use a t-test, specifically the one-sample t-test, independent samples t-test, and dependent samples t-test. The common characteristic among each of the tests is the dependent variable being measured at the interval level. The one-sample t-test involves comparing a sample mean to a benchmark or comparison figure. The independent samples t-test involves comparing the means of unrelated groups on a variable of interest. The dependent samples t-test examines how the means change for related entities under study – essentially studying the same individuals at two or more points in time. T-tests do an incredible job of showing differences in means and whether these differences are statistically significant, or if the differences are statistically greater than 0. What t-tests do not do is control for other factors. They just determine if the means are different and do not control for other characteristics within the comparison groups that may affect the results or dependent variable. Because of this, a statistically significant difference from a t-test cannot be claimed to be causal. For example, in the independent samples t-test involving the IT supervisor randomly assigning some employees to work from home and others from the office, if there are systematic differences between the at-home and in-person workers (on characteristics like education, race, gender, job satisfaction, satisfaction with supervisor, etc.), and these systematic differences are not accounted for, then any results and conclusions from the t-test may be biased. We could not make a causal claim. In such an event, it would be necessary to control for these factors, usually in a regression, which is the topic of later chapters.

PRACTICE PROBLEMS

1. Explain the conceptual differences between the independent and dependent samples t-tests.
2. For each of the following scenarios, indicate which type of t-test (if any) should be used.

   a.
   Dependent Variable: Number of write-ups
   Independent Variable: Gender (Male v. Female)

   b.
   Dependent Variable: Reading scores (0–100)
   Independent Variable: Participated in Head Start program (0 = No; 1 = Yes)

   c.
   Dependent Variable: Reading scores (0–100) of ten students in a first grade classroom
   Independent Variable: first day of school v. last day of school

   d.
   Dependent Variable: Salary (in dollars)
   Independent Variable: Years of education

   e.
   Dependent Variable: Donated to charity (1 = Yes; 0 = No)
   Independent Variable: Political party identification (2 = Democrat; 1 = Republican; 0 = Other)

3. T-tests are known as difference of means tests. What does it mean if a t-test indicates a difference of means between two groups?
4. For Scenarios 3 and 4 listed in Section 10.1:
   a. Indicate the independent and dependent variables.
   b. List and explain a few other variables that could affect the dependent variable in addition to the independent variable.
5. For Scenarios 3 and 4 in Section 10.1, provide research and null hypotheses.
6. Why is random sampling an important assumption for conducting a t-test. How does non-random sampling affect the results of a t-test?
7. Attendance at last year's city concert series averaged 125 patrons. This year, the city has removed admissions fees in the hopes of increasing attendance. A sample of this year's attendance average is 150 patrons per concert (n = 5 concerts) with a standard deviation of 35 patrons.
   a. Develop research and null hypotheses for this scenario.

b. What type of t-test should be conducted in this scenario? Why?
c. Conduct the t-test by hand and interpret the results.

R Commander Problems

8. An MPA director is interested in knowing if this year's undergraduate GPAs are different from last year's. Last year, the GPAs of undergraduate students in the unit was an average of 3.2. The director randomly samples ten students' files. The GPAs are: 4.0, 2.5, 3.1, 3.0, 2.7, 2.9, 3.3, 3.2, 2.0, 1.7.
   a. Enter the data into Excel. Load the data in the R Commander and run the appropriate t-test. Interpret your results.
9. Open the *floridacounties* dataset that contains county level voter turnout for Florida. It also contains a variable coded 1 if the county has an urban area with greater than 100,000 people, and 0 otherwise. Test the hypothesis that urban counties (counties with a city greater than 100,000 people) have higher voter turnout than rural counties.
10. Head Start is a government program that aims to help underprivileged children develop educationally through enrichment and social development activities prior to enrolling in kindergarten. Assume a researcher collects information from a classroom with twelve students, obtaining scores on a developmental test (0–100) for each student along with whether or not they participated in the Head Start program. The dataset is located in the Companion Site (*headstart* dataset).
    a. Run the appropriate t-test.
    b. Interpret the results and statistical significance.
    c. What conclusions can you make?
    d. Discuss whether or not the sample size is conducive to making a causal argument.

Appendix 10.1–Levene's Test of Equal Variances

When conducting a t-test, it is assumed that the variances between the two groups on the dependent variable are equal. To test the equal variances assumption, a Levene's test can be conducted. The null hypothesis of the Levene's test is that the variances are equal. Therefore, if the Levene's test reveals a p-value greater than 0.05, we can reject the null hypothesis, thus confirming unequal variances. Following the IT example from Section 10.3, the Levene's test can be run before conducting the t-test to confirm equal variances on the dependent variable between the two categories of the independent variable. To conduct the Levene's test:

Step 1: Click Statistics → Variances → Levene's test (Figure 10.16).

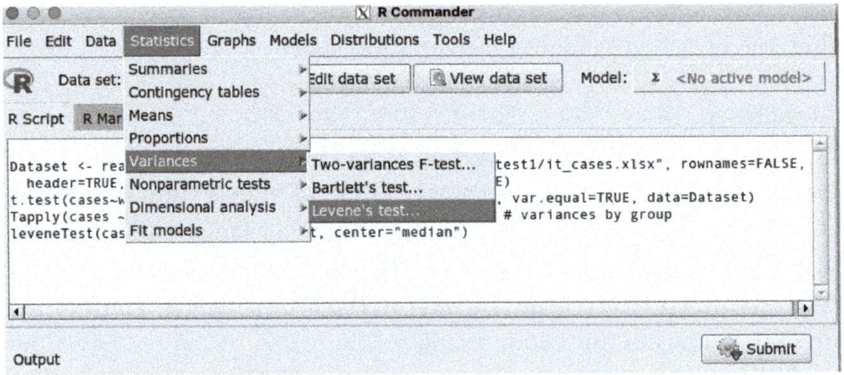

Figure 10.16 Levene's test, part 1

Step 2: In the "Factors" box, highlight the independent or grouping variable. For this example, it is the "work" variable. In the "Response Variable" box, highlight the dependent variable. In this example, it is the "cases" variable (Figure 10.17).

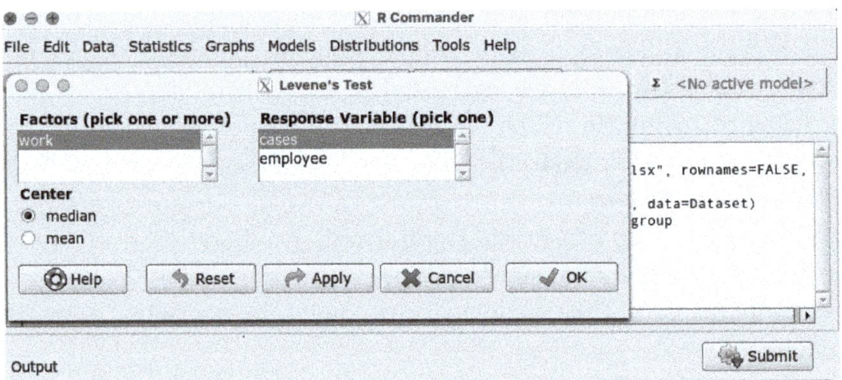

Figure 10.17 Levene's test, part 2

Step 3: Click OK. The R Commander will report the Levene's test (Figure 10.18).

```
Levene's Test for Homogeneity of Variance (center = "median")
      Df F value Pr(>F)
group  1  0.0492  0.827
      18
```

Figure 10.18 Levene's test result

The p-value for the Levene's test is 0.827, statistically insignificant. This p-value means that the null hypothesis of equal variances cannot be rejected; it is accepted, and thus equal variances are assumed. In the event that variances are not equal, one can indicate that equal variances are not assumed in the independent samples t-test box.

11

Analysis of Variance (ANOVA)

11.1 Introduction

The previous two chapters focused on the relationship between an interval level dependent variable and a nominal level independent variable with *two* categories. For example, if political party affiliation is measured as only Democrat or Republican, race is measured as White or non-White, job description is measured only as managerial or not, these codings are nominal with two categories. If the dependent variable of interest is interval level, then a t-test would be an appropriate statistical test. However, each of the aforementioned are often disaggregated into more than two categories. Party affiliation can be analyzed using Democrat, Republican, Libertarian, Independent, and Other. Job description could include upper management, middle management, and rank-and-file employees. Race is also often disaggregated into White, African-American, Asian/Pacific Islander, Other, etc. Certainly, each of these variables could have more categories. The central point is that if the independent variable is nominal with more than two categories, and the dependent variable is measured at the interval level, then a t-test is not the appropriate statistical test to use. Analysis of Variance (ANOVA) is the test to be used. It comes with some nuances (it uses an F distribution), and it has some assumptions that must be met; however, it is an oft-used test in the social sciences.

This chapter discusses the appropriate use of ANOVA – when to use it and the assumptions that should be met. The main focus of the chapter is on the correct data setup for running ANOVA, how to run an ANOVA in the R Commander, and then interpreting the results reported by the R Commander. One can mathematically conduct an ANOVA by hand, but the calculations are lengthier in their steps/computations, and they become time-consuming if the independent variable has more than four categories. Computations are not as convenient to conduct by hand like the t-tests in Chapter 10 or the chi-square (Chapter 12) or even bivariate regression (Chapter 16). The ease of computation with software makes calculation by hand a bit unnecessary. However, if you want to know the mathematics behind ANOVA and want to practice on your own, the Recommended Reading at the end of this chapter are excellent sources that provide step-by-step mathematical instruction on conducting ANOVA by hand. The goal of this chapter is to familiarize you with when to use ANOVA, its operation in software, and interpretation of results.

11.2 Assumptions of ANOVA

As may be guessed from the previous section, the first assumption to be met when using ANOVA is that the dependent variable is measured at the interval level and the independent variable is nominal with more than two categories. This is the first criteria that must be met.

Suppose one wants to know the relationship between type of pool of a home and its assessed value by the county assessor. The value is measured in dollars and is therefore an interval level dependent variable. Also, assume the type of pool for a home is coded as no pool, above ground pool, or in-ground pool. This independent variable is nominal with three categories. Therefore, ANOVA would be an appropriate test to measure the relationship between type of pool and assessed home value. Additionally, ordinal level independent variables can also be used with ANOVA. For brevity, the focus of this chapter is on nominal independent variables, but if treated like nominal variables, ordinal categories can be used with ANOVA. For example, if one wants to know how the condition of a house affects the county assessor's valuation of the home for tax purposes, the dependent variable would be the assessed value of the home (interval level). Suppose the condition of the house is rated Poor, Average, Good, or Very Good. This independent variable is measured at the ordinal level, and with the dependent variable at the interval level, ANOVA could be used. More often than not, however, you will likely see ANOVA used in public administration research with nominal independent variables simply because most of the trends in research examine multi-category nominal variables like party identification, race, gender, job title, etc.

The second assumption for ANOVA is that if you are using samples of data, the samples have been independently randomly selected. Therefore, in the previous example, if you are examining assessed home values and relying on a sample of data, it is assumed that you have randomly selected the homes to include or have taken a random sample of the assessor's housing data. Think about if a researcher only examined assessed values of homes within one or two zip codes of a city instead of randomly selecting homes throughout the city. It could be the case that the one or two zip codes sampled are systematically biased or different from homes in the other zip codes. Maybe the sampled homes from the few zip codes are in the exclusive neighborhoods where most homes have an in-ground pool or are in a zip code with substantially new housing stock. You can see how this might bias the results and conclusions made from analyses. Though a minor but important detail, the "independent" component of the assumption of independent random sample simply means that there is no correlation between being sampled or not being sampled. It is totally random.

ANOVA is often used in academic research involving experiments where there are two or more treatment groups and a control group, with an interval level outcome as the dependent variable. Experiments are often difficult to conduct in public administration, but for the sake of illustration, let's assume a large federal agency with offices in Washington D.C. is trying to decide on upgrades to their anti-virus and security software systems. They are interested in whether or not to switch to new software compared to the old software. The director of IT in the agency engages in a pilot program, where a randomly selected group of employees will have the VirusGone software installed on their computers, another group of randomly selected employees will have the SteelWall security software installed on their computers, and the remaining employees will have no upgrades, using the existing security software. After a period of three months, the IT director collects data on each computer, noting the number of viruses and/or security breaches. The director seeks to determine if a certain software program is more effective than others. Assuming that the director randomly assigns the pilot software to employees, ANOVA can be used. Without random assignment, it cannot be determined if the dependent variable (in this case, the count of viruses and security breaches) is a function of the software or some other characteristic. The "independent" requirement of independent random sampling in this case would mean that no employee is more or less likely to be in one of the pilot groups compared to the status quo/control group. Selection into a particular group is completely random, and if one individual is selected into a group, it does not affect another employee being selected into the same or different group.

The final assumptions of ANOVA are somewhat complex statistical theory assumptions. They are briefly discussed herein, but should you decide to pursue more advanced study of statistics or higher degrees in public administration, you may find yourself delving deeper into these assumptions. ANOVA assumes that the dependent variable for each group of the independent variable is normally distributed in the population. Therefore, for each sample, we assume the larger population is normally distributed on the dependent variable. It is also assumed that the variances across the independent variable groups in the larger population are equal across groups. As discussed, these assumptions concerning normality and variance are rooted in statistical theory. Public administrators likely are not actively dealing with these issues in their daily analyses; however, they are important to mention as assumptions in a similar manner that the theories of supply and demand assume perfect information among consumers and producers.

Sample sizes across groups in an ANOVA analysis should also be equal or very close to equal. Applied to the IT example, the director would want to ensure as best as possible that the number of computers assigned to the VirusGone software was roughly the same as the number of computers assigned to the SteelWall software as the same to the number of computers with the status quo software. When these assumptions have been met, we can place more confidence in our results from an ANOVA analysis.

The final assumption of ANOVA is in the construction of the null hypothesis. Assuming the use of random samples from a population, the null hypothesis is that there is no difference across the categories of the independent variable on the dependent variable in the population. The means of the dependent variable are the same across categories of the independent variable in the larger population. The research or alternative hypothesis is that at least one category of the independent variable is statistically different from another category on the dependent variable. The research/alternative hypothesis in ANOVA does not denote a direction of relationship. We will construct examples in the next section.

11.3 ANOVA in the R Commander

Running ANVOA in the R Commander is fairly simple. To do so, let's set up a hypothetical example. Every May, the U.S. Postal Service (USPS) solicits customers to donate canned food in their mailboxes during the Stamp Out Hunger food drive. Residents usually receive information about a week prior in the regular mail that mail carriers will be collecting canned foods and to leave them in their mailboxes to be picked up. Suppose the USPS wants to see if certain appeals to residents are more likely to increase canned food donations compared to their extant method of using a reminder postcard a week before. This year, a local office wants to try two new appeals postcards a week before the collection drive. Postcard A is the traditional postcard informing residents that they may place canned goods in their mailbox on a particular day to be collected. Postcard B is one of two new trial postcards. It appeals to individuals with information on the percent of people in the local community in need of food assistance and the number of families in the community that use the local food bank where the canned goods will be delivered. Postcard C tries to appeal to residents' emotions by showing a picture of a young, malnourished child and asks residents to donate canned goods to help feed hungry children. Postcards A, B, and C are randomly assigned to addresses in the community and placed in the respective mailboxes.

On collection day, each mail carrier is asked to count the number of cans for each address for which they deliver. Data analysts at the USPS then count the number of canned goods given at each address and match them to the address' assigned postcard. The administrators and analysts at the USPS hypothesize that donations will be the highest for Postcard C, then Postcard B, and the fewest donations will come from the traditional appeal postcard, Postcard A. Because the ANOVA research/alternative hypothesis does not stipulate a direction, the research/alternative hypothesis would technically be that at least one of the postcards differ from another on canned good donation behavior. The null hypothesis would be that the mean number of cans donated are equal for those receiving Postcard A to those receiving Postcard B to those receiving Postcard C.

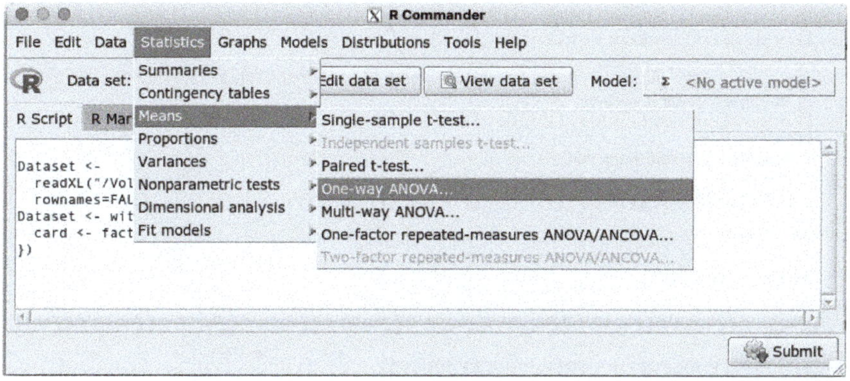

Figure 11.1 ANOVA in the R Commander, part 1

The corresponding dataset for this hypothetical example is the *canned_good* dataset in the Companion Site (www.cambridge.org/scheller). Download the dataset and first open it in Excel along with the codebook just to view the data and coding scheme. There are three columns: "address_id," "cans," and "card." The "address_id" variable is a unique identifier for each address. If this were a real dataset, addresses would be in the cells, or the same coding style could be used for privacy purposes by the analyst. The "cans" column represents the number of cans donated at each address while the "card" column indicates the type of postcard received by the residents at each address. The codebook indicates that a value of 0 is for an address that received Postcard A, 1 for Postcard B, and 2 for Postcard C.

With this background information, upload the data into the R Commander. The R Commander prefers the nominal variable to be non-numeric or string. Therefore, recode the "card" variable in line with the codebook and from instruction in Chapter 5. You can simply replace 0 with A, 1 with B, and 2 with C. Follow the Data → Manage variables in active data set → Convert numeric variables to factors steps as covered in Chapter 5.

The "cans" variable is the dependent variable, an interval level variable, while the "card" variable is the independent variable (nominal with three categories). Therefore, ANOVA is an appropriate statistical test. With one independent variable, the specific type of ANOVA is the one-way ANOVA. To run the one-way ANOVA:

Step 1. Click Statistics → Means → One-way ANOVA (Figure 11.1).

Step 2. A new box appears requesting an input for the "Groups" box and the "Response Variable" box. The "Groups" "represents the independent variable. In this case, it is the "card" variable. The "Response Variable" box corresponds to the dependent variable. In this example, select "cans." Then, click OK (Figure 11.2).

The output should now be available in the R Commander output window. It is reproduced in Figure 11.3.

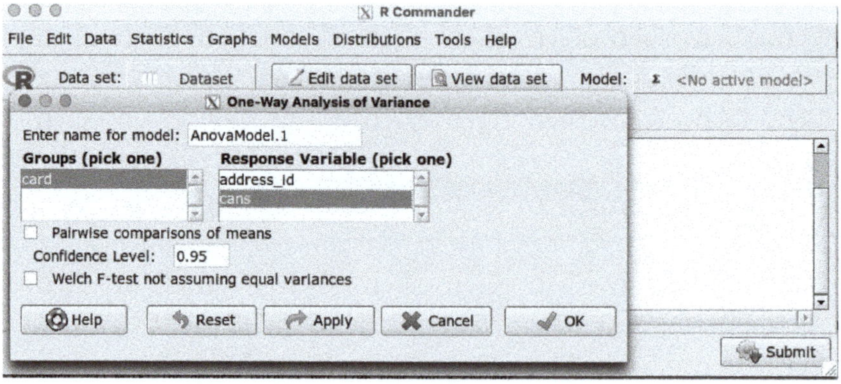

Figure 11.2 ANOVA in the R Commander, part 2

```
Rcmdr>  AnovaModel.1 <- aov(cans ~ card, data=Dataset)

Rcmdr>  summary(AnovaModel.1)
              Df Sum Sq Mean Sq F value Pr(>F)
card           2    176    88.0    6.47 0.0016 **
Residuals   1293  17587    13.6
---
Signif. codes:  0 '***' 0.001 '**' 0.01 '*' 0.05 '.' 0.1 ' ' 1

Rcmdr>  with(Dataset, numSummary(cans, groups=card, statistics=c("mean", "sd")))
      mean       sd data:n
A 5.773148 3.848575    432
B 5.849537 3.608195    432
C 6.590278 3.602165    432
```

F Value

p-value with significance stars

Independent variable categories

Category sample sizes

Dependent variable means per category

Figure 11.3 ANOVA in the R Commander output

11.4 Interpreting ANOVA

The ANOVA output above has a number of important pieces of information. In the bottom section of the output is a rudimentary table with each value of the independent variable – in this case, A, B, and C for each respective postcard. The "mean" column lists the mean value of the dependent variable for each category of the independent variable. In this particular example, the mean number of cans donated by those receiving Postcard A was 5.77. The mean number of cans donated by those individuals receiving Postcard B was about 5.85 cans. The mean number of cans donated by residents receiving Postcard C was 6.59 cans. The last column shows the number of observations for each category of the independent variable. The sample sizes were equal for each Postcard at 432. Remember that ANOVA is most robust when the sample sizes are nearly equal. From the results, it appears that the new, pilot postcards (Postcards B and C) compelled residents to donate more cans on average compared to the traditional or control group postcard (Postcard A). The difference between Postcard A and Postcard B appears slight, while Postcard C appears to have had the most impact. Postcard C was the card with the image of a malnourished child, which tried to appeal to residents' emotions. Are the differences statistically significantly different?

Unlike the t-test, which uses a t-distribution, ANOVA uses an F distribution. Thus, ANOVA output includes an F statistic, which may also be called an F Ratio or F Value. As with other tests covered, the p-value depicts the probability of obtaining the observed relationships by chance. Therefore, the F statistic is statistically significant at the 95% confidence level if the p-value is 0.05 or less. It is statistically significant at the 99% confidence level if the p-value is less than or equal to 0.01.

In the example above, the F value is 6.47 with a p-value of 0.0016. The F value is statistically significant at the 99% confidence level. The null hypothesis of no difference in the population for canned good donations across the three different postcards is rejected. The research/alternative hypothesis is accepted – at least one of the postcard groups significantly differs from another on the mean number of canned goods donated.

Which category of the independent variable is driving the statistically significant relationship? A limitation of the ANVOA F test is that the results do not indicate which group or category is responsible for the differences in the means. Eyeballing the results could reveal the pattern if it is obvious. In this example, we see that the mean can donations are 5.77, 5.85, and 6.59 for postcard groups A, B, and C respectively. It is safe to assume that postcard C is driving this result, probably from the difference in donations from individuals receiving Postcard C compared to Postcard A. However, do we know if the difference in donations from those receiving Postcard C are statistically significantly different from Postcard B? We cannot determine this simply from the ANOVA output. A common method to better establish which category is driving the statistically significant relationship(s) in ANOVA is to conduct a post-hoc test. One common post-hoc test is the Tukey HSD test that compares the means for each pair of categories. Only one additional step is needed when conducting the ANOVA in the R Commander. To obtain the Tukey HSD test of comparisons, follow the same steps as above using the Statistics → Means → One-way ANOVA process in the R Commander. In the resulting popup box where you enter your groups and response variables, make sure "Pairwise comparisons of means" is checked. Leave the confidence level set at the 0.95 default. See Figure 11.4 for the correct setup.

Clicking OK will return the same results from the previous ANOVA along with the additional Tukey HSD test of comparisons. The particular additional information to concentrate on appears in Figure 11.5.

The "Multiple Comparisons of Means: Tukey Contrasts" are presented as linear hypotheses and under such a label. Notice on the far left each pairing for categories of the independent variable. In this example, "B – A" is the first pairing, corresponding to Postcard B and Postcard A. The "Estimate" column shows the mean difference of the pair. For our example, this mean difference is the difference in donation

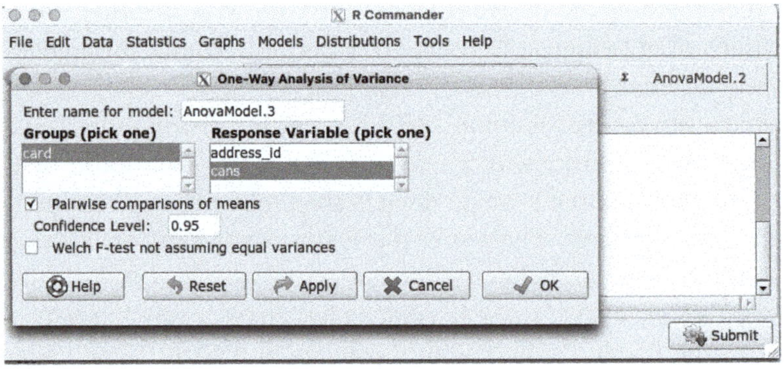

Figure 11.4 Tukey HSD test in the R Commander

```
         Simultaneous Tests for General Linear Hypotheses

Multiple Comparisons of Means: Tukey Contrasts


Fit: aov(formula = cans ~ card, data = Dataset)

Linear Hypotheses:
           Estimate Std. Error t value Pr(>|t|)
B - A == 0  0.07639    0.25094   0.304   0.9502
C - A == 0  0.81713    0.25094   3.256   0.0033 **
C - B == 0  0.74074    0.25094   2.952   0.0091 **
---
Signif. codes:  0 '***' 0.001 '**' 0.01 '*' 0.05 '.' 0.1 ' ' 1
(Adjusted p values reported -- single-step method)
```

Annotations: Pairwise comparison (pointing to "B - A"); Difference of means (pointing to "Estimate"); Tukey HSD p-value (pointing to "Pr(>|t|)")

Figure 11.5 Tukey HSD in the R Commander output

mean for Postcard B and Postcard A, depicted as 0.07639. This value is calculated by simply taking the mean donation of Postcard B respondents and subtracting the mean donation of Postcard A respondents. Remember that these means are reported in the original ANOVA output. The mean donation for Postcard B residents was 5.85 cans, or if extending the decimal places as fully presented in the ANOVA output, 5.849537 cans. The mean donation for Postcard A residents was 5.77, or 5.773148 if using all decimal places reported by the R Commander output. Therefore, 5.849537 − 5.773148 is 0.076389, or 0.07639 as rounded to the fifth decimal place by the R Commander. The Tukey HSD uses a t-test to determine if the difference is statistically significant. The t-value and associated p-value and significance level are reported by the R Commander. As with the t-test, p-values less than or equal to 0.05 indicate a statistically significant difference in the means for the particular pairing. In this case, the p-value is 0.9502; therefore, the 0.07639 difference in average cans donated between Postcard B residents and Postcard A residents is not statistically significant. Yes, residents that received Postcard B donated more cans (an average of 0.07639 cans), but this difference is not statistically significant, or, stated differently, this 0.07639 difference is no different from 0.

As may have been expected/suspected, the driving factor in the statistically significant relationship between postcard appeals and canned good donations is being driven by Postcard C. From the ANOVA and related Tukey HSD post-hoc test results, residents receiving Postcard C donated an average of 0.81713 more cans than residents receiving Postcard A. The p-value of 0.0033 of the Tukey HSD t-test indicates this relationship is significant at the 99% confidence level since the p-value is less than 0.01. Similarly, residents receiving Postcard C donated more cans on average than residents receiving Postcard B, by about 0.74074 cans, also statistically significant at the 99% confidence level since the p-value is less than 0.01. Thus, the post-hoc test indicates that while Postcard C is driving the statistically significant relationship, it is not only because the difference in donations is high comparing donations from Postcard C residents to Postcard A residents, but also from Postcard C to Postcard B. Using this information, one can make a conclusion that Postcard C was the most effective even when compared to the other pilot postcard (Postcard B) and may be the most effective appeal to solicit donations. Of course, as with all statistical results, one needs to also examine the substantive significance. Is a difference of 0.81713 cans from Postcard C compared to the control group of Postcard A substantively important? It is less than one can on average. As a public administrator, it may be your choice at some point to make a program/policy decision. In this case, would it be worth switching all Stamp Out Hunger advertising appeals to the message and image on Postcard C? Do the printing costs increase? Are there ethical implications for including an image of a malnourished child on an appeal? That is up to the decision makers. The statistics simply show the patterns.

11.5 Summary

This chapter covered a common statistical test used in public administration and other social science research known as Analysis of Variance (ANOVA). It is used when a researcher's dependent variable is at the interval level and the independent variable is at the nominal variable with more than two categories. ANOVA is particularly useful when dealing with data generated from experiments; however, it is also commonly used with non-experimental data like surveys. Independent variables of interest in survey data, like job title, gender, party identification, quality scores (poor, fair, excellent) are hypothesized to have relationships with dependent variables measured at the interval variable.

The bulk of the chapter focused on how to conduct ANOVA in the R Commander to obtain interpretable results from the ANOVA output and Tukey HSD post-hoc tests. Similar to other statistical tests, correlation still does not indicate causation with ANOVA despite its advantages in analyzing relevant data. It cannot account for other independent variables that may simultaneously have an impact on the dependent variable. A common theme with these tests is that multivariate regression (Chapter 15) can help researchers account for these other variables.

Recommended Reading

Iversen, G.R., & Norpoth, H. (1976). *Analysis of variance.* Sage.
Salkind, N.J. (2008). *Statistics for people who (think they) hate statistics.* Sage.

PRACTICE PROBLEMS

Conceptual Problems

1. Street engineers for a city are interested in traffic counts on three roads that are commonly used to enter downtown. For three workweeks, they count the number of cars using each type of street. The three types of streets are coded as 1 for the major arterial street, 2 for the minor arterial street, and 3 for a connector street. Determine if ANOVA is an appropriate test and why.
2. The same street engineers from Problem #1 are interested in traffic counts along Main Street during different scenarios. They take a sample of fifty days. Each day, they count the number of cars using main street. Determine if ANOVA is an appropriate test for the following and why? If not, explain why.
   a. If they are interested in traffic counts for days that are coded as being Rainy, Sunny, or Overcast.
   b. If they are interested in traffic counts and the level of snowfall measured in inches each day.
   c. If they are interested in traffic counts and whether or not the day is during the workweek (coded 1 if Monday through Friday) or a weekend day (coded 0 if Saturday or Sunday).
3. A survey of neighborhood and homeowners associations is conducted to compare neighborhood associations to homeowners associations on the following dependent variables:
   a. Number of times the association has filed suit against a resident.
   b. Number of homes in the association.
   c. If the association is located in a section of the city labeled as: elite, middle class, or lower class.

   A researcher runs an ANOVA and finds statistically significant results. A critic says the researcher has not conducted the research correctly. Why?
4. In a survey of residents, a researchers asks them how many hours a week they walk outside in their neighborhood. The researcher wants to compare walking activity across family type, coded (Single = 0; Married = 1; Divorced = 2; Other = 3). The researcher's sampling method leads to the following sample sizes of analysis:

   Other (n = 10)
   Single (n = 256)
   Divorced (n = 175)
   Married (n = 199)

   The researcher conducts an ANOVA and finds statistically significant results. What is one critique with the use of ANOVA and its results in this example?

R Commander Problems

5. Open the *competency_exam* dataset from the Companion Site (www.cambridge .org/scheller). It is a hypothetical dataset of employee competency scores (from 0 to 100). Three different versions of the test were given to avoid cheating (versions 1, 2, 3, and 4). The test administrator wants to determine if there are any differences in scores that can be attributed to the version of the exam given. Test this question using ANOVA and interpret the results.
6. Using the *competency_exam* dataset, test whether or not job type is related to the competency score. The "job" variable is coded 0 for clerical staff, 1 for middle manager, and 2 for upper management. What conclusions can you make?

12

Chi-Square

12.1 Introduction

In the previous chapter, we covered Analysis of Variance, otherwise known as ANOVA. The use of ANOVA is appropriate when studying the relationship between variables involves an interval level dependent variable and an independent variable with more than two categories. With chi-square, we are *ONLY* dealing with two variables measured at the nominal level (e.g. job title and whether or not they received a raise, city department and over/under budget, race and religious denomination, party identification and whether or not one voted last year, etc.). Both the dependent and independent variables are at the nominal level. The number of categories in each variable is of no importance. Chi-square can handle multiple categories. With t-tests and ANOVA, we were examining the relationship between variables, an independent variable and a dependent variable. In both of these tests, the dependent variable is measured at the interval level. In a similar vein, chi-square examines the relationship between an independent variable and a dependent variable, with both the dependent and independent variables measured at the nominal level. It helps us to determine if there is a statistically significant relationship between variables, but accounts for the fact that the dependent variable is limited in the number of values it can take.

This chapter covers the appropriate use of the chi-square test, focusing on when to use it based upon the level of measurement of the dependent and independent variable. The remainder of the chapter follows with a discussion of contingency tables, or how data are presented prior to running a chi-square test. Then, the assumptions of the test are covered, the chi-square distribution/table, how to run the test by hand and in the R Commander, followed by interpretation of the results of a chi-square test.

12.2 Constructing and Reading Contingency Tables

Race and police relations has been a topic of research and political discussion for many years. The murder of George Floyd at the hands of Minneapolis police officers not only ushered in a renewed interest in police–citizen interactions, but also public service equity in government. Many government agencies began to review their practices in response to greater attention to systemic racism and discrimination. For the sake of illustration, let's assume a hypothetical situation where a county's health department is interested in the experiences of its citizens with the county health department. There is concern among the directors that citizen experiences may differ by race, and that minority citizens may experience greater dissatisfaction with the department's staff and services, based upon a few complaints sent to the directors that staff have been rude and unhelpful in providing information about services offered at the department. In this particular city, the population is approximately 100,000, with 63% of the population identifying as white, and the remaining 37% identifying as an underrepresented minority, or non-white. The directors for the county health department send a survey to twenty citizens in the county that had used services from the county health department. One of the questions on the survey asks whether or not the respondent had a negative experience with the health department's staff in the past two years. Another question asks the race of the respondent. The results of the survey reveal that fifteen respondents identified as white, with six respondents indicating that they had a negative experience with staff in the past two years, and nine respondents indicating that they had not had a negative experience with staff. A total of five respondents identified as non-white, with three of them indicating they had a negative experience with staff, and two indicating that they had not had a negative experience.

A first step in displaying the data coded in this manner is to organize it into a contingency table, also known as a cross-tabulation. Convention is to display the independent variable arrayed in the columns, and the dependent variable arrayed in the rows. Table 12.1 illustrates an appropriate display for contingency tables.

Cross-reference this table with the description in the previous paragraph, and you will see the numbers match to their respective cells. With the exception of the Total in the bottom righthand cell (20), the other Totals represent marginals that will become useful very shortly. Each row total is considered a *row marginal.* The row marginals are 9 and 11, respectively. Each column total is considered a *column marginal.* The column marginals in Table 12.1 are 15 and 5, respectively.

Table 12.1 Contingency table – race and negative experience with health staff

	White	Non-White	Total
Yes to Neg. Experience	6	3	9
No to Neg. Experience	9	2	11
Total	15	5	20

12.3 Assumptions of Chi-Square

For all of the previous hypothesis tests covered so far (t-tests and analysis of variance), the dependent variable has been measured at the interval level. The t-test and the analysis of variance assume that the dependent variable is normally distributed, or that the sample of data is drawn from a normally distributed population. The chi-square test does not assume a normal distribution. It may also be referred to as a nonparametric test, as no underlying distribution of the data is assumed (Healey, 2002; Wonnacott & Wonnacott, 1990). The main assumptions to meet when using chi-square are simply that both the dependent and independent variables be measured at the nominal level. The null hypothesis for the chi-square test is of no relationship between the independent and dependent variables, or that they are independent. When running the chi-square test, rejection of the null hypothesis indicates a statistically significant relationship.

Let us assume that the county health department directors have a hypothesis that non-white individuals are more likely to report a negative experience with health department staff. This would be their research or alternative hypothesis. The null hypothesis would be of no relationship. Therefore, the null hypothesis would be that there is no relationship between race and negative experiences with health department staff. So, for the data represented in Table 12.1, with answers to whether or not respondents had a negative experience with staff based upon race, the independent variable is race (white v. non-white) and the dependent variable is whether or not the individual had a negative experience with staff (Yes or No).

12.4 Chi-Square Test by Hand

The chi-square test is relatively easy to conduct by hand, especially for simple contingency tables like Table 12.1 that is a 2 × 2 table. There are two rows and two columns in Table 12.1. One may state that there are actually three rows and three columns. However, we do not consider the Totals rows and columns as substantive rows and columns. There are two categories of race, the independent variable (white and non-white). There are two categories of negative interactions with staff (Yes and No). Hence, we consider Table 12.1 as a 2 × 2 table – two rows, two columns.

How can we test whether or not there is a statistically significant relationship between the independent variable and the dependent variable, or in this case, the relationship between race and negative interactions with health department staff? The null hypothesis is that there is no relationship between the independent and dependent variables. After you have stated your null hypothesis, you must go through several steps to get to the chi-square statistic, which is represented by Equation 12.1:

$$\chi^2 = \Sigma \frac{(f_o - f_e)^2}{f_e}, \qquad (12.1)$$

where f_o is the observed frequencies in your table (Table 12.1 for this example), and f_e is the expected frequencies in your table (what we need to calculate first). f_e is the frequencies we would expect to see if there is *NO* relationship between race and negative experiences with staff. They are not in your table, and you must calculate them. Essentially, you are going to create an identical table as the one provided, but will be calculating f_e for *each cell.*

For the data reported in Table 12.1, the directors pose a research hypothesis that race is correlated with negative experiences with health department staff. Specifically, the PR officer believes that non-white respondents are more likely to respond that they have had a negative experience with staff compared to white respondents. The null hypothesis is that there is no relationship between race and negative experiences with staff. More specifically, non-white respondents are neither more or less likely to report a negative experience with staff. To calculate the chi-square statistic, a number of steps should be followed.

Step 1: Calculate f_e and put them into an "expected values" table.

$$f_e = \frac{RowMarginal \times ColumnMarginal}{N}$$

The Row Marginal is the respective row's total, and the Column Marginal is the respective column's total, which are given to you in the original table provided. Therefore, the row marginals are 9 and 11. The column marginals are 15 and 5. All of the observed values (f_o) are in Table 12.1. Beginning in the upper left corner and reading clockwise, the f_o's are in each cell and are 6, 3, 2, and 9. For the upper left cell (value of 6), the respective row marginal is 9, and the respective column marginal is 15. In the lower right cell (value of 2), the respective row marginal is 11, and the respective column marginal is 5. For each of the substantive cells in Table 12.1, we must calculate the expected values we would observe if there was no relationship between race and negative experiences with health staff. Table 12.2 depicts the respective row (row marg.) and column marginals (column marg.). It also labels the raw data frequencies as f_o, observed frequencies for each cell.

For each substantive cell in the 2 × 2 table, calculate f_e. Beginning in the upper left cell (White, Yes), the observed value (f_e) is 6. The respective row

Table 12.2 Contingency table with marginals

	White	Non-White	Total
Yes to Neg. Experience	$f_o = 6$	$f_o = 3$	9 (row marg.)
No to Neg. Experience	$f_o = 9$	$f_o = 2$	11 (row marg.)
Total	15 (column marg.)	5 (column marg.)	20 (N)

marginal is 9, and the respective column marginal is 15. Therefore:

$$f_e = \frac{9 \times 15}{20}$$

$$f_e = \frac{135}{20}$$

$$f_e = 6.75$$

For the upper left cell, we observed 6 white individuals indicating they had a negative experience with health department staff. Based upon the sample of 20 respondents, if there was no relationship between race and negative experiences with staff, the expected value of whites indicating a negative experience with staff would be 6.75. The value of 6.75 is greater than 6, so is there a statistically significant relationship? This cannot be determined at this point. We must generate the expected values for all of the other cells and calculate the chi-square statistic.

For the upper right cell (Non-White, Yes), the observed value (f_o) is 3. The respective row marginal is 9, and the respective column marginal is 5. Therefore:

$$f_e = \frac{9 \times 5}{20}$$

$$f_e = \frac{45}{20}$$

$$f_e = 2.25$$

Continuing clockwise in the 2 × 2 table, in the bottom right cell (Non-White, No), the observed value (f_o) = 2. The respective row marginal is 11, and the respective column marginal is 5. Therefore:

$$f_e = \frac{11 \times 5}{20}$$

$$f_e = \frac{55}{20}$$

$$f_e = 2.75$$

Continuing clockwise to the final cell of the table, in the bottom left (White, No), the observed value (f_o) = 9. The respective row marginal is 11, and the respective column marginal is 15. Therefore:

$$f_e = \frac{11 \times 15}{20}$$

$$f_e = \frac{165}{20}$$

$$f_e = 8.25$$

To help illustrate the expected values versus the observed values, Table 12.3 includes the original observed values from Tables 12.1 and 12.2 but then

Table 12.3 Contingency table with expected values

	White	Non-White	Total
Yes to Neg. Experience	$f_o = 6$	$f_o = 3$	9 (row marg.)
	$f_e = 6.75$	$f_e = 2.25$	
No to Neg. Experience	$f_o = 9$	$f_o = 2$	11 (row marg.)
	$f_e = 8.25$	$f_e = 2.75$	
Total	15 (column marg.)	5 (column marg.)	20 (N)

also adds in the expected values if there was no relationship between the independent variable (race) and the dependent variable (negative experience with health department staff).

Step 2: Calculate your chi-square statistic using the chi-square equation:

$$\chi^2 = \Sigma \frac{(f_o - f_e)^2}{f_e}.$$

For each substantive cell in Table 12.3, subtract the expected value from the observed value ($f_o - f_e$). Then, square that value. Next, divide the squared value by expected value (f_e). Do this for each cell, and then add/sum all of the values. This leaves the chi-square test statistic value. Beginning in the upper lefthand cell,

$$\frac{(6 - 6.75)^2}{6.75}$$
$$\frac{(-0.75)^2}{6.75}$$
$$\frac{(0.5625)}{6.75}$$
$$= \mathbf{0.08}$$

The same process needs to be used for the other substantive cells. In this example, there are three more cells to calculate values. Moving to the upper right cell,

$$\frac{(3 - 2.25)^2}{2.25}$$
$$\frac{(0.75)^2}{2.25}$$
$$\frac{(0.5625)}{2.25}$$
$$= \mathbf{0.25}$$

Now for the bottom right cell,

$$\frac{(2-2.75)^2}{2.75}$$
$$\frac{(-0.75)^2}{2.75}$$
$$\frac{(0.5625)}{2.75}$$
$$= \mathbf{0.20}$$

On to the bottom left cell,

$$\frac{(9-8.25)^2}{8.25}$$
$$\frac{(0.75)^2}{8.25}$$
$$\frac{(0.5625)}{8.25}$$
$$= \mathbf{0.07}$$

Finally, sum up all of the values you calculated (in bold). This step aligns with the Σ value in the equation. Therefore:

$$\chi^2 = \Sigma\frac{(f_o - f_e)^2}{f_e} = \mathbf{0.60}$$

The value of 0.60 is the calculated χ^2 value for the relationship between race and negative experiences with health department staff. What does this statistic mean? On its own, it cannot be interpreted like a mean, median, mode, or standard deviation. It will always be a positive value due to the squaring in the equation. The chi-square statistic is a calculated value of the relationship between race and experience with the health department staff, but needs to be compared to a reference value to determine if the relationship is statistically significant. Appendix A lists all of the reference values across different levels of statistical significance (0.1 = 90%; 0.05 = 95%; 0.01 = 99%; 0.001 = 99.9%). However, in the first row is a category called *d.f.* This represents the degrees of freedom in our analysis and will affect which reference value to compare our calculated chi-square statistic.

Step 3: We will be using a chi-square distribution/table for these tests, so you must calculate degrees of freedom. For the chi-square test, the equation for calculating degrees of freedom is:

$$d.f. = (r-1)(c-1),$$

where r is the number of rows in your table, and c is the number of columns in your table. The number of rows and columns is the *substantive* rows and columns, or the rows and columns with observed data. The Totals rows and columns are not counted. Therefore, Table 12.1 is a 2 × 2 table – two rows and two columns. The degrees of freedom for Table 12.1 is then:

$$d.f. = (2-1)(2-1)$$
$$d.f. = (1)(1) = 1$$

Step 4: Go to the chi-square table (Appendix A) and find the critical value for the particular level of significance and degrees of freedom. If your calculated value of chi-square meets or exceeds the critical value, you may reject the null hypothesis. If your calculated value of chi-square does not meet or exceed the critical value, you cannot reject the null hypothesis.
With 1 degree of freedom, the 95% confidence critical value (0.05 column) is 3.84. Therefore, the calculated value of the chi-square statistic must be equal to or greater than 3.84 to state that there is a relationship between the independent and dependent variable significant at the 95% confidence level. The variables are independent of each other. Recall that the calculated chi-square value was 0.60, which is less than 3.84. Therefore, we fail to reject the null hypothesis that race and negative experiences with health department staff are related. Based upon this particular sample, we cannot conclude that race and negative experiences with health department staff are related in the larger population.

12.4.1 Evaluating Results

In the previous example, the results came out statistically insignificant. Does this mean that we can definitively conclude that race and negative experiences with health staff are unrelated? By now, you should know this to not necessarily be the case. It is important to evaluate the research design – sampling, data distribution, logic of results, etc. A good researcher always questions the results with a critical eye.

What might be some red flags from the previous example? First, the sample size. Even though we can calculate test statistics like the chi-square with small samples and generate results, small sample sizes make it more difficult to generalize to the larger population. A sample size of 20 is really very small, especially when considering the size of the true population, which was 100,000 in the example. It is certainly understandable that a researcher would be unable to obtain a 10% sample from a population of 100,000. Given that response rates to surveys are often below 25%, it would take an enormous amount of resources to get to 10,000. Surveys can be expensive to implement (especially if mailed or if paying people to make phone calls) and very time-consuming (sending reminders and/or sending out new surveys). However, it may be reasonable and feasible to obtain a sample of 1,000, 500, or even 200, which would lend greater confidence in the results of a study.

A second issue in the previous example is the characteristics of the sample population in relation to the larger population. Recall from the race and health staff

Table 12.4 Random sample of health survey respondents

	White	Non-White	Total
Yes to Neg. Experience	48	41	89
No to Neg. Experience	98	25	123
Total	146	66	212

example that the population of the city was 63% white and 37% underrepresented minority. In the sample, only 5 of the 20 respondents identified as underrepresented minority, or only 25% of the sample. The sample is 75% white (15 of 20 respondents). This overrepresentation of white respondents in the sample may skew or bias the results as minority respondents are underrepresented in the sample.

In the previous example, it was not indicated whether or not the directors used a random sample. Ideally, engaging in a random sample would generate a sample reflective of the population. This may not always be the result, especially if certain segments of the population are less likely to respond to a survey (e.g. older citizens reluctant to fill out an internet survey; younger citizens less likely to be contacted for a survey conducted via telephone or even snail mail; certain segments of the population that are less trusting of surveys; etc.). If we find that certain segments of the population are underrepresented in the sample compared to the population, oversampling in these segments may help overcome limited responses.

Let us assume in the previous example that the directors engaged in convenience sampling – sampling people they saw on the street from noon – 2:00 PM on a weekday. The directors decide to redo the study, randomly sampling in the population. They use voter registration data containing voter contact information (address, email, and phone number). The directors randomly select 1,000 individuals to receive the survey in an attempt to reach all demographics. A total of 212 individuals respond to the survey. The directors then organize the data into a contingency table, shown in Table 12.4 A total of 66 non-white individuals responded (31.1% of the sample), and 146 white individuals responded (68.9% of the sample). These percentages are more in line with the larger population's demographics from the previous example (37% non-white and 63% white).

Table 12.4 shows vastly different numbers from Table 12.1 A total of 48 white individuals out of 146 surveyed indicated that they had a negative experience with health department staff, or 32.88% of white respondents. Compare that to 41 out of 66 non-white individuals, or 62.12% of non-white respondents. These difference appear stark, but are they statistically significant? Re-running the chi-square test for the new data will help determine a statistically significant relationship between race and negative experiences with staff. Follow the previous steps to calculate the chi-square statistic.

Step 1: Calculate Expected Frequencies

As before, use the following equation to calculate expected frequencies:

$$f_e = \frac{RowMarginal \times ColumnMarginal}{N}$$

Beginning in the upper left cell (White, Yes), the observed value (f_o) is 48. The respective row marginal is 89, and the respective column marginal is 146. Therefore:

$$f_e = \frac{89 \times 146}{212}$$
$$f_e = \frac{12994}{212}$$
$$f_e = 61.29$$

For the upper right cell (Non-White, Yes), the observed value (f_o) is 41. The respective row marginal is 89, and the respective column marginal is 66. Therefore:

$$f_e = \frac{89 \times 66}{212}$$
$$f_e = \frac{5874}{212}$$
$$f_e = 27.71$$

Continuing clockwise in the 2 × 2 table, in the bottom right cell (Non-White, No), the observed value (f_o) = 25. The respective row marginal is 123, and the respective column marginal is 66. Therefore:

$$f_e = \frac{123 \times 66}{212}$$
$$f_e = \frac{8118}{212}$$
$$f_e = 38.29$$

Continuing clockwise to the final cell of the table, in the bottom left (White, No), the observed value (f_o) = 98. The respective row marginal is 123, and the respective column marginal is 146. Therefore:

$$f_e = \frac{123 \times 146}{212}$$
$$f_e = \frac{17958}{212}$$
$$f_e = 84.71$$

Now, update Table 12.4 with the expected frequencies. It should look like Table 12.5.

Table 12.5 Contingency table with expected frequencies, example 2

	White	Non-White	Total
Yes to Neg. Experience	$f_o = 48$	$f_o = 41$	89 (row marg.)
	$f_e = 61.29$	$f_e = 27.71$	
No to Neg. Experience	$f_o = 98$	$f_o = 25$	123 (row marg.)
	$f_e = 84.71$	$f_e = 38.29$	
Total	146 (column marg.)	66 (column marg.)	212 (N)

Step 2: Calculate the Chi-Square Statistic

Calculate your chi-square statistic using the chi-square equation (Equation 12.1):

$$\chi^2 = \Sigma \frac{(f_o - f_e)^2}{f_e}.$$

Beginning in the upper lefthand cell,

$$\frac{(48 - 61.29)^2}{61.29}$$
$$\frac{(-13.29)^2}{61.29}$$
$$\frac{(176.62)}{61.29}$$
$$= \mathbf{2.88}$$

Moving to the upper right cell,

$$\frac{(41 - 27.71)^2}{27.71}$$
$$\frac{(13.29)^2}{27.71}$$
$$\frac{(176.62)}{27.71}$$
$$= \mathbf{6.37}$$

Now for the bottom right cell,

$$\frac{(25 - 38.29)^2}{38.29}$$
$$\frac{(-13.29)^2}{38.29}$$
$$\frac{(176.62)}{38.29}$$
$$= \mathbf{4.61}$$

On to the bottom left cell,

$$\frac{(98 - 84.71)^2}{84.71}$$

$$\frac{(13.29)^2}{84.71}$$

$$\frac{(176.62)}{84.71}$$

$$= \mathbf{2.09}$$

Finally, sum up all of the values you calculated (in bold). Therefore:

$$\chi^2 = \Sigma \frac{(f_o - f_e)^2}{f_e} = 2.88 + 6.37 + 4.61 + 2.09$$

$$\chi^2 = 15.95$$

Step 3: Calculate Degrees of Freedom

The equation for calculating degrees of freedom is:

$$d.f. = (r - 1)(c - 1),$$

where r is the number of rows in your table, and c is the number of columns in your table. The number of rows and columns is the *substantive* rows and columns, or the rows and columns with observed data. The Totals rows and columns are not counted. Therefore, Table 12.4 is a 2 × 2 table – two rows and two columns. The degrees of freedom for Table 12.4 is then:

$$d.f. = (2 - 1)(2 - 1)$$

$$d.f. = (1)(1) = 1$$

Step 4 Go to the chi-square table (Appendix A) and find the critical value for the particular level of significance and degrees of freedom. With 1 degree of freedom, the 95% confidence critical value (0.05 column) is 3.84. Therefore, the calculated value of the chi-square statistic must be equal to or greater than 3.84 to state that there is a relationship between the independent and dependent variable at the 95% confidence level. The variables are independent of each other. Recall that the calculated chi-square value was 15.95, which is greater than 3.84. Therefore, we reject the null hypothesis that race and negative experiences with health department staff are related. We can conclude, based upon the sample, that there is a statistically significant relationship between race and negative experiences with health department staff in the larger population.

12.4.2 Evaluating Results, Part II

As a best practice, always evaluate the results – do they make sense, was the research design sound, does the sample reflect the larger population? With this relatively

Table 12.6 Contingency table with column percentages

	White	Non-White	Total
Yes to Neg. Experience	$f_o = 48$	$f_o = 41$	89 (row marg.)
	(32.88%)	(62.12%)	
No to Neg. Experience	$f_o = 98$	$f_o = 25$	123 (row marg.)
	(67.12%)	(37.88%)	
Total	146 (column marg.)	66 (column marg.)	212 (N)

simple 2 × 2 table, we can simply eyeball the results and see the relationship – non-whites are statistically more likely to indicate that they had a negative experience with health department staff compared to white residents. Another good practice when constructing and interpreting contingency tables is to add the percentages for each of the cells with frequencies. Work down the columns to create percentages. Table 12.6 updates Table 12.4 with percentages.

For white respondents, 32.88% indicated that they had a negative experience with health department staff, compared to 62.12% of non-white respondents. Additionally, 67.12% of white respondents indicated that they had not had a negative experience with staff compared to 37.88% of non-white respondents. These percentages help to better clarify the relationship between race and negative health department staff experiences as presented in Table 12.4. It also helps to show the pattern leading to the statistically significant relationship. In the sample, 32.88% of white respondents indicated a negative experience with staff compared to 62.12% of non-white respondents. Since the relationship is statistically significant from the chi-square test, the percentages indicate that non-white individuals are statistically more likely to indicate they had a negative experience with staff compared to white individuals.

Why the change in results from the previous analysis? With the larger sample size, the results change dramatically. Whereas before, the relationship between race and negative staff experience was not statistically significant, once a larger, more representative sample is taken, the results change. We see that race has a statistically significant relationship with negative experiences with staff. This example highlights the importance of sampling, sample sizes, representative sampling, and also continually evaluating results.

12.5 Calculating Chi-Square in R Commander

More often than not, researchers will not be presented with a contingency table of results like Tables 12.4 and 12.6. The likely scenario is that they will have a spreadsheet of data or will be required to enter data into a spreadsheet and then run the chi-square test. As with any statistical test, the setup of the data is very

	A	B	C	D
1	id	race	neg	
2	1	1	1	
3	2	0	1	
4	3	0	0	
5	4	1	1	
6	5	1	1	
7	6	1	0	
8	7	1	1	
9	8	1	1	
10	9	1	1	
11	10	1	1	
12	11	1	1	
13	12	1	1	
14	13	1	1	
15	14	1	1	

Figure 12.1 Race and negative experience with staff data screenshot

important. However, keeping the data organization simple using the KISS method (Keep It Simple, Sam) will allow the researcher to easily run analyses in any software system and allow the data to be archived for later use should other researchers want to use the dataset for their own analyses.

The raw data from Table 12.6 is available in the Companion Site (*staff_race_data*) (www.cambridge.org/scheller), and a screenshot of part of the dataset is shown in Figure 12.1. The codebook is also included in the Companion Site, but the coding is simple. The "id" variable is simply a unique identifier for each of the respondents to the hypothetical survey. The "race" column indicates the respondent's race, with a value of 1 indicating a white respondent, and a value of 0 indicating a non-white respondent. Finally, the "neg" column is each respective respondent's answer to the question of whether or not they had a negative experience with health department staff. A value of 1 indicates a yes response – they had a negative experience. A value of 0 indicates no negative experience with staff. Looking at the data in Figure 12.1, respondent number 2 (id = 2) has values of 0 for "race" and 1 for "neg," meaning this particular respondent was non-white and indicated that they had a negative

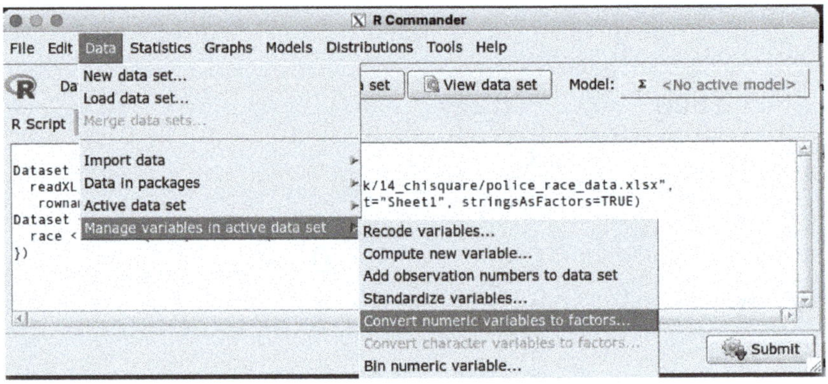

Figure 12.2 Recoding numeric to factor, part 1

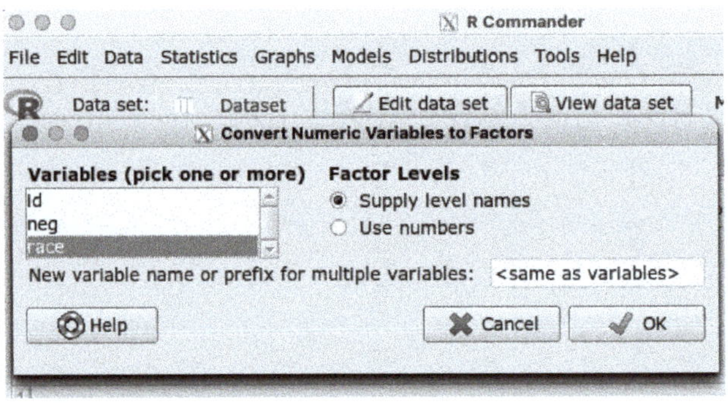

Figure 12.3 Recoding numeric to factor, part 2

experience with staff. Respondent number 3 (id = 3) has values of 0 for "race" and 0 for "neg," indicating that this is a non-white individual that reported *not* having a negative interaction with staff.

Unlike other software programs, the R Commander prefers to have numeric values, as they are coded in this dataset turned into factor (string) variables for conducting the chi-square test. Instead of having the datasets ready in the correct form for you to analyze, I have included the numeric version of the datasets so that you can practice recoding numeric variables into factor variables. It is good practice in case you are not faced with having the best case scenario of the data already in a form ready for analysis. Therefore, load the *staff_race_data* file into the R Commander. Make sure you have access to the codebook in the Companion Site so that you correctly recode the variables.

Begin with the race variable. Recode the value of 0 into "non-white" and the value of 1 into "white." To do this, do the following:

Step 1: Click Data → Manage variables in active data set → Convert numeric variables to factors (Figure 12.2).

Step 2: Highlight the variable needing to be converted to factor. In this case, it is the "race" variable. Click OK (Figure 12.3).

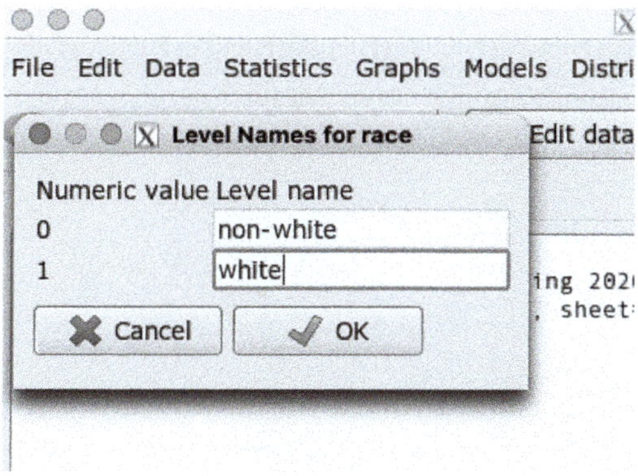

Figure 12.4 Recoding numeric to factor, part 3

Step 3: A warning box will appear stating "Variable race already exists. Overwrite variable?" Click Yes. This permanently changes the race variable from numeric to factor. If desired, you may create a new variable, "race2," as we have done in previous chapters. It is up to you based upon your preference. Either will work.

Step 4: A new box will emerge with the numeric values of the variable and text boxes for you to type in their description. Use the codebook for the dataset. A value of 0 corresponds to "non-white." Enter that into the text box for 0. A value of 1 corresponds to "white". Enter that into the text box for 1. Then click OK (Figure 12.4).

The changes should be applied to the dataset. You can always click the "View data set" button in the R Commander to visually inspect the changes.

Step 5: Following Steps 1–4, recode the "neg" variable from numeric to factor. Per the codebook, a value of 0 corresponds to "No" and a value of 1 corresponds to "Yes."

Once the variables have been recoded from numeric to factor, a chi-square test can be conducted using the R Commander. To conduct the chi-square test, do the following:

Step 1: Click Statistics → Contingency tables → Two-way table (Figure 12.5). A pop-up box will appear.

Step 2: Highlight the dependent variable in the row box. For this example, the dependent variable is "neg."

Step 3: Highlight the independent variable in the column box. For this example, the independent variable is "race" (Figure 12.6).

Step 4: Click the Statistics tab.

Step 5: Make sure the "Column percentages" bubble is checked along with the "Chi-square test of independence" box (Figure 12.7). Click OK.

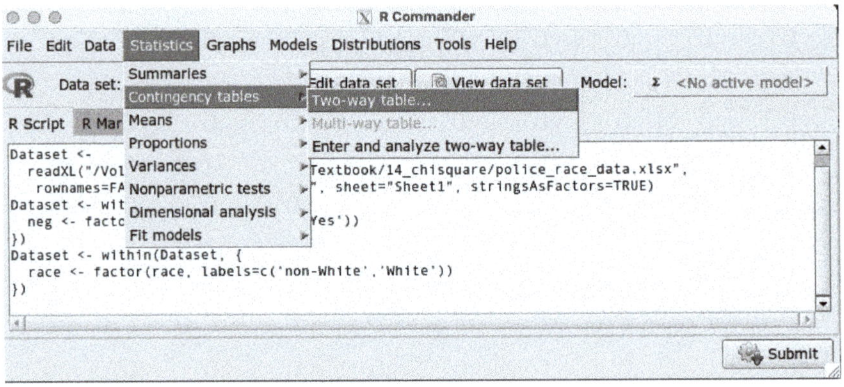

Figure 12.5 Chi-square in R Commander, part 1

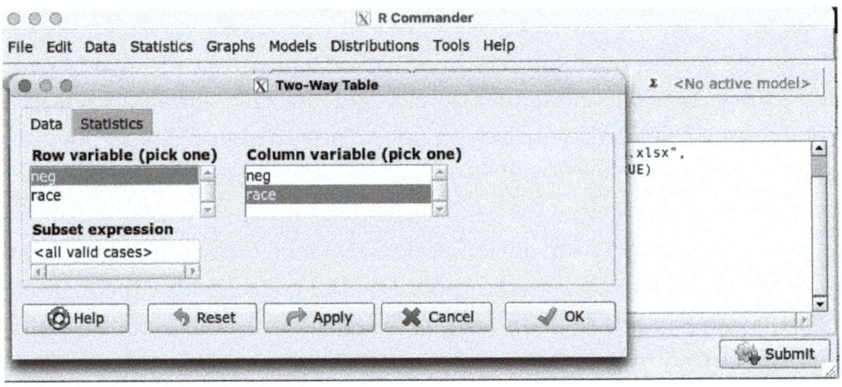

Figure 12.6 Chi-square in R Commander, part 2

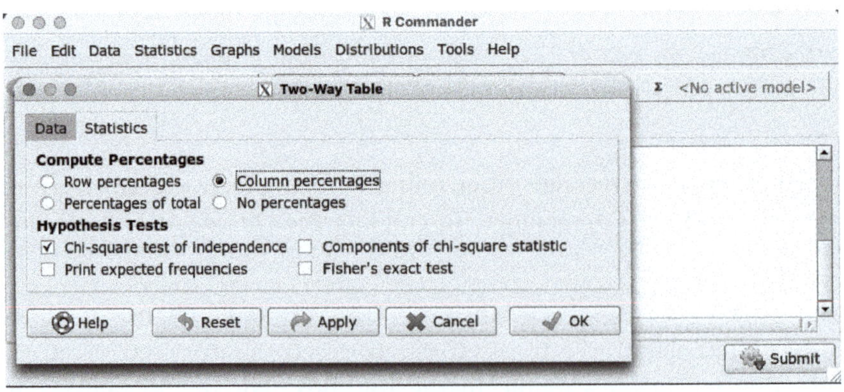

Figure 12.7 Chi-square in R Commander, part 3

The resulting output should look like Figure 12.8.

The R Commander output presents a frequency table that should correspond to Table 12.4. Check the rows/columns and the numbers. The only difference is the position of the rows. Whereas Table 12.4 has the first row as “Yes,” the R Commander output has the first row as “No.” The same juxtaposition exists for the R Commander

```
Frequency table:
      race
neg   non-White White
  No         25    98
  Yes        41    48

        Pearson's Chi-squared test

data:  .Table
X-squared = 15.96, df = 1, p-value = 0.0000647
```

Figure 12.8 Chi-square in R Commander output

output and Table 12.6. However, all of the substantive values for each row/column cell/category should match.

The R Commander output lists the chi-square value as 15.96. When we calculated the chi-square value, we came up with 15.95. The 0.01 difference is due to rounding when calculating by hand – substantively, there is no major difference. The R Commander output also lists the statistical significance level as 0.0000647. This p-value is obviously less than 0.05 (95% confidence level) and less than 0.01 (99% confidence level). Therefore, as with our by-hand calculation, we see that there is a statistically significant relationship between race and negative interactions with health department staff. As before, to determine what is driving this relationship, we can look at the column percentages in the R Commander output. Among the non-white respondents, 37.9% indicated that they had not had a negative experience with staff. 62.1% of non-white respondents indicated that they had a negative experience with staff. Among the white respondents, 67.1% indicated that they had not had a negative experience with staff. 32.9% indicated that they had experienced a negative experience with staff. With the statistically significant chi-square statistic and the column percentages, the pattern of the relationship is fairly clear. We can conclude that white respondents in the survey were statistically less likely to indicate that they had a negative experience with health department staff compared to non-white respondents.

12.6 Limitations of Chi-Square

The biggest substantive limitation of the chi-square test is that it *DOES NOT* show the direction of that relationship, but more importantly, it *DOES NOT* show the strength of the relationship between the independent and dependent variables. We will need to use regression to help understand these limitations. In the previous example with race and negative experiences with health staff, the data revealed a statistically significant relationship between race and negative experiences. The chi-square statistic did not show the direction of the relationship. We had to calculate the column percentages to get a sense of the direction of the relationship. What about the strength of the relationship? We know that the relationship is statistically significant at the 99% confidence level. But what does that really tell us? How much more likely are non-white individuals to have a negative experience with health staff compared to white individuals? To better understand the independent effect of race on negative experiences with health staff, a regression analysis would need to be conducted. In this example, given that the dependent variable is coded Yes/No, it would be a logistic regression, which is covered in Chapter 18.

Another limitation of chi-square analysis is that when there are multiple categories of the independent and/or dependent variable, interpretation of the results and determining what affects the significance becomes much more difficult. In this chapter, we have only analyzed 2 × 2 contingency tables, or tables with two categories for the independent variable and two categories for the dependent variable. The race and health department staff example had two categories for race (white v. non-white) and two categories for negative experiences with staff (Yes v. No). What if there were more categories regarding the dependent and independent variables? For example, suppose we were interested in surveying citizens on whom they voted for in the 2020 U.S. Presidential election based upon party identification. The dependent variable would be whom they voted for, and let's assume the options are Trump, Biden, Other, or Did Not Vote. This variable has four categories. Now, suppose the party identification categories asked are Democrat, Republican, Green, Independent, and Other. There are five party identification categories. We now have a 4 × 5 contingency table. Even with the ability to include column percentages, the table could become messy, hard to read, and with a chi-square statistic, nearly impossible to determine a relationship. Thus, this is a limitation of chi-square that can better be addressed using a type of regression analysis discussed in later chapters.

12.7 An Applied Example

Neighborhood organizations like neighborhood and homeowners associations are common citizen-led groups of residents that work to improve neighborhood conditions and promote community in neighborhoods. Neighborhood associations are often registered as 501c(3) nonprofit organizations. They usually have bylaws and a governing board, but the board and association have no legal authority over residents. If residents are upset about a neighbor that painted their house in camouflage, there is no recourse as long as the neighbor is not violating any municipal codes. A neighborhood association usually cannot govern its residents in a contractually binding manner. Therefore, most neighborhood associations engage in activities like block parties, neighborhood cleanup, and working with local government officials on neighborhood issues of concern/interest.

On the contrary, homeowners associations (HOAs) are much more formally organized with greater governing powers and can impose rules and regulations on residents that are contractually binding. The HOA has a governing board, bylaws, and rules that all residents must abide by. Residents usually know this once they purchase a property in an HOA, since the HOA charges dues to each unit and provides the neighborhood's rules and regulations. The dues are usually used for neighborhood maintenance and amenities like tennis courts, pools, community centers, etc. The rules/regulations, known as the neighborhood covenants, are legal documents. The neighbor that painted their house camouflage would likely be in violation of an HOA's rules (most HOAs restrict the types of changes and improvements that can be made to properties – often the construction materials and the colors of houses). Since HOA rules are binding, the HOA board could cite (through a property lien) the neighbor and require them to repaint their house to an approved color. All of this is to say that HOAs are more formally organized associations than neighborhood associations – essentially their own micro-governments – but growing in popularity, especially for new housing communities.

Some researchers attempt to understand the differences between neighborhood associations and HOAs. The *associations_survey* in the Companion Site (www.cambridge.org/scheller) is a real survey that was sent to neighborhood association and HOA presidents, with questions asking about their association's structure and activities. One of the questions in the survey (available in the *Associations_Codebook* in the Companion Site) asks whether or not the association engages in lobbying at the municipal level. A potential research/alternative hypothesis could be that HOAs engage in more lobbying at the municipal level than neighborhood associations. This hypothesis may be based upon the fact that HOAs charge membership dues that are usually much higher than neighborhood associations. Maybe HOAs are in a better position in regards to resources to lobby municipal government officials to pursue policies/actions to the neighborhood's benefit. A null hypothesis for this relationship would be that there is no relationship between association type and whether or not the association engages in lobbying at the municipal level.

To test the research/alternative hypothesis, it will be necessary to use the "type" variable as the independent variable. It is coded 0 for a neighborhood association and 1 for an HOA. The dependent variable will be the "lobby" variable. It is coded 0 for a No response and 1 for a Yes response. If you want to follow along, you may run this test by first recoding each of the variables from numeric to factor using the steps outlined in this chapter. The next step is to run the chi-square test in the R Commander with "lobby" as the dependent variable and "type" as the independent variable. The chi-square results appear in Figure 12.9.

The contingency table with percentages in Figure 12.9 reveals that 48.6 percent of neighborhood associations lobby local government, compared to 28.1 percent of HOAs. The difference appears fairly large, but is it statistically significant? No. The chi-square statistic is 2.94 with a p-value of 0.086. The relationship is statistically significant at the 90% confidence level, but not the 95% confidence level widely used in social science research. Therefore, we would accept the null hypothesis of no relationship between neighborhood organization type and whether or not they lobby local government. Based upon this sample, we would conclude that there is no

```
Frequency table:
     type
lobby NA HOA
  No  18  23
  Yes 17   9

Column percentages:
       type
lobby      NA   HOA
  No     51.4  71.9
  Yes    48.6  28.1
  Total 100.0 100.0
  Count  35.0  32.0

        Pearson's Chi-squared test

data:  .Table
X-squared = 2.9429, df = 1, p-value = 0.08626
```

Figure 12.9 Lobbying by neighborhood organization chi-square test

difference in lobbying activity between neighborhood v. homeowners associations in the larger population.

12.8 Summary

This chapter focused on an important statistical test widely used in the social sciences known as chi-square. It is appropriate to use when both the independent and dependent variables are measured at the nominal level. The number of categories is of no importance for running the test. It is considered a nonparametric test and does not rely on a Z or t distribution like previous chapters. Despite this, the chi-square distribution is easily interpretable from the statistical output and interpreted in a similar manner as t-tests in regards to rejecting the null hypothesis and understanding the p-values.

As with other tests previously covered in this textbook, one should not engage in making definitive causal statements based upon statistically significant results from a chi-square test. Causality cannot be determined from a chi-square test – remember correlation does not necessarily mean causation. The chi-square test can show statistically significant relationships/patterns between variables, but is limited to this conclusion unless the elements of experimental design have been met. With most social science research, especially surveys like the one used in this chapter, experimental design was not used, so we must stop at simply noting any statistically significant relationships. With a nominal dependent variable with two categories, one recourse is to use a logistic regression, the topic of Chapter 18 in this textbook. A nominal variable with more than two categories will likely use a multinomial regression – an advanced topic not covered in many public administration courses and texts – but a very useful technique for those interested in advanced statistics and for those whose careers will be focused on advanced data analysis.

PRACTICE PROBLEMS

Conceptual Problems

1. Explain the differences between the t-test, ANOVA, and chi-square. Create a table showing when each is appropriate to use based upon the level of measurement for the dependent and independent variables.
2. For each of the scenarios below, indicate whether or not chi-square would be an appropriate statistical test. Explain why/why not. For each scenario, the dependent variable is labeled DV and the independent variable is labeled IV. Each variable's coding is presented in the parentheses if not apparent from the variable description/label.
   a. DV: Political party affiliation (Democrat, Republican, Independent, Other)
   IV: Age (years)
   b. DV: Voted in previous election (Yes, No)
   IV: Race (White, African-American, Other)
   c. DV: Attended public art exhibit (Yes, No)
   IV: Income (in dollars)
   d. DV: Gallons of Rio Grande water used by pecan farmers
   IV: Inches of rain during the previous year
   e. DV: State infrastructure quality (Good, Average, Poor)
   IV: Region (West, Midwest, South, Northeast)
   f. DV: Satisfaction with city comprehensive plan (Strongly Satisfied, Satisfied, Neutral, Dissatisfied, Strongly Dissatisfied)
   IV: Gender (Male, Female, Other)
   g. DV: Preferred choice of transportation (Bus, Rail, Car, Walking, Bike, Other)
   IV: College Graduate (Yes, No)
   h. DV: Type of employment (Government, Nonprofit sector, Private sector, Other)
   IV: College major (Science, Social Science, Arts, Humanities, Other)
3. For each of the research statements below, identify the independent and dependent variables, provide research and null hypotheses for the researcher, and come up with an operationalization of each variable appropriate to run a chi-square test.
   a. A researcher wants to understand if being a registered voter is related to an individual volunteering in a political campaign.
   b. A researcher has a state budgetary dataset that contains data on government revenues/expenditures and whether or not the state is a red state (Republican) or blue state (Democrat). She thinks blue states are more likely to have budget deficits than red states.
   c. A local animal shelter is trying to determine how to market pet adoptions to increase adoptions and prevent euthanization of sheltered animals. The

marketing director thinks that certain genders are more likely to adopt different animals. The director collects information on the type of animal adopted and gender.

4. With a chi-square test, an analyst has observed data based upon various categories of the dependent and independent variables. Without using mathematics, explain how these observed values are used to determine if there is a relationship between the independent and dependent variable. How does this connect to the research and null hypotheses of the chi-square test?

Problems by Hand

5. Local governments are increasingly faced with issues regarding sustainability related to population growth, environmental challenges, and climate change. Suppose a researcher is interested in comparing two forms of local government on whether or not they have a long-term, comprehensive sustainability plan. The researcher wants to compare cities with a council-manager system of government to cities with a strong mayor form of government. As a quick reference, council-manager local governments have an elected city council that serves as the legislative branch of government. The council usually appoints a city manager to handle the day-to-day executive tasks of the city. The mayor in this system is usually much weaker, with the bulk of executive implementation left to the city manager and his/her office. In a strong mayor system, an elected city council usually serves as the legislative branch of the government, and an elected mayor is responsible for the executive functions, much in the same manner as the U.S. national government, just on a smaller scale.

   Suppose the researcher believes cities with a strong mayor system will be more likely to have a comprehensive sustainability plan, based upon the idea that the council and mayor are both elected and thus likely to implement a sustainability plan for future electoral purposes. The researcher randomly selected cities and notes their form of government and whether or not the city has a sustainability plan. The data appear in the table below.

   Form of Government & Sustainability Plan

	Strong Mayor	Council-Manager	Total
Has Plan	29	17	46
No Plan	24	15	39
Total	53	32	85

   a. Identify the researcher's independent and dependent variables.
   b. What is the researcher's research/alternative hypothesis?
   c. What would be the researcher's null hypothesis?

d. Below each substantive cell in the table, include the percent of observations in each column (show the percentage of observations for each cell by column).
e. Conduct a chi-square test: calculate the chi-square value and determine if it is statistically significant. Interpret the result. Was the researcher's hypothesis supported?

6. A human resources director is concerned that there may be some bias in who advances to the interview stage in their large public organization. The director is concerned that applicants with veteran status are not advancing to the interview stage compared to non-veterans. The director collects data on all applicants in their organization, noting which applicants advanced to the interview stage and which applicants are veterans. The data appear below:

Applicant Interviews

	Veteran	Non-Veteran	Total
Interview	18	42	60
No Interview	105	175	280
Total	123	217	340

a. What is the researcher's research hypothesis?
b. What is the null hypothesis?
c. Below each substantive cell in the table, include the percent of observations in each column (show the percentage of observations for each cell by column).
d. Conduct a chi-square test: calculate the chi-square value and determine if it is statistically significant. Interpret the result. Was the researcher's hypothesis supported?

7. Suppose a different HR director is interested in whether or not there is a relationship between race and whether or not an applicant advanced to the interview stage. The director collects the following data and wants to conduct a chi-square test.

Applicant Interviews

	White	Afr. Amer.	Hispanic	Other	Total
Interview	41	7	14	21	83
No Interview	126	85	30	39	280
Total	167	92	44	60	363

a. What is a plausible research hypothesis?
b. What is the null hypothesis?
c. Below each substantive cell in the table, include the percent of observations in each column (show the percentage of observations for each cell by column).
d. How many degrees of freedom should be used in this analysis?
e. Conduct a chi-square test: calculate the chi-square value and determine if it is statistically significant. Interpret the result. Was the hypothesis supported?

R Commander Problems

8. Suppose a fictional city offers a tuition reimbursement for employees seeking to obtain a Master's degree. The idea behind the tuition reimbursement program is that supporting their employees' advanced educational goals may lead to more promotions within the city. The city manager collects data on employees that have successfully obtained a Master's degree using the city's reimbursement program and whether or not they were promoted within a year of graduation. The manager specifically wants to know if candidates with an MPA degree are more likely to be promoted than those with other types of Master's degrees. The data collected by the manager is located in the Companion Site (www.cambridge.org/scheller), with the dataset named *mpa* and the respective codebook *mpa_codebook*.

a. Present plausible null and research hypotheses for the city manager.
b. Conduct a chi-square test with the dependent variable of whether or not the employee was promoted and the independent variable whether or not the employee earned an MPA. Present the contingency table and interpret the chi-square statistic and its significance. What can you conclude?
c. Change the independent variable to the type of degree earned by the employee. Run the chi-square test, present the contingency table, and interpret the chi-square statistic and its significance.
d. What other factors/variables may account for the results? Explain.

9. The Transportation Security Administration (TSA) is responsible for inspecting traveler documents at airports before travelers are permitted to enter airport terminals. Travelers present their government-issued identification and pass through metal detectors and/or body image scanners to help prevent terrorists from sneaking weapons or incendiary devices onto airplanes. Sometimes, travelers are randomly selected to be further inspected with a pat-down and carry-on baggage inspection to check for weapons or incendiary devices. The supervisor at one airport is concerned that travelers wearing religious headwear are more likely to be "randomly" selected for additional inspection, thus questioning the randomness of the inspections. The supervisor observes TSA agent behavior for one hour, noting whether or not the traveler was selected for additional inspection and whether or not the traveler was wearing any form of religious headwear. The fictional data are located in the *tsa* file in the Companion Site. The "traveler" variable is a unique identifier for each traveler. The "inspected" variable is coded Yes if the traveler was issued a secondary inspection and No if not. The "headwear" variable is coded Yes if the passenger was observed wearing religious headwear and No if not.

a. Propose plausible null and research hypotheses for the supervisor.
b. Produce the contingency table with column percentages.
c. Run a chi-square test and report the chi-square statistic and its significance.
d. Interpret the findings.

10. Open the *associations_survey* dataset in the R Commander and the *Associations_Codebook* for reference. Run a chi-square test and interpret the results for each of the following situations comparing neighborhood to homeowners associations (independent variable):

a. Dependent variable: the association has a pool.
b. Dependent variable: representatives report government and agency rulings that affect your association.
c. Dependent variable: the association has a professional manager.

11. City councils usually hold public hearings on their agenda items. Some city councils review liquor license applications of establishments seeking new liquor licenses or additions to their licenses. The *liquor_license* dataset in the Companion Site contains a real city's liquor license decisions for a council term. The unit of analysis is the individual application. During public hearings regarding liquor licenses, concerned citizens have the opportunity to express their opposition to proposed liquor licenses. City councils may take this opposition into consideration when approving/denying a liquor license. Test the hypothesis that there is a relationship between the presence of an opposition speaker ("speaker" variable) and a license being denied ("denial") by the council. The "opp_speaker" variable is coded "1" if the application had a speaker in opposition to it and 0 otherwise. The "denial" variable is coded "1" if the application was denied and "0" if the application was approved. Note that the dataset is in STATA form when uploading into the R Commander.

13

Ordinal Dependent Variables

13.1 Introduction

Most statistics textbooks, especially in public administration, omit discussion of analysis of ordinal level dependent variables using statistical tests. This omission is despite the fact that many variables of interest in surveys and data collected by researchers and practitioners are measured at the ordinal level. Likert scales are one of the most often used measures to gauge information related to levels of approval or agreement (Strongly Agree, Agree, Neutral, Disagree, Strongly Disagree). Other typical ordinal measures include degree of passage (high pass, low pass, low fail, high fail), quality (Excellent, Fair, Poor), and even age if measured with ranges (Less than 18, 18–30, 31–50, 51–70, 70+), etc.

Up until this point, we have only known how to graph ordinal measures with bar graphs and to calculate the descriptive statistic (median) to report central tendency. However, what if we want to engage in hypothesis testing with an ordinal level dependent variable? One relatively easy, yet unknown test that researchers and practitioners can use is the Wilcoxon rank sum test. It is akin to a t-test (Field, Miles, & Field , 2012); however, t-tests should not be used for ordinal dependent variables. The Wilcoxon rank sum test involves different assumptions and calculations, but the essential foundations of its use are the same – test the difference between groups on a dependent variable measured at the ordinal level. This short chapter will introduce the logic behind the Wilcoxon rank sum test, its assumptions, and when it is appropriate to use it. Then, a by-hand illustration will be used to explain the steps of the test, followed by how to run the test in the R Commander. Interpretation of the output and implications for hypothesis testing are also covered. Finally, a presentation on a test for dependent samples with ordinal level dependent variables (Wilcoxon signed rank test) in the R Commander concludes the chapter.

13.2 Logic of Wilcoxon Rank Sum Test

Let's look at a hypothetical research design example involving a public works department. The department is considering asking in the next fiscal year's budget for

Table 13.1 Streetlight safety survey

Neighborhood A	Neighborhood B
0	−2
1	−1
1	−1
2	−1
−1	0
2	1
2	1
2	

new, brighter LED streetlights for the city's streets. The public works department thinks these lights will improve residents' perception of safety and compel residents to engage in more outdoor activities in the evenings. Wanting to have more reliable data and analysis before asking for a million dollars in the next budget for LED lights, managers in the public works department decide to conduct a pilot study. They identify two very similar neighborhoods in the city in terms of demographics (racial composition, income, percent owner-occupied housing, region of city, quality/number of streetlights, etc.). The managers determine that these two neighborhoods are very similar in nearly every respect. They decide to install new LED streetlights in Neighborhood A, and to make no changes to the streetlights in Neighborhood B.

A few months after the installation of the LED streetlights in Neighborhood A, the managers randomly send a survey to residents in both Neighborhood A and Neighborhood B, asking questions related to their recent outdoor activities and how safe they feel walking in the neighborhood at night. They ask respondents to answer how much they agree with the following statement, "I feel safe walking in my neighborhood at night":

Strongly Agree (2)
Agree (1)
Neither Agree nor Disagree (0)
Disagree (−1)
Strongly Disagree (−2)

The coding for each response is in parentheses. A "Strongly Agree" response receives a value of 2, while a "Strongly Disagree" response receives a value of −2. Table 13.1 shows the data for each neighborhood.

The process to conduct the rank sum test begins with ordering the data from values of low to high. This step is depicted in Table 13.2, in the "Response"

Table 13.2 Streetlight safety survey with rank scores

Response	Neighborhood	Position	Rank Score
−2	B	1	1
−1	B	2	3.5
−1	B	3	3.5
−1	B	4	3.5
−1	A	5	3.5
0	A	6	6.5
0	B	7	6.5
1	A	8	9.5
1	A	9	9.5
1	B	10	9.5
1	B	11	9.5
2	A	12	13.5
2	A	13	13.5
2	A	14	13.5
2	A	15	13.5

and "Neighborhood" columns. Each individual response is listed in the "Response" column and its corresponding neighborhood in the "Neighborhood" column.

The "Position" column is simply a count of the order position of the respective response value. It is ordered numerically from 1 to infinity. In this example, it is ordered from 1 to 15, representing the fifteen unique observations/responses for Neighborhood A and Neighborhood B. The next step is to rank score each observation/response, starting with a rank score of 1. So, starting with the first row of Table 13.2, the response of −2 for Neighborhood B is in the first position. There are no other values of −2, so the rank score for this response is 1. This corresponds to the rank score value of 1 in the "Rank Score" column.

The next response value is −1, and from Table 13.2, we see that the response of −1 appears four times (three times for Neighborhood B and one time for Neighborhood A). What do we make of this? Those four response values of −1 correspond to Positions 2, 3, 4, and 5. Since they are equal response values, we have to average the rank score by position. Therefore, we add each position value and divide by the number of responses at that particular value. For a of −1, we thus have:

$$\frac{2+3+4+5}{4} = 3.5$$

All −1 responses receive a rank score of 3.5.

Likewise, with the response value of 0, those responses correspond to a position of 6 and 7, respectively. We thus have:

$$\frac{6+7}{2} = 6.5$$

There are two responses of 0, hence the denominator containing a value of "2." These two responses are in positions 6 and 7, hence the addition of 6 and 7 in the numerator.

For the response value of 1, there are four responses populating positions 8–11. The calculation for the rank score is:

$$\frac{8+9+10+11}{4} = 9.5.$$

The same logic can be applied to the value of 2, occupying positions 12–15. The calculation for the rank score for the responses of 2 is thus:

$$\frac{12+13+14+15}{4} = 13.5.$$

The next step is to sum the rank scores for each neighborhood. Rank scores for Neighborhood A are: 3.5, 6.5, 9.5, 9.5, 13.5, 13.5, 13.5, and 13.5. Therefore, the sum of rank scores for Neighborhood A is 83. Rank scores for Neighborhood B are: 1, 3.5, 3.5, 3.5, 6.5, 9.5, and 9.5. Therefore, the sum of rank scores for Neighborhood B is 37.

Though we will not go further in the mathematical calculations, the Wilcoxon rank sum score test determines if there is a statistically significant difference between Neighborhood A and Neighborhood B, or the values of 83 and 37, respectively. In the terms of a null hypothesis, the Wilcoxon rank sum test determines if we can reject the null hypothesis that Neighborhood A and Neighborhood B do not differ in their perception of safety after Neighborhood A receives the new, LED streetlights. Just eyeballing the rank sum data, we would likely conclude that there are statistically significant differences between Neighborhood A and Neighborhood B. The R Commander can conduct a relatively easy test to determine if these differences are statistically significant.

13.3 Wilcoxon Rank Sum Test in the R Commander

Proper data input and organization are imperative to correctly conducting the Wilcoxon rank sum test for any statistical software. The data from Table 13.1 should be entered into Excel in a particular format to ensure ease of computation for the software. Figure 13.1 depicts a screenshot of the correct data entry in Excel. The column labeled "response" indicates each piece of data or individual response to the survey question regarding perceived neighborhood safety. The "neighborhood" column indicates the neighborhood from each respective response. Neighborhood A is coded as a 1, and Neighborhood B is coded as a 0. This 1/0 coding is arbitrary and by preference. Neighborhood A could be coded 0 and Neighborhood B coded as 1.

	A	B
1	response	neighborhood
2	0	1
3	1	1
4	1	1
5	2	1
6	-1	1
7	2	1
8	2	1
9	2	1
10	-2	0
11	-1	0
12	-1	0
13	-1	0
14	0	0
15	1	0
16	1	0

Figure 13.1 Neighborhood streetlight safety data

One can now upload this spreadsheet *safety* dataset in Companion Site into the R Commander. Every piece of statistics software has its own preferences for how data is to be labeled depending upon the test. Recall from Chapter 4 that best practices of data entry are to use numbers since some software programs are unable to compute values in words or letters (string variables). For the Wilcoxon rank sum test, we need to convert the grouping variable, or the "neighborhood" variable, into a string or factor variable. This is the first step in conducting the Wilcoxon rank sum test. Additional steps for running the test and the output appear below.

Step 1: Convert the grouping variable to a string or factor variable. Click Data → Manage variables in active dataset → Convert numeric variables to factors (Figure 13.2).

Step 2: Highlight the grouping variable (in this case, the "neighborhood" variable). Make sure "Supply level names" is checked, and then click OK (Figure 13.3).

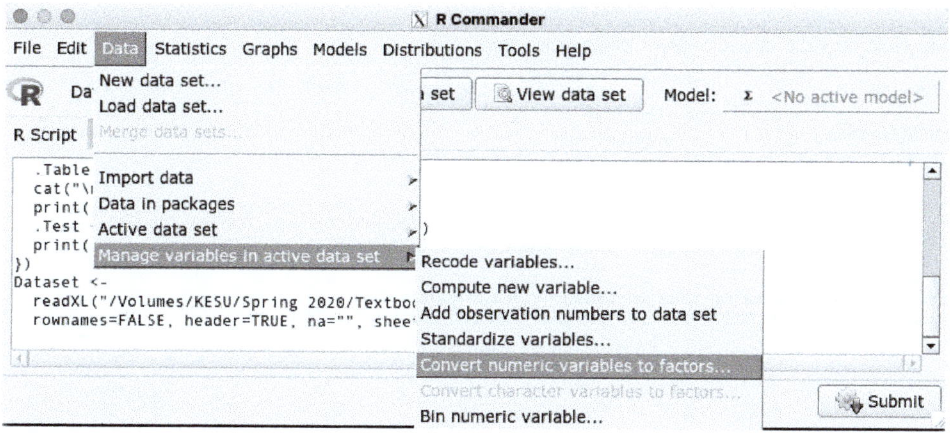

Figure 13.2 Numeric to factor, part 1

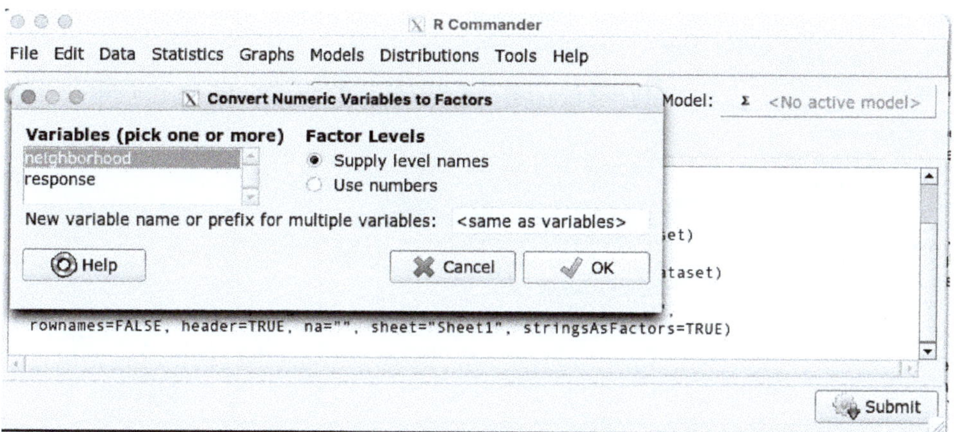

Figure 13.3 Numeric to factor, part 2

Step 3: Click Yes if a box appears asking you to overwrite the variable. Doing so will make the changes permanent in the dataset. Alternatively, you could just create a new variable name in Step 2 in the "New variable name..." box.

Step 4: Another box will emerge asking to provide a name for each numeric variable. Enter accordingly. In this particular example, a value of 0 represents Neighborhood B, and a value of 1 represents Neighborhood A, as shown in Figure 13.4. Once your variable names have been added, click OK.

Step 5: To run the Wilcoxon rank sum test, click Statistics → Nonparametric tests → Two-sample Wilcoxon test (Figure 13.5).

Step 6: Select the appropriate grouping variable (in the example, the "neighborhood" variable) and the appropriate response variable ("response" in the example) (Figure 13.6).

Step 7: Click the "Options" tab and look for the "Type of Test" options. Check "Exact" (Figure 13.7).

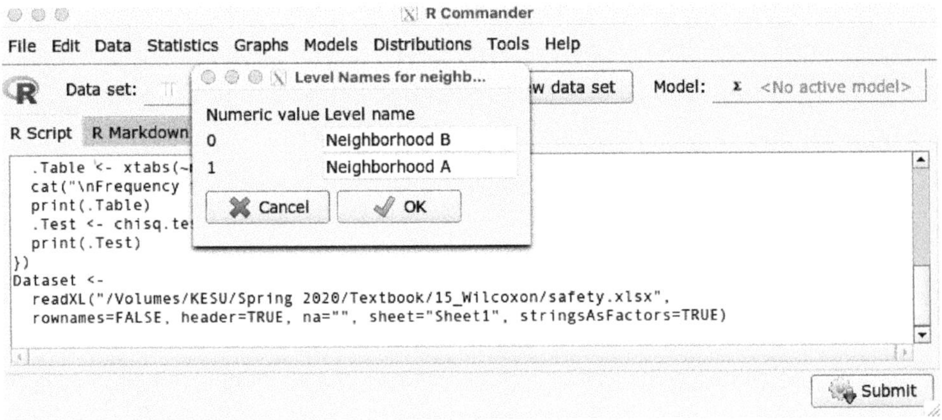

Figure 13.4 Numeric to factor, part 3

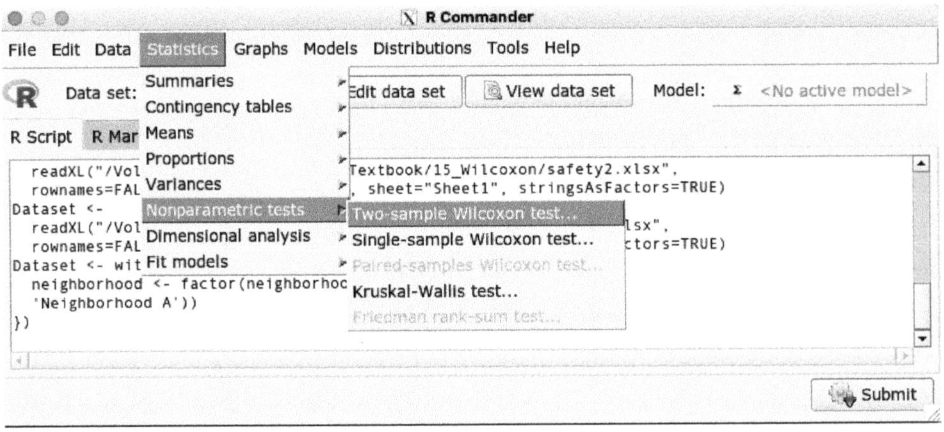

Figure 13.5 Wilcoxon rank sum test, part 1

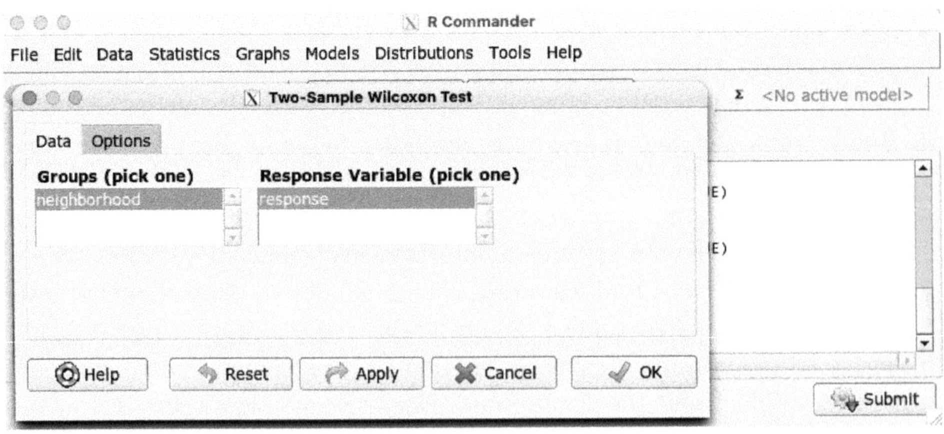

Figure 13.6 Wilcoxon rank sum test, part 2

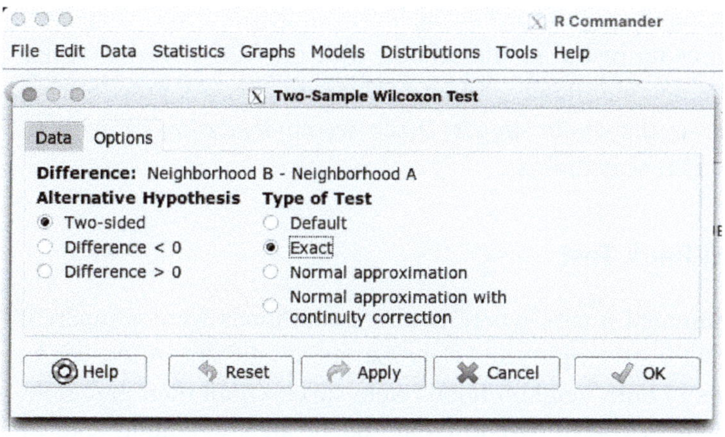

Figure 13.7 Wilcoxon rank sum test, part 3

Step 8: Click OK, and the output should look like Figure 13.8.

```
Rcmdr> Tapply(response ~ neighborhood, median, na.action=na.omit, data=Dataset)
Rcmdr+    # medians by group
Neighborhood B Neighborhood A
          -1.0            1.5

Rcmdr> wilcox.test(response ~ neighborhood, alternative='two.sided', exact=TRUE,
Rcmdr+    correct=FALSE, data=Dataset)

        Wilcoxon rank sum test

data:  response by neighborhood
W = 9, p-value = 0.02368
alternative hypothesis: true location shift is not equal to 0
```

Figure 13.8 Wilcoxon rank sum test output

While the R Commander does not report the rank sums that were calculated by hand, it does provide one crucial statistic – the significance level. It does provide the group medians, with Neighborhood A having a median rating score of 1.5 to Neighborhood B's −1.0. This helps you to know that, overall, Neighborhood A has a higher rating. The R Commander implicitly calculates the rank sums and then compares them against each other, calculating whether or not the difference between the groups (in this case, Neighborhood A and Neighborhood B) in neighborhood safety is statistically significant. The output shows a p-value of 0.02368, indicating a statistically significant difference between Neighborhood A and Neighborhood B on perceptions of safety. From our calculations by hand, we know that the rank sum for Neighborhood A was 83 and Neighborhood B was 37. Therefore, given how the safety measure is coded (higher values indicating more with feeling safe), we can conclude that residents in Neighborhood A feel safer than residents in Neighborhood B. Neighborhood A's safety ratings are higher than Neighborhood B's safety ratings, and this difference is statistically significant at the 95% confidence level. Therefore, we can conclude that residents in the neighborhood with the LED streetlights felt safer than residents in the neighborhood without LED streetlights. As practitioners and policy evaluators, the results would suggest that a recommendation be made to the city to invest more in LED streetlights.

13.4 Wilcoxon Signed Rank Test

The previous example presented a case where two neighborhoods were compared: Neighborhood A received LED streetlights and Neighborhood B did not. A few weeks after installation, residents in both neighborhoods were surveyed on their perceived levels of safety. This example involved two different, independent neighborhoods or samples and then a statistical test of the difference in safety perceptions through the Wilcoxon rank sum test. This test is similar to an independent samples t-test. What if a researcher examines one group, studying the effects of a policy or program on a sample by observing the sample before the policy and then observing the sample after the policy? There is only one sample, which is comprised of the same individuals/entities. All individuals/entities are the same before the policy and after the policy. Such a situation is analogous to a dependent samples t-test, where the same group of individuals are studied over time. Let's return to the same LED streetlight example, but alter the scenario.

Suppose the public works department surveys residents of Neighborhood A before implementation of the installation of LED streetlights. They would like to get a sense of residents' perception of safety prior to the policy as a type of baseline test or pre-test. They ask respondents to answer how much they agree with the following statement, "I feel safe walking in my neighborhood at night":

Strongly Agree (2)
Agree (1)
Neither Agree nor Disagree (0)
Disagree (−1)
Strongly Disagree (−2)

The data appear in Table 13.3, with the respondents' names in the first column, their score of safety before the installation of LED streetlights in the second column, and then their responses to safety after installation of the streetlights in the last column.

Calculating the Wilcoxon signed rank test has a number of steps, more involved than calculating the rank sum test. It is much easier to have software run the test. The data from Table 13.3 are contained in the *safety2* dataset in the Companion Site (www.cambridge.org/scheller). Opening the dataset, there are three columns, each representative of the columns in Table 13.3. To run the Wilcoxon signed rank test in the R Commander:

Step 1: Click Statistics → Nonparametric tests → Paired-samples Wilcoxon test (Figure 13.9).

Table 13.3 Streetlight safety survey, example 2

Respondent	Pre-Policy	Post-Policy
Deandre	0	0
Jane	−1	0
Danielle	−1	1
Maria	−2	−1
Osborne	0	0
Fernando	1	2
Isabel	1	2
Ashok	1	0

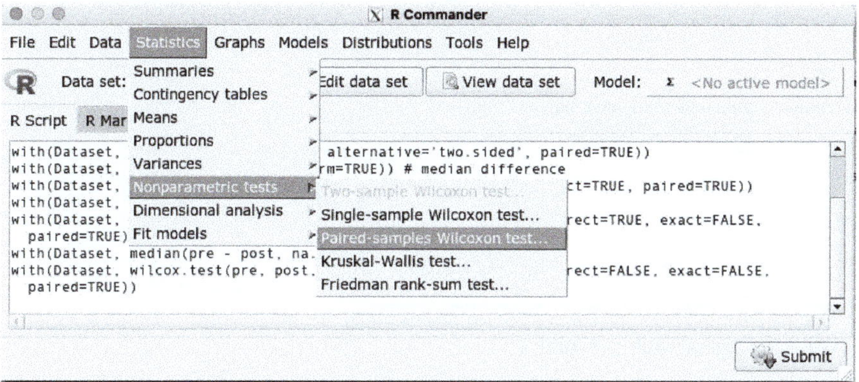

Figure 13.9 Wilcoxon signed rank test, part 1

Step 2: A box will appear asking for a selection of a "First variable" and a "Second variable." Before we select the variable, click the "Options" tab, so that we can tell the R Commander what type of test options it should include. Change the "Type of Test" to "Normal approximation" (Figure 13.10). The Wilcoxon signed rank test is sensitive to sample sizes, with sample sizes less than forty affecting the output if you select "Normal approximation" versus the "Default" or "Exact." Field, Miles, and Field (2012), in their chapter on nonparametric tests, do an excellent job explaining the intricacies of the different options for the Wilcoxon signed rank test that are beyond the scope of this textbook. For our purposes, we will select the normal approximation, because if one were to run this same dataset in STATA and SPSS (as shown on the Online Appendix), the results will match if using the "Normal approximation" option in the R Commander.

Step 3: Now, click back on the "Data" tab in the same window. In this example, we want the "pre" variable to be the "First variable," as it is the individuals' scores for neighborhood safety before the policy. The "Second variable"

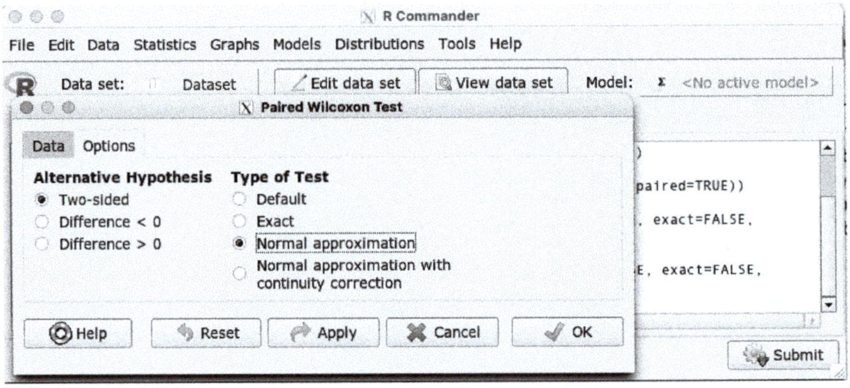

Figure 13.10 Wilcoxon signed rank test, part 2

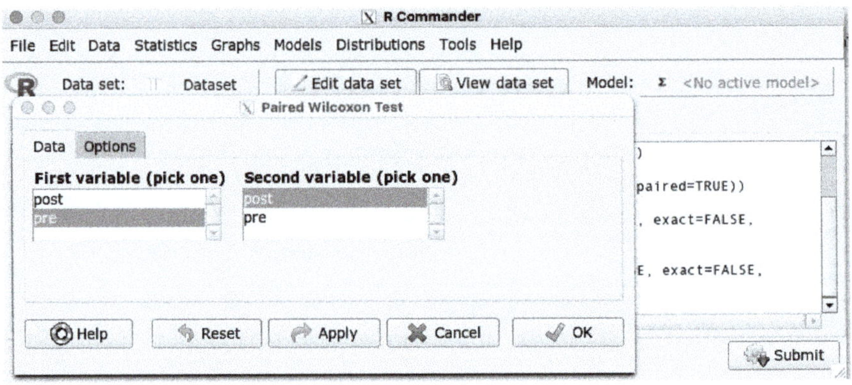

Figure 13.11 Wilcoxon signed rank test, part 3

```
        Wilcoxon signed rank test

data:  pre and post
V = 3, p-value = 0.09558
alternative hypothesis: true location shift is not equal to 0
```

Figure 13.12 Wilcoxon signed rank test output

should be "post" for our example as it is the individuals' neighborhood safety score after the new light policy. Highlight each of these respectively, and then click OK (Figure 13.11).

The results should emerge in the R Commander output window and look like Figure 13.12

The value to pay attention to is the p-value of significance. In this case, it is 0.0956, not less than or equal to 0.05 for the 95% confidence level of significance. Therefore, we cannot conclude that the safety scores changed significantly after the installation of the new streetlights. One key note is that the sample size is very small ($n = 8$), which we know makes it difficult to make conclusions regarding relationships between variables. A good researcher would likely try to obtain more observations. We should continue to interpret the results given by the R Commander, but make note of the small sample size.

13.5 Summary

This chapter has focused on the use of a lesser-known, but still valuable statistical tool for conducting public administration research – the Wilcoxon test. The Wilcoxon rank sum test is analogous to the independent samples t-test, but used when the dependent variable is ordinal and the observations are independent. Like the paired samples t-test, the Wilcoxon Signed Rank Test is used for ordinal level dependent variables that are dependent, usually resulting from repeat observations/sampling of the unit of analysis. However, unlike the t-test, the Wilcoxon tests (like ANOVA and chi-square) are considered nonparametric tests, relying on different test distributions and calculations.

The next four chapters shift back to parametric tests with interval dependent variables that are assumed to follow a normal distribution. Regressions constitute the bulk of statistical tests in the remaining chapters. It is a very common statistical method that helps researchers move closer to making stronger causal claims. The limitations of the tests we have covered so far have been their limited ability to establish causality as they test the strength, direction, and significance of relationships between variables. However, the oft-used phrase "correlation does not necessarily mean causation" has limited us from making causal claims. While OLS regression cannot definitively establish causality (conditions of causality must be met), it is a more robust test that better enables researchers to provide stronger evidence of causal relationships between variables.

PRACTICE PROBLEMS

Conceptual Problems

1. For each of the following scenarios, identify if a Wilcoxon test should be used. If so, identify which type of Wilcoxon test. If not, explain why, and which test may be better for the scenario.
   a. The relationship between number of speeding tickets issued by a police department and the color of the speeding car's paint (coded red, yellow, black, white, other).
   b. A study is proposed that would survey residents of a community on whether or not they are registered to vote (Yes/No), with a hypothesis that those living in a particular part of town (coded North, South, East, West, and Central) are more likely to be registered.

c. Employee performance is rated by the individual employee as "Poor, Average, Good, Superior," and the researcher wants to compare this measure based upon whether or not the employee attended a professional development conference in the past year (Yes/No).
d. A researcher is trying to understand the relationship between the amount an organization received in grant money (in dollars) and whether or not the organization is a faith-based organization.
e. A researcher is surveying 100 people in May and then the same 100 people in October, asking them how much they approve of the President's handling of the economy. Survey responses include Strongly Approve, Approve, Neutral, Disapprove, Strongly Disapprove. Fifty of the respondents were randomly assigned to watch a presidential debate in late September, and fifty were randomly assigned to not watch a September presidential debate.
f. A public hospital is trying to determine the effect of their post-natal nutrition classes on infant weights. Through a grant program, twenty randomly selected mothers/infants are enrolled in the program. A "control" group of twenty randomly selected mothers/infants are selected to be observed. Infants' weights are taken at one month of age and three months of age. The nutrition classes occur during month two.

2. Explain the differences between the Wilcoxon rank sum test and:
a. The Wilcoxon signed rank test
b. ANOVA
c. Chi-square
d. Independent samples t-test

Problems by Hand

3. A large public organization is debating whether or not to move to three-day in-person workdays with two days for remote work. One department (Department A) is test-piloting with this program, while Department B works a traditional five-day workweek. The manager of the public organization randomly selected six individuals from each department and asks, "How much do you like your current workday arrangement: Strongly like, Like, Neutral, Dislike, Strongly dislike." The manager codes the responses:

$2 =$ Strongly like
$1 =$ Like
$0 =$ Neutral
$-1 =$ Dislike
$-2 =$ Strongly dislike

The response data are presented in the following table:

Workweek data

Dept. A	Dept. B
2	0
2	0
1	0
1	−2
−0	−2
−1	−1

Calculate the rank scores and the sum of rank scores for each department. By how much do the sums differ?

R Commander Problems

4. Enter data from Problem #3 into Excel and then load into the R Commander.

a. Run the appropriate Wilcoxon test to test the differences between Department A and Department B. Show your results.

b. Do your R Commander results reflect your by-hand calculations?

c. Interpret whether or not the results are statistically significant. How do you know?

d. What are some limitations of making conclusions from this analysis?

5. Open the Associations Codebook and the *associations_survey* dataset in the Companion Site (www.cambridge.org/scheller). It is a survey of neighborhood and homeowners associations (HOA) presidents. Use the Wilcoxon rank sum test to test the following hypotheses. For each, report the results, interpret the findings, and determine if the hypothesis is supported:

a. HOAs are more likely than neighborhood associations to indicate that the association's main goal is to protect property values.

b. HOAs are more likely than neighborhood associations to indicate that city officials pay attention to the association's opinions.

c. HOAs are more likely than neighborhood associations to indicate that the association helps maintain the neighborhood's appearance.

d. HOAs are more likely than neighborhood associations to indicate that the association is an effective conduit between residents and city and county governments.

e. Neighborhood associations are more likely than HOAs to indicate that the association helps residents get to know one another.

f. Neighborhood associations are more likely than HOAs to indicate that the association helps foster a sense of community.

6. Suppose a school administrator is trying to determine if a new reading program introduced to students in their first month of school improves reading levels. Prior to the program, children are rated on their kindergarten reading levels on a scale from Deficient, Average, Above Average. The scores are coded as −1 for Deficient, 0 for Average, and 1 for Average. The trial reading program is implemented among the students in the first month and their reading levels measured according to the same scale and coding scheme. Results from the trial appear in the table below:

Student reading scores

Student	Pre-Policy	Post-Policy
1	−1	0
2	0	0
3	−1	0
4	−1	0
5	1	2
6	0	1

a. Enter the data into Excel and then upload into the R Commander.
b. Run the appropriate Wilcoxon test in the R Commander and report the results.
c. Interpret the results and any statistical significance.
d. What are some limitations of this data and test result? Explain.

PART 4

14

Bivariate Regression

14.1 Introduction

In Chapter 10 on t-tests, we examined data comparing fire department turnout times between stations that underwent a training module and those that did not. The dependent variable, turnout time, was an interval level measure, while the independent variable, before and after receiving training, was a two-category nominal variable. The dependent samples t-test revealed a statistically significant relationship between participation in the training module and shorter turnout times. However, correlation does not mean causation. Likewise, a statistically significant t-test that shows a relationship between two variables does not indicate causation. In the absence of a true experimental design, with a randomly assigned control group and treatment group(s), we cannot easily establish a causal relationship between an independent and a dependent variable. We can only say that the two variables are statistically related or correlated. Remember from Chapter 2 the conditions to establish a causal relationship, and most importantly, correlation does not necessarily mean causation! Our research design and statistical tests should stem from theory and our theoretical expectations of the relationship between an independent and dependent variable.

In this chapter, we will focus on total response times, and begin discussing regression as a new statistical test. This test is called bivariate regression, and this chapter goes into great detail to explain the fundamentals of regression and its ability to show the direction, strength, and statistical significance of relationships between variables, a dependent variable and an independent variable. While bivariate regression (and multivariate regression and logistic regression that are discussed in later chapters) cannot determine causality, it is a tool to help better understand relationships between independent and dependent variables. With regression, researchers can control for the effect of other variables that may affect the dependent variable. With the t-test, ANOVA, and chi-square, we only dealt with an independent variable and a dependent variable. In the social sciences, we rarely are able to conduct experiments, but we often have many datapoints and variables at hand to conduct analysis. Regression allows us to better understand the relationship between our independent variable of interest and the dependent variable, while taking into account the independent effects/relationships of other independent variables. Steps to conduct a regression by hand and with the R Commander are discussed in step-by-step detail. Graphing the relationship between variables is covered along with engaging in predictive relationships through bivariate regression.

14.2 Bivariate Regression by Hand

Even though most of the datasets public administrators use to analyze data contain hundreds, thousands, and maybe even millions of observations, it is much easier to understand the logic of bivariate regression and what the R Commander does when it runs a regression by conducting a regression by hand with a small dataset. Statistical software is only useful for analysis and research when the user knows what code or drop-down commands to utilize. First, we will examine a hypothetical emergency response dataset, then go into graphing the data, conducting the regression by hand, then conducting regression with the R Commander, and finally interpreting the findings.

Suppose a fire chief wants to know the effect of distance to an emergency on emergency response times. They want to be able to explain and predict response times knowing the distance from the fire station to the emergency when the station receives the emergency dispatch. For each emergency response covered by their station, the station's distance from the emergency in miles is collected, along with the amount of time in seconds it takes for the unit to arrive on scene. The fire chief hypothesizes a causal relationship between the two variables, with distance in miles as the independent variable, and the response time in seconds as the dependent variable. Their hypothesis is that response time *depends* upon the miles from the emergency. To formally show the relationship between the independent variable and the dependent variable, we represent the independent variable by X and the dependent variable by Y. This is standard convention in the social sciences. Therefore, the hypothesized relationship is:

$$\text{Response Time } (Y) \leftarrow \text{Distance to Emergency}(X)$$

The left-pointing arrow indicates that Distance to Emergency (X) affects Response Time (Y). The chief takes a random sample of their station's emergency responses and the data appear in Table 14.1.

The first step in understanding the statistical relationship between the independent variable and dependent variable is to plot the datapoints in a graph. The dependent variable should be represented on the y-axis and the independent variable on the x-axis, hence the use of Y to represent the dependent variable and X to represent the independent variable.

Plot each of the datapoints in Table 14.1 in a graph. Your graph should look something like Figure 14.1.

Table 14.1 Emergency response times

Table #	Distance (miles) (*X*)	Response Time (sec.) (*Y*)
1	3.1	491
2	2.5	364
3	1.7	253
4	0.8	163
5	0.5	125
6	1.9	310
7	1.3	210

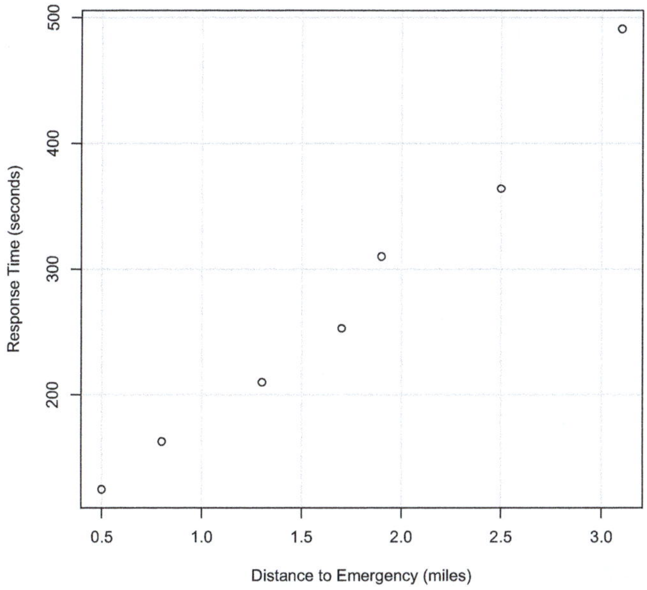

Figure 14.1 Emergency response times by distance to emergency

Bivariate regression involves putting a best fitting line through the datapoints in your graph. When you run a bivariate regression using computer software, the computer implicitly graphs the data and puts a best fitting line through the data array. Try to put a best-fitting line through your graph that you just drew. It should look like something similar to Figure 14.2.

The R Commander can generate the plot of data with a best-fitting regression line (Figures 14.1 and 14.2), along with the regression slope/coefficient and y-intercept, which we can solve by hand. It is easy to check how accurate your by-hand graph is compared to the computer-generated graph shown in Figure 14.2 To reproduce Figure 14.2, use the following steps. Load the dataset *regression_fire_example* from

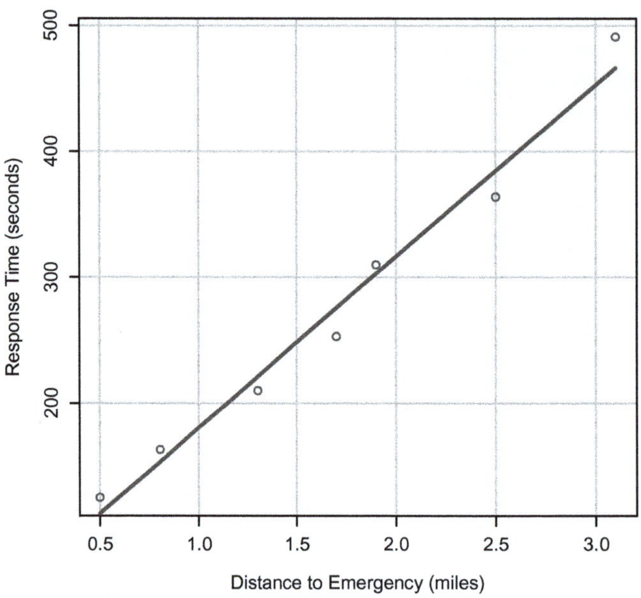

Figure 14.2 Emergency response times by distance to emergency with regression line

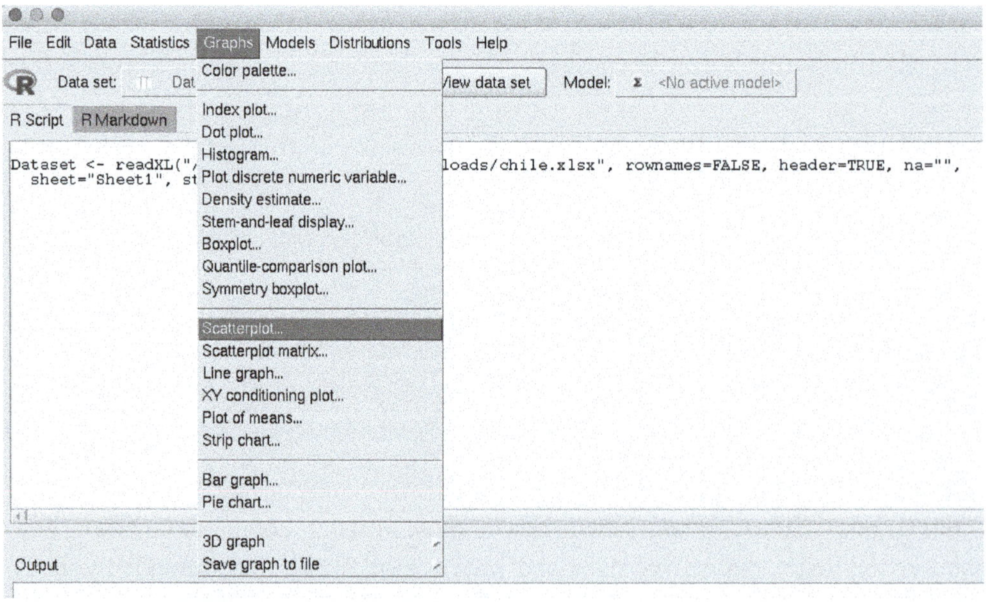

Figure 14.3 Scatterplot with regression line, part 1

the Companion Site (www.cambridge.org/scheller) into the R Commander. Once the dataset is loaded, do the following:

Step 1: Click Graphs → Scatterplot (Figure 14.3)

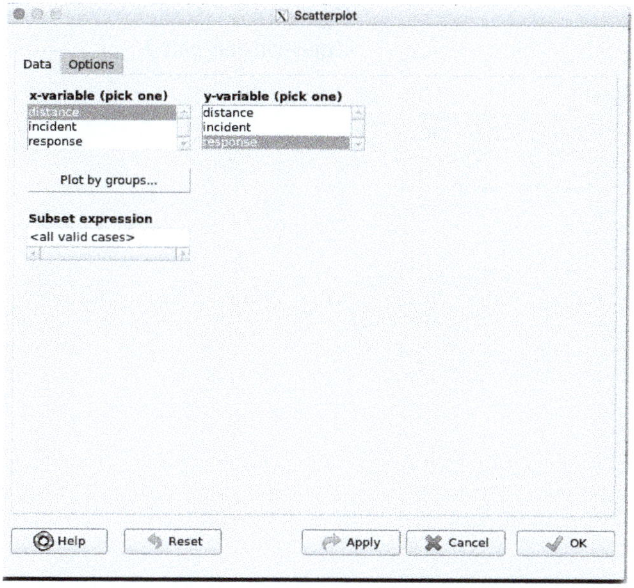

Figure 14.4 Scatterplot with regression line, part 2

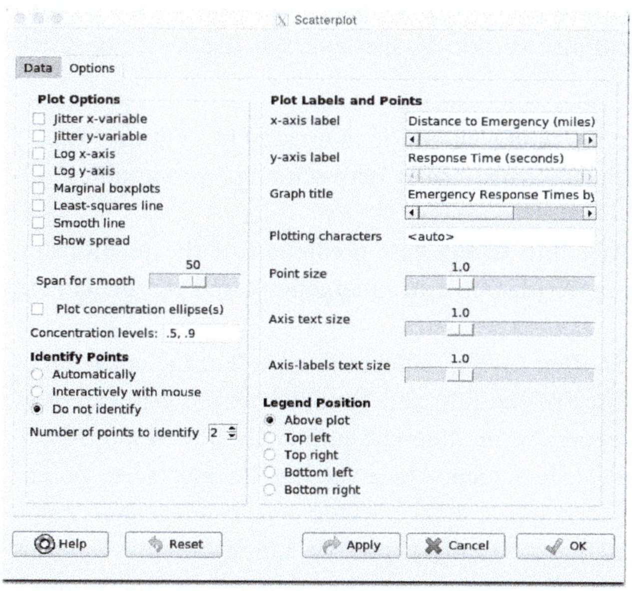

Figure 14.5 Scatterplot with regression line, part 3

Step 2: In the pop-up box, select the independent variable (X variable) and the dependent variable (Y variable). In our example, select "distance" for the x variable and "response" for the y variable (Figure 14.4).

Step 3: Click the "Options" tab to create labels and titles for your scatterplot. In the "Plot Labels and Points" area, label your x-axis (independent variable) and your y-axis (dependent variable) as appropriate. You can also include a title for your graph by typing in the "Graph title" box (Figure 14.5).

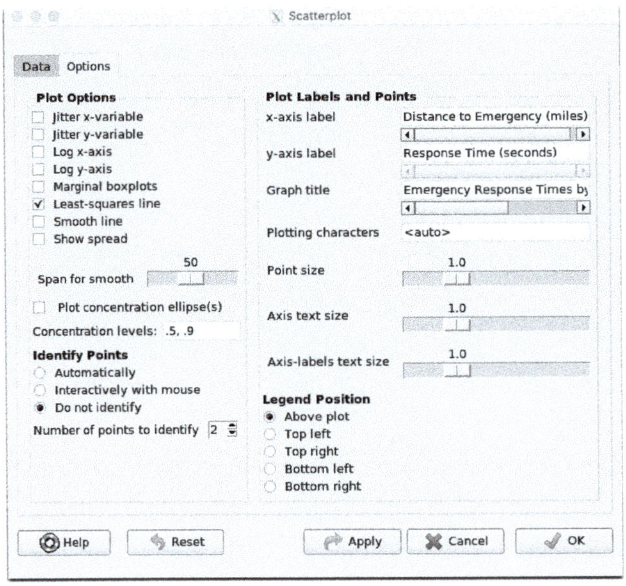

Figure 14.6 Scatterplot with regression line, part 4

Step 4: To include the best-fitting regression line, make sure the "Least-squares line" under the "Plot Options" section is also checked (Figure 14.6). Click OK.

You should now see your scatterplot, which should look exactly like Figure 14.2.

These steps will allow you to create a scatterplot between any two variables you choose.

The equation of that best-fitting line is our best prediction of the relationship between the independent variable, X (distance to emergency), and the dependent variable, Y (response time).

The expression, $Y = mX + b$ is often used in algebra to represent the equation of a line, where m represents the slope of the line and b represents the y-intercept of the line. The slope shows the steepness of the line and ultimately how responsive Y is to a change in X. The y-intercept, b, depicts where the line intersects the y-axis, or the value of Y when X is 0.

In statistics, the equation of the line is usually expressed a bit differently in terms of notation, but not in substance. The equation of the best-fitting line is often represented in statistics by:

$$Y = b_0 + b_1 X, \tag{14.1}$$

where b_0 represents the y-intercept and b_1 represents the slope, or beta/beta coefficient. We represent the relationship between Y and X in statistics more specifically as:

$$Y_i = b_0 + b_1 X_i + e_i, \tag{14.2}$$

where Y_i is an individual observation of the variable Y that corresponds with an individual observation of X, represented by X_i. Referring back to Table 14.1, each value in the Distance column represents an individual observation of X, represented by X_i. Each X_i has its respective Y observation, represented by Y_i. For example, the third observation has an X_i of 1.7 miles from the emergency, with a corresponding Y_i of 253 seconds to respond. b_0 and b_1 still represent the y-intercept and slope, respectively.

The term e_i is new, and represents the error, and is often called the error term. To understand the error term, look back at Figures 14.1 and 14.2. Figure 14.1 plots the data from Table 14.1. These plots are *observed* data – in this case, data observed by the fire chief. Each dot represents an X_i observation and its corresponding Y_i observation.

We then put in a best-fitting line through the data as in Figure 14.2. Of course, not every dot, or even a single dot, may lie along this line. This fact is where the error term comes in with Equation 14.2 to make it more comprehensive of the relationship between Y and X. Equation 14.2 basically says that each Y value (Y_i) is a function of its corresponding X value (X_i) multiplied by the slope (b_1) plus a constant value represented by the y-intercept (b_0) and some error (e_i). The distance each dot lies above or below the best-fitting line is its respective e_i. Alternatively, and maybe more simplistically, Equation 14.2 is Equation 14.1 plus some random error.

When considered altogether, the observed datapoints from the sample can be used to make inferences about the larger population, or the true relationship between Y and X. Remember from Chapter 9 that social scientists rarely ever have the entire population of data to analyze; they rely on samples and use information from the samples to extrapolate up to the population. The sample of data is also used to *predict* the relationship between Y and X. The best-fitting line that is drawn through the data in Figure 14.2 is the *predicted* relationship between Y and X based upon the sample data. As such, once the best-fitting line is calculated, the relationship between Y and X is usually expressed as:

$$\hat{Y} = \hat{b}_0 + \hat{b}_1 X_1 \tag{14.3}$$

Equation 14.3 is the prediction equation and the equation used to represent the relationship between X and Y based upon the sample data. It is the equation of the best-fitting line through the sample data in Figure 14.2. The ^, or "hat" symbol, indicates a predicted value based upon the observed data. So, Equation 14.3 says that the predicted value of Y for any value of X is the respective X value multiplied by the predicted slope, plus the predicted y-intercept. Enter any value of X you may be interested in knowing the predicted Y, and you can predict Y once you have calculated the predicted y-intercept ($\hat{b}_0$) and the predicted slope ($\hat{b}_1$).

Calculating the predicted slope and the predicted y-intercept by hand is relatively easy for small samples. The equation used to calculate the slope of the best-fitting line through the sample data is represented by Equation 14.4:

Table 14.2 Completion of step 2

$X_i - \bar{X}$	$Y_i - \bar{Y}$
(3.1 − 1.69) = 1.41	(491 − 273.71) = 217.29
(2.5 − 1.69) = 0.81	(364 − 273.71) = 90.29
(1.7 − 1.69) = 0.01	(253 − 273.71) = − 20.71
(0.8 − 1.69) = − 0.89	(163 − 273.71) = − 110.71
(0.5 − 1.69) = − 1.19	(125 − 273.71) = − 148.71
(1.9 − 1.69) = 0.21	(310 − 273.71) = 36.29
(1.3 − 1.69) = − 0.39	(210 − 273.71) = − 63.71

$$\hat{b}_1 = \frac{\Sigma(X_i - \bar{X})(Y_i - \bar{Y})}{\Sigma(X_i - \bar{X})^2} \tag{14.4}$$

This equation can be broken down into its component parts using mathematical order of operations following these steps:

Step 1: Calculate the mean of the X and Y values from the data in Table 14.1. The mean of X, represented by $\bar{X}$, is calculated with Equation 6.1 from Chapter 6:

$$\bar{X} = \frac{\Sigma X_i}{N}$$

Therefore,

$$\bar{X} = \frac{3.1 + 2.5 + 1.7 + 0.8 + 0.5 + 1.9 + 1.3}{7} = \frac{11.8}{7}$$

$$\bar{X} = \mathbf{1.69}$$

The mean of Y, represented by $\bar{Y}$, is calculated with the equation below as covered in previous chapters as:

$$\bar{Y} = \frac{\Sigma Y_i}{N}$$

Therefore,

$$\bar{Y} = \frac{491 + 364 + 253 + 163 + 125 + 310 + 210}{7} = \frac{1916}{7}$$

$$\bar{Y} = \mathbf{273.71}$$

Step 2: Subtract the mean of X, $\bar{X}$, from each individual observation of X. Subtract the mean of Y, $\bar{Y}$, from each individual observation of Y. Table 14.2 depicts this step.

Step 3: Multiply the respective differences: $(X_i - \bar{X})$ multiplied by $(Y_i - \bar{Y})$. Table 14.3 updates Table 14.2 to include this step.

Step 4: Add the products of $(X_i - \bar{X}) \times (Y_i - \bar{Y})$ as seen in Table 14.4. You now have the numerator for Equation 14.4.

Table 14.3 Completion of step 3

$X_i - \bar{X}$	$Y_i - \bar{Y}$	$(X_i - \bar{X}) * (Y_i - \bar{Y})$
$(3.1 - 1.69) = 1.41$	$(491 - 273.71) = 217.29$	$(1.41 * 217.29) = \mathbf{306.38}$
$(2.5 - 1.69) = 0.81$	$(364 - 273.71) = 90.29$	$(0.81 * 90.29) = \mathbf{73.13}$
$(1.7 - 1.69) = 0.01$	$(253 - 273.71) = -20.71$	$(0.01 * -20.71) = \mathbf{-0.21}$
$(0.8 - 1.69) = -0.89$	$(163 - 273.71) = -110.71$	$(-0.89 * -110.71) = \mathbf{98.53}$
$(0.5 - 1.69) = -1.19$	$(125 - 273.71) = -148.71$	$(-1.19 * -148.71) = \mathbf{176.96}$
$(1.9 - 1.69) = 0.21$	$(310 - 273.71) = 36.29$	$(0.21 * 36.29) = \mathbf{7.62}$
$(1.3 - 1.69) = -0.39$	$(210 - 273.71) = -63.71$	$(-0.39 * -63.71) = \mathbf{24.85}$

Table 14.4 Completion of step 4

$X_i - \bar{X}$	$Y_i - \bar{Y}$	$(X_i - \bar{X}) * (Y_i - \bar{Y})$
$(3.1 - 1.69) = 1.41$	$(491 - 273.71) = 217.29$	$(1.41 * 217.29) = 306.38$
$(2.5 - 1.69) = 0.81$	$(364 - 273.71) = 90.29$	$(0.81 * 90.29) = 73.13$
$(1.7 - 1.69) = 0.01$	$(253 - 273.71) = -20.71$	$(0.01 * -20.71) = -0.21$
$(0.8 - 1.69) = -0.89$	$(163 - 273.71) = -110.71$	$(-0.89 * -110.71) = 98.53$
$(0.5 - 1.69) = -1.19$	$(125 - 273.71) = -148.71$	$(-1.19 * -148.71) = 176.96$
$(1.9 - 1.69) = 0.21$	$(310 - 273.71) = 36.29$	$(0.21 * 36.29) = 7.62$
$(1.3 - 1.69) = -0.39$	$(210 - 273.71) = -63.71$	$(-0.39 * -63.71) = 24.85$
		$\mathbf{\Sigma = 687.26}$

Table 14.5 Completion of step 5

$(X_i - \bar{X})$	$(X_i - \bar{X})^2$
$(3.1 - 1.69) = 1.41$	$(1.41)^2 = \mathbf{1.99}$
$(2.5 - 1.69) = 0.81$	$(0.81)^2 = \mathbf{0.66}$
$(1.7 - 1.69) = 0.01$	$(0.01)^2 = \mathbf{0.0001}$
$(0.8 - 1.69) = -0.89$	$(-0.89)^2 = \mathbf{0.79}$
$(0.5 - 1.69) = -1.19$	$(-1.19)^2 = \mathbf{1.42}$
$(1.9 - 1.69) = 0.21$	$(0.21)^2 = \mathbf{0.04}$
$(1.3 - 1.69) = -0.39$	$(-0.39)^2 = \mathbf{0.15}$

Step 5: Subtract the mean of X from each individual observation of X, and then square the difference $(X_i - \bar{X})^2$. Table 14.5 shows this process.

Table 14.6 Completion of step 6

$(X_i - \bar{X})$	$(X_i - \bar{X})^2$
$(3.1 - 1.69) = 1.41$	$(1.41)^2 = 1.99$
$(2.5 - 1.69) = 0.81$	$(0.81)^2 = 0.66$
$(1.7 - 1.69) = 0.01$	$(0.01)^2 = 0.0001$
$(0.8 - 1.69) = -0.89$	$(-0.89)^2 = 0.79$
$(0.5 - 1.69) = -1.19$	$(-1.19)^2 = 1.42$
$(1.9 - 1.69) = 0.21$	$(0.21)^2 = 0.04$
$(1.3 - 1.69) = -0.39$	$(-0.39)^2 = 0.15$
	$\Sigma = 5.05$

Step 6. Sum the products of $(X_i - \bar{X})^2$. Table 14.6 shows this step. You now have your denominator for Equation 14.4.

Step 7. Divide your numerator by the denominator:

$$\hat{b}_1 = \frac{687.26}{5.05} = 136.09.$$

How do we interpret this number? The slope of the best-fitting line through the data is 136.09. The sign on the coefficient is positive, indicating a positive relationship between X and Y, or a positive relationship between distance from the emergency and response time. Therefore, X and Y go in the same direction. As X increases, Y increases; as X decreases, Y decreases. In our example, we can say that on average, as the distance to the emergency increases, so does the emergency response time. As the distance to the emergency decreases, so does the emergency response time. Please note that slope, slope coefficient, beta, and beta coefficient are often used interchangeably. Beta or beta coefficient are the most often used terms.

As in algebra, the slope represents "rise over run," or the vertical increase in Y from an increase in X. More specifically, the slope tells us how much Y changes in response to a one-unit increase in X. So, for our example, as X increases by one unit, Y increases by 136.09 units, on average. More specifically, as the distance to the emergency increases by one mile, the response time increases by 136.09 seconds (on average). Likewise, if the distance to the emergency decreases by one mile, we can expect the response time to decrease by an average of 136.09 seconds.

A good habit to get into when interpreting regression coefficients is to use a template. One such template to use is depicted below. Items in brackets indicate where you need to include relevant information based upon your regression results.

On average, ceteris paribus, a one unit increase in [whatever X is] is associated with a [value of slope without sign] unit [increase if value of slope is +; decrease if value of slope is −] in [whatever Y is].

For our example, we can say, "On average, ceteris paribus, a one unit increase in distance to the emergency is associated with a 136.09 unit increase in response time." More specifically, "On average, ceteris paribus, a one mile increase in the distance to the emergency is associated with a 136.09 second increase in response time." The term "ceteris paribus" may be unfamiliar. It is Latin for "all other things being equal," or for regression purposes, all other variables (independent variables) being considered or held constant. For bivariate regression, there are no other independent variables to be held constant. The "ceteris paribus" phrasing is most important for multivariate regression, when the interpretation of one variable's effect is calculated when other independent variables are considered or held constant; however, it is a good habit to begin using the phrasing. To be sure, "ceteris paribus" is more of an academic term, and practitioners are unlikely to use it in daily discussion. It can certainly be substituted with "holding other variables constant."

Now having the slope of the best-fitting regression line, we simply need the y-intercept ($\hat{b}_0$), or where the line intersects the y-axis, to come up with the equation for the regression line. The equation to calculate the y-intercept ($\hat{b}_0$) is:

$$\hat{b}_0 = \bar{Y} - \hat{b}_1\bar{X} \tag{14.2}$$

We multiply the slope just calculated ($\hat{b}_1$) by the mean of X ($\bar{X}$) and then subtract the result from the mean of Y ($\bar{Y}$). Therefore, the equation setup is:

$$\begin{aligned}\hat{b}_0 &= 273.71 - 136.09(1.69)\\ &= 273.71 - 229.99\\ &= \mathbf{43.72}\end{aligned}$$

The interpretation of the y-intercept ($\hat{b}_0$) can be formalized with a template. As with the template for the interpretation of the slope, fill in the items in brackets with relevant information:

When [X's or independent variables] are 0, the expected [Y or the dependent variable] is [$\hat{b}_0$].

Applied to our example, there is only one X or independent variable, distance to emergency in miles, so we would say: "When the distance to the emergency is 0 miles, the expected response time is 43.72 seconds." This means that if the fire personnel were 0 miles from the emergency, the expected response time would on average be 43.72 seconds. This suggests that if the emergency was at the fire department, we could expect the fire personnel to take 43.72 seconds to respond to it. In Figure 14.2, if we extend the regression line to the y-axis, it would intersect the y-axis at $Y = 43.72$.

As we will see in a moment, the y-intercept may or may not have a substantively important or even sensical interpretation. In this case, a distance of 0 miles to the emergency would be an emergency at the fire station. This may seem nonsensical that it would take 43.72 seconds for personnel to respond at the site of the emergency, but one could potentially argue that it could take 43.72 seconds for them to be alerted and obtain the equipment to resolve the emergency. Other examples will show much clearer situations where the y-intercept produces a substantively meaningful interpretation versus a nonsensical interpretation.

Combined, the slope and y-intercept allow us to know the equation of the best-fitting line through the sample data drawn in Figure 14.2:

$$\hat{Y} = 43.72 + 136.09X$$

This equation, based upon the sample data, best explains the relationship between the independent variable and the dependent variable. In the example, it is the relationship between distance from the emergency and emergency response time. By definition, the y-intercept (43.72) is found when you substitute a value of 0 for X. Along this line, you can also engage in prediction. For example, suppose the fire chief wanted to predict the response time for an emergency three miles away. Even though we do not have a value of three in the observed sample data in Table 14.1, we can still predict a "what if" scenario. What if an emergency is three miles away from the station? What would be the chief's best prediction of the emergency response time ($\hat{Y}$)? Insert the value of 3 for X and solve for Y:

$$\begin{aligned} \hat{Y} &= 43.72 + 136.09(3) \\ &= 43.72 + 408.27 \\ \hat{Y} &= 451.99 \end{aligned}$$

The chief's best prediction, based upon the sample data that they have available, is that it would take 451.99 seconds for the fire personnel to arrive on-scene at the emergency located three miles from the fire station, or slightly more than 7.5 minutes. This prediction is not a guarantee; it is a best-guess or "guesstimate" of the amount of time it would take. This prediction is based upon the small sample. As discussed in Chapter 9, the more data we have, the better our prediction will be. Because this is such a small sample size, the 451.99 second prediction could be either a high or a low estimate. Ideally, therefore, the chief would have a larger random sample, allowing them to place greater confidence in their results.

14.2.1 Least Squares Principle

One may wonder why Equation 14.4 generates the best-fitting line through a scatterplot of data. Refer back to Figure 14.2, the scatterplot with the best-fitting regression line included. Look at each of the dots, or datapoints, in the figure. No dot fits perfectly on the best-fitting regression line. Remember that the dots are our observed data from Table 14.1. Based upon this data, the best-fitting regression line is drawn in and is the prediction line from the sample for the entire population of data (remember that in this case and in most cases in public administration, we do not have the full population of data). The distance from each dot to the best-fitting line is the error, as introduced in Section 14.2. We want to minimize these errors. If we think of the dots above the line as positive and the dots below the line as negative, one may assume the goal is to reach 0 – to have the positive and negative values cancel each other. But think about a scenario where one dot is 100 units above the line (−100) and another dot is 100 units below the line (−100). They would cancel each other out, but the line is probably not a best-fitting line. To account for negative values, the least squares criterion is used, which minimizes the sum of the squared distances from the best-fitting line. Squaring eliminates negative values, thus the error will always be positive. The key is to minimize this sum.

14.2.2 Nonsensical Y-Intercept

When might the y-intercept be nonsensical? After generating the regression equation and calculating the y-intercept, we must ask ourselves if it is likely or theoretically possible for X to take on a value of 0 and have a meaningful interpretation. Let's take a basic example to understand when the y-intercept may not make substantive sense. If a researcher collected data on public sector workers' ages and their salaries, they could run a regression. Suppose they run such a regression and find the relationship of age on salary to be positive according to the regression equation:

$$\hat{Y} = 15{,}000 + 500(X)$$

When X is 0, the value of Y is 15,000, or more specifically, if the worker has an age of 0, they will earn $15,000. This example is nonsensical. A public sector employee cannot have an age of 0. It is not only illegal, but nonsensical. No living person has an age of 0. However, when we plot data and generate a best-fitting line equation, there will always be a y-intercept. A line will always intersect the y-axis, even if X cannot have a meaningful 0 value. This does not affect the significance of the results, but only the interpretation of the y-intercept in that it is unlikely to exist in the real world. The interpretation of the beta coefficient is not affected. Also remember that we are usually dealing with samples, and the y-intercept may generate a value that just would not/could not exist in the larger population, making it nonsensical.

14.3 Bivariate Regression with R Commander

The bivariate regression can also be run in the R Commander, and this will give us the slope/coefficient and the y-intercept. Such a tool becomes very useful when we want to run regressions with hundreds or thousands of observations. Using the response time example, we can get the R Commander to generate the slope/coefficient and the y-intercept by running the bivariate regression. Use the *regression_fire_example* dataset.

Step 1: Click Statistics → Fit Models → Linear Model (Figure 14.7).

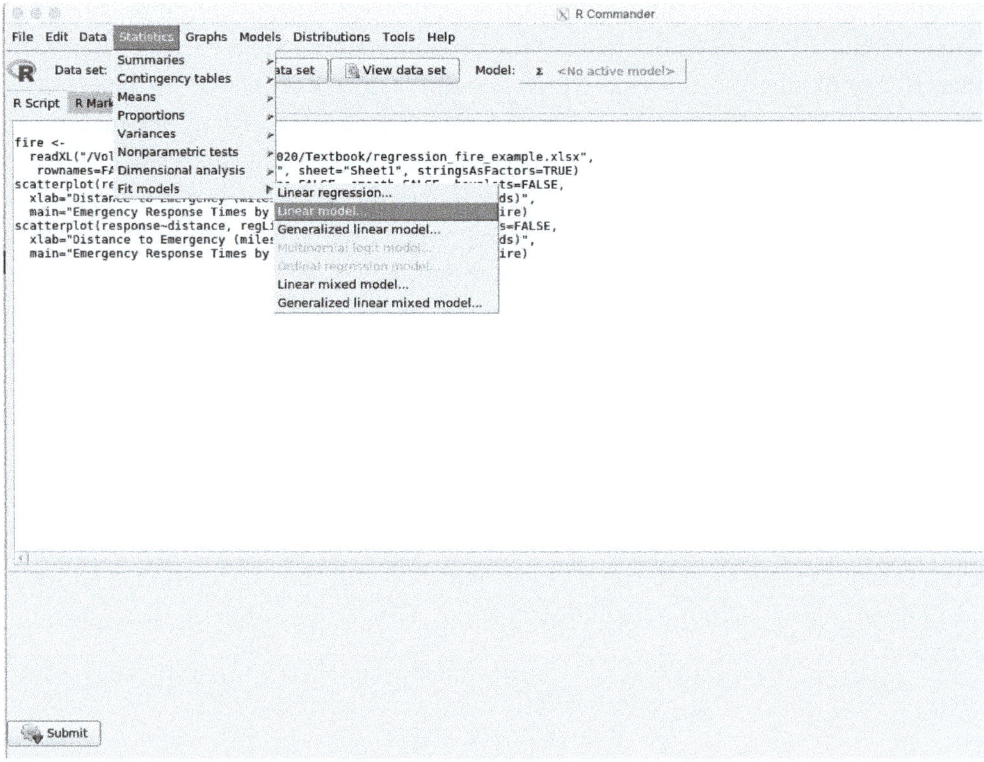

Figure 14.7 Bivariate regression in R Commander, part 1

Step 2: The box that opens may appear intimidating, but the necessary information is simple to input. The cursor is automatically placed in the short, empty rectangular box to the left of the ˜ symbol. All of the variables in the dataset appear in the "Variables" box. Place the dependent variable into this box by double-clicking the respective dependent variable from the "Variables" box. In this example, we are using the "response" variable as the dependent variable. The cursor then automatically moves to the longer rectangular box to the right of the ˜ symbol. Place your independent variable ("distance") in this box by double-clicking on it in the "Variables" box. The box "Enter name for model" contains the name/label for your model. It is automatically generated, and there is no need to change it unless you want to (Figure 14.8).

Step 3: Click OK, and your output should generate in the R Commander and look like Figure 14.9.

Statistics of interest are primarily in the "Estimate" column. The "(Intercept)" row is the y-intercept or the $\hat{b}_0$. Under the "(Intercept)" row are all of the independent variables in the regression model. For our example, there is just one independent variable, "distance," the distance in miles from the emergency. The value under the

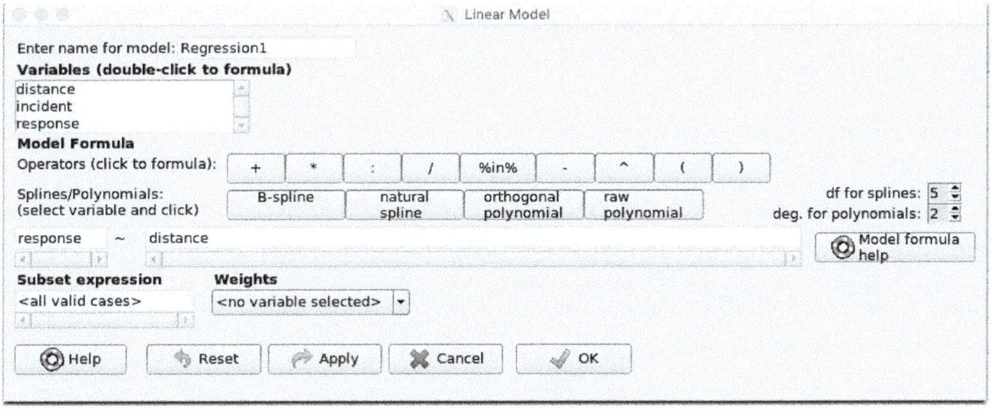

Figure 14.8 Bivariate regression in R Commander, part 2

```
Call:
lm(formula = response ~ distance, data = Dataset)

Residuals:
      1       2       3       4       5       6       7
 24.756 -20.565 -22.659   9.860  12.699   7.115 -11.206

Coefficients:
            Estimate Std. Error t value  Pr(>|t|)
(Intercept)   44.235     16.734   2.643    0.0458 *
distance     136.132      8.865  15.356 0.0000213 ***
---
Signif. codes:  0 '***' 0.001 '**' 0.01 '*' 0.05 '.' 0.1 ' ' 1

Residual standard error: 19.92 on 5 degrees of freedom
Multiple R-squared:  0.9792,    Adjusted R-squared:  0.9751
F-statistic: 235.8 on 1 and 5 DF,  p-value: 0.00002125
```

Figure 14.9 Bivariate regression output

"Estimate" column is the beta coefficient value for the "distance" variable. It is the slope of the best-fitting regression line through the data.

The results should mirror your by-hand calculations. Rounding may cause the statistics to differ slightly. The R Commander gives us a $\hat{b}_1$ of 136.132 to our by-hand calculations of 136.09. Likewise, the R Commander gives us a $\hat{b}_0$ of 44.235 to our by-hand calculations of 43.72. The differences are minuscule and likely due to rounding when we calculate these figures by hand to two decimal places. When in doubt, and since you'll likely be using large datasets necessitating software, go with the software's calculations.

```
Rcmdr> Regression1 <- lm(response ~ distance, data=fire)

Rcmdr> summary(Regression1)

Call:
lm(formula = response ~ distance, data = fire)

Residuals:
      1       2       3       4       5       6       7
 24.756 -20.565 -22.659   9.860  12.699   7.115 -11.206

Coefficients:
            Estimate Std. Error t value  Pr(>|t|)
(Intercept)   44.235     16.734   2.643    0.0458 *
distance     136.132      8.865  15.356 0.0000213 ***
---
Signif. codes:  0 '***' 0.001 '**' 0.01 '*' 0.05 '.' 0.1 ' ' 1

Residual standard error: 19.92 on 5 degrees of freedom
Multiple R-squared:  0.9792,    Adjusted R-squared:  0.9751
F-statistic: 235.8 on 1 and 5 DF,  p-value: 0.00002125
```

Standard Error of the Slope

Figure 14.10 Standard Error in regression output

14.4 Statistical Significance

So far, we have calculated the slope or beta coefficient of the best-fitting line through the sample data. For our example, the R Commander reveals the slope to be 136.132. For a one second increase in the distance to the emergency, we can expect, on average, a 136.132 second increase in the emergency response time. How do we know that this value is statistically significant? Stated another way, how can we be sure that the value of 136.132 is meaningful and not a value due to chance or equivalent to a value of 0, as discussed in Chapter 9? Remember, with inferential statistics, the idea is to use a sample to make claims about the larger population. As such, Berry and Sanders (2000) best reflect the question to ask to understand statistical significance: "How likely is it that a researcher would observe a [beta coefficient] of the magnitude found in the *sample* if the true [beta coefficient] in the *population* were zero?" (p. 46). To determine if the value of $\hat{b}_1$ is statistically significant, we need to look at its standard error, also called the standard error of the slope. The arrow in Figure 14.10 points to the standard error for the coefficient on the distance variable that we have been using. Meier, Brudney, and Bohte (2015) state that, "The standard error of the estimate may be interpreted as the amount of error that one makes when predicting a value of Y for a given value of X" (p. 336). With this error, a 95% confidence interval can be created for the beta coefficient and thus statistical significance determined.

One way to determine if the coefficient is significant is by eyeballing and dividing the coefficient by its standard error. If the coefficient is roughly two (or more) times its standard error (specifically 1.96 times for large samples), then the coefficient is statistically significant at at least the 95% confidence level. In our example, the coefficient ($\hat{b}_1$) is 136.132 and its standard error is 8.865 (see Figure 14.10). Obviously, 136.121 is considerably more than double 8.865. Therefore, we know that the coefficient is statistically significant at at least the 95% confidence level.

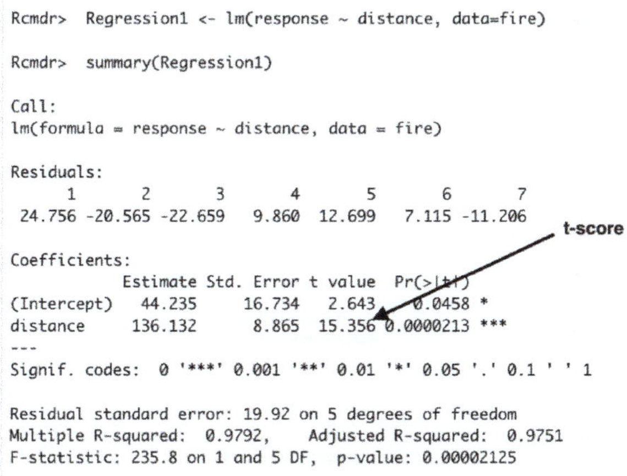
```
Rcmdr> Regression1 <- lm(response ~ distance, data=fire)

Rcmdr> summary(Regression1)

Call:
lm(formula = response ~ distance, data = fire)

Residuals:
      1       2       3      4      5      6       7
 24.756 -20.565 -22.659  9.860 12.699  7.115 -11.206

Coefficients:
            Estimate Std. Error t value  Pr(>|t|)
(Intercept)   44.235     16.734   2.643 0.0458 *
distance     136.132      8.865  15.356 0.0000213 ***
---
Signif. codes:  0 '***' 0.001 '**' 0.01 '*' 0.05 '.' 0.1 ' ' 1

Residual standard error: 19.92 on 5 degrees of freedom
Multiple R-squared:  0.9792,    Adjusted R-squared:  0.9751
F-statistic: 235.8 on 1 and 5 DF,  p-value: 0.00002125
```


Figure 14.11 T-Score in regression output

A second way to determine if the beta coefficient is statistically significant is to look at its t-value. In our example, the t-value (also called a t-score) for the distance variable's coefficient is 15.356, as shown in the output in Figure 14.11.

The $\hat{b}_1$ is 136.132 and its standard error is 8.865. Dividing 136.132 by 8.865 yields the t-value of 15.356, and the coefficient is statistically significant if the t-value is at least 1.96.

The third way to determine statistical significance is also likely the easiest to observe. The p-value is the t-value of the null hypothesis that the coefficient is equal to 0, hence the reason R Commander reports the t-value of the variable's coefficient. The R Commander reveals the coefficient's p-value under the "Pr(> | t |)" column. A p-value $\leq$ 0.05 indicates statistical significance at the 95% confidence level. A p-value $\leq$ 0.01 indicates statistical significance at the 99% confidence level. Finally, a p-value of $\leq$ 0.001 indicates a 99.9% confidence level.

A p-value of less than 0.05 indicates a statistically significant relationship between its respective independent variable and the dependent variable. It indicates that the null hypothesis of the coefficient being statistically no different than 0 is rejected. Specifically, the p-value gives the probability of observing the independent variable's coefficient in the sample (136.132 in our example) if the true population coefficient was 0, or if the independent variable has no effect on the dependent variable. In our example, the p-value is 0.0000213, or turned into a percentage by multiplying by 100, the probability of observing the distance variable's coefficient of 136.132 in the sample if the true effect of distance on response time in the population was 0, is 0.00213%.

Why not just say there is a 0% chance of this error since 0.002125% is so negligible? In the social sciences we can rarely ever be 100% certain about anything. Even if the probability is small, there is a chance we are wrong and that our sample does not reveal the true relationship between the independent variable and dependent

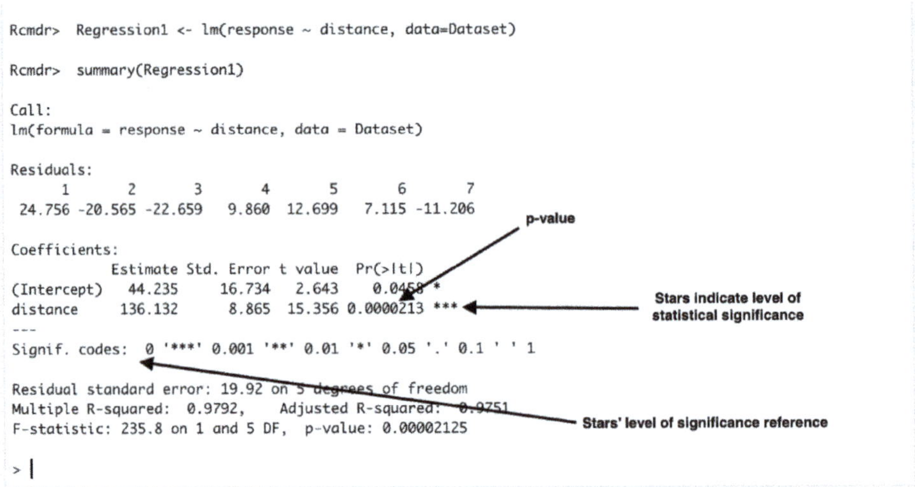

```
Rcmdr> Regression1 <- lm(response ~ distance, data=Dataset)

Rcmdr> summary(Regression1)

Call:
lm(formula = response ~ distance, data = Dataset)

Residuals:
      1       2       3       4       5       6       7
 24.756 -20.565 -22.659   9.860  12.699   7.115 -11.206

Coefficients:
            Estimate Std. Error t value  Pr(>|t|)
(Intercept)   44.235     16.734   2.643    0.0458 *
distance     136.132      8.865  15.356 0.0000213 ***
---
Signif. codes:  0 '***' 0.001 '**' 0.01 '*' 0.05 '.' 0.1 ' ' 1

Residual standard error: 19.92 on 5 degrees of freedom
Multiple R-squared:  0.9792,    Adjusted R-squared:  0.9751
F-statistic: 235.8 on 1 and 5 DF,  p-value: 0.00002125

> |
```


Figure 14.12 Statistical significance in regression output

variable in the population. Social scientists are usually "OK" with having at most a 5% chance of error, hence the importance placed on a p-value of less than or equal to 0.05, or 5%.

The output in Figure 14.12 labels the items to look for with the information provided by the R Commander. It shows the p-value and the stars next to the p-value that indicate the level of significance. One star reflects statistical significance at the 95% confidence level, two stars reflect the 99% confidence level, and three stars reflect the 99.9% confidence level.

With this information, social scientists usually interpret the results as we have done before, but they add the level of significance for the relationship between the independent and dependent variables. It is therefore reasonable to add to our earlier observation and interpret the relationship between the variables in our example more fully as, "On average, ceteris paribus, a one unit increase in distance to the emergency leads to a 136.132 unit increase in response time. This relationship is statistically significant at the 99.9% confidence level." More specifically, we could also say, "On average, ceteris paribus, as the distance to the emergency increases by one mile, the response time increases by 136.132 seconds. This relationship is statistically significant at the 99.9% confidence level." Social scientists also often refer to the variable being statistically significant. "The distance variable is statistically significant at the 99.9% confidence level."

14.5 Coefficient of Determination – R-Squared (R^2)

In Chapter 15, we will be discussing our regression model, or the independent variables we use to explain the dependent variable. In this chapter, we have only one

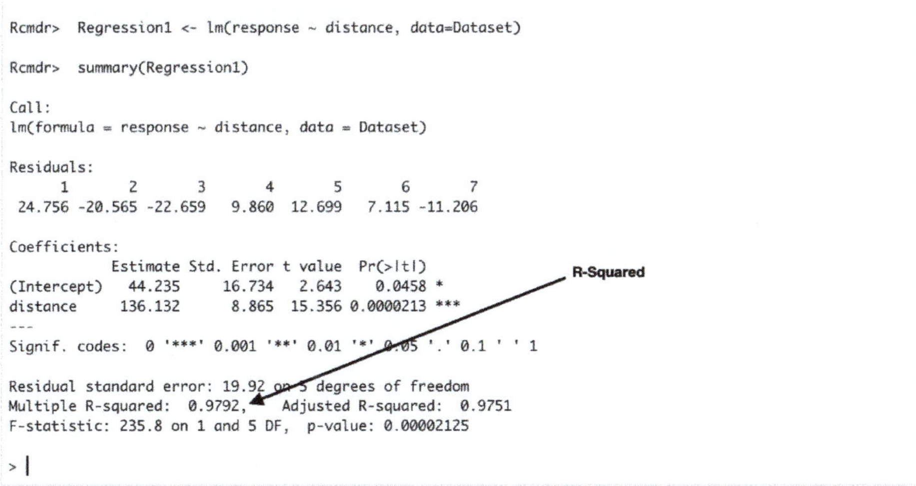

```
Rcmdr>  Regression1 <- lm(response ~ distance, data=Dataset)

Rcmdr>  summary(Regression1)

Call:
lm(formula = response ~ distance, data = Dataset)

Residuals:
      1       2       3       4       5       6       7
 24.756 -20.565 -22.659   9.860  12.699   7.115 -11.206

Coefficients:
            Estimate Std. Error t value  Pr(>|t|)
(Intercept)   44.235     16.734   2.643    0.0458 *
distance     136.132      8.865  15.356 0.0000213 ***
---
Signif. codes:  0 '***' 0.001 '**' 0.01 '*' 0.05 '.' 0.1 ' ' 1

Residual standard error: 19.92 on 5 degrees of freedom
Multiple R-squared:  0.9792,    Adjusted R-squared:  0.9751
F-statistic: 235.8 on 1 and 5 DF,  p-value: 0.00002125

> |
```


Figure 14.13 R-Squared in regression output

independent variable, distance to emergency, to explain emergency response time. In our example, how well does distance to the emergency explain or predict emergency response time? Stated differently, how well does our best-fitting regression line "fit" the data? Answering these questions helps us to determine how well our regression model/equation explains the data and whether or not we should include additional independent variables (hint: Social scientists rarely, if ever, use bivariate regression, instead modeling the dependent variable as a function of multiple independent variables, but bivariate regression is a good starting point for understanding multivariate regression). To answer these questions, refer back to Figure 14.2.

How well does the data "fit" the regression line? In our hypothetical example, the fit seems strong. The R Commander regression output we have been analyzing tells us how well the data fit the regression line or how well the independent variable explains the dependent variable. The particular statistic is the R-Squared value. You will see in Figure 14.13 where to look for the R-Squared.

The R-Squared value is listed as the "Multiple R-squared" value in the output. The value is 0.9792. Multiplying the R-Squared value by 100 yields the percent variation in the dependent variable explained by the independent variable. So, 97.92% of the dependent variable is explained by the independent variable. Therefore, the correct and most specific interpretation is, "97.92% of the variation in emergency response times is explained by distance to the emergency." Chapter 15 will discuss how the R-Squared changes with the addition of multiple independent variables and will cover the Adjusted R-Squared value.

R-Squared values can range from 0 to 1. The larger the R-Squared value, the more concentrated the data lie along the regression line. An R-Squared of 0 reflects

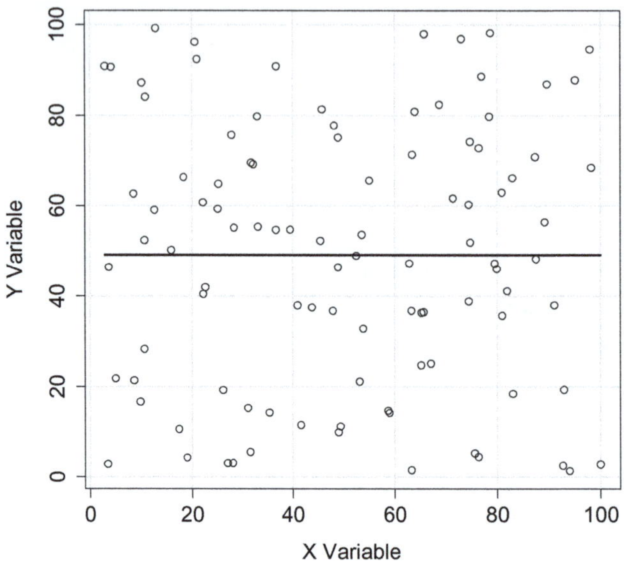

Figure 14.14 R-Squared = 0

a relationship where the independent variable explains no variation in the dependent variable. An R-Squared value of 1 represents a perfect fit. Our R-Squared value of 0.9792 is a very strong fit. Figure 14.14 shows a relationship between *X* and *Y* with an R-Squared value of 0. The R Commander put a best-fitting regression line through the data, but you can see that it is flat. *X* does not help to predict *Y*, hence the data appears to be a random cloud of data with no discernible pattern. On the other hand, Figures 14.15 and 14.16 show R-Squared values of 1, where all observations fit perfectly on the regression line. Figure 14.15 shows a perfectly positive relationship while Figure 14.6 shows a perfectly negative relationship.

14.6 Public Administration Example with Hypotheses

Using a large dataset, let's look at another example. Open the *state_politics* dataset located in the Companion Site (www.cambridge.org/scheller). This dataset contains information on transportation spending for all fifty states over several years. Transportation spending is operationalized as the percent of the state budget allocated to transportation. Also in the dataset is a variable measuring the percentage of workforce unionized for the state in each year. One potential research question could be: "What effect do state unionization levels have on state transportation spending?" You may not have any a priori inclinations as to the direction of the relationship between unionization and transportation spending, so a plausible research hypothesis could be:

H_{1a}: State unionization levels affect state transportation spending.

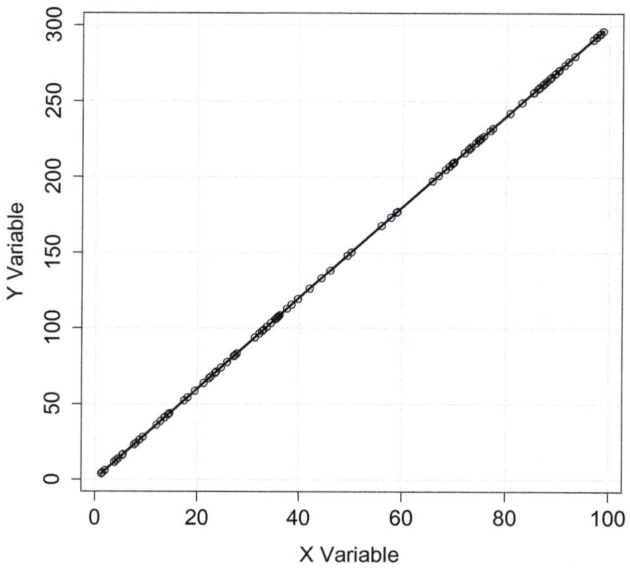

Figure 14.15 R-Squared = 1, example 1

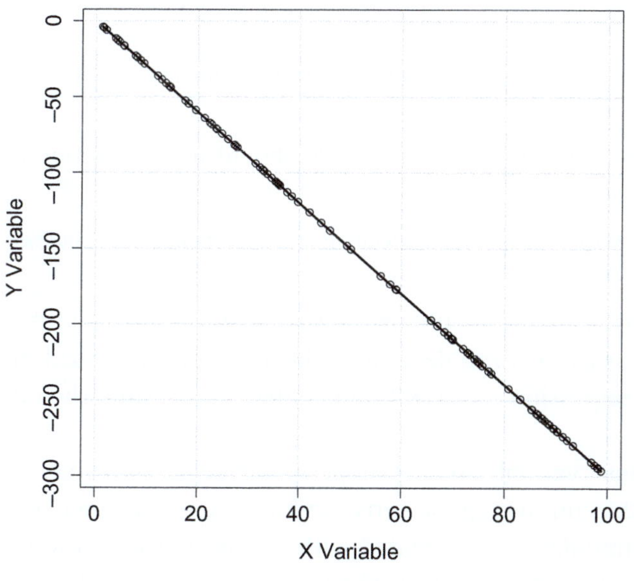

Figure 14.16 R-Squared = 1, example 2

You may also have a directional hypothesis for the relationship between unionization and transportation spending based upon previous research findings or logic. Let's assume we think states with a high percentage of the workforce unionized will spend more on transportation as a percent of the budget. We may think this because labor costs may be higher in these states due to higher union wages. Therefore, we may be able to offer such a directional hypothesis:

```
Call:
lm(formula = tport ~ unions, data = Dataset)

Residuals:
   Min     1Q Median     3Q    Max
-7.268 -2.248 -0.341  1.554 19.888

Coefficients:
            Estimate Std. Error t value Pr(>|t|)
(Intercept)  9.65216    0.24031  40.166   <2e-16 ***
unions      -0.04097    0.01894  -2.163   0.0308 *
---
Signif. codes:  0 '***' 0.001 '**' 0.01 '*' 0.05 '.' 0.1 ' ' 1

Residual standard error: 3.069 on 845 degrees of freedom
  (3 observations deleted due to missingness)
Multiple R-squared:  0.005505,  Adjusted R-squared:  0.004328
F-statistic: 4.678 on 1 and 845 DF,  p-value: 0.03084
```

Figure 14.17 Transportation spending bivariate regression

H_{1b}: State transportation spending as a percentage of the budget increases as the state's percentage of the workforce unionized increases.

H_{1b} is a more specific hypothesis, and when possible, we should offer directional hypotheses. The null hypothesis is:

H_0: There is no relationship between state transportation spending as a percentage of the budget and the state's percentage of the workforce unionized.

In the R Commander, the "unions" variable should be used as the X variable, and the "tport" variable should be used as the Y variable. Follow the directions described in Section 14.3 to run a bivariate regression in the R Commander. Your results should look like Figure 14.17.

The coefficient on the "unions" variable, or the slope of the regression line, is −0.04. Therefore, we can say that on average, ceteris paribus, a one unit increase in the state workforce that is unionized is associated with a 0.04 unit decrease in the percentage of the state budget allocated to transportation. More specifically, on average, ceteris paribus, a one percent increase in the state workforce that is unionized leads to a 0.04 percent decrease in the percentage of the state budget allocated to transportation. The p-value is 0.0308. So, this relationship is significant at the 95% confidence level. We find a statistically significant result that is in the opposite direction to our original hypothesis. We supposed that a state's level of unionization would increase the percent of the state budget allocated to transportation. We found the exact opposite. Therefore, we should say that our hypothesis was not supported, but that a statistically significant relationship in the opposite direction was found.

Combined with the y-intercept of 9.65, we can now generate the regression equation, or the equation of the best-fitting regression line:

$$\hat{Y} = 9.65 - 0.04X$$

The plus sign in the equation disappears because the coefficient is negative. It could be included, but a + and a − results in a −.
The R-squared value is 0.005505, so 0.55% of the variation in percent of the state budget allocated to transportation can be explained by the percent of the state's workforce that is unionized. This is a very low R-Squared, which should be expected given the inclusion of only one independent variable. We know that social science phenomena are a function of more than one independent variable. In this example, a state's percentage of budget spent on transportation is affected by more than simply the state's unionization percentage. The state's level of debt, political climate, and quality of infrastructure are a few variables that likely have an effect on the state's transportation budget. These variables could fairly easily be operationalized with existing data to run a multivariate regression.

14.7 Summary

Over the course of this chapter, we learned how to visually depict the relationship between two variables using a scatterplot and how to properly place the independent and dependent variables on the axes. This visual inspection provided the basis for conducting a statistical test to determine the strength, direction, and statistical significance of a relationship between an independent variable and a dependent variable. This test was the bivariate regression, and we learned how to run it by hand and in the R Commander, followed by the interpretation of bivariate regression output. In the next chapter, we will add more variables to the analysis, also known as a multivariate regression.

PRACTICE PROBLEMS

Conceptual Problems

1. When producing a scatterplot, what variable goes on the x-axis? The y-axis?
2. Suppose a manager hypothesizes that employee morale is a function of when an employee last received a raise.
   a. Identify the independent and dependent variables in this statement.
   b. How would you measure or operationalize the independent and dependent variables? How could you go about collecting or obtaining this data?

c. Develop null and directional research hypotheses for the relationship between employee morale and time since receiving a raise.
d. Sketch a graph to visually depict your hypothesized relationship, correctly labeling the axes.
e. What other independent variables would you eventually want to include? Explain.

3. Hypothesize a positive relationship between two variables of interest.
   a. Explain the logic behind your hypothesis.
   b. Explain how you would operationalize your variables – what data would you collect?
   c. Sketch a graph to visually depict your hypothesized relationship, correctly labeling the axes.
4. Explain what the regression line in a scatterplot depicts.
5. Define and explain the following components of a regression line:
   a. Slope
   b. y-intercept

Problems by Hand

6. Suppose a city transportation authority wants to know the effect of winter weather on light-rail ridership. The director of the transit authority hypothesizes that as the amount of snow in the city increases, so will the ridership on the light rail. She believes that winter weather, especially increases in snowfall, compels workers in the city to abandon their vehicles for public transportation. She collects data of ridership on days when there is measurable snowfall.
   a. Create a scatterplot by hand of the data. Be sure to correctly label the axes. Draw a best-fitting regression line in your plot.
   b. Describe the relationship between the independent and dependent variables. Is it a positive or a negative relationship?

Light-rail ridership on snowy days

Observation (Day)	Snow (in.)	Ridership
1	0.5	6253
2	1.0	7002
3	3.25	8350
4	6.25	9994
5	2.30	7513
6	4.70	8731

   c. Calculate the slope or beta coefficient of the best-fitting regression line.

d. Interpret the slope or beta coefficient of the best-fitting regression line.
e. Calculate the y-intercept of the best-fitting regression line.
f. Interpret the y-intercept of the best-fitting regression line.
g. What is the regression equation or the equation of the best-fitting regression line?
h. The local weather forecaster is predicting 3.5 inches of snow in two days. The director of the city transportation authority wants to ensure enough staff are available for light-rail operations. Predict the number of people riding the light rail if there is 3.5 inches of snow.
i. What other variables might you want to eventually include to explain light rail ridership on snowy days and how might you go about collecting that information?

7. The superintendent of the local school system is interested in understanding the effect of student absences on standardized test scores. The superintendent takes a random sample of five students in the district, noting the number of days absent and their score on the state standardized test (0–100). The data appear in the table below.

Student absences and test scores

Student	Absences	Test Score
1	0	96
2	3	88
3	1	95
4	7	62
5	5	73

a. Create a scatterplot by hand of the data. Be sure to correctly label the axes. Draw a best-fitting regression line in your plot.
b. Describe the relationship between the independent and dependent variables. Is it a positive or a negative relationship?
c. Calculate the slope or beta coefficient of the best-fitting regression line.
d. Interpret the slope or beta coefficient of the best-fitting regression line.
e. Calculate the y-intercept of the best-fitting regression line.
f. Interpret the y-intercept of the best-fitting regression line.
g. What is the regression equation or the equation of the best-fitting regression line?

8. The director of the Texas Health and Human Services is interested in how the state unemployment rate affects the number of households each month on food stamps. The director's staff collects information on the monthly unemployment rate (percent unemployed) in the state for the past ten years, along with the number of households each month receiving food stamps. A bivariate regression is run with unemployment rate as the independent variable and the number of households on food stamps in the state as the dependent variable. s.e. represents the standard error of the respective slope. The results appear below:

$\hat{b}_0 = 236,931$
$\hat{b}_1 = 75,521$
$s.e._{\hat{b}1} = 22,483$
R-Squared $= 0.54$

a. Interpret the beta coefficient on the unemployment variable if it is statistically significant. How do you know if it is statistically significant or not? If it is not significant, explain what may be the reason.
b. Interpret the y-intercept. Does it make substantive sense?
c. Using the beta coefficient and y-intercept, write down the equation of the best-fitting regression line.
d. Interpret the R-Squared value.
e. Predict the number of households on food stamps if the unemployment rate is 10.5%.

9. The director of international bridges in Nogales, Arizona, is trying to understand the effect of bridge wait times on the number of border crossings at the international bridge. The director collects a year's worth of data, including each day's average wait time (in minutes) at the bridge and the day's total number of crossings. s.e. represents the standard error of the respective slope. The bivariate regression results appear below:

$\hat{b}_0 = 17,317$
$\hat{b}_1 = -42.88$
$s.e._{\hat{b}1} = 17.25$
R-Squared $= 0.19$

a. Interpret the beta coefficient on the wait time variable if it is statistically significant. How do you know if it is statistically significant or not? If it is not significant, explain what may be the reason.
b. Interpret the y-intercept. Does it make substantive sense?
c. Using the beta coefficient and y-intercept, write down the equation of the best-fitting regression line.
d. Interpret the R-Squared value.
e. Predict the number of crossings if the average wait time is 120 minutes.

10. A researcher for the Parks Service is interested in knowing the effect of park admission prices on the number of weekend visitors. The researcher generates a random sample of parks across the United States and collects information

on the price of park admission along with the total number of weekend visitors for the year. She regresses the total number of weekend visitors on park admission prices and finds the following results:

$\hat{b}_0 = 6,899$
$\hat{b}_1 = -500.35$
$s.e._{\hat{b}1} = 400.23$
R-Squared = 0.08

a. Interpret the beta coefficient on the price of admission variable if it is statistically significant. How do you know if it is statistically significant or not? If it is not significant, explain what may be the reason.
b. Using the beta coefficient and y-intercept, write down the equation of the best-fitting regression line.
c. Interpret the R-Squared value.
d. What other variables should we consider that affect weekend park attendance?

R Commander Problems

11. Suppose a minor league baseball team plays in a stadium owned by its city. Attendance at games is of importance since the city receives revenue from ticket sales and purchases from concessions and souvenirs. Suppose city leaders are interested in attendance at games. They are trying to understand the factors that affect attendance so that they can begin to project revenues from ticket sales. They hypothesize that the temperature at game time affects attendance. They think heat may deter attendance. They have a dataset from the 2017 season, but need help analyzing the data. Using the *baseball* dataset and the *baseball_codebook* in the Companion Site (www.cambridge.org/scheller), test their hypothesis by doing the following:
a. Generate a scatterplot depicting attendance and temperature at game time. What pattern do you see?
b. Run a bivariate regression, testing the effect of temperature on attendance.
c. Is their hypothesis supported by the results? Why/why not?
d. What might explain these results?
e. Interpret the R-Squared value.
f. What other variables may affect attendance that we should consider?
g. Write down the regression equation of the best-fitting line through the data based upon the results from the analysis.
h. Interpret the y-intercept. Does it make substantive sense?

12. Open the *state politics codebook* and load the *state_politics* dataset into the R Commander. Let's test the effect of state government ideology (0–100) on the state's percent of budget allocated to transportation.

a. Generate a scatterplot depicting ideology and percent of budget allocated to transportation spending. What pattern do you see?
b. Regress the percent of state budget spent on transportation on state government ideology and copy/paste the results.
c. Interpret the beta coefficient on state government ideology if statistically significant.
d. Interpret the R-Squared value.
e. Write down the regression equation of the best-fitting line through the data based upon the results from the analysis.
f. Interpret the y-intercept. Does it make substantive sense?
g. Predict the percent of state budget allocated to transportation if the state government ideology score is 50.

13. Using the same *state politics codebook* and the *state_politics* dataset, run a regression with the dependent variable as percent of the state budget allocated to transportation and the independent variable as state legislative professionalism. Assume the research hypothesis is that there is a positive relationship between state legislative professionalism and the percent of the state budget allocated to transportation spending.
a. Do the results support the hypothesis? Why/why not?
b. Interpret the beta coefficient if statistically significant.
c. Interpret the y-intercept.
d. Interpret the R-Squared value.

14. Take the data from Problem #6, enter it into Microsoft Excel, and then load into the R Commander.
a. Create a scatterplot of the data with the best-fitting regression line. Be sure to correctly label the axes. Compare the R Commander's output to your own sketch from problem #6.
b. Interpret the slope or beta coefficient of the best-fitting regression line if it is statistically significant.
c. Interpret the y-intercept of the best-fitting regression line.
d. What is the regression equation or the equation of the best-fitting regression line?

15. Take the data from Problem #7, enter it into Microsoft Excel, and then load into the R Commander.
a. Create a scatterplot of the data with the best-fitting regression line. Be sure to correctly label the axes. Compare the R Commander's output to your own sketch from problem #7.
b. Interpret the slope or beta coefficient of the best-fitting regression line if it is statistically significant.
c. Interpret the y-intercept of the best-fitting regression line.
d. What is the regression equation or the equation of the best-fitting regression line?

15

Multivariate Regression

15.1 Introduction

Are emergency response times *only* affected by how far emergency responders are from the emergency? Like many phenomena in the world, the answer is no. Multiple variables affect emergency response times in the same manner that multiple variables affect incomes of MPA graduates (years of experience, gender, professional certifications, etc.), local economic output (education of population, tax incentives, population growth, etc.), and employee satisfaction (wages, vacation time, satisfaction with retirement benefits, etc.). Time of day, weather, road construction, type of emergency, number of personnel required, and even fire station layout may also affect how long it takes emergency responders to arrive on scene. If we collect data on emergency response times, and only model them as a function of distance to an emergency, we cannot and will not truly understand what affects emergency response times. However, we can collect data and run a multivariate regression to understand the impact of any number of independent variables on a dependent variable of interest. In the end-of-chapter problems, we will return to the emergency management example, allowing you to practice running different regression models with the emergency response dataset. To diversify our understanding of how statistics can be useful in a wide variety of public administration examples, the next section introduces a new example likely of interest to those in human resources management.

15.2 Logic of Multivariate Regression

Multivariate regression is a common statistical test used to model a dependent variable as a function of multiple (hence multivariate) independent variables. What affects employee raises in a public organization? Probably multiple variables, hence the need for a multi-variable or multivariate regression. Table 15.1 contains fictional data, but can be applied to a public administration example. Suppose a human resources (HR) department manager in a public agency is curious about whether or not employee raises in a unit are being allocated fairly and in accordance with performance. Let's assume the HR manager takes a random sample of twenty employees

Table 15.1 Employee raise data

Raise %	Performance Rating (0–100)	Years in Organization
6.3	89	9
4.9	82	3
1.3	70	2
4.6	72	4
7.9	95	12
3.8	74	3
10	100	14
7.2	91	10
2.3	73	3
5.9	87	2
9.2	98	5
5.3	80	7
0.1	40	1
0.9	49	1
7.5	95	11
4.8	74	7
6.3	88	5
8.1	93	13
7.9	90	11
1.1	62	2

from a particular department, and collects data for each employee's percent raise for the previous year allocated by the employee's supervisor, along with the number of years the employee has been employed in the organization. We can hypothesize that both an employee's performance rating and the number of years in the organization would be positively related to their raise percentage. The data for this hypothetical situation appear in Table 15.1.

If we think that an employee's raise is *only* a function of their performance rating, we can model that with a bivariate regression. However, if an employee's raise is also a function of other variables, like their years in the organization, then we will draw biased conclusions if we run a bivariate regression with performance rating as the only independent variable. We will obtain an effect of performance rating on the raise, but it will not be accurate, because we will not have correctly considered other variables.

```
Output                                                              Submit

Call:
lm(formula = raise ~ perf, data = HR_Data)

Residuals:
     Min       1Q   Median       3Q      Max
-2.33888 -0.58219 -0.02246  0.81006  2.25231

Coefficients:
            Estimate Std. Error t value      Pr(>|t|)
(Intercept) -8.25472    1.35502  -6.092 0.00000934030 ***
perf         0.16991    0.01671  10.167 0.00000000691 ***
---
Signif. codes:  0 '***' 0.001 '**' 0.01 '*' 0.05 '.' 0.1 ' ' 1

Residual standard error: 1.154 on 18 degrees of freedom
Multiple R-squared:  0.8517, Adjusted R-squared:  0.8435
F-statistic: 103.4 on 1 and 18 DF,  p-value: 0.000000006914
```

Figure 15.1 Employee raise bivariate regression

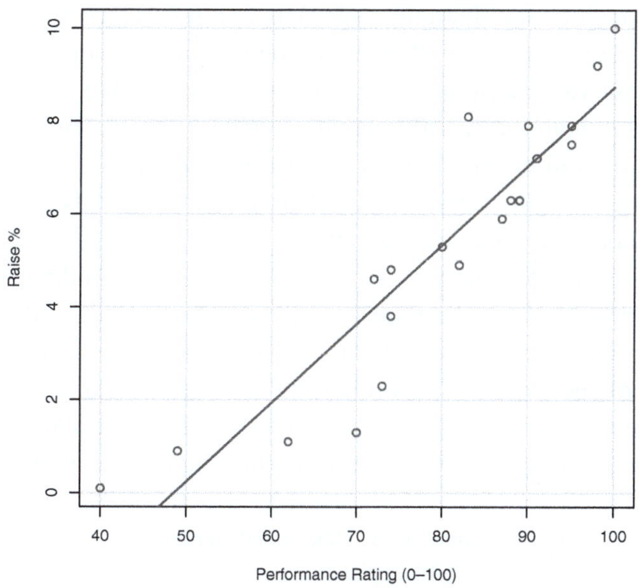

Figure 15.2 Raise percentage and performance rating

To illustrate the biased results from not including relevant variables, we can first run a bivariate regression with the Raise % as the dependent variable and the Performance Rating as the independent variable. The output appears in Figure 15.1 The bivariate regression interpretation would be that on average, ceteris paribus, a one unit increase in the performance rating leads to a 0.17% increase in the employee's raise. This relationship is significant at greater than the 99% confidence level.

Figure 15.2 depicts the bivariate relationship between raise percentage and performance rating with a scatterplot. The least squares line is drawn in to better illustrate the positive relationship between performance rating and the raise percentage.

What if we think years experience also affects the raise percentage? How can we model and depict that relationship, acknowledging the effect of the supervisor performance rating? Whereas the bivariate regression can be depicted two-dimensionally, when another independent variable is included, we enter the three-dimensional world.

Multivariate regression is the method to examine the effect of multiple variables (hence "multivariate") on a dependent variable. In the bivariate world, we are dealing with two dimensions, a dependent variable Y and an independent variable X. Figure 15.2 shows the two-dimensional relationship between performance rating and raise percentage. As such, the relationship is depicted as a best-fitting line through the data as discussed in Chapter 14. For our example, we hypothesized that employee performance rating positively affected the raise percentage. If we think that the years of experience or number of years the employee has worked for the organization may affect the raise percentage, then we have another independent variable and dimension for consideration.

We can model this relationship with a multivariate regression. In our case, we may think that the raise percentage (Y) is a function of not only the performance rating (X_1), but also another independent variable, years in the organization (X_2). We now have two independent variables explaining the dependent variable. Now, we enter a three-dimensional world, and instead of estimating a best-fitting line through the data between X and Y, we must estimate a best-fitting plane through the data of X_1, X_2, and Y. Figure 15.3 depicts such a relationship.

The plane depicted best fits the plotted data of X_1, X_2, and the corresponding Y values. The vertical axis represents Y, or the raise percentage. The X_1 axis and the X_2 axis represent the performance rating and years in the organization, respectively. Each dot represents one of the twenty datapoints from Table 15.1. Thinking three-dimensionally, each of the dots is suspended in the "air" with the linear plane representing the best-fitting plane through the data incorporating the least squares

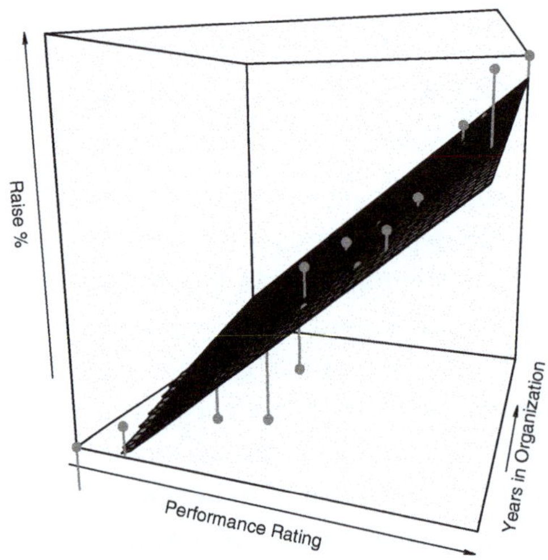

Figure 15.3 Multivariate regression best-fitting plane

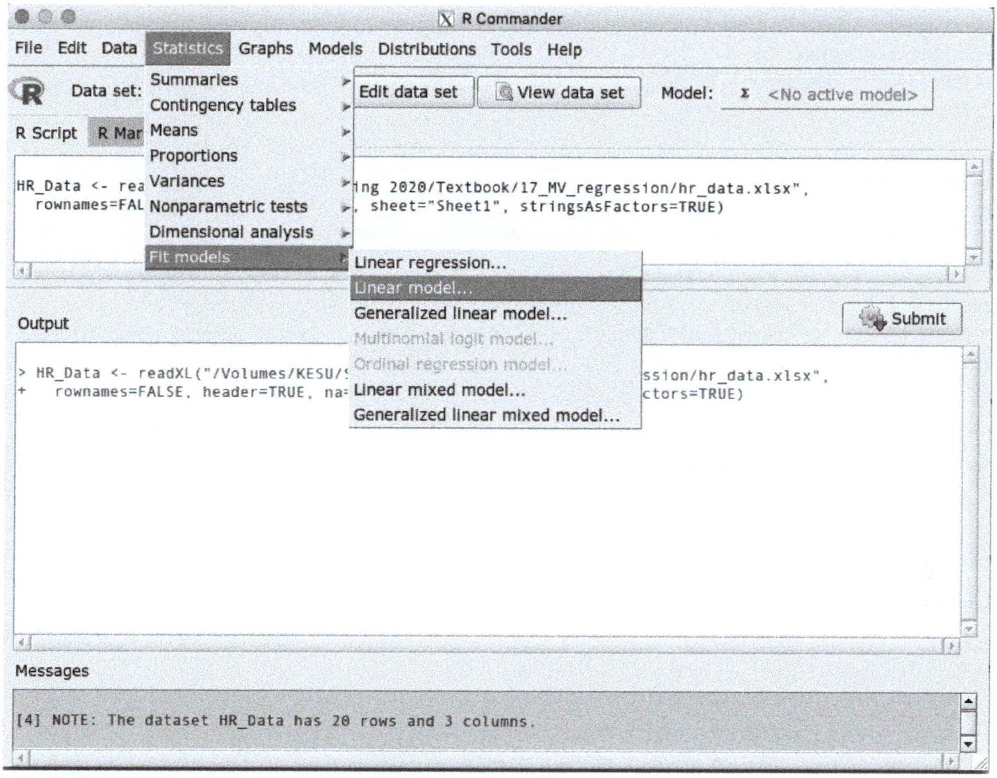

Figure 15.4 Multivariate regression, part 1

criterion discussed in Chapter 14. Visually, the general relationship is one in which as both the performance rating and years in the organization increase, so does the raise percentage. To what specific effect, it is difficult to see in the graph.

Running the multivariate regression model in the R Commander gives us the specific effects, measured by the beta coefficients. The steps are identical to those for the bivariate regression described in Chapter 14, with the only difference being the addition of an independent variable. In the multivariate world, we will likely always include *even* more variables, entering dimensions that cannot be depicted on paper.

To run the multivariate regression, load the dataset *hr_data* from the Companion Site (www.cambridge.org/scheller) into the R Commander. Once the dataset is loaded:

Step 1: Click Statistics → Fit models → Linear model (Figure 15.4).

Step 2: Double click the "raise" variable, our dependent variable, to put it into the small dependent variable box towards the middle-left of the popup box. Then, double click the "perf" variable. It should naturally populate into the long independent variable box. Then, double click the other independent variable, "years." It populates to the independent variable box with a "+"

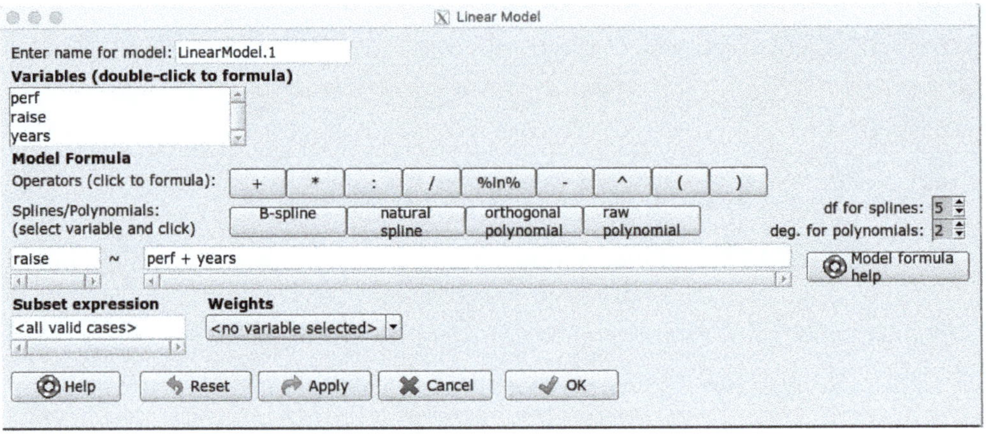

Figure 15.5 Multivariate regression, part 2

```
Rcmdr> LinearModel.1 <- lm(raise ~ perf + years, data=HRdata)

Rcmdr> summary(LinearModel.1)

Call:
lm(formula = raise ~ perf + years, data = HRdata)

Residuals:
     Min       1Q   Median       3Q      Max
-1.80417 -0.64762  0.06227  0.65326  1.88279

Coefficients:
            Estimate Std. Error t value   Pr(>|t|)
(Intercept) -6.19685    1.28582  -4.819    0.00016 ***
perf         0.12647    0.01940   6.518 0.00000526 ***
years        0.22393    0.07105   3.152    0.00582 **
---
Signif. codes:  0 '***' 0.001 '**' 0.01 '*' 0.05 '.' 0.1 ' ' 1

Residual standard error: 0.9434 on 17 degrees of freedom
Multiple R-squared:  0.9064,    Adjusted R-squared:  0.8954
F-statistic: 82.31 on 2 and 17 DF,  p-value: 0.000000001803

>
```

y-intercept

Coefficient for performance rating

p-values & significance of coefficients

Coefficient for years in organization

Figure 15.6 Multivariate regression results

sign separating it from the first independent variable. Your screen should look like Figure 15.5.

Step 3: Click OK, and your R Commander output should look like Figure 15.6.

15.3 Interpreting Multivariate Regression Coefficients

The interpretation template of the coefficients for the independent variables is exactly the same as with the bivariate regression. It is here where the ceteris paribus term becomes particularly important, as it means "all other things being equal." In statistical terms, ceteris paribus means holding the other independent variables in our model constant (Berry and Sanders, 2000). To illustrate, we would interpret the coefficient on the performance rating (0.126) by saying, "On average, ceteris paribus, a one-unit increase in the performance rating leads to a 0.126 unit (or %) increase in an employee raise." Stated differently, we can say, "On average, holding years in the organization constant, a one-unit increase in the performance rating leads to a 0.126% increase in an employee raise." Essentially, once years in the organization has been accounted for, the independent effect of the performance rating is a 0.126% increase in the employee raise (on average) for each one-unit increase in the performance rating.

Likewise, the interpretation of the coefficient on years in the organization (0.224) is, "On average, ceteris paribus, a one-unit increase in the number of years served in the organization leads to a 0.224% increase in the employee raise." Stated differently, we can say, "On average, holding performance rating constant, a one-unit increase in the years served in the organization leads to a 0.224% increase in an employee raise." Alternatively, but saying the same thing, you can state, "On average, ceteris paribus, an additional year served in the organization leads to a 0.224% increase in the employee raise." These simply represent different ways to say the same thing.

At this point, one needs to consider whether or not to add additional variables to the multivariate regression. If, in theory, only the performance rating and years in the organization affect employee raises, then the modeling can stop and we can be confident in the results. Most likely, we'll want to collect data for more variables, such as gender or even job title. You may want to know the number of variables to include in a multivariate regression. There is no definitive answer. A regression model needs to be driven by theory and include all relevant variables that affect the dependent variable. Of course, the inclusion of additional variables should be taken within reason – data that is impossible or unethical to collect cannot and should not be included in the regression model. It is also impossible to collect every single independent variable that affects a dependent variable – there is simply not enough time, ability to collect the variable, and/or money to collect the data.

15.4 Interpreting the Y-Intercept

Much like the interpretation template for the coefficients, interpreting the y-intercept, or constant, is the same – we simply now have two independent variables to set at a value of 0. The interpretation of the y-intercept for the example is, "When the performance rating is 0 and the years served in the organization is 0, the expected employee raise is −6.20%." Though difficult to see as drawn since the y-axis stops at 0 in Figure 15.3, if one were to continue to extend the plane down and to the left, it would intersect the y-axis (Raise %) at −6.20. This y-intercept is a bit nonsensical. While it is certainly possible for an employee to receive a performance rating of 0, it is unlikely for them to have 0 years experience in the organization. This particular example would involve the scenario of the employee walking into their job on the first day, receiving a performance evaluation, and then a raise decision. So, in this particular example, the y-intercept is not very useful.

15.5 R-Squared and Adjusted R-Squared – Which One to Use?

The R Commander reports both the R-Squared and the Adjusted R-Squared values. When conducting multivariate regression, it is best to get into the habit of using the Adjusted R-Squared. The Adjusted R-Squared value controls for, and mathematically discounts, the number of independent variables used in a multivariate regression model. Therefore, it will usually be smaller than the R-Squared value. The interpretation is exactly the same as the R-Squared. The difference is that no matter how many independent variables you add to your regression model, the R-Squared value will increase. Even though the R-Squared is bounded between values of 0 and 1, you could run a model with ten independent variables, then eleven, then twelve, then thirteen, and each time, the R-Squared would increase (even if only by very small amounts). This would occur even with the addition of nonsensical independent variables. In the employee raise example, suppose we collected data on each of the twenty employee's feelings towards Taylor Swift's music on a scale of 1 (Strongly Dislikes) to 10 (Die-Hard "Swiftie"). Even though there is no theoretical or likely logical reason to think an employee's affinity towards Taylor Swift's music affects their raise, the inclusion of this variable in the regression model would lead to an increase (albeit, a very small increase) in the R-Squared value.

In the human resource data example, the Adjusted R-Squared is 0.8954, so if rounding, we would interpret it as, "89.5% of the variation in employee raises is explained by performance rating and years in the organization." This value is a large Adjusted R-Squared, suggesting that our model does a very good job of explaining employee raises.

15.6 Multivariate Regression Equation

Equation 14.2 (restated here) on bivariate regression shows the mathematical relationship between an independent variable X and dependent variable Y:

$$Y_i = b_0 + b_1 X_i + e_i \tag{14.2}$$

In our two independent variables example, the regression equation becomes:

$$Y_i = b_0 + b_1 X_{1i} + b_2 X_{2i} + e_i \tag{15.1}$$

Equation 15.1 represents the equation of the best-fitting plane through the data. Values of 1 and 2 have been added to each X value to represent X_1 and X_2, respectively, or in our example, employee performance rating and years in the organization.

In general, the multivariate regression equation is often represented by the following equation to account for the inclusion of more than two independent variables, up to an infinite number (in practice, models will often have fewer than twenty independent variables):

$$Y_i = b_0 + b_1X_{1i} + b_2X_{2i} + \ldots + b_kX_{ki} + e_i, \tag{15.2}$$

where k represents the kth number, or final number of independent variables in the regression model.

15.7 Prediction with Multivariate Regression

As with bivariate regression, multivariate regression results can be used to engage in prediction. From Chapter 14, the bivariate prediction equation is:

$$\hat{Y} = \hat{b}_0 + \hat{b}_1X_1 \tag{14.3}$$

With multivariate regression, the prediction equation becomes:

$$\hat{Y} = \hat{b}_0 + \hat{b}_1X_1 + \hat{b}_2X_2 + \ldots + \hat{b}_kX_k, \tag{15.3}$$

where k represents the total number of independent variables in the multivariate regression model. So, if you have 10 independent variables in your regression model, k would equal 10 and be X_{10}.

With the output from the regression on the human resources data, the prediction equation is:

$$\hat{Y} = -6.20 + 0.13X_1 + 0.22X_2, \tag{15.4}$$

where X_1 is the performance rating, and X_2 is years in the organization. Alternatively, the prediction equation can also be expressed as:

Raise Percentage $= -6.20 + 0.13$ (Peformance Rating) $+ 0.22$ (Years in Organization)

Suppose the HR manager wanted to predict the raise percentage of an employee with 18 years experience in the organization and a performance rating of 75. What is the best guess for the expected raise percentage? To solve, enter the relevant information into equation 15.4, remembering that X_1 represents the performance rating and that X_2 represents the years in the organization:

$$\hat{Y} = -6.20 + 0.13(75) + 0.22(18)$$
$$\hat{Y} = -6.20 + 9.75 + 3.96$$
$$\hat{Y} = 7.51$$

The HR manager's best guess or predicted raise for the employee would be 7.51%.

An HR manager may simply be interested in understanding the independent effects of employee performance ratings and years in the organization on raises. However, in the real world, the manager may also be interested in knowing if supervisors are giving raises equitably, consistently, and based upon certain criteria. In this case, both the employee performance rating and their years working in the organization have a statistically significant positive effect on employee raises. It would be concerning if only years in the organization determined an employee's wage and their performance rating had no effect. Such a pattern would indicate that the supervisors are allocating raises solely based upon seniority (measured in years worked at the organization). In the next section, we will see an example of when there could be some problematic trends in the data. It also will introduce you to using categorical or dummy variables in multivariate regression.

15.8 Categorical/Dummy Independent Variables

A different HR manager collects data from one of their departments regarding employee raises, wanting to know the effect of performance rating, years in the organization, and gender on employee raises. The data are depicted in Table 15.2. Eyeballing the data regarding gender and raises appears to show a pattern to the

Table 15.2 Employee raise data

Raise %	Performance Rating (0–100)	Years in Organization	Gender 1 = F: 0 = M
6.3	55	5	0
4.9	81	8	0
1.3	88	4	1
4.6	90	15	1
7.9	80	10	0
3.8	77	1	1
10	89	16	0
7.2	90	17	1
2.3	79	2	1
5.9	93	18	0
9.2	84	6	0
5.3	84	3	1
0.1	74	11	1
0.9	45	8	1
7.5	72	9	0
4.8	91	1	0
6.3	77	5	0
8.1	85	3	0
7.9	100	10	0
1.1	82	7	1

human resource manger – it appears that women receive lower raises than men. We can run a multivariate regression to determine if the HR manager's supposition has merit and is supported by statistical analysis. Run the multivariate regression with the employee raise as the dependent variable and performance rating, years in organization, and gender as the independent variables. It is the *hr_data2* dataset in the Companion Site.

Your R Commander interface with the correct variable inputs should look like Figure 15.7.

The resulting regression output should look like Figure 15.8.

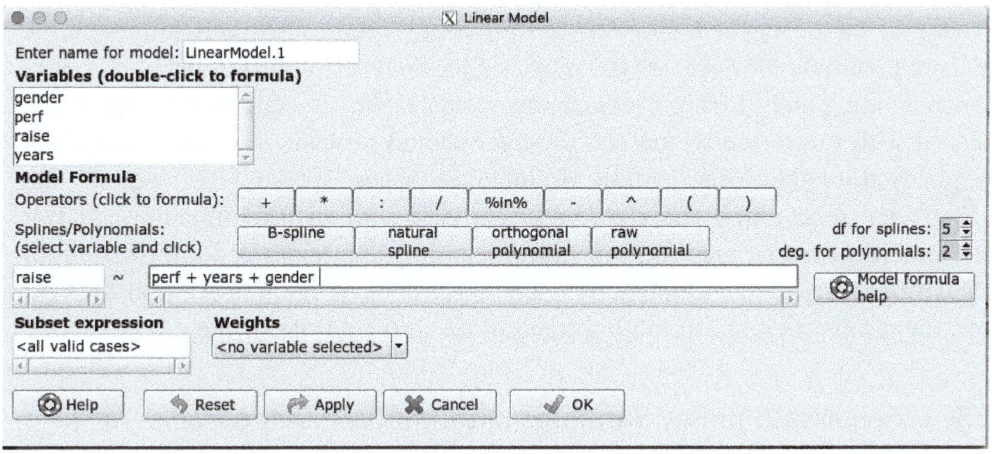

Figure 15.7 Multivariate regression with dummy variables

```
Call:
lm(formula = raise ~ perf + years + gender, data = HR_Data2)

Residuals:
    Min      1Q  Median      3Q     Max
-2.9385 -1.8183  0.1406  1.3445  2.8717

Coefficients:
            Estimate Std. Error t value Pr(>|t|)
(Intercept)  2.54160    2.99205   0.849  0.40816
perf         0.04709    0.03671   1.282  0.21795
years        0.08941    0.08695   1.028  0.31915
gender      -3.97084    0.88419  -4.491  0.00037 ***
---
Signif. codes:  0 '***' 0.001 '**' 0.01 '*' 0.05 '.' 0.1 ' ' 1

Residual standard error: 1.944 on 16 degrees of freedom
Multiple R-squared:  0.6257,	Adjusted R-squared:  0.5556
F-statistic: 8.917 on 3 and 16 DF,  p-value: 0.001049

>
```

Figure 15.8 Multivariate regression with dummy variables results

Employee performance rating and years in the organization are not statistically significant; however, the coefficient on gender is negative and statistically significant at greater than the 99% confidence level. How can we interpret the −3.97 coefficient for gender? The dummy variable is coded such that a value of 1 is an observation for a woman, while a value of 0 is an observation for a man. When interpreting categorical or dummy variables with only two categories (in this case, female v. male), a good template to use is: "On average, ceteris paribus, [having or being whatever is a 1] is associated with a [beta] unit increase or decrease in the dependent variable." For our example, the interpretation of the gender coefficient is that on average, ceteris paribus, being a woman is associated with a 3.97% lower raise. This is compared to men. We use "lower" instead of "decrease," because there's not really a decrease in the raise which connotes getting a pay cut. Context will determine the best interpretation. In this example, only gender is statistically significant. The performance rating and years in organization variables are not statistically significant.

Faced with these results, the HR manager should probably be concerned about unequal and unethical distribution of employee wages. The analysis suggests that only gender affects an employee's raise – a clear case of discrimination. At this point, the HR manager may want to collect additional variables and information for analysis (if theory dictates and/or there are likely omitted variables), but at the very least, the results suggest a troubling trend in the particular department.

15.9 Categorical/Dummy Variables with Multiple Categories – An Applied Example

Sometimes, categorical/dummy variables important for analysis do not have two categories like "Yes/No"; they may have multiple categories like "Political party," "Religious denomination," "Job title," and "Gender" (if surveys and information collected go beyond male and female categories to include "non-binary," "prefer not to say," etc.). Building off an analysis from Chapter 14, we can understand how to interpret these types of dummy variables using the *state_politics* dataset. Recall from Chapter 14 that we examined the effect of unionization on state transportation spending. We ran a bivariate regression analysis and obtained the results reproduced as Figure 15.9.

The bivariate regression showed that a one unit increase in unionization, or a one percent increase in the workforce being unionized, leads to a 0.04 unit or 0.04% decrease in the state budget allocated to transportation.

During President Joe Biden's first term as President, Pete Buttigieg served as Secretary of Transportation. Suppose Secretary Buttigieg is interested in understanding the factors that affect state transportation spending. Specifically, he wants to know the factors that affect the percentage of the state budget allocated to transportation spending across the United States. Joanna, a data analyst in the Department of Transportation, is tasked with putting together a dataset on state transportation

```
Call:
lm(formula = tport ~ unions, data = Dataset)

Residuals:
   Min     1Q Median     3Q    Max
-7.268 -2.248 -0.341  1.554 19.888

Coefficients:
            Estimate Std. Error t value Pr(>|t|)
(Intercept)  9.65216    0.24031  40.166   <2e-16 ***
unions      -0.04097    0.01894  -2.163   0.0308 *
---
Signif. codes:  0 '***' 0.001 '**' 0.01 '*' 0.05 '.' 0.1 ' ' 1

Residual standard error: 3.069 on 845 degrees of freedom
  (3 observations deleted due to missingness)
Multiple R-squared:  0.005505,	Adjusted R-squared:  0.004328
F-statistic: 4.678 on 1 and 845 DF,  p-value: 0.03084
```

Figure 15.9 Union data bivariate regression

budget spending, identifying possible variables affecting state transportation spending and reporting back to the Secretary.

She is able to collect data from 2000 to 2016 on state transportation spending, along with other variables like state budget surplus, state debt, state government ideology, state percentage of the workforce unionized, etc. Growing up in the Midwest, Joanna remembers driving on pothole-filled roads, especially after long, snowy winters. To her, it seemed that the roads were never in great condition. She thinks regional variations exist and hypothesizes that Midwest states spend less on transportation compared to other states. She therefore also collects information on the census region for each state. A screenshot of the data appears in Figure 15.10.[1]

The variables collected by Joanna, their labels, descriptions, and coding are shown in Table 15.3.

The dependent variable is state transportation spending, measured as the percent of the state budget allocated to transportation. As we tested in Chapter 14, Joanna decides to include the state unionization variable. She adds state government ideology, a measure of the state government's partisanship on a scale from 1 (most conservative) to 100 (most liberal) from data collected by Berry et al. (2010). She thinks that ideology may impact the percent of the state budget devoted to transportation.

She also collects information on each state legislature's level of professionalism from research by Bowen and Greene (2014). The level of professionalism of a state legislature is a measure of resources available to legislators. More professional legislatures have more resources. The Bowen and Greene (2014) measure of state legislative professionalism is a variable accounting for the staff expenditures of legislators along with the length of the legislative session. It is a kind of index variable whereby high professionalism scores (positive values) indicate legislatures with high

[1] Dataset comes from research published in Boyer and Scheller (2018).

	A	B	C	D	E	F	G	H	I
1	state	year	unions	ideology	prof	tport	debt	surplus	region
2	AL	2000	9.7	51.504	0.373988	15	1245.04	-12.6113	South
3	AL	2001	11	83.0738	0.318725	15.9	1298.44	-56.922	South
4	AL	2002	9.6	83.0738	0.318725	6.9	1480.86	-79.1338	South
5	AL	2003	9.9	83.0738	0.294768	7.1	1512.25	183.225	South
6	AL	2004	9	83.0738	0.294768	8.1	1704.91	-46.3844	South
7	AL	2005	8.1	46.0997	0.342273	7.6	1627.16	-112.675	South
8	AL	2006	9.7	46.0997	0.342273	7.5	1595.21	-43.1837	South
9	AL	2007	10.2	46.0997	0.501254	3.9	1505.16	120.167	South
10	AL	2008	8.8	46.0997	0.501254	3.7	1465.14	231.157	South
11	AL	2009	9.5	45.2192	0.564682	3.4	1563.14	-16.8268	South
12	AL	2010	9.8	45.6199	0.564682	6.3	1789.15	-182.556	South
13	AL	2011	10.9	42.3333	0.14458	6.5	1714.18	-469.101	South
14	AL	2012	10.1	41.7827	0.14458	8.2	1806.25	-162.919	South
15	AL	2013	10	20.5436		6.4	1801.78	-202.135	South
16	AL	2014	9.2	19.956		6	1691.76	-336.997	South
17	AL	2015	10.8	19.0589	0.527612	6.5	1726.68	-351.249	South
18	AL	2016	10.8	19.0589	0.527612	6.4	1666.69	-290.667	South
19	AK	2000	20.4	51.1142	0.292487	14.7	8067.3	5824.02	West
20	AK	2001	20.4	51.1305	0.1483	21.6	8059.9	760.644	West
21	AK	2002	21.9	51.1305	0.1483		8234.73	2694.65	West
22	AK	2003	22	50.8119	0.099077		8615.73	-707.844	West

Figure 15.10 State politics dataset

levels of staff expenditures and short legislative sessions. Legislators have short sessions with highly paid staff resources to help with legislative duties. Negative values indicate low professionalism scores, or legislatures with low staff expenditures and long legislative sessions, an indication that legislators often have to do many of the administrative tasks themselves during long legislative sessions. Joanna thinks that highly professional legislatures may be in a better position to understand transportation issues in the state, and therefore be more likely to spend a greater percentage of the state budget on transportation.

She also thinks that a state's fiscal condition affects levels of transportation spending. Specifically, she thinks the more a state is in debt, the less likely it is to spend a greater percentage of its budget on transportation. Additionally, if a state is running a budget surplus (revenues > expenditures), she thinks the state will be more likely to allocate funds to transportation. Finally, she hypothesizes that states in the Midwest allocate less of their budget towards transportation. This hypothesis is based upon her own anecdotal observations, but can certainly be empirically tested.

Joanna formalizes her model of state transportation spending as:

$$\begin{aligned}\text{State Transportation Spending} &= b_0 + b_1(\text{State Unionization}) \\ &+ b_2(\text{State Government Ideology}) + b_3(\text{State Legislative Professionalism}) \\ &+ b_4(\text{State Debt}) + b_5(\text{State Budget Surplus}) + b_6(\text{Region})\end{aligned}$$

The Region variable is a factor variable containing four categories (Northeast, South, Midwest, and West). When Joanna and we run the multivariate regression, our inputs should look like Figure 15.11

Table 15.3 State transportation spending data

Variable	Label	Description	Coding
State	*state*	State name	State name
Year	*year*	Year	Year
State Unionization	*unions*	Percentage of state Workforce Unionized	% of state workforce unionized
State Government Ideology	*ideology*	Measure of state government ideology from conservative to liberal (Berry et al., 2010)	Scale from 1 (Most Conservative) to 100 (Most Liberal)
State Legislative Professionalism	*prof*	Level of professionalism of state legislature regarding staffing and session length (Bowen and Greene 2014)	Negative scores = low professionalism; positive scores = high professionalism
State Transportation Spending	*tport*	Percentage of state budget allocated to transportation	% of state budget allocated to transportation
State Debt	*debt*	Real per capita state debt	Dollars (thousands of 2009 dollars)
State Budget Surplus	*surplus*	Real per capita state budget surplus (revenues – expenditures)	Dollars (thousands of 2009 dollars)
Region	*region*	Census region	Region (Northeast, South, Midwest, West)

The corresponding results should appear like Figure 15.12.

The region variable gets disaggregated into its component categories (essentially new variables) in the results, but Midwest is missing. Why? Region is a factor or categorical or nominal variable with more than two categories. One category needs to be left out of the analysis to serve as the reference category. The reference category is what we compare the other categories of the variable to. Therefore, the beta coefficients on the Northeast (−1.93), South (−1.22), and West (−0.05) variables are the effect of those regions *as compared to* the Midwest. This is the reason why the Midwest variable is not seen in the results. It is serving as the reference category.

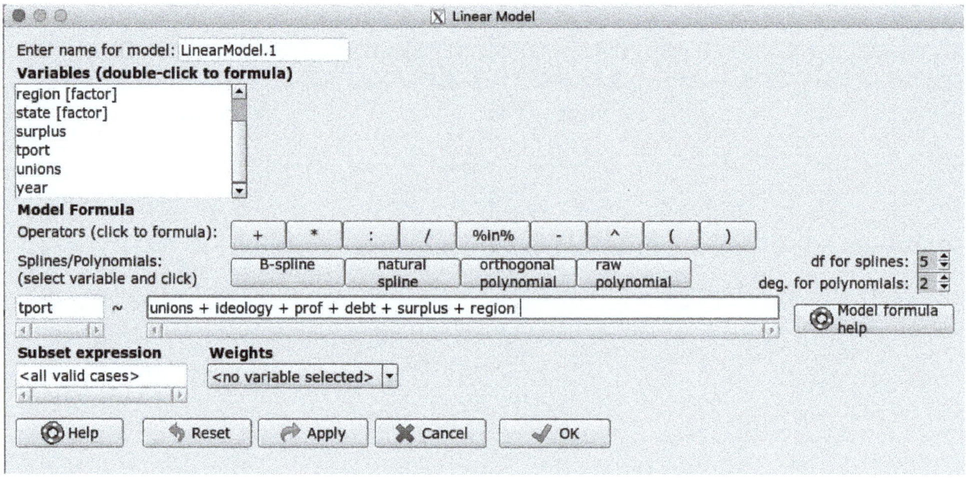

Figure 15.11 State transportation spending multivariate regression

```
Residuals:
    Min      1Q  Median      3Q     Max
-8.7373 -1.8936 -0.1638  1.5420 18.1115

Coefficients:
                       Estimate  Std. Error t value Pr(>|t|)
(Intercept)         10.50515970  0.34383067  30.553  < 2e-16 ***
unions              -0.10492748  0.02518717  -4.166 3.44e-05 ***
ideology            -0.02027481  0.00469517  -4.318 1.77e-05 ***
prof                 0.48083678  0.14411026   3.337 0.000887 ***
debt                 0.00045792  0.00007281   6.289 5.25e-10 ***
surplus              0.00064978  0.00016533   3.930 9.23e-05 ***
region[T.Northeast] -1.92750623  0.39403753  -4.892 1.21e-06 ***
region[T.South]     -1.22401663  0.31654153  -3.867 0.000119 ***
region[T.West]      -0.05185729  0.29816238  -0.174 0.861970
---
Signif. codes:  0 '***' 0.001 '**' 0.01 '*' 0.05 '.' 0.1 ' ' 1

Residual standard error: 2.873 on 799 degrees of freedom
  (42 observations deleted due to missingness)
Multiple R-squared:  0.1468,    Adjusted R-squared:  0.1383
F-statistic: 17.19 on 8 and 799 DF,  p-value: < 2.2e-16
```

Figure 15.12 State transportation spending multivariate regression results

To interpret the coefficients on the region variables, we can use a new template that applies to interpreting variables with multiple categories: "On average, ceteris paribus, [having or being whatever is a 1], compared to the reference category of [whatever the reference category is], is associated with a [beta] unit increase or decrease in the dependent variable." So, for the Northeast, we would say, "On average, ceteris paribus, being a state in the Northeast, compared to the reference category of Midwest, leads to a 1.93 unit (1.93%) decrease in the percent of the state budget allocated to transportation." This relationship is significant at at least the 99% confidence level. For the South, we would say, "On average, ceteris paribus, being a state in the South, compared to the reference category of Midwest, leads to a 1.22 unit (1.22%) decrease in the percent of the state budget allocated to transportation."

This relationship is also significant at the 99% confidence level. Therefore, Joanna's hypothesis that Midwest states spend poorly on transportation compared to other states is not supported by the evidence. Midwest states, on average, actually spend more money as a percentage of their state budget on transportation than states in the Northeast and the South. The beta coefficient on the West variable is not statistically significant. Therefore, there are no statistical differences in spending between Midwest and Western states on transportation.

15.9.1 Regression Equation

We can update Joanna's regression equation from above to provide more specific information with the disaggregation of the Region variable into its component categories. Her original regression equation expression was:

$$\begin{aligned}\text{State Transportation Spending} &= b_0 + b_1(\text{State Unionization}) \\ &+ b_2(\text{State Government Ideology}) + b_3(\text{State Legislative Professionalism}) \\ &+ b_4(\text{State Debt}) + b_5(\text{State Budget Surplus}) + b_6(\text{Region})\end{aligned}$$

With the results, we can update it to:

$$\begin{aligned}\text{State Transportation Spending} &= b_0 + b_1(\text{State Unionization}) \\ &+ b_2(\text{State Government Ideology}) + b_3(\text{State Legislative Professionalism}) \\ &+ b_4(\text{State Debt}) + b_5(\text{State Budget Surplus}) + b_6(\text{Northeast}) + b_7(\text{South}) + b_8(\text{West})\end{aligned}$$

Inserting the beta coefficients gives Joanna the regression equation:

$$\begin{aligned}\text{State Transportation Spending} &= 10.51 - 0.10(\text{State Unionization}) \\ &- 0.02(\text{State Government Ideology}) + 0.48(\text{State Legislative Professionalism}) \\ &+ 0.0005(\text{State Debt}) + 0.0006(\text{State Budget Surplus}) - 1.93(\text{Northeast}) \\ &- 1.22(\text{South}) - 0.05(\text{West})\end{aligned}$$

15.9.2 Engaging in Prediction

As with other examples, we can engage in prediction. Suppose Joanna wanted to estimate the percent of a state's budget allocated to transportation spending for a state that has:

- unionization of 8.3%
- government ideology score of 55
- legislative professionalism score of −1
- no state debt
- no state surplus
- is in the Northeast

Enter the relevant information into Joanna's regression equation to help her answer her question:

$$\text{State Transportation Spending} = 10.51 - 0.10(8.3) - 0.02(55) + 0.48(-1) + 0.0005(0) + 0.0006(0) - 1.93(1) - 1.22(0) - 0.05(0)$$

Since the state is in the Northeast, the "Northeast" component receives a value of 1, while the "South" and "West" components receive values of 0. Working through the equation yields:

$$\text{State Transportation Spending} = 10.51 - 0.83 - 1.1 - .48 + 0 + 0 - 1.93 + (0) + 0 = 6.17$$

Her best prediction for this particular state would be 6.17% of the state budget allocated to transportation. She may note that the Adjusted R-Squared is only 13.83%, so she might conclude that she may need to collect additional information to have better confidence in her results and predictions.

15.10 Summing Up: Implications of Bivariate v. Multivariate Regression

The state transportation spending example shows what happens to our results, confidence, and prediction abilities when we move from the bivariate to the multivariate world. In the bivariate example, we modeled state transportation spending only as a function of a state's percent of the workforce unionized. When we added other theoretically relevant independent variables, the results changed, especially the beta coefficient on the "unions" variable.

In the bivariate example, unionization had a beta coefficient of −0.04, significant at the 95% confidence level. When we included other variables in the multivariate analysis, the beta coefficient on the unionization variable chaged to −0.10, significant at greater than the 99% confidence level. Unions now appear to have a stronger effect on state transportation spending than previously hypothesized. Before, each 1% increase in the number of unions in the state led to an average decrease in the state budget allocated to transportation by 0.04%. Now, with the inclusion of other relevant variables, each 1% increase in the number of unions in the state leads to an average decrease in the state budget allocated to transportation by 0.10%. Though these differences may seem miniscule (0.04% to 0.10%), remember that state budgets involve millions of dollars; therefore, what appears to be a miniscule increase of effect may be hundreds of thousands or even millions of dollars.

The changing values of coefficients and their significance levels highlight the importance of correctly modeling statistical relationships. Where possible, researchers should include all theoretically relevant independent variables that affect their dependent variable. Otherwise, they may suffer from omitted variable bias (excluding relevant variables), and violate a key assumption of linear regression (more detail in

Chapter 16). Such a violation introduces bias into our results, causing us to get an incorrect coefficient in them. These results would report a relationship between an independent and dependent variable incorrectly, and thus we could not understand the independent effect of that independent variable on the dependent variable.

PRACTICE PROBLEMS

Conceptual Problems

1. Explain what linear regression depicts between a dependent variable, Y, and two independent variables, X_1 and X_2.
2. Suppose a manager hypothesizes that employee morale is a function of when an employee last received a raise, their age, and number of years the employee has been in the organization.
   a. Identify the independent and dependent variables in this statement.
   b. How would you measure or operationalize the independent and dependent variables? How could you go about collecting or obtaining this data?
   c. Develop null and directional research hypotheses for the relationship between employee morale and age, on the one hand, and number of years in the organization, on the other.
   d. What other independent variables would you eventually want to include? Explain.
   e. What would happen to our regression results if we did not include these additional variables that you think affect employee morale - if we only included when an employee last received a raise, their age, and the number of years the employee has been in the organization? How does this affect the confidence of our results?
3. Hypothesize a negative relationship between two variables of interest.
   a. Explain the logic behind your hypothesis.
   b. Explain how you would operationalize your variables - what data would you collect?
4. What is a reference category in a regression? Identify a variable that would likely need a reference category and explain why.
5. Find a journal article in public administration where the researcher(s) utilizes a multivariate regression model in their analysis. Answer the following:
   a. What is the research question of the article?
   b. What hypotheses are tested?
   c. List the dependent variable and the independent variables.
   d. Explain how the dependent and independent variables are measured and coded. Do the measurement and coding schemes make sense? Why/why not?
   e. Interpret the statistically significant variables in their analysis.

f. Interpret the Adjusted R-Squared if reported.
g. Are there other variables the researcher should consider? Why/why not?

Problems By Hand

6. The director of the Texas Health and Human Services is interested in how the state unemployment rate affects the number of households each month on food stamps. The director's staff collects information on the monthly unemployment rate (percent unemployed) in the state for the past ten years, along with the number of households each month receiving food stamps. A bivariate regression is run with unemployment rate as the independent variable and the number of households on food stamps in the state as the dependent variable. The results appear below:

$\hat{b}_0 = 236,931$
$\hat{b}_1 = 75,521$
$s.e._{\hat{b}1} = 22,483$
R-Squared $= 0.54$

The director's chief data analyst points out that other variables may need to be included. The data analyst collects data on the state's estimated population for each of the ten years, along with the state's median family income for the previous ten years. The analyst then runs a multivariate regression with unemployment rate, estimated population, and median family income (in thousands of dollars) as the independent variables and the number of households on food stamps in the state as the dependent variable. The multivariate regression results appear below. X_1 is the unemployment rate, X_2 is the estimated population, and X_3 is the median family income.

$\hat{b}_0 = 111,426$
$\hat{b}_1 = 68,745$
$s.e._{\hat{b}1} = 30,001$
$\hat{b}_2 = 0.0002$
$s.e._{\hat{b}2} = 0.0001$
$\hat{b}_3 = -150.35$
$s.e._{\hat{b}3} = 15.65$
R-Squared $= 0.89$
Adjusted R-Squared $= 0.89$

a. Interpret the beta coefficient on each independent variable if it is statistically significant. How do you know if it is statistically significant or not? If it is not significant, explain what may be the reason.
b. What happened to the coefficient on the unemployment rate from the bivariate regression to the multivariate regression. Why?

c. Interpret the y-intercept. Does it make substantive sense? Why/why not?
d. Using the beta coefficients and y-intercept, write down the equation of the best-fitting regression plane.
e. Interpret the Adjusted R-Squared value.
f. Predict the number of households on food stamps if the unemployment rate is 10.5%, the estimated population is 15,000,000, and the median family income is $25,031.

7. The director of international bridges in Nogales, Arizona, is trying to understand the effect of bridge wait times on the number of border crossings at the international bridge. They think as wait times increase, the number of crossings decrease. Basically, they hypothesize that as wait times increase, people will be deterred from crossing. The director collects a year's worth of data, including each day's average wait time (in minutes) at the bridge (X_1), and the day's total number of crossings (Y). They also collect data to control for the effect of the exchange rate of the Peso to the Dollar (X_2), and daily high temperature (X_3). The multivariate regression results appear below:

$$\hat{b}_0 = 16,999$$
$$\hat{b}_1 = -15.6$$
$$s.e._{\hat{b}1} = 10.25$$
$$\hat{b}_2 = 89.34$$
$$s.e._{\hat{b}2} = 46.23$$
$$\hat{b}_3 = 3,451$$
$$s.e._{\hat{b}3} = 535.6$$
$$\text{R-Squared} = 0.54$$
$$\text{Adjusted R-Squared} = 0.49$$

a. Which variables are statistically significant? How do you know?
b. Interpret all statistically significant variables.
c. Interpret the y-intercept. Does it make substantive sense?
d. Using the beta coefficients and y-intercept, write down the equation of the best-fitting regression plane.
e. Interpret the Adjusted R-Squared value. What other variables should be included?
f. Predict the number of crossings if the average wait time is 30 minutes, the exchange rate is 35, and the high temperature is 95 degrees.

8. The executive director of a local nonprofit organization is interested in understanding the factors that affect an individual's level of donations during their local fundraising campaign. The director has access to a database containing the names of all of this year's and last year's donors. The database contains information on the total dollar amount of donation from the individual this year and in the previous year, along with the donor's gender, and the donor's political party identification pulled from public records. They regress this year's donation dollar amount on the donor's previous year's contribution, their gender, and their political party identification. Gender is coded 1 if the donor is a male, and 0 if the donor is a female. The political party identification variable contains the categories of Democrat, Independent, Republican, Libertarian, and Other. The director believes Democrats to be predisposed to donating more to the organization, so she makes Democrat the reference category. The results appear below:

$\hat{b}_0 = 24$
$\hat{b}_1$ (Previous Donation) $= 25$
$s.e._{\hat{b}1} = 2.56$
$\hat{b}_2$ (Gender) $= 78.93$
$s.e._{\hat{b}2} = 55.89$
$\hat{b}_3$ (Independent) $= 55.31$
$s.e._{\hat{b}3} = 22.98$
$\hat{b}_4$ (Republican) $= -17.57$
$s.e._{\hat{b}4} = 10.85$
$\hat{b}_5$ (Libertarian) $= 27.88$
$s.e._{\hat{b}5} = 16.09$
$\hat{b}_6$ (Other) $= -32.18$
$s.e._{\hat{b}6} = 8.76$
R-Squared $= 0.32$
Adjusted R-Squared $= 0.28$

a. Which variables are statistically significant? How do you know?
b. Interpret all statistically significant variables.
c. Interpret the y-intercept. Does it make substantive sense?
d. Using the beta coefficients and y-intercept, write down the equation of the best-fitting regression plane.
e. Interpret the Adjusted R-Squared value. What other variables should be included?
f. What other variables should the director try to collect to better understand donor donations?

R Commander Problems

9. In Chapter 14's problems, you looked at the effect of temperature on attendance at a minor league team's baseball games. Attendance at games is of importance since the city receives revenue from ticket sales and purchases from concessions and souvenirs. City leaders now think that attendance is a function of more than temperature. They task you with trying to figure out what variables affect attendance. Using the *baseball* dataset and the *baseball codebook* in the Companion Site (www.cambridge.org/scheller), do the following and answer the questions:

a. For reference, re-run the bivariate regression from Chapter 14, testing the effect of temperature on attendance.
b. Interpret the coefficient on the temperature variable if statistically significant.
c. Now, add in the "wind" variable to the regression model and run the analysis with temperature and wind speed as the two independent variables.
d. Interpret the statistically significant variables.
e. What happened to the coefficient for temperature and its significance? Explain why these changed.
f. Hypothesize a relationship between whether or not a promotion occurs on the game day, whether or not the game is on a weekend, and the team's win percentage.
g. Add the variables from "f" into the regression model and show the results. Interpret any statistically significant variables.
h. What happened to the coefficient for temperature and its significance? Why might this be the case?
i. Interpret the y-intercept. Does it make substantive sense?
j. Interpret the Adjust R-Squared.
k. Predict attendance at a baseball game if the temperature is 75 degrees, the wind speed at game time is 5 mph, there is a promotion, the game is on a weekday, and the team's win percentage is 55.

10. Open the *emergency_response* dataset. It contains data on emergency response times.

a. Run a bivariate regression with response time as the dependent variable and distance to the emergency as the independent variable. Interpret the coefficient on the distance variable.
b. The chief thinks the presence of supervisors known as battalion chiefs may decrease response times – employees may be more motivated to hurry if a supervisor is present. Add this variable ("chief_station") to the regression model along with the time of day for the emergency. The chief thinks graveyard shift emergencies will take longer to respond to since personnel may be asleep. Four dummy variables comprise the time of day variable ("day," "evening," "night," and "graveyard"). Run the multivariate regression.
c. Interpret any statistically significant variables.
d. Were the chief's expectations supported? Why/why not?
e. Predict the response time for an emergency if the distance to the emergency is 3 miles, a chief is present, and the incident happens during the graveyard shift.

11. The superintendent of the local school system is interested in understanding the effect of student absences on standardized test scores. The superintendent takes a random sample of twenty students in the district, noting the number of days absent, student race/ethnicity, and their score on the state standardized test (0–100). Student race/ethnicity is coded as 1 if the student is White, 2 if the student is African American, 3 if the student is Hispanic, and 4 if the student is of any Other race or multi-racial. The data appear in the Table below.
    a. Enter the data into Excel and then upload into the R Commander.
    b. Run a bivariate regression with the dependent variable as the test score and the independent variable as the number of absences.
    c. What is the effect of absences on test scores and is it statistically significant?

Student absences and test scores

Student	Absences	Race/Ethnicity	Test Score
1	0	Hispanic	96
2	3	White	88
3	1	White	95
4	7	African American	62
5	5	Hispanic	73
6	0	Other	100
7	15	White	22
8	0	African American	78
9	2	Hispanic	95
10	5	White	82
11	3	White	99
12	4	African American	62
13	1	Other	78
14	7	White	63
15	0	Hispanic	91
16	2	African American	86
17	3	White	76
18	2	Other	89
19	11	White	53
20	3	African American	88

d. What is the interpretation of the Adjusted R-Squared value?
e. Run a multivariate regression with the dependent variable as the test scores and the independent variables as the number of absences and the student's race.
f. Interpret any statistically significant variables.
g. What happened to the coefficient on absences and its significance? Why?

12. The state of New Mexico is known for growing green chiles. Three counties are especially essential for the state's green chile crop – Doña Ana, Luna, and Sierra. They are located in Southern New Mexico and have a favorable climate for growing green chiles. You have been hired by the state agriculture department to analyze green chile crop production from 2017 to 2021 from these three coutnies. You are given the available dataset containing data from the US Department of Agriculture (USDA, 2022) and National Centers for Environmental Information (NCEI, 2022). The dataset is named the *chile* dataset and is located in the Companion Site. Variables in the dataset compiled from the USDA are:

county = county
year = year
cwt = county chile production in hundredweight (1 hundredweight = 100 pounds) per acre
acres = county number of acres of chile planted

Variables compiled from the NCEI include:
rain = average county rainfall in inches during growing season (March–July)
temp = average county temperature in Fahrenheit during growing season (March–July)

a. Your first task as an analyst is to come up with hypotheses and expected relationships between the "cwt" variable and the independent variables "acres," "rain," and "temp."
b. Run a multivariate regression with "cwt" as the dependent variable and "acres," "rain," and "temp" as the independent variables.
c. Interpret each of the beta coefficients for the independent variables.
d. Interpret the y-intercept. Does it make substantive sense? Why/why not?
e. Interpret the Adjusted R-Squared.
f. As the analyst, you are tasked with determining whether or not there is enough data to make conclusions. What do you think? Take a look at the data and examine what might be missing in terms of observations and variables. What steps do you recommend to increase available data?

g. As a quick preview to the next chapter, do you think that rain and temperature have perfectly linear relationships with production (the effects of rain and temperature on production is the same for 0.5 inches of rain and 25 inches of rain; average temperature of 60 degrees and average temperature of 90 degrees)? Why/why not? You may need to do some independent reading on growing green chiles in New Mexico to better help you answer this question.

16

Regression Assumptions

16.1 Introduction

In the previous two chapters, we went into great detail regarding OLS regression, a powerful statistical test to help determine not only the relationships among variables, but also to better understand the causal relationship between independent and dependent variables. As with all statistical tests and models, there are some theoretical and mathematical assumptions that must be met in order for our conclusions to be robust and valid. Violating one or more of these assumptions can lead to biases in our analysis, faulty conclusions, and ultimately, ill-informed conclusions for decision making in public administration and policy. Sometimes, with violation of assumptions, an easy fix exists to help overcome the violation and associated biases. Other times, more advanced statistical methods and/or tests, well beyond the scope of this textbook, are needed to remedy the problems.

You may have already noticed some patterns in the types of variables and their measurement from the previous two chapters. It is no coincidence that the examples have all involved interval level variables. It is also not coincidental that we do not include more than one independent variable to measure a concept. Studies will usually not include two or more measures of poverty, like a measure of a household's annual income *and* a variable identifying whether or not the household falls below the poverty line. These two measures are likely highly correlated.

When using multivariate OLS regression, there are a number of assumptions that need to be met, some more complicated to understand than others. We'll start with some of the more basic assumptions (not more or less important) that need to be met, and then discuss some of the more complicated, mathematical assumptions. An in-depth discussion of some of the more complicated mathematical assumptions is beyond the scope of this book, but they are important to know and understand as one does research. Terms like "autocorrelation" and "heteroscedasticity" are likely not common parlance in daily office discussions; however, a basic understanding of them can help public administrators become better consumers of public administration research and applied research findings. Readers interested in more advanced instruction of regression assumptions can utilize the citations in the Recommended Reading section at the end of the chapter.

16.2 Assumption 1: Dependent Variable Is Interval

The first and most basic assumption to meet to run OLS regression is to make sure the dependent variable is interval level. Technically, the dependent variable should be able to range from $-\infty$ to ∞, or as Berry (1993) notes, able to take on any value. For example, personal wealth can range from $-\infty$ (highly in debt) to ∞ (super wealthy). In practice, however, it is OK to use bounded dependent variables assuming they can take on a relatively large number of values. Attendance at a baseball game ranges from 0 to the stadium's capacity. It is completely appropriate to use this measure as a dependent variable. Test scores (ranging from 0–100) are often used in analyses, along with crime rates (crimes per 100,000 people), city gross domestic product (GDP), percent of population receiving a vaccine, number of work absences, deaths from a natural disaster, etc. These examples are all viable dependent variables for analysis.

Even a ranking scale of 1–10 is often used as a dependent variable in a regression analysis. When the number of categories begins to drop below 10, however, linear regression is not such a good method to use and biases may be introduced in analyses. For example, if a researcher is interested in measuring employee job satisfaction on a scale from 1–5 according to the following,

1 = Highly Dissatisfied
2 = Satisfied
3 = Neither Satisfied nor Dissatisfied
4 = Satisfied
5 = Highly Satisfied

OLS regression would not be appropriate. This measure is really an ordinal level of measurement of satisfaction. Sure, one could run an OLS regression with this measure as the dependent variable, and any statistical program would "spit out" numerical results. However, the coefficients/results would be biased, and we could draw incorrect conclusions on the effect of the independent variables in the model on job satisfaction. A more appropriate statistical test would be an ordered logistic regression.

As an example, suppose a probation officer is interested in collecting data on whether or not a client recidivated, or committed another crime during their probation. The manager collects data on the age of the client, race, gender, nature of original crime, time on probation, etc., to help explain whether or not the client committed a crime. The dependent variable is recidivism, and the officer codes each client as to whether or not they recidivated. A value of 1 is a "Yes" in the spreadsheet, while a value of 0 represents "No." This categorical or dummy variable contains only two categories - Yes or No. It can be used as a dependent variable, *BUT* not in an OLS regression. If one were to use such a dependent variable in an OLS regression, statistical software would report results, but they would be incorrect/biased. When dealing with these Yes/No or 1/0 coded dependent variables, the appropriate statistical test is a logistic regression, which is the topic of Chapter 18. Remember, to run an OLS regression, the dependent variable should be interval! Otherwise, you may need to use a different statistical test. If the probation officer had percent recidivated, say from yearly data from the city that included the percent of citizens on probation that recidivated, this measure would be at the interval level.

One may wonder about the independent variables for OLS regression. It is recommended to measure independent variables at the interval level when able. Dummy or dichotomous independent variables may also be used in OLS regression, and in fact are very common when measuring categorical variables like gender, party identification, job title, yes/no, urban versus rural, etc.

16.3 Assumption 2: Linear Relationship between Independent and Dependent Variables

In an OLS or linear regression, the relationship between the independent variables (X) and the dependent variable (Y) is assumed to be linear. The effect of X on Y is therefore assumed to not change across all values of X, hence the logic behind interpreting regression coefficients as "a one unit change in X leads to a [beta] unit change in Y." If the effect of X on Y varies depending upon the value of X (for example, the effect of X on Y is larger for smaller values of X), the linearity assumption for OLS regression has been violated.

Let's take a look at a hypothetical example involving county vaccine rates for a dangerous virus and death rates. The vaccine rate is measured as the percent of the county vaccinated against a dangerous virus. The death rate is the number of people dying from the virus per 100,000 people in the county. Figure 16.1 depicts one potential scenario.

The relationship is a strong negative relationship. As the percent of the county population vaccinated rises, the county deaths per 100,000 from the virus declines. The regression line shows that most of the observations fall very close along it. Even if the regression line was not present, it is clearly a negative linear relationship from observing the datapoints. Figure 16.2 shows a different hypothetical relationship between vaccination rates and deaths.

In this example, there is obviously some sort of negative relationship between vaccination rates and death rates. The best-fitting regression line is drawn through the data; however, something appears off. Some observations appear to fall close to the regression line, but others appear far away in a systematic pattern. Between vaccination rates of 20% and 60%, nearly all of the observations fall below the regression line for death rate. At the extreme low and high values of vaccination rates (below 20% and above 60%), a disproportionate number of observations fall above the regression line. This can be very problematic for running analyses.

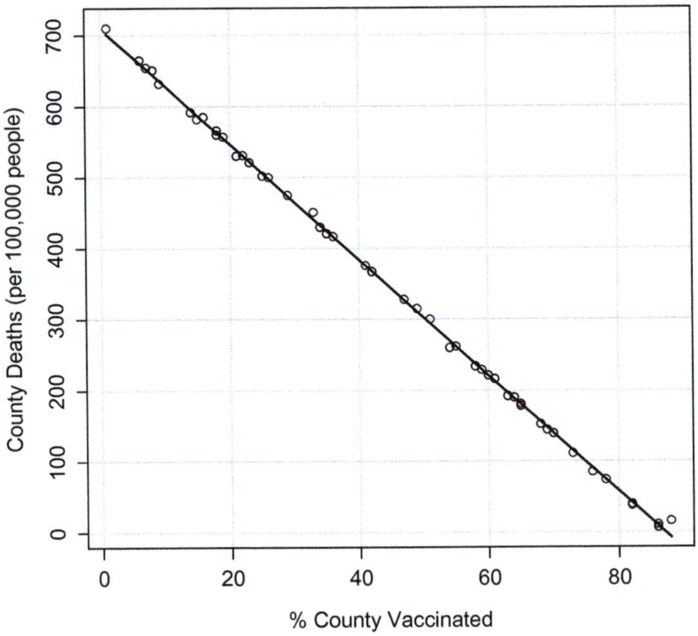

Figure 16.1 Linear relationship between independent (X) and dependent variables (Y)

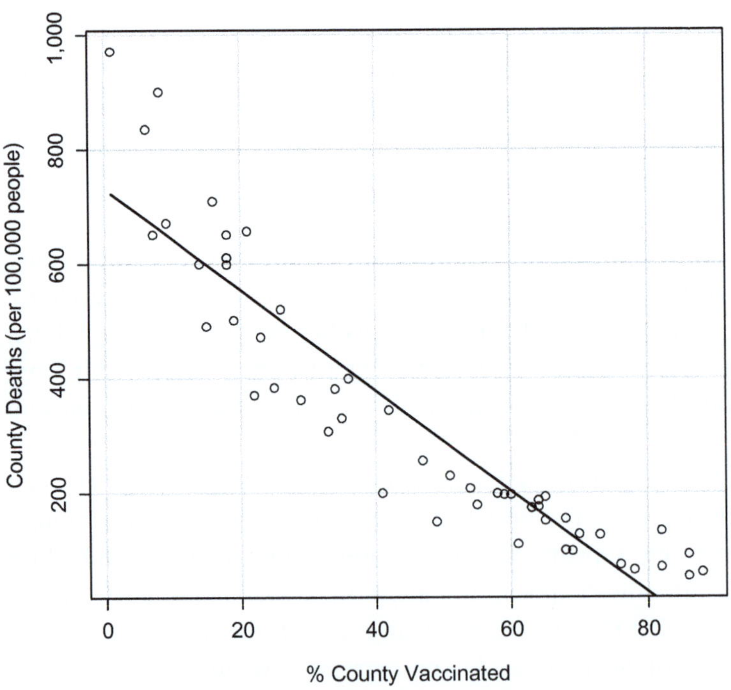

Figure 16.2 Nonlinear relationship with best-fitting regression line

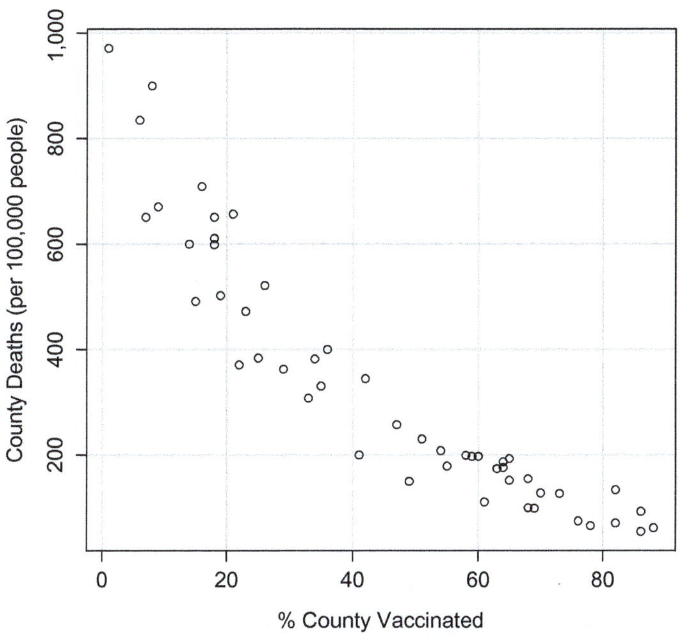

Figure 16.3 Nonlinear relationship without best-fitting regression line

We are interested in the data-generating process of the variables in our analysis. Linear regression assumes a *linear* data-generating process between the independent variable (X) and the dependent variable (Y). The data in Figure 16.2 does not appear to be linear. This fact is much clearer once the best-fitting regression line is removed from the data as shown in Figure 16.3.

There appears to be a curvature to the data, or a convex pattern relative to the origin of the graph. One can envision drawing a curved line through the scatterplot's datapoints, starting from the northwest corner of the graph down to the southeast corner – something along the lines seen in Figure 16.4 with a smoothing line placed through the data to better show the relationship between the percent vaccinated and the death rate.

With this data-generating process, OLS regression should not be used in an analysis of the effect of vaccination rates on death rates. The software would still report results, but they would be biased.

Relationships do not have to be perfectly linear in practice – such relationships really only exist in the hard sciences like the relationship between degrees Fahrenheit and degrees Celsius:

$$C = \frac{5}{9}(F - 32)$$

There is no deviation from this relationship between Fahrenheit and Celsius. It exists as a perfectly linear and predictable relationship. Most relationships in the social sciences will not be even remotely as clear as the Fahrenheit–Celsius relationship.

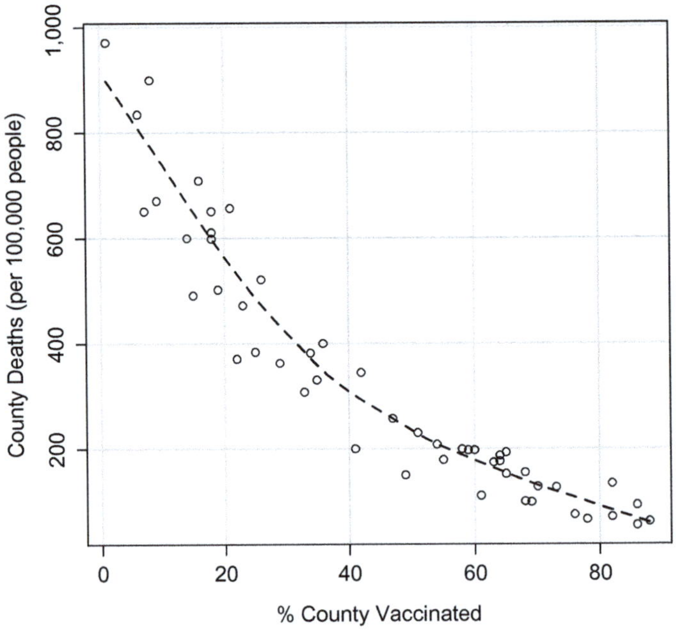

Figure 16.4 Nonlinear relationship with smoothing line

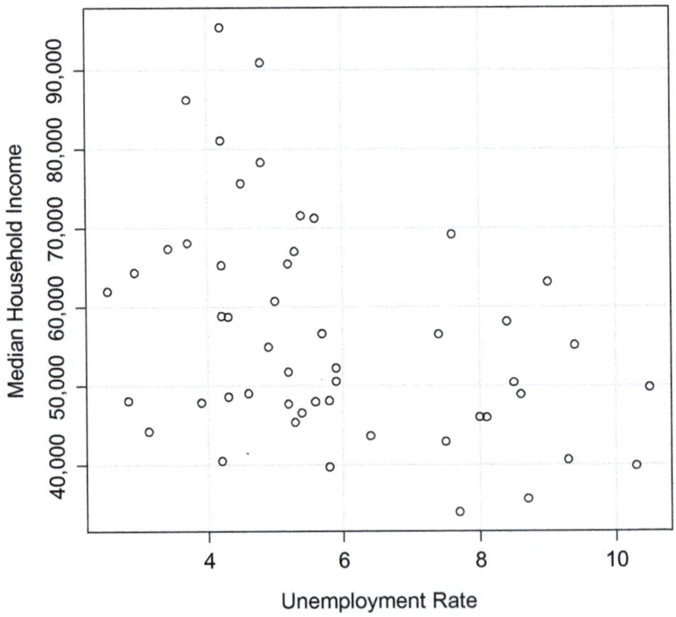

Figure 16.5 County unemployment rates and median household income

More often than not, relationships between two variables may appear more like Figure 16.5, which plots some datapoints regarding county unemployment rates and county median household incomes in Texas (where available) from the 2015 American Community Survey (U.S. Census Bureau, 2015).

Obviously, there is not a perfectly linear relationship between unemployment rate and median household income. We do see a general, negative relationship – as the unemployment rate increases, median household income decreases. Some deviations exist, which are likely explained by a multitude of other variables that affect county median household income (county level measures of educational attainment, race, age, etc.).

A variety of non-linear relationships could appear in your data that you need to notice in order to recognize that OLS regression may not be the appropriate method to analyze the relationships between variables. Each of the figures (Figures 16.6 through 16.10) depict non-linear relationships preventing the use of OLS regression.

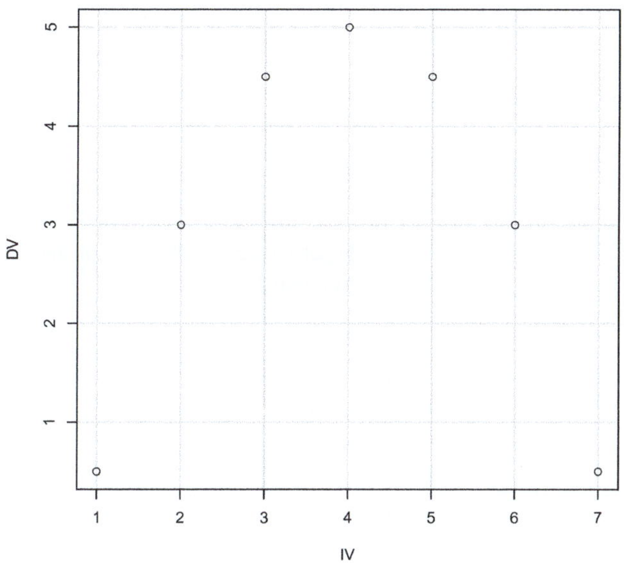

Figure 16.6 Quadratic relationship, example 1

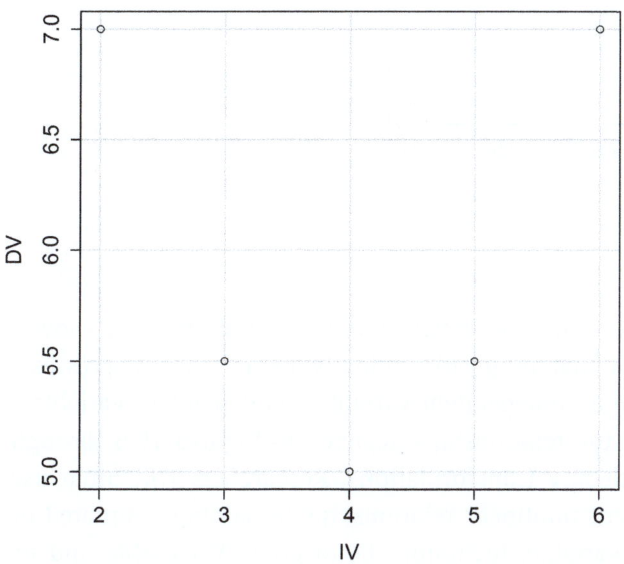

Figure 16.7 Quadratic relationship, example 2

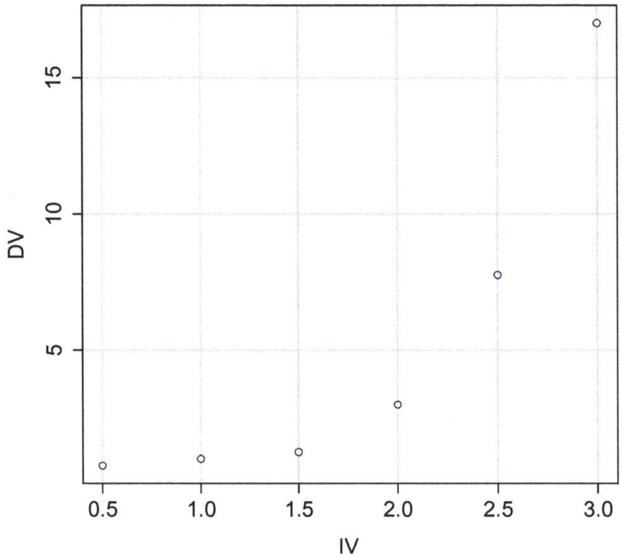

Figure 16.8 Cubic relationship, example 1

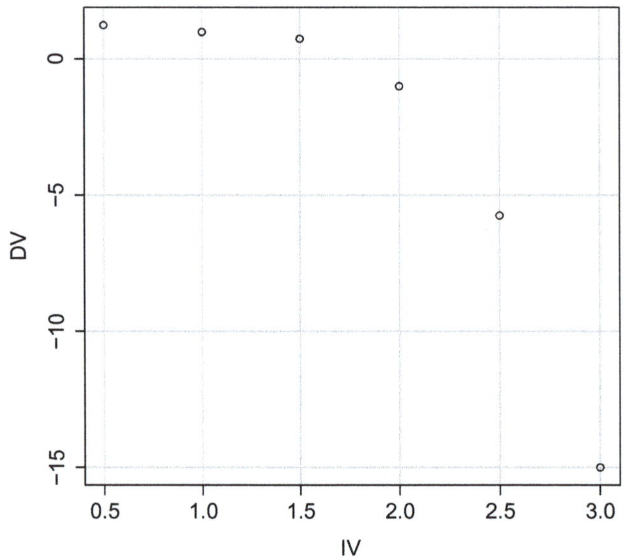

Figure 16.9 Cubic relationship, example 2

Figures 16.6 and 16.7 depict quadratic relationships. Figures 16.8 and 16.9 show a cubic relationship for values of X that are positive. Finally, Figure 16.10 expresses a logarithmic relationship between an independent variable and dependent variable.

Running OLS regression with the relationships depicted in Figures 16.6 through 16.10 is not appropriate without any transformations. Researchers will often use polynomial equations to represent nonlinear relationships by adding a squared or cubed transformation of an X variable, including the original X variable and its

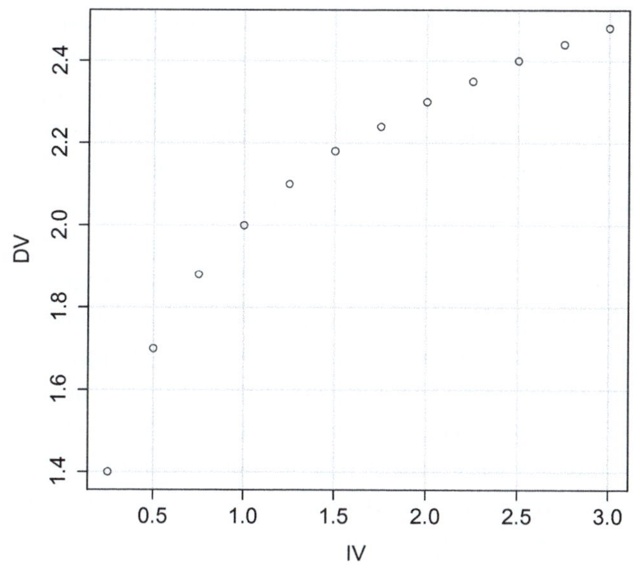

Figure 16.10 Logarithmic relationship

transformed variable (X^2) if dealing with a quadratic relationship. The Fox (2016) citation in the Recommended Reading section is an excellent resource if interested in understanding nonlinear relationship transformation and the use of OLS regression.

16.4 Assumption 3: Model Correctly Specified

A major assumption of OLS regression is that the regression model is correctly specified, or that the researcher has correctly modeled the data generating process by including the relevant independent variables in the regression. There should not be any omitted independent variables that affect the dependent variable (a problem known as omitted variable bias). Likewise, any theoretically irrelevant variables should not be included in the regression model. Finally, X should affect Y in a causal relationship and not Y affecting X, or X and Y simultaneously affecting each other. OLS regression assumes the theoretical causal direction is solely in the manner that independent variables (X) affect the dependent variable (Y). If a regression model is not correctly specified, the researcher may not accurately draw conclusions based upon the research.

A typical concern for researchers is in the form of omitted variable bias, or excluding a relevant variable from the regression model. In Chapter 14, we examined bivariate regression with a dependent variable being explained by one independent variable. Chapter 15 introduced and explained the importance of multivariate regression where a dependent variable is explained by more than one independent variable. Examples in the chapter and end-of-chapter problems had you run a bivariate regression and then run a multivariate regression with additional variables. You should have noted how the coefficients on the independent variables along with their significance changed with the inclusion of other relevant variables. Omitting relevant variables biases the beta coefficient estimates, giving us an incorrect assessment of the independent effect of a particular variable on the dependent variable. Additionally, omitting relevant variables affects our ability to engage in predictions. If we use the regression results to make predictions about the dependent variable for various values of independent variables, our predictions will be biased or incorrect if we omit relevant variables.

Students often wonder how many independent variables to include in the regression model. As Berman and Wang (2018) correctly note, the inclusion of independent variables should be driven by theory, recognizing the impossibility of collecting and analyzing every single variable that may affect a social science phenomenon. Therefore, their recommendation is to include the most relevant variables. The same logic applies to the issue of irrelevant variables. Irrelevant is not the same as statistically insignificant. Variables that are not statistically significant in a regression should not simply be dropped from the model and the regression re-run. Theory dictates the inclusion of variables to a regression model, even if they end up being statistically insignificant.

One quick test to determine if you have omitted variable bias is to run your regression models with different independent variables, noting how the Adjusted R-Squared changes with the inclusion/omission of variables. As a caveat, you should include any theoretically relevant variable even if it is not statistically significant. Theory, first and foremost, should drive your regression models and what independent variables you include. However, if the Adjusted R-Squared increases when you include another independent variable, it should likely be included in the model.

16.5 Assumption 4: No Measurement Error

We assume that our variables are measured correctly. As basic examples, if a police officer's radar gun sometimes inaccurately reported the speed of a vehicle, or if a camera tracking the number of cars through an intersection sometimes double-counts large vehicles as two vehicles, or if a digital temperature gauge occasionally reports temperatures off by 3 degrees, then there is measurement error. Logically, if there is error in the manner in which data are collected, then we do not have accurate data, and therefore, results from analyses would be biased and conclusions inaccurate and faulty.

16.6 Assumption 5: Independent Variables Must Vary

By definition, variables vary. Therefore, if you have collected an independent variable that is constant, or contains the same values, it cannot be used in a regression model. For example, if you were studying the effect of education on income levels in a community, and everybody in the community had a bachelor's degree, there would be no way to determine the effect of education on income, even if people had differing income levels. Since everybody has a bachelor's degree, no comparison can be made. We could not say, "On average, ceteris paribus, a one-unit increase in education leads to a [beta] unit increase/decrease in income." Everybody has the same education level, and there are no observations where education varies by 1 or more units.

16.7 Assumption 6: There Is No Perfect Multicollinearity

The assumption of no perfect multicollinearity dictates that no variables in a regression can perfectly correlate with each other. With perfect multicollinearity, two variables predict each other or move/vary perfectly with each other. If X_1 correlated perfectly with X_2, they would move lock-step with each other by a specific factor. For example, if $X_2 = 2X_1$, the two variables are perfectly correlated with each other by a factor of 2. X_1 perfectly predicts X_2. If X_1 and X_2 were included in an OLS regression, it would be impossible to generate coefficients for either variable given their perfect collinearity. In fact, software will generate a warning or error message of perfect collinearity. Perfect multicollinearity is unlikely to exist in public administration and similar fields of research, unless sample sizes and datasets have a small number of observations (Berry, 1993; Berry & Feldman, 1985; Lewis-Beck and Lewis-Beck, 2016). Nevertheless, variables may be highly correlated with each other or present a situation with high multicollinearity in an OLS regression. What effect does this have?

High multicollinearity leads to inflated standard errors (Berry & Feldman, 1985; Gujarati, 2003). Remember that a variable's significance in OLS regression is determined by dividing the variable's coefficient by its standard error. Therefore, with high multicollinearity, the significance of a variable(s) is not estimated correctly, thus leading to faulty conclusions about the level of significance of the effect of an independent variable.

Additionally, when multicollinearity is high, it becomes difficult to determine the independent effects of each of the collinear variables on the dependent variable. Remember that with multivariate regression, we want to be able to explain the effect of one independent variable while holding all other independent variables constant. If two variables are highly collinear with each other, say X_1 and X_2, it is difficult to determine how each variable uniquely affects the dependent variable. Software will report beta coefficients, but since there is so much similarity/overlap between the two variables, it is difficult to know how much of the beta coefficient on one variable is attributed to its independent effects on Y compared to the other collinear variable (Wonnacott & Wonnacott, 1990). One manner to help overcome high multicollinearity is to ensure you use the one-concept, one-variable principle. There is no need to have multiple measures of the same concept, like using percent of the population living below the poverty line and percent of the population receiving government

```
Call:
lm(formula = gradrate ~ income + lunch + masters, data = Dataset)

Residuals:
    Min      1Q  Median      3Q     Max
-4.7472 -0.5937 -0.0600  0.6292  3.5856

Coefficients:
               Estimate  Std. Error t value    Pr(>|t|)
(Intercept) 57.55074003  6.63433742   8.675 0.000000191 ***
income       0.00041248  0.00006594   6.255 0.000011482 ***
lunch       -0.07497556  0.04630578  -1.619       0.125
masters      0.09623018  0.06677574   1.441       0.169
---
Signif. codes:  0 '***' 0.001 '**' 0.01 '*' 0.05 '.' 0.1 ' ' 1

Residual standard error: 1.97 on 16 degrees of freedom
Multiple R-squared:  0.9706,	Adjusted R-squared:  0.9651
F-statistic: 176.3 on 3 and 16 DF,  p-value: 1.817e-12
```

Figure 16.11 Graduation rate regression output

welfare assistance. Both measure the same concept of poverty or wealth (or lack of wealth). Nevertheless, multicollinearity may occur in less obvious situations among variables, so it is important to test for it.

Let's take a look at the effects of multicollinearity, how to detect it, and how to remedy it using a hypothetical example. Returning to the graduation rate and income example, load the *graduationrate* data from the Companion Site (www.cambridge.org/scheller) into the R Commander. Run a multivariate regression model with "gradrate" as the dependent variable and "income," "lunch," and "masters" as the independent variables. The "gradrate" variable is the school's four-year percentage of students who graduate. "Income" is the median household income for the school, "lunch" is the percent of students in the school on the free/reduced lunch program, and "masters" is the percent of teachers in the school with a master's degree. Your regression output should look like Figure 16.11.

The coefficient on the income variable is significant at the 99.9% significance level while the coefficients on the lunch and masters variables are not statistically significant. Interpreting the coefficient on income, we would say, "On average, ceteris paribus, a one dollar increase in median household income leads to a 0.0004% increase in the graduation rate." Since a one dollar increase is miniscule, we can multiply it out to a degree of our choosing. To understand the effect of a $10,000 increase in median household income, move the decimal point over four places to the right (ten-thousands increase). Therefore, we can now say, "On average, ceteris paribus, a $10,000 increase in median household income leads to a 4.12% increase in the graduation rate." However, is this an accurate reflection of the effect of income on graduation rate? As you may surmise, income and percent of students

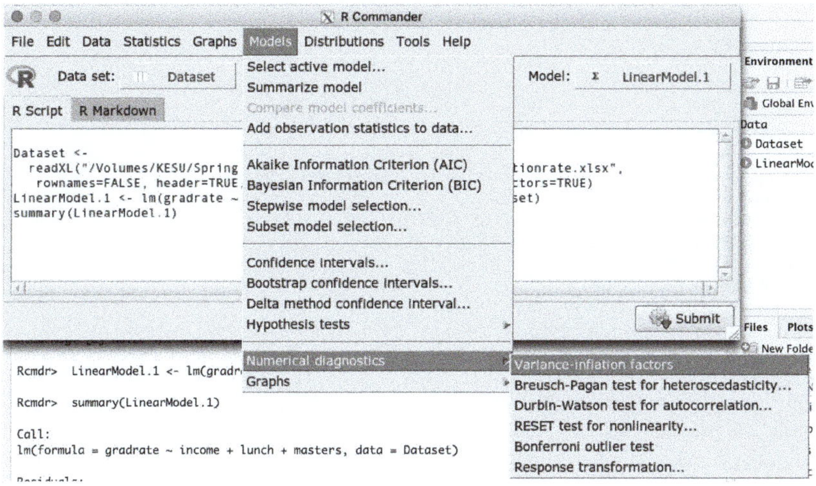

Figure 16.12 Calculating VIFs in the R Commander

on free/reduced lunch are likely collinear. How can we determine if we have a multicollinearity problem?

One method of determining multicollinearity is to generate correlation coefficients. Correlations of 0.80 or more generally indicate a high degree of multicollinearity (Field, Miles, & Field , 2012). Another easy method to determine if your regression model suffers from multicollinearity is to obtain the Variance Inflation Factor (VIF). If one independent variable is highly collinear with other independent variables, the VIF will be large (Fox, 2016). How large is large? Generally speaking, if a variable has a VIF of ten or more, then your regression model likely suffers from multicollinearity.

To see if our previous regression model suffers from multicollinearity, we can have the R Commander report the VIFs. Once you run the multivariate regression, you should click:

Models → Numerical diagnostics → Variance-inflation factors

Visually, your steps should look like Figure 16.12.

Following these steps generates the output in Figure 16.13.

The VIF for the "lunch" variable is 11.77, above the threshold value of 10. How can we remedy this multicollinearity issue? The simple solution is to eliminate a collinear variable, or the variable with the VIF greater than 10. Remember, one concept, one measure/variable. We can logically conclude that the lunch variable, with its high VIF score, is likely measuring the same concept as the "income" variable – that of household wealth or socioeconomic status. Therefore, we should remove the "lunch" variable from the regression model and simply use the "income" and the "masters" variables as the independent variables. Doing this, and re-running the multivariate regression model, yields the results in Figure 16.14.

```
Rcmdr>  library(lmtest, pos=17)

Rcmdr>  vif(LinearModel.3)
   income     lunch   masters
 5.306880 11.769773  7.119488  <------------  VIFs

Rcmdr>  round(cov2cor(vcov(LinearModel.3)), 3) # Correlations of parameter estimates
            (Intercept) income  lunch masters
(Intercept)       1.000 -0.850 -0.934  -0.542
income           -0.850  1.000  0.629   0.034
lunch            -0.934  0.629  1.000   0.741
masters          -0.542  0.034  0.741   1.000
>
```

Figure 16.13 VIF output in the R Commander

```
Call:
lm(formula = gradrate ~ income + masters, data = Dataset)

Residuals:
    Min      1Q  Median      3Q     Max
-3.8957 -1.3333 -0.1181  1.0211  4.0019

Coefficients:
               Estimate  Std. Error t value Pr(>|t|)
(Intercept) 47.51816681  2.48139265  19.150 6.08e-13 ***
income       0.00047965  0.00005365   8.941 7.78e-08 ***
masters      0.17638594  0.04690208   3.761  0.00156 **
---
Signif. codes:  0 '***' 0.001 '**' 0.01 '*' 0.05 '.' 0.1 ' ' 1

Residual standard error: 2.062 on 17 degrees of freedom
Multiple R-squared:  0.9658,	Adjusted R-squared:  0.9618
F-statistic: 240.3 on 2 and 17 DF,  p-value: 3.432e-13

>
```

Figure 16.14 Regression without multicollinear variables

While the coefficient on "income" does not change drastically, it does change. Now, we can say, "On average, ceteris paribus, a $10,000 increase in median household income leads to a 4.80% increase in the graduation rate." This is a 0.68% increase from the previous model. Additionally, the "masters" variable, measuring the percent of teachers with a Masters degree, is now significant at the 99% confidence level and indicates a positive relationship. In the previous model with the inclusion of multicollinear variables, the "masters" variable was statistically insignificant. These changing results highlight the importance of not only correct model specification, but also the importance of ensuring low multicollinearity in regression models.

16.8 Assumption 7: Error Term Normally Distributed with Mean of 0

The next sections of regression assumptions involve assumptions with the error term or errors from a regression model. Most public administrators will not worry themselves with the minutiae of analyzing the error terms; however, it is important to at

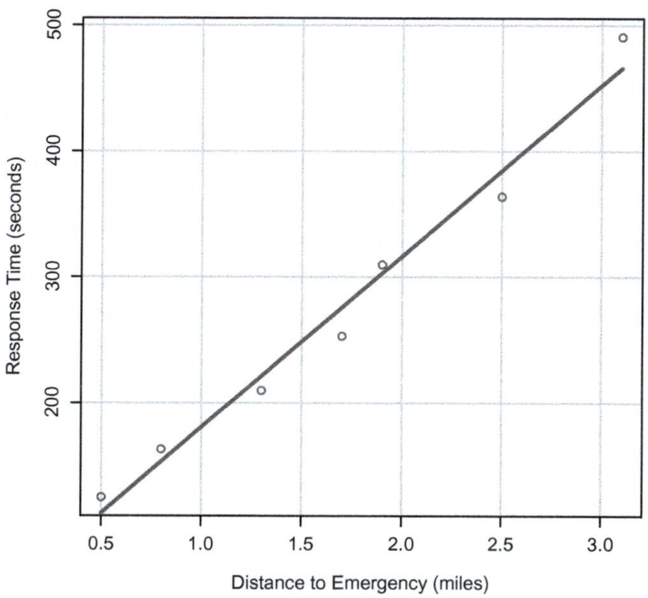

Figure 14.2 Emergency response times by distance to emergency with regression line

least be familiar with these assumptions if you suspect they may affect your analyses and if you are interested in becoming more skilled in statistics and econometrics. Regarding these errors, more specifically, you can think about these errors as the distance from each datapoint in a scatterplot from the best-fitting regression line. For better visualization, Figure 14.2 is reproduced to allow you to recall the bivariate regression model of emergency response times (Y) as a function of distance to the emergency (X).

The distance from each dot to the best-fitting regression line represents the error term. Recall that the best-fitting regression line equation is:

$$\hat{Y} = \hat{b}_0 + \hat{b}_1 X \tag{14.3}$$

If we want to represent the relationship between Y and X in Figure 14.2 to account for the errors or distances from the dots to the best-fitting regression line, we can express this relationship as:

$$Y_i = b_0 + b_1 X_i + e_i, \tag{16.1}$$

where Y_i is each observed value of Y. This equation states that each value of Y is a function of a value of X, multiplied by the beta coefficient (b_1), plus the value of the y-intercept (b_0) along with some error, e_i. The component of the equation represented by $Y_i = b_0 + b_1(X_i)$ is the best-fitting line equation. The e_i component accounts for why each dot does not align perfectly along the best-fitting regression line. It is the error and the distance from each respective dot to the best-fitting regression line.

It is assumed that the value of these errors or the distances from the observations to the best-fitting regression line are normally distributed (follow a normal distribution like we saw in Chapter 9), with a mean of zero. In Figure 14.2, think of the dots above the best-fitting line as positive errors, or more specifically, the distance between the dot and the best-fitting line as + values. Think of the dots below the best-fitting line as negative errors, or more specifically, the distance between the dot and the best-fitting line as having – values. The assumption states that the mean of all of the values is 0. If, on average, the errors above the line cancel out the errors below the line, the mean is 0. The effect of having an error term with a mean other than 0 is that it biases the y-intercept (b_0) (Lewis-Beck and Lewis-Beck, 2016). If this intercept if not of importance to the researcher, the issue of a non-zero mean error term is less problematic.

Thinking about the errors being normally distributed may be more difficult to visualize. This component of the assumption states that if you calculated the distance from the best-fitting line for each dot and then plotted their values in a histogram, the histogram would appear normally distributed. Gujarati (2003) notes that meeting the normality assumption for the error terms allows us to assume the beta coefficients for the independent variables in the regression are normally distributed (and thus we can use the t-distribution to determine their statistical significance). In the absence of normality, Gujarati (2003) argues that running the analysis with large sample sizes eliminates issues related to a non-normal error term. To determine if the error term is normally distributed with a mean of zero, researchers will often plot the errors (also known as residuals), looking for patterns, and/or implement other specific statistical tests on the residuals. The Gujarati (2003) citation provides good instruction on these methods.

16.9 Assumption 8: Error Term Uncorrelated with Independent Variables

If the error term is correlated with an independent variable(s), then the beta coefficients will be biased (Lewis-Beck and Lewis-Beck, 2016). If the error term is correlated with an independent variable(s), then there is a systematic component of the error term that makes it non-random, thus introducing bias. Lewis-Beck and Lewis-Beck (2016) suggest ensuring that all relevant independent variables that affect the dependent variable have been included in the regression model.

16.10 Assumption 9: Homoscedasticity

Whereas the assumption of normal distribution of errors assumes that the errors are normally distributed with a mean of 0, the assumption of homoscedasticity of the errors assumes that there are no changes to the patterns of the errors as X increases/decreases. The distribution of the errors should be uniform across various values of X. If the errors become larger/smaller as X increases/decreases, then heteroscedasticity is present. Figure 16.15 depicts a situation of *heteroscedasticity*

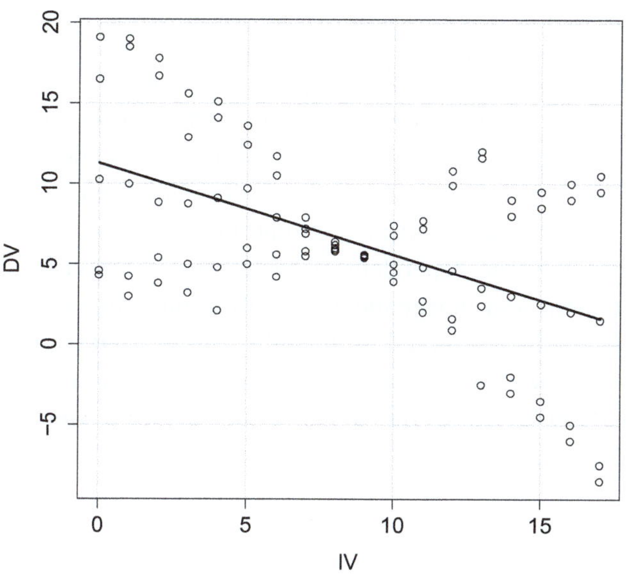

Figure 16.15 Heteroscedasticity

between an independent variable on the x-axis and a dependent variable on the y-axis.

Though extreme in its depiction, it shows that for smaller values of X the observations are much spread out, then get closer to the best-fitting regression line for X values of about 5 to 11. Then, the observations fan out again away from the line as the X values increase. This "fanning" out shows heteroscedasticity. If you were to draw vertical lines from each observation to the best-fitting regression line, those lines would be longer for low and high values of X in Figure 16.15, and shorter for X values of 5 to 11. Ideally, our scatterplot should depict homoscedasticity, or no discernible patterns or "fanning out" across the values of X. OLS regression models assume homoscedasticity. In the absence of homoscedasticity, our standard errors become incorrect and thus prevent us from understanding the true significance level of the coefficients on our independent variables (Gujarati, 2003).

16.11 Assumption 10: No Autocorrelation

The final regression assumption is that there is no autocorrelation, or that the errors are not correlated with each other. The errors associated with one independent variable should not be correlated to the errors of another independent variable. Lewis-Beck and Lewis-Beck (2016) describe it best: "The assumption of no autocorrelation means that the error corresponding to an observation is not correlated with any of the errors for the other observations" (pp. 27–28). This means that the distance an observation is from the best-fitting regression line should not be dependent upon or correlated with the distance from the best-fitting regression line for another or other observations. For public administrators, autocorrelation is rarely an issue unless working with time series data (Kellstedt & Whitten, 2009), which is a topic beyond the scope of this text.

16.12 Summary

This chapter delved into the assumptions of OLS, or linear regression models – a kind of "under the hood of the car" examination. While most public administrators do not worry themselves with the details of these assumptions, a basic understanding of them is important to master to ensure accuracy in analyses. The more common assumptions public administrators likely deal with are Assumptions 1–3 and Assumption 6. To run a linear regression, the dependent variable must be interval, the relationship between the dependent and independent variable(s) must be linear in nature, all relevant independent variables should be included in the regression, and researchers should avoid multicollinearity. Examples of violations of these assumptions along with testing for them in the R Commander were covered to allow researchers to gain greater confidence in their results.

Recommended Reading

Berry, W.D. (1993). *Understanding regression assumptions.* Sage.

Fox, John (2016). *Applied regression analysis & generalized linear models* (3rd ed.). Sage.

Gujarati, Damodar N. (2003). *Basic econometrics.* McGraw-Hill (4th ed.).

Lewis-Beck, C., & Lewis-Beck, M. (2016). *Applied regression: An introduction* (2nd ed.) Sage.

PRACTICE PROBLEMS

Conceptual Problems

1. For each of the dependent variables and their coding listed below, determine if linear regression can be used and explain why/why not.
   a. # of student absences by school
   b. Mayoral approval rating on a scale from 0 (Strongly Disapprove) to 100 (Strongly Approve)
   c. Voted in the 2020 election (1 = Yes; 0 = No)
   d. Mayoral approval rating on a scale where 5 = Strongly approve; 4 = Approve; 3 = Neither approve nor disapprove; 2 = Disapprove; 1 = Strongly disapprove
   e. Party identification (1 = Democrat; 2 = Republican; 3 = Other)
   f. Median household income in dollars
   g. Public service motivation of employees on a scale where 3 = High; 2 = Medium; 1 = Low
   h. Attended a professional development training (1 = Yes; 0 = No)

2. For each of the below data scenarios between an independent variable X and dependent variable Y, graph the data by hand. Then, enter each of the scenarios into an Excel spreadsheet. Upload to the R Commander and generate a scatterplot of the data for each scenario. Based upon your by-hand and R Commander graphs, explain whether or not if linear regression could be used for these relationships and why/why not. Looking at the data, speculate on what type of relationship exists between X and Y (linear, cubic, quadratic, logarithmic, etc.).

Scenario A

Observation #	X	Y
1	0	0.5
2	1	0.75
3	2	1.5
4	3	2.75
5	4	4.5
6	5	6.75
7	6	9.5

Scenario B

Observation #	X	Y
1	1	0.5
2	2	0.75
3	3	1.5
4	4	2.75
5	5	4.5
6	6	6.75
7	7	9.5

Scenario C

Observation #	X	Y
1	2	3.5
2	3	5
3	4	6.5
4	5	8
5	6	9.5
6	7	11

3. Suppose the League of Women Voters is interested in knowing the determinants of people turning out to vote on Election Day. They collect precinct level voter turnout percentages for each precinct in a large city. They run a regression analysis where the precinct level voter turnout is a function of the median age of the precinct voter and the percent of the precinct identifying as a racial minority. They receive results suggesting that age has a significantly positive effect on turnout and percent minority has a significantly negative effect on turnout. Critique their findings and explain why their results may be biased. What other information should they collect?
4. A public manager is interested in knowing the effect of gender on job satisfaction. They hypothesize that female employees are less satisfied than male employees. To test this hypothesis, the researcher interviews all female employees and asks them to rank their satisfaction on a scale of 1 to 10. They also collect information regarding the number of years they've been employed in the organization, their salary, and the number of write-ups they have received ($n = 10$). They set up the regression model according to the form:

$$Satisfaction = b_0 + b_1(Gender) + b_2(YearsEmployed) + b_3(Salary) + b_4(Write - Ups)$$

Critique this research design and variables used and their measurement.

R Commander Problems

5. Open the *baseball* dataset from the Companion Site (www.cambridge.org/scheller) into the R Commander and open the codebook in Microsoft Word. The chief marketing strategist for the team is trying to figure out what affects attendance at baseball games. They hypothesize that attendance is dependent upon a number of variables: temperature at game time, winds at game time, the team's win percentage, whether or not there is a promotion on gameday, and whether or not the game is on a weekend. Run a multivariate regression with these variables and determine if multicollinearity is an issue. Explain why/why not. Remedy the multicollinearity issue if it exists. Interpret all statistically significant variables.
6. Open the *state politics codebook* and load the *state_politics* dataset into the R Commander. Let's determine what affects the percent of the state budget allocated to transportation spending. Include the independent variables of state legislative professionalism, state government ideology, debt, surplus, and percent of the state workforce that is unionized.
   a. Run the multivariate regression.
   b. Determine if multicollinearity is an issue. Explain why/why not.
   c. If multicollinearity is an issue, run a new model and interpret the statistically significant results.

17

Interactive Relationships and Interaction Terms in Regression

17.1 Introduction

The previous three chapters dealt with the topic of Ordinary Least Squares (OLS) regression, or linear regression, focusing on how/when to use linear regression and the assumptions underlying linear regression that allow researchers to make better causal claims from a sample to the population. The use of multivariate regression is a common method of analyzing the effects of various independent variables on a dependent variable. In your own current or future research and readings of studies, you have or likely will come across multivariate regression or other more advanced statistical methods using linear regression. One more advanced use of linear regression is the inclusion of interaction terms to model interactive (or conditional) relationships between independent variables. The terms "conditional" and "interactive" are used interchangeably in this chapter to denote the relationship modeled by interaction terms. An interactive or conditional relationship indicates that the effect of one variable, X_1, is conditional upon values of another independent variable, X_2. More specifically, the *effect* of X_1 on the dependent variable, Y, depends upon and varies as values of X_2 change. The vice versa relationship could also exist, but the manner in which to model either situation is to interact or multiply these two variables.

To understand the logic of interaction terms in the linear regression model, refer back to the OLS regression models of Chapters 14 and 15. Inherent in the previous linear regression models is their additive nature. Recall from Chapter 15 the multivariate equation, Equation 15.2:

$$Y_i = b_0 + b_1X_{1i} + b_2X_{2i} + \ldots + b_kX_{ki} + e_i, \tag{15.2}$$

A particular observed value of the dependent variable, Y_i, is equal to the value of the y-intercept (b_0) **PLUS** the observed value of X_1 multiplied by its coefficient (b_1), **PLUS** the observed value of X_2 multiplied by its coefficient (b_2), **PLUS** the observed values for all other independent variables up to X_k, multiplied by their respective coefficients (b_k), **PLUS** some error (e).

There may be instances where in reality, or in theory, the effect of X_1 may depend upon various values of X_2, and vice versa. Stated differently, the effect of X_1 may differ (be larger or smaller) across various values of X_2, and vice versa. Stated in yet another manner, the coefficient on X_1 may differ across various values of X_2, and vice versa. With this relationship between independent variables, we must account for this *interactive* or *conditional* relationship and the effect on the dependent variable.

This chapter presents some introductory information and instruction on why, when, and how to use interaction terms in linear regression. As it is one of the more involved lessons in the textbook, the chapter goes step-by-step into understanding interaction terms. A fictional dataset and example begins the chapter's introduction to interaction terms and interactive relationships, followed by modeling them in the R Commander. The bulk of the chapter focuses on interpretation of interaction terms.

17.2 Interactive Relationship Examples

Let's begin with a simple example of an interactive relationship before delving into specific public administration examples, so as to better understand the logic behind interactive relationships and interaction terms in regression.

A university professor of a large undergraduate section of an Introduction to Public Administration course is interested in understanding how study and sleep habits affect exam scores. The professor is interested in understanding the grades from the recent midterm (0% to 100%). They think that the number of hours a student studies has a positive impact on the exam grades, along with the number of hours the student slept the night before the exam. However, they also hypothesize that there is an interactive relationship – namely that the number of hours studied only positively affects exam grades if students get a decent amount of sleep the night before the exam (6 or more hours). The professor takes a random sample ($n = 20$) of their students and surveys them asking them the approximate number of hours they studied for the exam during the week and the number of hours of sleep they had the night before the exam. They record the data for each student, including their midterm exam grade. The data appear in Table 17.1 Enter the data into Excel on your own, save the file to your computer, and then upload the data into the R Commander.

Previously, we would model the effect of hours of study and hours of sleep on student grades as:

$$Y_i = b_0 + b_1X_{1i} + b_2X_{2i} + e_i, \tag{17.1}$$

or for our example:

$$Grade_i = b_0 + b_1(HoursStudied)_i + b_2(HoursSleep)_i + e_i$$

The resulting output of this non-interactive model is shown in Figure 17.1.

Table 17.1 Student exam score data

Student	Grade	Hrs. Studied	Hrs. Sleep
1	74	14	1
2	100	15	10
3	99	13	8
4	87	9	6
5	72	10	3
6	96	11	8
7	98	11	9
8	62	7	3
9	71	8	5
10	78	8	4
11	58	4	2
12	75	10	2
13	77	15	3
14	95	12	8
15	63	12	1
16	68	10	2
17	85	1	7
18	74	2	6
19	70	1	6
20	81	15	3

If we think that there is an interactive relationship between the number of hours studied and the hours of sleep like the professor hypothesizes, we must account for this interactive relationship by multiplying X_1 by X_2, or multiplying *HoursStudied* by *HoursSleep*.

The multivariate regression equation depicting an interactive relationship now looks like:

$$Y_i = b_0 + b_1X_{1i} + b_2X_{2i} + b_3(X_{1i} \times X_{2i}) + e_i, \quad (17.2)$$

For the exam grade example:

$$\begin{aligned} Grade_i = b_0 + b_1(HoursStudied)_i + b_2(HoursSleep)_i \\ + b_3(HoursStudied_i * HoursSleep_i) + e_i, \end{aligned}$$

```
Call:
lm(formula = grade ~ study + sleep, data = Dataset)

Residuals:
   Min     1Q Median     3Q    Max
-7.021 -3.219 -0.205  3.114  7.658

Coefficients:
            Estimate Std. Error t value Pr(>|t|)
(Intercept)  48.2910     3.0475  15.846 1.29e-11 ***
study         1.2324     0.2320   5.313 5.72e-05 ***
sleep         3.9741     0.3699  10.744 5.35e-09 ***
---
Signif. codes:  0 '***' 0.001 '**' 0.01 '*' 0.05 '.' 0.1 ' ' 1

Residual standard error: 4.535 on 17 degrees of freedom
Multiple R-squared:  0.8915,    Adjusted R-squared:  0.8787
F-statistic: 69.84 on 2 and 17 DF,  p-value: 0.000000006329
```

Figure 17.1 Non-interactive student exam score regression

where the coefficient b_3 is the beta coefficient on the interaction term of $(HoursStudied) \times (HoursSleep)$. This interaction term models the interactive/conditional relationship between the two variables on the dependent variable.

17.3 Modeling Interactions in the R Commander

Implementing this regression equation/model in the R Commander is not difficult. Doing so requires using the same steps as before when running a multivariate regression, with one small addition. We must create the interaction term in the R Commander by multiplying the X_1 variable by the X_2 variable, or in our case, multiplying *HoursStudied* by *HoursSleep*. To create the interaction term:

Step 1: Click Data → Manage variables in active data set → Compute new variable (Figure 17.2).

Step 2: A new box will pop up. In the "New variable name box" enter any name you would like to use to represent the interaction. I have named it "interaction." In the next box to the right, labeled "Expression to compute," you will enter the command to create the interaction term. Double-click the "study" variable. Doing so puts the variable in the box. Next, enter the command to multiply this variable, which is simply the asterisk, or * symbol. Once you have typed that, double-click the "sleep" variable. It now should appear to the right of the *. Before clicking OK, your window should look like Figure 17.3.

Step 3: Click OK, and the R Commander will have produced the interaction term. To double-check, you can always click the "View data set" button in the R

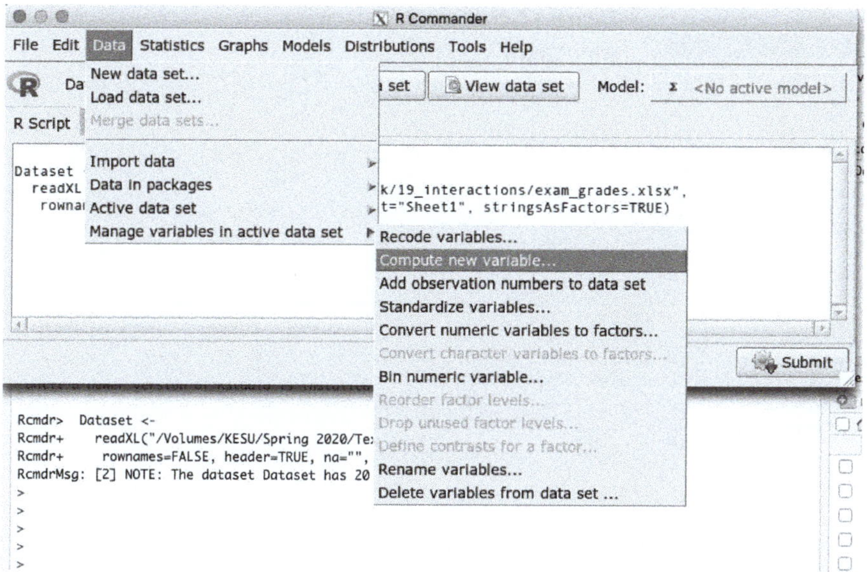

Figure 17.2 Creating interaction term, step 1

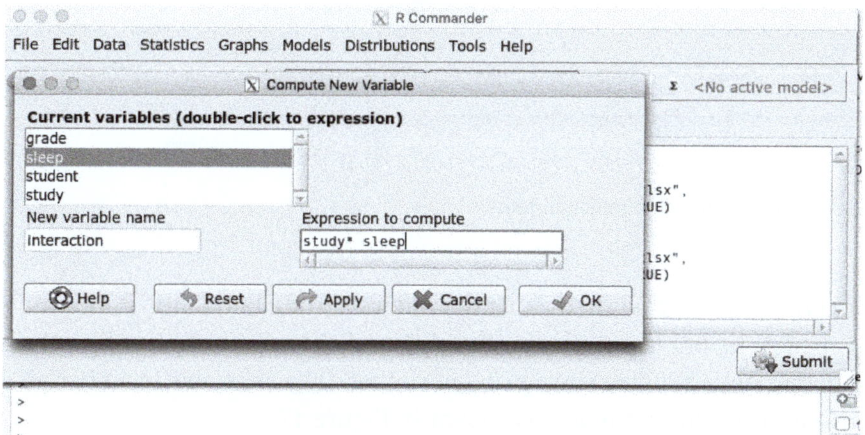

Figure 17.3 Creating interaction term, step 2

Commander. A popup window with a data view will appear. Off to the right should be your newly created interaction term (Figure 17.4).

Step 4: Now, to run the following model:

$$Grade_i = b_0 + b_1(HoursStudied)_i + b_2(HoursSleep)_i + b_3(HoursStudied_i \times HoursSleep_i) + e_i,$$

simply run a traditional multivariate regression model in the R Commander as you did before. This time, your dependent variable will be "grade," and your independent variables will be "study," "sleep," and "interaction." When running interaction models, you must include not only the newly formed

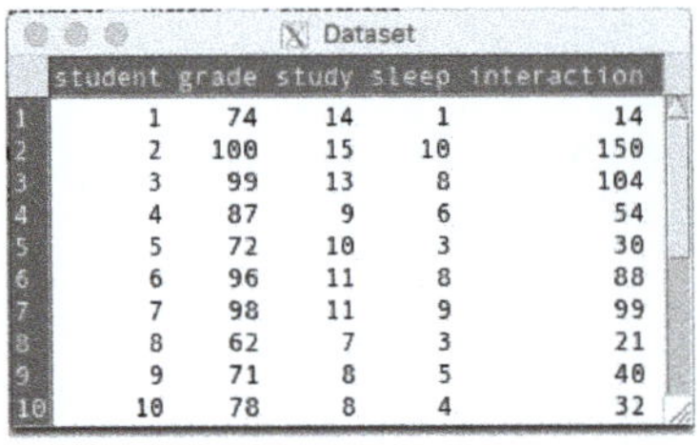

	student	grade	study	sleep	interaction
1	1	74	14	1	14
2	2	100	15	10	150
3	3	99	13	8	104
4	4	87	9	6	54
5	5	72	10	3	30
6	6	96	11	8	88
7	7	98	11	9	99
8	8	62	7	3	21
9	9	71	8	5	40
10	10	78	8	4	32

Figure 17.4 Creating interaction term, step 3

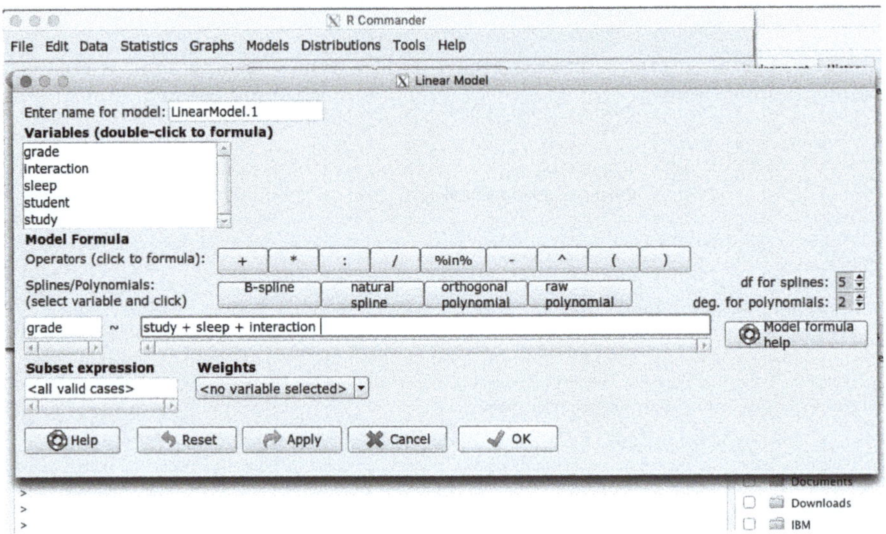

Figure 17.5 Linear regression with interaction term

interaction term, but also their constitutive terms (Brambor, Clark, & Golder, 2006), which in our case are the "study" and "sleep" variables. Shortly, we will see why, but for now, just know that they must be included. A screenshot of the correct inputs is shown in Figure 17.5.

Step 5: Click OK and the R Commander will report the regression results in R Studio (Figure 17.6).

17.4 Interpreting Interactive Models, Interaction Terms, and Results

In the output, we see that all of the independent variables, including the interaction between hours studied and hours of sleep, are statistically significant. Equation 17.2 can be updated to:

$$Y_i = 35.30 + 2.39X_{1i} + 6.38X_{2i} - 0.21(X_{1i} \times X_{2i}) + e_i, \quad (17.3)$$

with Y_i representing the exam grade, X_1 representing the number of hours studied, and X_2 representing the number of hours slept.

```
Rcmdr>  LinearModel.1 <- lm(grade ~ study + sleep + interaction, data=Dataset)

Rcmdr>  summary(LinearModel.1)

Call:
lm(formula = grade ~ study + sleep + interaction, data = Dataset)

Residuals:
    Min      1Q  Median      3Q     Max
-6.8546 -3.3663  0.2713  2.3947  7.2996

Coefficients:
            Estimate Std. Error t value  Pr(>|t|)
(Intercept) 35.29605    6.66398   5.297 0.0000723 ***
study        2.38614    0.57795   4.129  0.000788 ***
sleep        6.38341    1.17302   5.442 0.0000543 ***
interaction -0.21119    0.09851  -2.144  0.047757 *
---
Signif. codes:  0 '***' 0.001 '**' 0.01 '*' 0.05 '.' 0.1 ' ' 1

Residual standard error: 4.12 on 16 degrees of freedom
Multiple R-squared:  0.9157,    Adjusted R-squared:  0.8999
F-statistic: 57.94 on 3 and 16 DF,  p-value: 0.000000008184

>
```

Figure 17.6 Linear regression with interaction term output

How do we interpret the interaction term and the beta coefficients on the constitutive terms of hours studied and hours of sleep, respectively? You see that the beta coefficient on the interaction term is negative. Does this mean that the interaction of hours studied and hours of sleep actually *decreases* test scores?! Has the professor's hypothesis been shown to have no support? Should students actually study less and sleep less if they want to improve their test scores?!

As you may imagine, the interpretation of interactive models is more complicated than simply looking at the coefficient on the interaction term. Studying and sleeping less leading to higher grades is likely an absurd conclusion, but we must interpret what the data report. We must also know *how* to interpret the data and use some basic mathematical skills to understand if the professor's hypothesis is correct. Doing so requires a bit of basic calculus instruction.

Refer back to the general multivariate regression model, Equation 15.2:

$$Y_i = b_0 + b_1 X_{1i} + b_2 X_{2i} + \ldots + b_k X_{ki} + e_i, \tag{15.2}$$

The beta coefficients represent a rate of change, or how responsive Y is to a one-unit increase in the respective X. Alternatively stated, we are modeling the change in Y with respect to a change in X. In calculus, this relationship is mathematically translated to:

$$\frac{\delta Y}{\delta X}, \tag{17.4}$$

or also depicted as:

$$\frac{\Delta Y}{\Delta X} \tag{17.5}$$

Both Equations 17.4 and 17.5 state "change in Y with respect to a change in X." These are also called derivatives. Therefore,

$$\frac{\delta Y}{\delta X_1} = b_1,$$
$$\frac{\delta Y}{\delta X_2} = b_2,$$

Referring to Equation 15.2, the same rules can be applied to show marginal effects for the independent variables:

$$Y_i = b_0 + b_1 X_{1i} + b_2 X_{2i} + b_3(X_{1i} \times X_{2i}) + e_i,$$
$$\frac{\delta Y}{\delta X_1} = b_1 + b_3(X_2),$$
$$\frac{\delta Y}{\delta X_2} = b_2 + b_3(X_1),$$

Referring back to Equation 17.3:

$$Y_i = 35.30 + 2.39X_{1i} + 6.38X_{2i} - 0.21(X_{1i} \times X_{2i}) + e_i, \qquad (17.3)$$

or

$$Grade = 35.30 + 2.39(HoursStudied) + 6.38(HoursSleep) - 0.21(HoursStudied \times HoursSleep) + e_i$$

The individual effect of *HoursStudied* is now measured by b_1 and b_3 (*HoursSleep*). Its individual effect is conditional upon or interactive with *HoursSleep*. Therefore,

$$\frac{\delta Y}{\delta HoursStudied} = b_1 + b_3(HoursSleep),$$

or

$$\frac{\delta Y}{\delta HoursStudied} = 2.39 - 0.21(HoursSleep),$$

This derivative states that a one-unit change in X_1 leads to a $2.39 - 0.21(X_2)$ unit change in Y. So, the effect of hours studied on exam grades varies as a function of hours slept.

The individual effect of *HoursSleep* is now measured by b_2 and b_3 (*HoursStudied*). Its individual effect is conditional upon or interactive with *HoursStudied*. Therefore,

$$\frac{\delta Y}{\delta HoursSleep} = b_2 + b_3(HoursStudied),$$

or

$$\frac{\delta Y}{\delta HoursSleep} = 6.38 - 0.21(HoursStudied),$$

This derivative states that a one-unit change in X_2 leads to a $6.38 - 0.21(X_1)$ unit change in Y. So, the effect of hours of sleep on exam grades varies as a function of hours studied.

What is the effect of hours studied if a student sleeps for 2.5 hours the night before an exam? 8 hours?

For 2.5 hours of sleep:

$$\frac{\delta Y}{\delta HoursStudied} = 2.39 - 0.21(2.5) = 2.39 - 0.53 = \mathbf{1.86}$$

The results state that each additional hour studied (assuming/conditional upon 2.5 hours slept) leads to a 1.86 point/unit increase in the exam score.

For 8 hours of sleep:

$$\frac{\delta Y}{\delta HoursStudied} = 2.39 - 0.21(8) = 2.39 - 1.68 = \mathbf{0.71}$$

Each additional hour studied (assuming/conditional upon 8 hours slept) leads to a 0.71 point/unit increase in the exam score.

Even though the 0.71 effect for 8 hours of sleep is smaller than the 1.86 effect for 2.5 hours of sleep, the results are not saying increasing the number of hours studied is ineffective. They just state that essentially, as hours slept increases, the effect of more studying is positive, but just at a smaller rate. This effect is akin to the law of diminishing marginal productivity in economics.

Each effect that we just calculated is considered a marginal effect. For example, the marginal effect of hours studied is 1.86 if the number of hours slept is 2.5. The marginal effect of hours studied for 8 hours of sleep is 0.71. Researchers may want to see these effects in one graph, known as a marginal effects graph. Some of the readings in the Recommended Reading section at the end of the chapter provide resources for more advanced topics with interaction terms, like the production of

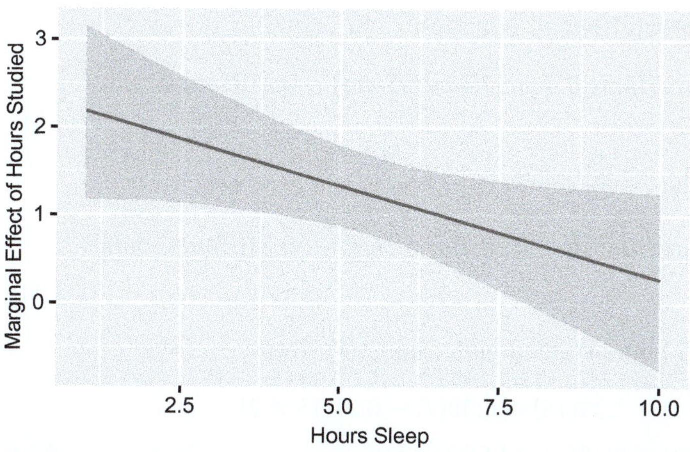

Figure 17.7 Marginal effect of hours studied across various values of hours of sleep

marginal effects graph, which is beyond the scope of this textbook. For illustrative purposes, though, Figure 17.7 is the marginal effects graph for hours studied (y-axis) across various values of hours of sleep (x-axis). Recall that for 2.5 hours of sleep, the marginal effect of studying on the exam is an average increase of 1.86. In Figure 17.7, find 2.5 on the x-axis, and then visually draw a vertical line up to where it hits the negatively sloped line. Now, move horizontally over to the y-axis. What value does this correspond to? 1.86, the value we calculated. Do the same for 8 hours of sleep. The marginal effect should be 0.71. The shaded region around the marginal effects line represents the 95% confidence interval for the marginal effect. When the shaded region is either fully above or below the horizontal 0 line, then the marginal effect is statistically significant. In this graph, the marginal effect of hours studied is statistically significant for X values ranging from 0 to approximately 8. For greater than approximately 8 hours of sleep, the marginal effect of hours studied is not statistically significant at the 95% confidence level.

Switching to hours of sleep, what is the marginal effect of sleep if the hours studied is 1 compared to 12? For 1 hour studied,

$$\frac{\delta Y}{\delta HoursSleep} = 6.38 - 0.21(1) = \mathbf{6.17}$$

Each additional hour of sleep given only 1 hour studied leads to a 6.17 point/unit increase in the exam score.

For 12 hours studied:

$$\frac{\delta Y}{\delta HoursSleep} = 6.38 - 0.21(12) = 6.38 - 2.52 = \mathbf{3.86}$$

Each additional hour of sleep, given 12 hours studied, leads to a 3.86 point/unit increase in the exam score.

Finally, interaction terms do not preclude the ability to engage in predictions. What is the expected grade of a student that studied 15 hours for the exam and slept for 7 hours the night before? Recall Equation 17.3:

$$Y_i = 35.30 + 2.39(HoursStudied) + 6.38(HoursSleep) - 0.21(HoursStudied \times HoursSleep) + e_i, \quad (17.3)$$

The prediction equation simply removes the error term and becomes:

$$\hat{Y}_i = 35.30 + 2.39(HoursStudied) + 6.38(HoursSleep) - 0.21(HoursStudied \times HoursSleep) \quad (17.4)$$

For the specific example (15 hours studied and 7 hours of sleep):

$$\hat{Y}_i = 35.30 + 2.39(15) + 6.38(7) - 0.21(15 \times 7)$$
$$\hat{Y}_i = 35.30 + 35.85 + 44.66 - 22.05$$
$$\hat{Y}_i = 93.76$$

The expected grade for the student that studied 15 hours and slept for 7 hours the night before the exam is a 93.76.

17.5 Interactions with Dummy Variables

Sometimes, researchers may be interested in the interaction of dummy variables with other variables. Common dummy variables used in interactions include male/female, Democrat/Republican, employed/unemployed, etc. Suppose that a nonprofit director hypothesizes that income and party affiliation interact in terms of the amount of donations made by individuals. They think people with more income donate more money to the nonprofit, but that this effect is more pronounced among Democrats. The director collects donation data as the dependent variable (amount of money donated by a respective individual), and the independent variables of the individual's income (in thousands) along with their party affiliation (coded 1 for Democrat; 0 for all other parties). Suppose the director runs the multivariate regression, and obtains the following results:

$$\hat{Y}_i = 10.15 + 5.05(Income) + 8.29(Party) + 15.88(Income \times Party)$$

$$s.e._{Income} = 1.20$$
$$s.e._{Party} = 3.68$$
$$s.e._{Income \times Party} = 2.96$$

All of the beta coefficients are at least double their respective standard errors; therefore, all three variables, including the interaction term, are statistically significant. The marginal effect of income is represented by the derivative:

$$\frac{\delta Y}{\delta Income} = 5.05 + 15.88(Party)$$

When the donor is a Democrat (Party = 1), then the marginal effect of income is 5.05 + 15.88(1) = 20.93. So, given that the donor is a Democrat, each one thousand dollar increase in income (one-unit increase) yields an average increase in donation by 20.93, or $20.93.

When the donor is of another party (Party = 0), then the marginal effect of income is 5.05 + 15.88(0) = 5.05. So, given that the donor is not a Democrat, each one thousand dollar increase in income (one-unit increase) yields an average increase in donation by 5.05, or $5.05.

17.6 When to Use Interaction Terms and an Application

One of the first rules of using interaction terms is to ensure there are theoretical reasons to include them. Theory dictates the statistical model; therefore, if you have an interactive or conditional hypothesis, then include an interaction term. Interaction terms should not be included in regression models "just because," or to see if they come out statistically significant to improve one's results. There needs to be a theoretical reason(s) to include them.

In a 2021 issue of *Public Administration*, Choi and Hong have a study examining policing disparities of minority citizens as a function of the racial and ethnic makeup of the local city council and police force. Their dependent variable is the ratio of police searches for minority citizens to white citizens. To simplify their complex models, their main independent variables are essentially the percent of city council composed of minority members (X_1) and the percent of the local police force composed of minority members (X_2). They also interact these two variables to determine if there is an interactive effect between minority representation on city council and minority composition in the local police force. Their study is a test of representation's effect on policing disparities. They find that increasing minority representation on city council decreased the search ratio, *conditional* upon having the local police force having substantial minority representation among officers. The Choi and Hong (2021) study not only illustrates the use of interaction terms, but how they can be used for applied research that can have real-world implications. It highlights the importance not only of minority representation on local government bodies like city councils, but also bureaucratic agencies like police departments reflecting the population they serve.

17.7 Summary

This chapter introduced a new way to construct regression models for interactive or conditional hypotheses – the use of interaction terms. If a researcher thinks that the effect of one independent variable is dependent upon the value of another independent variable, or if the effect of one independent variable varies across values of another independent variable, then an interaction term should be used. Interaction terms are created by simply multiplying one independent variable by another. We examined how to do this in the R Commander along with how to interpret interaction terms in regression models. We first examined interactions between two interval independent variables, and then when one independent variable is a dummy variable.

This chapter does not cover every aspect of interaction terms – whole books and journal articles are dedicated to using interaction terms. Increasingly popular in academic research, but much beyond the scope of this textbook or even typical public administration courses, is the visual depiction of interactions in regression – plotting marginal effects; plotting predicted probabilities; using interaction terms with multi-category nominal variables; and using interaction terms in other types of statistical tests like time series analysis, panel data analysis, and logistic regression (the topic of Chapter 18). Some of the most recent developments in political methodology and analysis are occurring along the lines of understanding interaction terms in advanced models beyond OLS regression.

Recommended Reading

Berry, William D., DeMeritt, Jacqueline, H.R., & Esarey, Justin (2010). Testing for interaction in binary logit and probit models: Is a Product Term Essential? *American Journal of Political Science,* 54(1), 248–266.

Brambor, Thomas, Clark, William Roberts, & Golder, Matt (2006). Understanding interaction models: Improving empirical analyses. *Political Analysis,* 14(1), 63–82.

Fox, John (2016). *Applied regression analysis & generalized linear models.* Sage.

Kaufman, Robert L. (2019). *Interaction effects in linear and generalized linear models.* Sage.

PRACTICE PROBLEMS

Conceptual Problems

1. Explain what a derivative is and how it relates to interpreting beta coefficients.
2. For each of the following equations, what is the marginal effect of X_1 on Y?
   a.) $Y_i = 12.30 - 3.25X_1 + 5.90X_2$
   b.) $Y_i = 100.78 + 82.67X_1 + 35.01X_2 - 21.35(X_1 \times X_2)$
   c.) $Y_i = -4.59 + 6.78X_1 - 0.871X_2 + 5.76(X_1 \times X_2)$
3. Develop two interactive hypotheses. For each:
   a. Identify the dependent variable and independent variables.
   b. Explain the interaction between independent variables and your logic.
4. Search for a journal article in your field of interest where the author(s) used an interactive hypothesis with an interaction term.
   a. What was the author's hypothesis?
   b. Explain the use of the interaction term and why the author(s) included it.
   c. Was the interaction term statistically significant? How do you know?
   d. What did the author conclude about their hypothesis?

R Commander Problems

5. Open the *emergency_response* dataset from the Companion Site (www.cambridge.org/scheller). The fire chief is interested in what affects emergency response times. The chief thinks graveyard shift emergencies will take longer to respond to since personnel may be asleep. Four dummy variables comprise the time of day variable ("day," "evening," "night," and "graveyard"). Make the "day" variable the reference category. She thinks that distance to the emergency also affects response times. She thinks the presence of supervisors known as battalion chiefs may decrease response times – employees may be more motivated to hurry if a supervisor is present – but that it interacts with distance to the emergency. She hypothesizes that when a supervisor is present,

personnel may be more inclined to hurry when they know the emergency is farther away. The regression model she seeks to test is:

$$ResponseTime = b_0 + b_1(Graveyard) + b_2(Evening) + b_3(Night) + b_4(Distance) + b_5(Chief) + b_6(Chief \times Distance)$$

a. Create the interaction term in the R Commander.
b. Run the regression model for her equation.
c. Is the interaction term significant?
d. What is the marginal effect of having a chief at the station?
e. What is the marginal effect of distance to the emergency?

6. There is a variable called turnout time in the *emergency_response* dataset from the Companion Site. The turnout time is different from the response time. It is the time from when the fire personnel have been alerted to an emergency to when they leave the fire station. It is a component of response time, but does not include the actual time traveled to the emergency after leaving the station. The fire chief thinks that maybe her hypotheses should reflect turnout time instead of response time since travel issues are not always controlled by the personnel.

a. What factors might affect travel time that may increase the total response time?
b. Why might response time be a poor measure of effort/speed by fire personnel compared to turnout time?
c. Run the same multivariate regression as in Problem 5, but with turnout time as the dependent variable.
d. Is the interaction term significant?
e. What is the marginal effect of having a chief at the station?
f. What is the marginal effect of distance to the emergency?
g. Based upon the findings from Problems 5 and 6(d–f), what conclusions and policy recommendations can the fire chief make?

7. Earlier in this chapter, there was a scenario presented where a professor was curious about the effect of hours studied and hours slept on exam grades. They hypothesized that hours studied and hours slept interacted with each other to affect exam grades. Suppose in addition to this hypothesis, they update their hypotheses and believe there is an interactive relationship between gender and student age. They recently read a study suggesting that women mature earlier than males. Therefore, they hypothesize that older, female students will have higher exam scores than younger, male students. They update their data to include gender (coded 1 for female; 0 otherwise) and collect data on the student's age. The data appear below:

a. Enter the data into Excel and upload into the R Commander.
b. Write the regression equation based upon the professor's hypotheses.
c. Run the multivariate regression in the R Commander.

d. Interpret any statistically significant findings – were the professor's hypotheses supported?
e. What is the marginal effect of gender on the exam score? Show this mathematically.
f. What is the marginal effect of age on the exam score? Show this mathematically.
g. Predict the exam score for a male student, age 21, that studied 3 hours for the exam, and did not sleep the night before the exam.

Student exam score data

Student	Grade	Hrs. Studied	Hrs. Sleep	Gender	Age
1	74	14	1	0	21
2	100	15	10	1	22
3	99	13	8	1	24
4	87	9	6	1	20
5	72	10	3	0	25
6	96	11	8	1	21
7	98	11	9	0	28
8	62	7	3	0	19
9	71	8	5	1	18
10	78	8	4	0	26
11	58	4	2	0	18
12	75	10	2	1	22
13	77	15	3	0	19
14	95	12	8	1	30
15	63	12	1	0	23
16	68	10	2	0	21
17	85	1	7	1	30
18	74	2	6	0	42
19	70	1	6	0	23
20	81	15	3	1	22

18

Logistic Regression

18.1 Introduction

Researchers do not always have hypotheses containing dependent variables measured at the interval level. Sometimes, they may be interested in observing whether or not a phenomenon occurred – a yes/no situation where no logical interval level measure could exist. For example, using individual level voter data, did a citizen vote or not? There is no interval level measure of voting for a person. They cannot have a percentage of whether or not they voted or have a scale of voting from 1–10. It is an either/or situation. The citizen voted or did not vote. Similarly, think of a public manager trying to determine if employees call in sick during certain days of the week or times of the year. Maybe they think employees are more likely to call in sick on Fridays so they can have a long weekend or they call in sick right before a holiday to extend their vacation. The dependent variable is whether or not an employee called in sick on a particular day of the week. They either called in sick (did not come to work) or they came to work. There is really no interval measure of calling in sick – it does not make sense that an employee called in 75% sick.

Throughout this text, these types of variables have been called dichotomous variables, dummy variables, binary variables, or nominal/categorical variables with two categories. All of these different terms refer to the same type of variable – coded 1 or 0. OLS regression should not be used when the dependent variable is dichotomous. If one were to use a dichotomous dependent variable in an OLS regression, most statistics software, including the R Commander, will report results, and beta coefficients will be generated for the independent variables in the model. An error message will not appear informing the researcher that they are using the incorrect statistical test. The result would be faulty conclusions and interpretations of the effects of independent variables on the dichotomous dependent variable. This fact highlights the emphasis in earlier chapters on correct variable measurement and knowing levels of measurement for dependent variables – how a dependent variable is measured dictates what statistical test is appropriate. This chapter covers how to run logistic regressions (when the dependent variable is dichotomous) and how to interpret findings from the results.

18.2 Assumptions and Hypothetical Data for Logistic Regression

To better understand logistic regression, it is important to start with a basic example. Some states require vehicles to pass an annual safety inspection – mechanics at state-approved businesses review a car's physical features for any safety issues like broken windows, loose parts, tire wear, etc., along with hooking up the car to an emissions measuring machine to ensure the vehicle's emissions mitigation systems are fully operable and the car is not polluting above a minimum standard.

Suppose a state transportation director is interested in collecting data on vehicle characteristics that may lead to an increase likelihood of it failing an inspection. The director thinks that cars with more mileage will be more likely to not pass a vehicle inspection. They collect a random sample of data, noting the approximate number of miles on the vehicle and whether or not the vehicle passed inspection. A screenshot of the Excel data appears in Figure 18.1. Under the "inspection" column,

	A	B	C
1	vehicle	inspection	miles
2	1	0	88
3	2	0	92
4	3	0	215
5	4	0	147
6	5	0	168
7	6	0	175
8	7	0	209
9	8	0	224
10	9	1	39
11	10	1	48
12	11	1	55
13	12	1	62
14	13	1	75
15	14	1	82
16	15	1	103
17	16	1	145

Figure 18.1 Vehicle inspection data

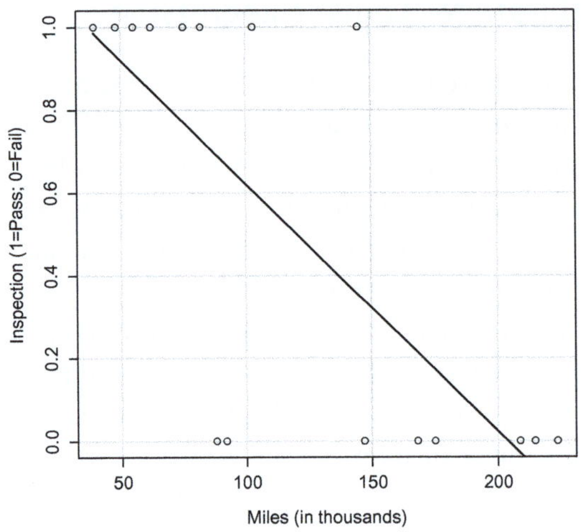

Figure 18.2 OLS regression line through data

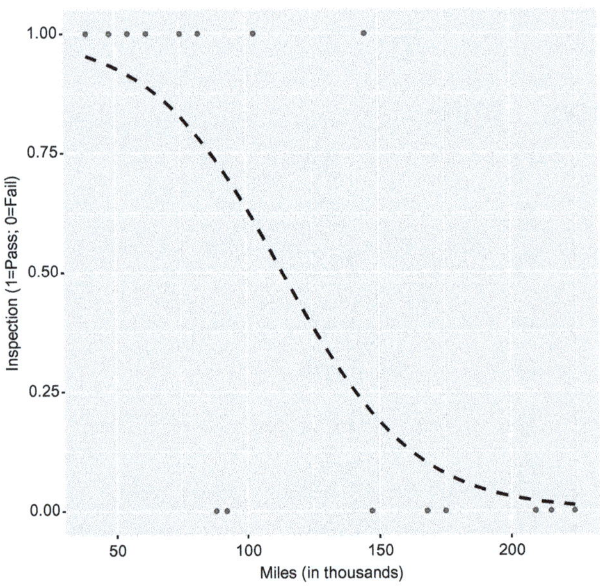

Figure 18.3 Logistic regression line through data

a vehicle is coded 1 if it passed inspection, and coded 0 if it did not pass inspection. The "miles" column indicates the number of miles on the vehicle (in thousands).

A visual inspection of the data in Figure 18.1 likely meets the "eyeball test" that vehicles with more miles are less likely to pass inspection and more likely to fail inspection. Graphing the data also shows an interesting pattern. The director wants to visually display this data and test whether or not their hypothesis is supported through statistical significance. Figures 18.2 and 18.3 show the data displayed in two separate graphs. In Figure 18.2, a best-fitting OLS regression line is plotted through the data. Something appears amiss as the line does not really "run" through the data. Towards the top of the graph, a number of observations systematically appear on the right side of the regression line. Towards the bottom of the graph, a number of observations appear to the left of the regression line. Not many observations lie on or near the "best-fitting" regression line. This pattern is a result of the dependent variable ("inspection") only being able to take on two values, a 1 or a 0. Therefore, the graph correctly shows the distribution of the dependent variable across the various values of the independent variable ("miles"). The fact that the dependent variable can only have a value of 1 or 0, however, makes fitting a best-fitting line through the data problematic. A straight line does not really fit the data well or show the data-generating process. A better reflection of the data-generating process and relationship between the independent variable of vehicle miles and whether or not a vehicle passed the inspection is represented in Figure 18.3. It is a logistic regression line through the data, representing the probability of passing an inspection for various amounts of vehicle miles.

What does this all mean and how can a researcher interpret the data? The researcher needs to utilize a new method, instead of OLS regression, called logistic regression, which accounts for the fact that the dependent variable can only have a value of 1 or 0. The equation and interpretation of a logistic regression is different from the OLS regression and a bit less intuitive, but is important to master to ensure more accurate interpretation and presentation of results.

18.3 Logit Equation

The logistic regression equation with one independent variable can be represented by:

$$Pr(Y_i = 1) = \frac{e^{(b_0 + b_1 X_{1i})}}{1 + e^{(b_0 + b_1 X_{1i})}} \tag{18.1}$$

The term $Pr(Y_i = 1)$ can be read as "the probability that a particular value of the dependent variable, Y, equals 1 (as opposed to a 0)." The right-side of the equation represents the functional form to determine the probability that a particular vehicle containing a certain number of miles (X) passes inspection. It uses the values for b_0 and b_1 generated from the observed data on X_1 and Y to predict the probability of observing a 1 for various values of X. A deeper dive into logistic regression, its equation, and its estimation is beyond the scope of this textbook, and the mathematical properties and assumptions are usually reserved for more advanced graduate level courses. The citations from the Recommended Reading section at the end of this chapter provide a few noteworthy and more advanced treatments of logistic regression. Additionally, most public administrators are not actively getting deep into the mathematics; they want to know how to best interpret data correctly and how to present it to their stakeholders and supervisors. As such, the focus of this chapter

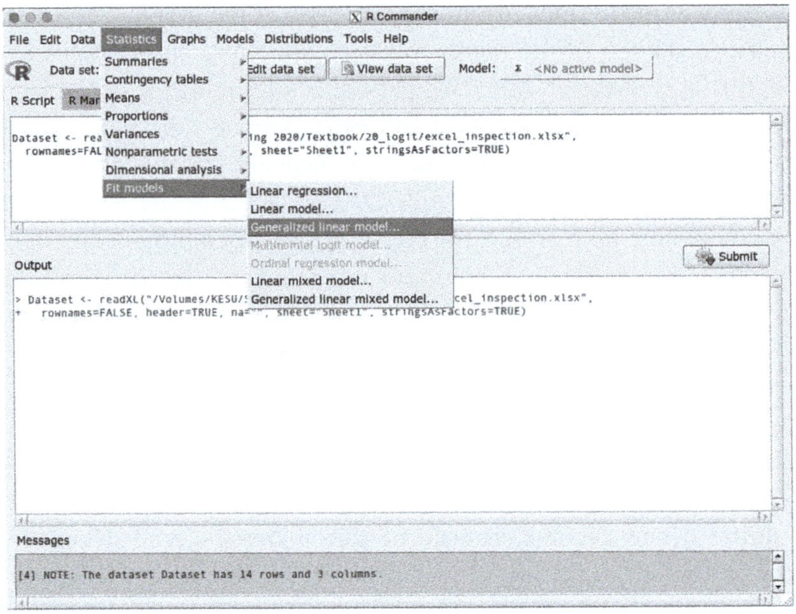

Figure 18.4 Logistic regression in R Commander, part 1

will be on how to correctly run a logistic regression and then meaningfully interpret the findings.

18.4 Logistic Regression in R Commander

The *excel_inspection* file in the Companion Site (www.cambridge.org/scheller) has the raw data from Figure 18.1. Once uploaded into the R Commander, a logistic regression can be run. The logistic regression is a test of the generalized linear model class. Therefore, the steps are:

Step 1: Click Statistics → Fit models → Generalized linear model (Figure 18.4). This opens a window allowing the input of the dependent and independent variable(s).

Step 2: Double-click the dependent variable to send it to the dependent variable box. For this particular example, the "inspection" variable is the dependent variable. Then, double-clicking the relevant independent variable(s) will send the independent variable(s) to the independent variable box. For this particular example, "miles" is the only independent variable in the model. To run the logistic regression, the highlighted option in the "Family" box should be "binomial," and the highlighted option in the "Link" function box should be "logit." These options should be automatically highlighted as default. The respective window should look like Figure 18.5.

Step 3: Click OK. The resulting output should look like Figure 18.6.

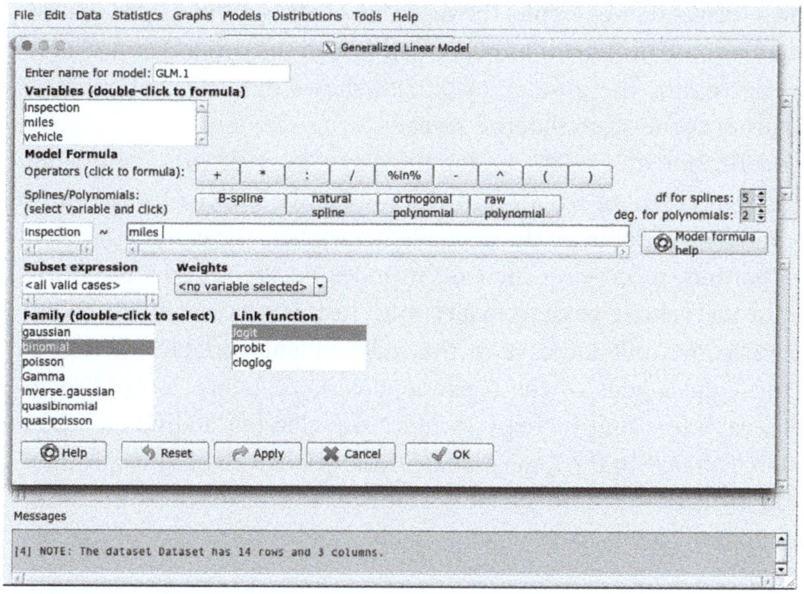

Figure 18.5 Logistic regression in R Commander, part 2

```
Call:
glm(formula = inspection ~ miles, family = binomial(logit), data = Dataset)

Deviance Residuals:
     Min        1Q    Median        3Q       Max
-1.63548  -0.41719   0.07899   0.51854   1.73905

Coefficients:
            Estimate Std. Error z value Pr(>|z|)
(Intercept)  4.57757    2.07811   2.203   0.0276 *
miles       -0.04028    0.01842  -2.186   0.0288 *
---
Signif. codes:  0 '***' 0.001 '**' 0.01 '*' 0.05 '.' 0.1 ' ' 1

(Dispersion parameter for binomial family taken to be 1)

    Null deviance: 22.181  on 15  degrees of freedom
Residual deviance: 11.607  on 14  degrees of freedom
AIC: 15.607

Number of Fisher Scoring iterations: 5


Rcmdr>  exp(coef(GLM.1))  # Exponentiated coefficients ("odds ratios")
(Intercept)       miles
 97.2772850   0.9605199
```

Figure 18.6 R Commander logistic regression output

18.5 Logit Interpretation

The coefficient on "miles" from the output is −0.040. Like OLS regression coefficients, the logit coefficient shows the direction of the relationship between the respective independent variable and dependent variable. A negative coefficient thus reveals a negative relationship between the independent variable and the dependent variable. In the vehicle inspection example, the negative coefficient indicates that as the vehicle miles increase, the likelihood of observing a 1 on the dependent variable (passing inspection) decreases. The p-value of 0.0288 shows that the coefficient is statistically significant at the 95% confidence level.

Interpreting the coefficient of −0.040 is not the same as with OLS regression. In the world of logistic regression, we are not examining the effect of a one-unit increase of the independent variable on the dependent variable. ***We cannot*** say that "on average, ceteris paribus, a one-unit increase in miles on the vehicle leads to a 0.040 unit decrease in the vehicle passing inspection." In this case, what is a 0.040 unit decrease? For each one unit increase in the independent variable, there is a 0.040 decrease in the logged odds of the dependent variable being 1. Applied to the specific example, each one unit increase in miles traveled (an additional 1,000 miles) leads to a 0.040 decrease in the logged odds of the vehicle passing inspection. Logged odds may be difficult for some or most students and researchers to grasp. Therefore, other calculations are usually made to make substantive sense of logistic regression coefficients.

18.5.1 Odds Ratio

The logit coefficient is not completely useless. It does indicate the direction of the relationship between the independent and dependent variable along with the variable's statistical significance. A more substantive interpretation requires additional calculations. A common statistic reported is the odds ratio. The odds ratio reports the change in odds of observing a phenomenon for each one-unit increase in the independent variable. It is simply the exponentiated form of the beta coefficient as shown in Equation 18.2. Stated another way, each one-unit increase in the respective independent variable leads to a change in the odds of Y being or equalling 1 ($\Pr(Y_i) = 1$) by a "factor of e^{β}" (Long, 1997, p. 80), or the odds are multiplied by e^{β} (Menard, 2002). To keep consistency with the notation throughout this textbook, we can substitute b for β and still refer to it as the beta coefficient as in previous chapters.

$$OddsRatio = \frac{Pr(Y_i = 1)}{Pr(Y_i = 0)} = e^{X_i b} \tag{18.2}$$

If the beta coefficient on the independent variable is positive, then logic would dictate that a one-unit increase in the independent variable leads to an increase in the odds of observing the dependent variable. For example, if the beta coefficient on X is 0.50, then $e^{0.50}$ equals 1.649, and the odds of Y being or equalling 1 changes by a factor of 1.649, or are 1.649 times greater. So the interpretation would be that each one-unit increase in X leads to an increase in the odds of Y occurring or Y equalling 1 by 1.649, or as Long (1997) states, "the odds are 1.649 times larger" (p. 80). Thinking mathematically to Equation 18.2,

$$OddsRatio = \frac{Pr(Y_i = 1)}{Pr(Y_i = 0)} = e^{X_i b} = 1.649,$$

the numerator would be larger than the denominator. The probability of Y equalling 1 is greater than the probability of Y equalling 0. Hence, we can say that for each one-unit increase in X, the odds change by a factor of 1.649, or are 1.649 times greater.

If the beta coefficient is negative, say −0.50, then the odds of Y occurring or Y equalling 1 decrease for every one unit change in X by e^b, or that the odds are multiplied by e^b. In this case, if the coefficient is −0.50, then the odds change by a factor of 0.607. An odds ratio less than 1 indicates a decrease in the odds of Y equalling 1, even though the odds ratio is positive. Thinking mathematically to Equation 18.2,

$$OddsRatio = \frac{Pr(Y_i = 1)}{Pr(Y_i = 0)} = e^{X_i b} = 0.607,$$

the numerator would be smaller than the denominator. The probability of Y equalling 1 is less than the probability of Y equalling 0. Hence, we can say that the odds change by a factor of 0.607, or the odds of Y equalling 1 are 0.607 times the odds of Y equalling 0. Such a statement may be somewhat difficult for people to understand. When dealing with odds ratios less than 1, Liu (2016) suggests taking the inverse of the odds ratio. The inverse of 0.607 is 1.65 (1/0.607). This inversion gives the odds of Y equalling 0 compared to Y equalling 1, or stating that the odds of Y equalling 0 are 1.65 times or 1.65 times greater than the odds of Y equalling 1.

Looking back at the vehicle inspection results, the coefficient on the "miles" variable is −0.040. Therefore, $e^{-0.040}$ equals 0.961. A one unit increase in the vehicle miles traveled (each additional 1,000 miles) leads to the odds of a vehicle passing inspection changing by a factor of 0.961. Taking its inverse (1/0.961) gives us a value of 1.04. Therefore, each one-unit increase in vehicle miles (each additional 1,000 miles) increases the odds of the vehicle *failing* inspection by 1.04, or the odds of the vehicle failing inspection are 1.04 times greater. The R Commander reports the odds ratio, or exponentiated coefficient for each of the logit coefficients in the model, which is located towards the bottom of Figure 18.6. Because students and general practitioners often have trouble understanding odds ratios, they are often converted into the percent change in odds, which is a bit more intuitive.

18.5.2 Percent Change in Odds

The percent change in the odds may be a more intuitive interpretation for some. The beta coefficient can be converted into the percent change in odds for a one-unit increase in X. Equation 18.3 depicts the equation for the percent change in odds for any beta coefficient in a logistic regression:

$$\%\Delta Odds = (e^{X_i b} - 1) \times 100 \qquad (18.3)$$

The particular b for a particular X variable is used in the exponentiation, a value of 1 is subtracted, and then the difference is multiplied by 100 to generate the percent change in the odds for a one-unit increase in the respective X. If, for example, the beta coefficient on a particular X variable is 0.50, then the percent change in odds would be:

$$\%\Delta Odds = (e^{0.50} - 1) \times 100,$$

$$\%\Delta Odds = (1.649 - 1) \times 100,$$

$$\%\Delta Odds = (0.649) \times 100 = 64.9$$

Therefore, we would say that the odds of passing inspection increase by 64.9% for each one-unit increase in X.

For the vehicle inspection example, the beta coefficient on the "miles" variable is −0.040. Therefore,

$$\%\Delta Odds = (e^{-0.040} - 1) \times 100,$$

$$\%\Delta Odds = (0.961 - 1) \times 100,$$

$$\%\Delta Odds = (- 0.039) \times 100 = -3.9$$

Therefore, we can say that for each one-unit increase in the miles on the vehicle (an additional 1,000 miles), the odds of the vehicle passing inspection decrease by 3.9%.

18.5.3 Predicted Probabilities

Another method of making substantive sense of logit output is to calculate predicted probabilities for interesting values of the independent variable, X. In the inspection example, one can calculate the predicted probability that a vehicle passes inspection for any amount of miles of interest. What is the predicted probability of a vehicle passing inspection if it has 100,000 miles? Since the variable is measured in thousands of miles, we would be interested in calculating the predicted probability of Y when X=100. Recall the logistic regression equation (Equation 18.1):

$$Pr(Y_i = 1) = \frac{e^{(b_0 + b_1 X_{1i})}}{1 + e^{(b_0 + b_1 X_{1i})}} \qquad (18.1)$$

Also recall from earlier in the chapter that the term $Pr(Y_i = 1)$ can be read as "the probability that a particular value of the dependent variable, Y, equals 1 (as opposed to a 0)." The right-side of the equation represents the functional form to determine the probability that a particular vehicle containing a certain number of miles (X) passes inspection. With the logit output from the R Commander, all of the relevant information is available to calculate the probability of observing a 1, or a vehicle passing inspection if it has 100,000 miles:

$b_0 = 4.578$
$b_1 = -0.040$
$X_{1i} = 100$ (the interesting value of X decided by the researcher)

Solving for Y, also known as $Pr(Y_i = 1)$, or the probability that the vehicle passed inspection:

$$Pr(Y_i = 1) = \frac{e^{(4.578+(-0.040)(100))}}{1 + e^{(4.578+(-0.040)(100))}}$$

Simplified, the equation becomes:

$$Pr(Y_i = 1) = \frac{e^{(4.578-0.040(100))}}{1 + e^{(4.578-0.040(100))}}$$

Multiplying 100 by −0.040 in the exponentiated components of the equation yields:

$$Pr(Y_i = 1) = \frac{e^{(4.578-4.00)}}{1 + e^{(4.578-4.00)}}$$

Subtraction within the parentheses leaves the remaining equation to be:

$$Pr(Y_i = 1) = \frac{e^{0.578}}{1 + e^{0.578}}$$

Completing the exponentiating elements of the equation results in:

$$Pr(Y_i = 1) = \frac{1.782}{1 + 1.782},$$

or simplified to:

$$Pr(Y_i = 1) = \frac{1.782}{2.782} = \mathbf{0.64}$$

After these computations, the researcher can say that the predicted probability of a vehicle passing inspection if it has 100,000 miles is 0.64 or 64%. The researcher can use the same equation for any number of vehicle miles of interest: 68,000 miles (X=68); 280,000 miles (X=280). The predicted probabilities of inspection passage of this model is based upon the independent variable(s) used. In this case, there was one independent variable, vehicle miles. As previously discussed in detail in the chapter on multivariate regression, a dependent variable is likely a function of more than one independent variable. Therefore, assumptions of correct model specification and no omitted variable bias are still assumed with the logistic regression models. If the researcher collected additional data on the vehicles like make/model of the car, age of car, number of oil changes, etc., they would need to be included in the model and the predicted probability would definitely change. While this bivariate model is used for simplifying the somewhat complicated nature of logistic regression and its interpretation, correct model specification is, as always, an important consideration. The next example will use a new public administration example to illustrate how to interpret a logistic regression and quantities of interest (odds ratios and predicted probabilities) when using more than one independent variable.

18.6 An Applied Example – Logistic Regression

Public administration spans nearly every aspect of citizens' lives, including what citizens eat and drink. Public health departments regulate food quality and engage in inspections for cleanliness and regulation adherence. Less publicly visible, but still impactful, are alcohol regulations. City, county, and state governments regulate the sale of alcohol – the who (restaurants, bars, convenience stores, grocery stores, caterers, etc.), the what (beer, wine, and/or distilled spirits), the where (in what types of businesses and their locations relative to schools, religious establishments, other alcohol establishments), and the when (days and hours of the week, holidays, etc.). Proprietors interested in selling alcohol must apply for a permit, which is often approved/denied by an elected governmental body, and monitored by a public agency like a beverage or liquor control commission of appointed/hired public servants.

City councils that review applications for liquor licenses may pay particular attention to local demographics, socioeconomics, density of alcohol establishments, and types of businesses requesting different types of licenses. Some public health research studies have indicated that certain types of establishments like convenience stores and liquor stores are more likely to locate in predominantly minority neighborhoods (LaVeist & Wallace, 2000; Lee et al., 2020). City councils may be more likely to heavily scrutinize or even deny liquor licenses in minority neighborhoods. City council meeting minutes, legislation, and voting are included in public records. Voting for/against, yay/nay, approve/disapprove, deny/not deny are binary or dichotomous decisions and can be coded 1/0 respectively for each category. Neighborhood demographic and socioeconomic data are also readily available from the Census Bureau at the Census tract level. Whether or not liquor licenses are more likely to be denied in a minority neighborhood is a testable, empirical inquiry.

Suppose a researcher hypothesizes that liquor licenses are more likely to be denied for business applicants in neighborhoods with a higher African American population. The researcher also wants to control for the type of liquor license, thinking that licenses for bars and licenses for liquor stores and convenience stores will be heavily scrutinized. The *liquor_license* dataset in the Companion Site (www.cambridge.org/scheller) contains data regarding liquor license denials by a city council for a period of time. The dataset contains a variable named "denial," coded 1 if a particular business was denied a liquor license and 0 if they were approved (not denied) for a liquor license. Using each business' address, the researcher is able to place the business seeking a liquor license within its respective Census tract. With this information, the researcher can collect economic and demographic information provided by the Census Bureau for each Census tract. The "black" variable represents the percent Black/African American population in the respective Census tract.

The type of liquor license may also affect the likelihood of denial. The researcher thinks that licenses for liquor/convenience stores may gain greater scrutiny among

```
Call:
glm(formula = denial ~ black + classD, family = binomial(logit),
    data = Dataset)

Deviance Residuals:
    Min       1Q   Median       3Q      Max
-0.8359  -0.1704  -0.1434  -0.1306   3.0872

Coefficients:
             Estimate Std. Error z value Pr(>|z|)
(Intercept) -4.89157    0.48816 -10.020  < 2e-16 ***
black        0.03545    0.01448   2.448 0.014369 *
classD       1.91761    0.57018   3.363 0.000771 ***
---
Signif. codes:  0 '***' 0.001 '**' 0.01 '*' 0.05 '.' 0.1 ' ' 1

(Dispersion parameter for binomial family taken to be 1)

    Null deviance: 131.78  on 576  degrees of freedom
Residual deviance: 112.51  on 574  degrees of freedom
AIC: 118.51

Number of Fisher Scoring iterations: 7


Rcmdr> exp(coef(GLM.1)) # Exponentiated coefficients ("odds ratios")
(Intercept)       black      classD
0.007509627 1.036082210 6.804669572
```

Figure 18.7 Liquor license denial logistic regression output

members of city council and be more likely to be denied. Liquor and convenience stores often pursue Class D licenses, allowing the sale of beer and distilled spirits for off-site consumption. The researcher creates a dummy variable, "classD," and it is coded 1 if the license application is for a Class D license, and 0 otherwise. Therefore, the logistic regression model would be:

$$Pr(Y_i = 1) = \frac{e^{(b_0+b_1X_{1i}+b_2X_{2i})}}{1 + e^{(b_0+b_1X_{1i}+b_2X_{2i})}} \tag{18.4}$$

Equation 18.4 is the representation of the multivariate logistic regression model, where X_1 is the percent Black/African American in the Census tract for the respective business requesting a liquor license. X_2 is the dummy variable representing if the establishment is requesting a Class D license ($X = 1$) versus all other types of licenses ($X = 0$). The steps to run the multivariate logistic regression are the same as the logistic regression from earlier. Simply ensure that all of the independent variables for analysis are double-clicked into the independent variables box. Following these steps returns the logistic regression results depicted in Figure 18.7.

Both the coefficients on the "black" and "classD" variables are statistically significant at the 95% and 99.9% confidence levels, respectively. Given that they are both positive, they have a positive relationship with the dependent variable of liquor license denials. As the black/African American population increases in the Census tract, the probability of a liquor license denial increases. The exponentiated coefficient on the "black" variable is 1.036; therefore, each one-unit increase in the black/African American population (one percent increase) increases the odds of denial 1.036 times.

The exponentiated coefficient for the "classD" variable is 6.805. Therefore, a Class D liquor license (compared to all other liquor licenses) increases the odds of denial by 6.805 times.

Predicted probabilities can be calculated even with multiple independent variables, just with a few more calculations and steps. For example, suppose a researcher is interested in knowing the probability of denial for a liquor license if the business seeking the license is seeking a Class D license and is located in a Census tract with a black/African American population of 50%. Inserting this information and the logit coefficients from the output into Equation 18.4 gives:

$$Pr(Y_i = 1) = \frac{e^{(-4.892+0.035(50)+1.918(1))}}{1 + e^{(-4.892+0.035(50)+1.918(1))}}$$

Going step-by-step through the order of operations:

$$Pr(Y_i = 1) = \frac{e^{(-4.892+1.75+1.918)}}{1 + e^{(-4.892+1.75+1.918)}}$$

$$Pr(Y_i = 1) = \frac{e^{(-1.224)}}{1 + e^{(-1.224)}}$$

$$Pr(Y_i = 1) = \frac{0.294}{1 + 0.294}$$

$$Pr(Y_i = 1) = \frac{0.294}{1.294}$$

$$Pr(Y_i = 1) = 0.227$$

or

$$Pr(Y_i = 1) = 22.7\%$$

Based upon the sample data and the logistic regression results, the best prediction for the probability of denial is 22.7%. Therefore, the predicted probability that a business seeking a Class D liquor license in a Census tract with 50% black/African American population is denied is 22.7%.

As good public administration researchers, we should look at the results and think about what they mean. The results from the logistic regression suggest that in this particular city, the city council is more likely to deny liquor licenses in areas with a high concentration of African Americans. Is this an example of government trying to limit predatory businesses attempting to locate within minority areas to serve alcohol? Research does indicate that liquor stores and convenience stores selling alcohol tend to locate in minority neighborhoods. Or is this an example of government attempting to regulate the economy of African American neighborhoods, preventing certain types of businesses based upon systemic stereotypes? The data cannot show this, which is one limitation of quantitative research. However, in the practice problems at the end of this chapter, further variables will be used to expand on the model. Nevertheless, the normative, equitable, and ethical implications should always be considered in the back of the researcher's mind as they interpret quantitative results.

18.7 Summary

Logistic regression is the final statistical model covered in this text. It is an important method to know and learn, because public administrators often want to try to predict or understand behavior that is dichotomous, or yes/no, observed/unobserved, passed/failed, etc. These dependent variables can only take on two values, usually coded as a 1 if occurred and 0 if not occurred. This chapter showed why linear regression is not the appropriate method to test hypotheses when the dependent variable is binary/dichotomous. The logistic regression model was introduced and the steps for conducting it in the R Commander were covered. The statistical output for logistic regression is different from linear regression, and the use of odds ratios and predicted probabilities were covered to make substantive sense of logistic regression output.

Logistic regression is an important and powerful method to use for correct analysis when dependent variables are binary/dichotomous. The mathematical computations are a bit involved compared to linear regression, but the conclusions drawn from correct use of logistic regression make for more accurate analysis of data and tests of hypotheses. As public administrators engage in more big data collection, the need for understanding advanced methods and correct model specification becomes ever more important. More advanced methods can be used as students of public administration learn more skills. This text covered the most elementary topics and should be a good basis for most data analysis for public administrators. However, as analytical skills become increasingly important for decision making, topics like time series, panel analysis, event count models, and structural equation modeling will become key tools for analysts. These terms may be foreign to you, but are just some of the burgeoning methods of importance in data analysis for practitioners in public administration.

Recommended Reading

Aldrich, J.H., & Nelson, F.D. (1984). *Linear probability, logit, and probit models*. Sage.

Long, J.S. (1997). *Regression models for categorical and limited dependent variables*. Sage.

PRACTICE PROBLEMS

Conceptual Problems

1. For each of the following dependent variables, determine if linear regression, logistic regression, or neither are appropriate:
   a. Gross Domestic Product (millions of dollars)
   b. Number of new business permits in a year for a city
   c. Met EPA standard/Did not meet EPA standard
   d. Satisfaction of public services (1 = Satisfied; 2 = Neutral; 3 = Not Satisfied)
   e. Voted/Not voted
   f. Party identification (1 = Democrat; 2 = Republican; 3 = Other)
   g. Lived/Died
   h. Satisfaction of public services from 1 (least satisfied) to 100 (most satisfied)
2. Why is a linear regression different from a logistic regression? When is it appropriate to use a linear regression versus a logistic regression?
3. Find a journal article where the author(s) uses a logistic regression to test their hypothesis.
   a. What is the hypothesis of the study?
   b. Identify the main dependent variable in the study.
   c. What are the independent variables in the study?
   d. What are the main findings of the study?
4. A researcher for the Environmental Protection Agency (EPA) is trying to determine what affects the likelihood that factories meet EPA standards. The researcher collects data on whether or not factories meet EPA standards (coded 1 if the factory meets standards; 0 if the factory fails standards). The researcher hypothesizes that age of the factory and whether or not it uses coal (coded 1 if the factory uses coal; 0 if not) are the independent variables of interest. The researcher finds that both the age of the factory and whether or not it uses coal are both statistically significant. The respective beta coefficients are:
   $b_{age} = 0.032$
   $b_{coal} = 2.76$
   a. Calculate and interpret the odds ratio.
   b. Calculate the predicted probability of meeting the EPA's standard if the age of the factory is sixty years old and the factory uses coal.
5. A housing director for the city sends out a survey to residents of a neighborhood asking residents whether or not they support upcoming project ideas the city is interested in pursuing. One project is converting an abandoned, historical building owned by the city into a new homeless shelter. The director asks residents if they support (Support) this conversion (1 = Yes; 0 = No). The director also asks the residents some demographic questions like their gender (1 = Male; 0 = Female), number of children (Children) living in their home,

and years lived in the neighborhood. Having their address, the director also calculates how far they live from the proposed shelter (Distance in miles). The director runs the following logistic regression model:

$$Pr(Support = 1) = \frac{e^{(b_0 + b_1 X_{Gender} + b_2 X_{Children} + b_3 X_{Years} + b_4 X_{Distance})}}{1 + e^{(b_0 + b_1 X_{Gender} + b_2 X_{Children} + b_3 X_{Years} + b_4 X_{Distance})}}$$

The coefficients resulting from the logistic regression are:

$b_{Gender} = -0.068$
$b_{Children} = -0.002$
$b_{Years} = -0.034$
$b_{Distance} = -1.25$

Gender and Distance are statistically signficant.

a. Interpret the findings for Gender and Distance by explaining their relationship (direction) with support for building the shelter.
b. Calculate and interpret the odds ratio.
c. Calculate the predicted probability of supporting the shelter if the respondent was female, with two children, living in the neighborhood for one year, and lives 0.5 miles from the proposed shelter.

R Commander Problems

6. Open the *liquor_license* dataset used earlier in the chapter from the Companion Site (www.cambridge.org/scheller). Using the independent variables of percent black/African American in the Census tract, income in the Census tract, and whether or not the license is a Class D license, run a logistic regression with denial of the license as the dependent variable.

a. Come up with research and null hypotheses for the effect of income on the likelihood of denial.
b. Interpret any statistically significant findings (direction of relationship between the independent variables and the dependent variable).
c. Calculate and interpret the odds ratio.
d. Calculate the predicted probability of denial if the black/African American percentage is 25, income is 30,000, and the license is not a Class D license.

7. There is another variable in the *liquor_license* dataset called "restrictions." It is coded 1 if the liquor license was approved, but with restrictions, and 0 if the license was approved without restrictions. Common restrictions include limitations on hours of operation/sales, type of alcohol sold, and size of alcohol sold.

a. What do you expect to be the effect of black/African American and liquor class on the probability of having restrictions?
b. Run the logistic regression with restrictions as the dependent variable, and the independent variables of black/African American, income, and Class D.
c. Calculate and interpret the odds ratio.

d. Calculate the predicted probability of restrictions if the black/African American percentage is 25, income is 30,000, and the license is not a Class D license.

8. The following data contains voter history information for eight voters and their level of education in years. Twelve years of education would be equivalent to having graduated from high school.

Voter turnout

Voter	Voted in 2020 (1 = Voted; 0 Did not vote)	Education (Years)
1	1	16
2	1	18
3	0	12
4	1	16
5	0	13
6	0	10
7	0	12
8	1	17

a. Enter the data in Excel and load into the R Commander.

b. Run a logistic regression with voting as the dependent variable and years of education as the independent variable.

c. Interpret the results and whether or not they are statistically significant. What other variables should be used in a study on voter turnout. Why?

9. Open the *ppp* dataset from the Companion Site. It contains information on the adoption of public-private partnerships (PPPs) by state-year. A public-private partnership is an agreement between a government (public sector) and a private company or companies to provide public services. They are commonly used for transportation projects like light-rails, harbors, airport improvements, new roads, etc. The codebook contains all of the variables in the dataset.

a. Think about why a state may want to adopt a PPP in transportation. What are two or three reasons?

b. Using the codebook, create two research and two corresponding null hypotheses that explain why a state would adopt a PPP.

c. Using the variables in the dataset, including your variables of interest and any relevant control variables, run a logistic regression on PPP adoption, and interpret your findings.

d. If you have not done so already, use the estimated per capita lane miles, state government ideology, state GDP, and percentage of the state budget spent on transportation as independent variables in the logistic regression model and write the logistic regression equation.

e. Calculate and interpret the odds ratios for any statistically significant variables.
f. Calculate the predicted probability of PPP adoption if the estimated per capita lane miles is 100,000, the state government ideology is 50 (neither conservative nor liberal – moderate), state GDP is 43,000 (as measured in the units in the codebook), and percentage of the state budget spent on transportation is 5.4.

APPENDIX A

Critical Values of χ^2

	Level of significance				
df	0.10	0.05	0.025	0.01	0.001
1	2.706	3.841	5.024	6.635	10.828
2	4.605	5.991	7.378	9.210	13.816
3	6.251	7.815	9.348	11.345	16.266
4	7.779	9.488	11.143	13.277	18.467
5	9.236	11.070	12.833	15.086	20.515
6	10.645	12.592	14.449	16.812	22.458
7	12.017	14.067	16.013	18.475	24.322
8	13.362	15.507	17.535	20.090	26.125
9	14.684	16.919	19.023	21.666	27.877
10	15.987	18.307	20.483	23.209	29.588
11	17.275	19.675	21.920	24.725	31.264
12	18.549	21.026	23.337	26.217	32.910
13	19.812	22.362	24.736	27.688	34.528
14	21.064	23.685	26.119	29.141	36.123
15	22.307	24.996	27.488	30.578	37.697
20	28.412	31.410	34.170	37.566	45.315
25	34.382	37.652	40.646	44.314	52.620
30	40.256	43.773	46.979	50.892	59.703
35	46.059	49.802	53.203	57.342	66.619
40	51.805	55.758	59.342	63.691	73.402
50	63.167	67.505	71.420	76.154	86.661

(cont.)

df	Level of significance				
	0.10	0.05	0.025	0.01	0.001
60	74.397	79.082	83.298	88.379	99.607
70	85.527	90.531	95.023	100.425	112.317
75	91.061	96.217	100.839	106.393	118.599
80	96.578	101.879	106.629	112.329	124.839
90	107.565	113.145	118.136	124.116	137.208
100	118.498	124.342	129.561	135.807	149.449

APPENDIX B

Critical Values of t

	Level of significance					
df	0.10	0.05	0.025	0.01	0.005	0.001
1	3.078	6.314	12.706	31.821	63.657	318.313
2	1.886	2.920	4.303	6.965	9.925	22.327
3	1.638	2.353	3.182	4.541	5.841	10.215
4	1.533	2.132	2.776	3.747	4.604	7.173
5	1.476	2.015	2.571	3.365	4.032	5.893
6	1.440	1.943	2.447	3.143	3.707	5.208
7	1.415	1.895	2.365	2.998	3.499	4.782
8	1.397	1.860	2.306	2.896	3.355	4.499
9	1.383	1.833	2.262	2.821	3.250	4.296
10	1.372	1.812	2.228	2.764	3.169	4.143
11	1.363	1.796	2.201	2.718	3.106	4.024
12	1.356	1.782	2.179	2.681	3.055	3.929
13	1.350	1.771	2.160	2.650	3.012	3.852
14	1.345	1.761	2.145	2.624	2.977	3.787
15	1.341	1.753	2.131	2.602	2.947	3.733
20	1.325	1.725	2.086	2.528	2.845	3.552
25	1.316	1.708	2.060	2.485	2.787	3.450
30	1.310	1.697	2.042	2.457	2.750	3.385
40	1.303	1.684	2.021	2.423	2.704	3.307
50	1.299	1.676	2.009	2.403	2.678	3.261
60	1.296	1.671	2.000	2.390	2.660	3.232

(cont.)

df	Level of significance					
	0.10	0.05	0.025	0.01	0.005	0.001
70	1.294	1.667	1.994	2.381	2.648	3.211
75	1.293	1.665	1.992	2.377	2.643	3.202
80	1.292	1.664	1.990	2.374	2.639	3.195
90	1.291	1.662	1.987	2.368	2.632	3.183
100	1.290	1.660	1.984	2.364	2.626	3.174
∞	1.282	1.645	1.960	2.326	2.576	3.090

APPENDIX C

Table of Probabilities Associated with the Standard Normal Distribution

z	0.00	0.01	0.02	0.03	0.04	0.05	0.06	0.07	0.08	0.09
0.0	.5000	.4960	.4920	.4880	.4840	.4801	.4761	.4721	.4681	.4641
0.1	.4602	.4562	.4522	.4483	.4443	.4404	.4364	.4325	.4286	.4247
0.2	.4207	.4168	.4129	.4090	.4052	.4013	.3974	.3936	.3897	.3859
0.3	.3821	.3783	.3745	.3707	.3669	.3632	.3594	.3557	.3520	.3483
0.4	.3446	.3409	.3372	.3336	.3300	.3264	.3228	.3192	.3156	.3121
0.5	.3085	.3050	.3015	.2981	.2946	.2912	.2877	.2843	.2810	.2776
0.6	.2743	.2709	.2676	.2643	.2611	.2578	.2546	.2514	.2483	.2451
0.7	.2420	.2389	.2358	.2327	.2296	.2266	.2236	.2206	.2177	.2148
0.8	.2119	.2090	.2061	.2033	.2005	.1977	.1949	.1921	.1894	.1867
0.9	.1841	.1814	.1788	.1762	.1736	.1711	.1685	.1660	.1635	.1611
1.0	.1587	.1562	.1539	.1515	.1492	.1469	.1446	.1423	.1401	.1379
1.1	.1357	.1335	.1314	.1292	.1271	.1251	.1230	.1210	.1190	.1170
1.2	.1151	.1131	.1112	.1093	.1075	.1056	.1038	.1020	.1003	.0985
1.3	.0968	.0951	.0934	.0918	.0901	.0885	.0869	.0853	.0838	.0823
1.4	.0808	.0793	.0778	.0764	.0749	.0735	.0721	.0708	.0694	.0681
1.5	.0668	.0655	.0643	.0630	.0618	.0606	.0594	.0582	.0571	.0559
1.6	.0548	.0537	.0526	.0516	.0505	.0495	.0485	.0475	.0465	.0455
1.7	.0446	.0436	.0427	.0418	.0409	.0401	.0392	.0384	.0375	.0367
1.8	.0359	.0351	.0344	.0366	.0329	.0322	.0314	.0307	.0301	.0294
1.9	.0287	.0281	.0274	.0268	.0262	.0256	.0250	.0244	.0239	.0233
2.0	.02275	.02222	.02169	.02118	.02067	.02018	.01970	.01923	.01876	.01831
2.1	.01786	.01743	.01700	.01659	.01618	.01578	.01539	.01500	.01463	.01426

(cont.)

z	0.00	0.01	0.02	0.03	0.04	0.05	0.06	0.07	0.08	0.09
2.2	.01390	.01355	.01321	.01287	.01255	.01222	.01191	.01160	.01130	.01101
2.3	.01072	.01044	.01017	.00990	.00964	.00939	.00914	.00889	.00866	.00842
2.4	.00820	.00798	.00776	.00755	.00734	.00714	.00695	.00676	.00657	.00639
2.5	.00621	.00604	.00587	.00570	.00554	.00539	.00523	.00508	.00494	.00480
2.6	.00466	.00453	.00440	.00427	.00415	.00402	.00391	.00379	.00368	.00357
2.7	.00347	.00336	.00326	.00317	.00307	.00298	.00289	.00280	.00272	.00264
2.8	.00255	.00248	.00240	.00233	.00226	.00219	.00212	.00205	.00199	.00193
2.9	.00187	.00181	.00175	.00169	.00164	.00159	.00154	.00149	.00144	.00139
3.0	.00135	.00131	.00126	.00122	.00118	.00114	.00111	.00107	.00103	.00100
3.1	.00097									
3.2	.00069									
3.3	.00048									
3.4	.00034									
3.5	.00023									
3.6	.00016									
3.7	.00011									
3.8	.00007									
3.9	.00005									
4.0	.00003									

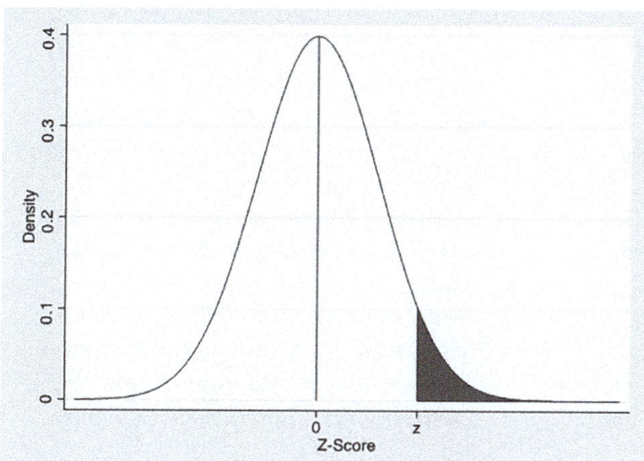

References

Aldrich, J.H., & Nelson, F.D. (1984). *Linear probability, logit, and probit models.* Sage.

An, B., Porcher, S., Tang, S., & Kim, E.E. (2021). Policy design for COVID-19: Worldwide evidence on the efficacies of early mask mandates and other policy interventions. *Public Administration Review*, 81(6), 1157–1182.

Baker, J.E. (2021). Subsidies for succulents: Evaluating the Las Vegas Cash-for-Grass Rebate Program. *Journal of the Association of Environmental and Resource Economics*, 8(3), 475–508.

Battaglio, R.P., & French, Jr., P.E. (2016). Public service motivation, public management reform, and organizational socialization: Testing the effects of employment at-will and agency on PSM among municipal employees. *Public Personnel Management*, 45(2), 123–147.

Bellé, N. (2013). Experimental evidence on the relationship between public service motivation and job performance. *Public Administration Review*, 73(1), 143–153.

Bereitschaft, B., & Scheller, D. (2020). How might the COVID-19 pandemic affect 21st century urban design, planning, and development? *City Science*, 4(4), 56.

Berman, E., & Wang, X. (2018). *Essential statistics for public managers & policy analysts* (4th ed.). Sage.

Berry, W.D. (1993). *Understanding regression assumptions.* Sage.

Berry, W.D., DeMeritt, J.H.R., & Esarey, J. (2010). Testing for interaction in binary logit and probit models: Is a product term essential? *American Journal of Political Science*, 54(1), 248–266.

Berry, W.D., & Feldman, S. (1985). *Multiple regression in practice.* Sage.

Berry, W.D., Fording, R.C., Ringquist, E.J., Hanson, R.L., & Klarner, C.E. (2010). Measuring citizen and government ideology in the U.S. states: A re-appraisal. *State Politics & Policy Quarterly*, 10(2), 117–135.

Berry, W.D., & Sanders, M.S. (2000). *Understanding multivariate research: A primer for beginning social scientists.* Westview Press.

Bowen, D.C., & Greene, Z. (2014). Should we measure professionalism with an index? A note on theory and practice in state legislative professionalism research. *State Politics & Policy Quarterly*, 14(3), 277–296.

Box, G.E.P., & Tiao, G.C. (1965). A change in level of a nonstationary time series. *Biometrika*, 52 (1/2), 181–192.

Box-Steffensmeier, J.M., Freeman, J.R., Hitt, M.P., & Pevehouse, J.C.W. (2014). *Time series analysis for the social sciences.* Cambridge University Press.

Boyer, E.J., & Scheller, D.S. (2018). An examination of state-level public-private partnership adoption: Analyzing economic, political, and demand-related determinants of PPPs. *Public Works Management & Policy*, 23(1), 283–309.

Boyle, A., Barrilleaux, C., & Scheller, D. (2014). Does walkability influence

housing prices? *Social Science Quarterly*, 95(3), 852–867.
Brambor, T., Clark, W.R., & Golder, M. (2006). Understanding interaction models: Improving empirical analyses. *Political Analysis*, 14(1), 63–82.
Bureau of Economic Analysis (n.d.). www.bea.gov.
Bureau of Transportation Statistics (n.d.). www.bts.gov/browse-statistical-products-and-data.
Carmody, T. (2016, February 26). How the Flint River got so toxic: Factories and people have been dumping sewage, chemicals, and road salt in the Flint River for more than a century. *The Verge*. www.theverge.com/2016/2/26/11117022/flint-michigan-water-crisis-lead-pollution-history.
Carr, J.B., & Feiock, R.C. (1999). Metropolitan government and economic development. *Urban Affairs Review*, 34(3), 476–488.
Census Bureau Quick Facts. (n.d.). www.census.gov/quickfacts/.
Centers for Disease Control and Prevention (2022). *Life expectancy at birth by state*. www.cdc.gov/nchs/pressroom/sosmap/life_expectancy/life_expectancy.htm.
Centers for Disease Control and Prevention (n.d.). *Covid data tracker*. https://covid.cdc.gov/covid-data-tracker/#trends_weeklydeaths_select_00.
Choi, H., & Hong, S. (2021). Linking political and bureaucratic representation: Does minority representation on city councils affect the outcomes of street-level service? *Public Administration*, 99, 405–421.
Christiani, L., Shoub, K., Baumgartner, F.R., Epp, D.A., & Roach, K. (2021). Better for everyone: Black descriptive representation and police traffic stops. *Politics, Groups, and Identities*, 10(5), 807–816.
Clay, K., Troesken, W., & Haines, M. (2014). Lead, mortality, and productivity. *Review of Economics and Statistics*, 96, 458–470.
Commission on Presidential Debates (2000). *October 3, 2000 transcript*. www.debates.org/voter-education/debate-transcripts/october-3-2000-transcript/.
Cottrell, D., Herron, M.C., & Smith, D.A. (2021). Vote-by-mail ballot rejection and experience with mail-in voting. *American Politics Research*, 49(6), 577–590.
De Vaus, D.A. (2001). *Research design in social research*. Sage.
Dillman, D.A. (1991). The design and administration of mail surveys. *Annual Review of Sociology*, 17, 225–249.
Dillman, D.A. (2000). *Mail and internet surveys: The tailored design method* (2nd ed.). John Wiley & Sons.
Durning, D., & Sanford, P. (2010). Unification promises and outcomes: The case of Athens and Clark County, Georgia. In S.M. Leland & K. Thurmaier (eds.), *City-county consolidation: Promises made, promises kept?* (pp. 215–244). Georgetown University Press.
Edwards, M. (2014). Fetal death and reduced birth rates associated with exposure to lead-contaminated drinking water. *Environmental Science & Technology*, 48, 739–746.
Elbel, B., Taksler, G.B., Mijanovich, T., Abrams, C.B., & Dixon, L.B. (2013). Promotion of healthy eating through public policy. *American Journal of Preventive Medicine*, 45(1), 49–55.
Faulk, D., & Schansberg, E. (2009). An examination of selected economic development outcomes from consolidation. *State and Local Government Review*, 41(3), 193–200.
Fenno, R. (1978). *Home style: House members in their districts*. Little, Brown.
Field, A., Miles, J., & Field, Z. (2012). *Discovering statistics using R*. Sage.

Fox, J. (2016). *Applied regression analysis & generalized linear models.* (3rd ed.). Sage.

Fox, J. (2017). *Using the R Commander: A point-and-click interface for R.* CRC Press.

Fox, J., & Bouchet-Valat, M. (2022). *Rcmdr: R Commander.* R package version 2.8-0. https://socialsciences.mcmaster.ca/jfox/Misc/Rcmdr/.

Frankfort-Nachmias, C., & Nachmias, D. (2008). *Research methods in the social sciences* (7th ed.). Worth Publishers.

Grossman, D.S., & Slusky, D.J.G. (2019). The impact of the Flint Water Crisis on fertility. *Demography*, 56, 2005–2031.

Gujarati, D.N. (2003). *Basic econometrics* (4th ed.). McGraw Hill.

Hansen, J.A., & Tummers, L. (2020). A systematic review of field experiments in public administration. *Public Administration Review*, 80(6), 921-931.

Hawkins, C.V., Krause, R.M., & Deslatte, A. (2023). Staff support and administrative capacity in strategic planning for local sustainability. *Public Management Review*, 25(5), 879–900.

Healey, J.F. (2002). *Statistics: A tool for social research* (6th ed.). Wadsworth Publishing.

Hock, S., Anderson, S., & Potoski, M. (2012). Invitation phone calls increase attendance at civic meetings: Evidence from a field experiment. *Public Administration Review*, 73(2), 221–228.

Houston, D.J. (2011). Implications of occupational locus and focus for public service motivation: Attitudes towards work motivations across nations. *Public Administration Review*, 71(5), 761–771.

Huber, A. (2016). Is seeing intriguing? Practitioner perceptions of research documents. *Journal of Interior Design*, 41(1), 13–32.

Isett, K.R., & Hicks, D.M. (2018). Providing public servants what they need: Revealing the "unseen" through data visualization. *Public Administration Review*, 78(3), 479–485.

Iversen, G.R., & Norpoth, H. (1976). *Analysis of variance.* Sage.

Johnson, J.B., & Reynolds, H.T. (2012). *Political science research methods* (7th ed.). Sage.

Kaufman, Robert L. (2019). *Interaction effects in linear and generalized linear models.* Sage.

Kellstedt, P.M., & Whitten, G.D. (2009). *The fundamentals of political science research.* Cambridge University Press.

Kim, S. (2006). Public service motivation and organizational citizenship behavior in Korea. *International Journal of Manpower*, 27(8), 722–40.

King, G., Keohane, R.O., & Verba, S. (1994). *Designing social inquiry: Scientific inference in qualitative research.* Princeton University Press.

LaVeist, T.A., & Wallace Jr., J.M. (2000). Health risk and inequitable distribution of liquor stores in African American neighborhood. *Social Science & Medicine*, 51, 613–617.

Lavrakas, P.J. (2008). Respondent fatigue. In P.J. Lavarkas (ed.), *Encyclopedia of survey research methods* (pp. 742–743). Sage.

Lee, J.P., et al. (2020). What explains the concentration of off-premise alcohol outlets in Black neighborhoods? *SSM-Population Health*, 12, 1–11.

Leedy, P.D., & Ormrod, J.E. (2010). *Practical research: Planning and design* (9th ed.). Pearson.

Leisink, P., & Steijn, B. (2009). Public service motivation and job performance of public sector employees in the Netherlands. *International Review of Administrative Sciences*, 75(1), 35–52.

Leland, S.M., & Thurmaier, K. (eds.) (2010). *City-county consolidation: Promises made, promises kept?* Georgetown University Press.

Lewis-Beck, M. (1995). *Data analysis: An introduction.* Sage.

Lewis-Beck, C., & Lewis-Beck, M. (2016). *Applied regression: An introduction* (2nd ed.). Sage.

Lim, J., Kourtit, K., Nijkamp, P., & Stream, C. (2022). Spatial deconcentration of tourism concentrations: A visitors' galaxy impact model of the COVID-19 crisis. *Sustainability*, 14(6), 3239.

Lipka, S. (2011, August 7). Want data? Ask students. Again and again. *Chronicle of Higher Education.* www.chronicle.com/article/want-data-ask-students-again-and-again/.

Liu, X. (2016). *Applied ordinal logistic regression using STATA.* Sage.

Long, J.S. (1997). *Regression models for categorical and limited dependent variables.* Sage.

Lyons, J., & Fowler, L. (2021). Is it still a mandate if we don't enforce it? The politics of COVID-related mask mandates in conservative states. *State and Local Government Review*, 53(2) 106–121.

McGregor, D.M. (1957). The human side of enterprise. *Management Review*, 46, 22–28.

Meier, K.J., Brudney, J.L., & Bohte, J. (2015). *Applied statistics for public and nonprofit administration.* (9th ed.). Cengage.

Menard, S. (2002). *Applied logistic regression analysis* (2nd ed.). Sage.

Minor League Baseball (2023). The official site of Minor League Baseball. *MiLB.com.* www.milb.com/.

Morin, R., Parker, K., Stepler, R., & Mercer, A. (2017, January 11). Police views, public views. *Pew Research Center.* www.pewresearch.org/social-trends/2017/01/11/police-views-public-views/.

Naff, K.C., & Crum, J. (1999). Working for America: Does public service motivation make a difference? *Review of Public Personnel Administration*, 19(4), 5–16.

National Academy of Public Administration (n.d.). *Grand Challenges in Public Administration.* Retrieved April 23, 2023, from https://napawash.org/grand-challenges/the-12-grand-challenges#jump-22640.

National Centers for Environmental Information (NCEI) (2022). *Climate at a Glance County Time Series.* Available at: www.ncei.noaa.gov/access/monitoring/climate-at-a-glance/county/time-series.

National Commission for the Protection of Human Subjects of Biomedical and Behavioral Research (1978). *The Belmont report: Ethical principles and guidelines for the protection of human subjects of research.* Bethesda, MD.

Nebraska Department of Education (n.d.). nep.education.ne.gov.

Nishishiba, M., Jones, M., & Kraner, M. (2014). *Research methods and statistics for public and nonprofit administrators: A practical guide.* Sage.

Nix, J. & Shjarback, J. (2021). Factors associated with police shooting mortality: A focus on race and a plea for more comprehensive data. *PLOS ONE*, 16(11), 1–14.

O'Brien, T.L. (2021, July 18). Can the Southwest survive with less water? *Bloomberg.* www.bloomberg.com/graphics/2021-opinion-us-drought-southwest-arizona-water-crisis/.

Osborne, J.W. (2013). *Best practices in data cleaning.* Sage.

Osborne, M. (2022, May 5). Officials will release less water into Lake Mead because of drought. *Smithsonian Magazine.* www.smithsonianmag.com/smart-news/officials-will-release-less-water-into-lake-mead-because-of-drought-180980030/#:~:text=In%20August%202021%2C%20the%20government,it%20unable%20to%20draw%20water.

Park, S.M., & Rainey, H.G. (2007). Antecedents, mediators, and consequences of affective, normative, and continuance commitment: Empirical tests of commitment effects in federal agencies. *Review of Public Personnel Administration*, 27(3), 197–226.

Park, S.M., & Rainey, H.G. (2008). Leadership and public service motivation in U.S. federal agencies. *International Public Management Journal*, 11(1), 109–142.

Perry, J.L., & Wise, L.R. (1990). The motivational bases of public service. *Public Administration Review*, 50(3), 367–373.

Peterson, B.E., & Lawrence, D.S. (2021). Do the effects of police body-worn cameras on use of force and complaints change over time? Results from a panel analysis in the Milwaukee Police Department. *Criminal Justice and Behavior*, 48(6), 734–754.

Pickup, M. (2015). *Introduction to time series*. Sage.

Pollock III, P.H. (2016). *The essentials of political analysis* (5th ed.). Sage.

Popper, K. (1968). *Logic of scientific discovery*. Hutchinson.

Porcher, S. (2020). Response2covid19, a dataset of governments' responses to COVID-19 all around the world. *Scientific Data*, 7(423), 1–9.

Pyo, S. (2021). Do body-worn cameras change law enforcement arrest behavior? A national study of local police departments. *American Review of Public Administration*, 51(3), 184–198.

Ramis, H. (2005). Ghostbusters – Commentary (DVD ts. 03:01–03:17).

Robinson, S.B., & Leonard, K.F. (2019). *Designing quality survey questions*. Sage.

Salkind, N.J. (2008). *Statistics for people who (think they) hate statistics*. Sage.

Scheller, D.S. (2015). The effects of neighborhood democracy on cooperation: A laboratory study. *Journal of Urban Affairs*, 37(5), 568–583.

Scheller, D.S. (2016). Neighborhood hierarchy of needs. *Journal of Urban Affairs*, 38(3), 429–439.

Scheller, D.S., & Reglen, D. (2021). Improving fire department turnout times: Training versus sanctions in a high public service motivation environment. *International Public Management Journal*, 24(6), 973–996.

Singleton, Jr., R.A., & Straits, B.C. (2005). *Approaches to social research* (4th ed.). Oxford University Press.

Skelley, G. (2020, June 5). How Americans feel about George Floyd's death and the protests. *FiveThirtyEight*. https://fivethirtyeight.com/features/how-americans-feel-about-george-floyds-death-and-the-protests/.

Troesken, W. (2006). Lead exposure and eclampsia in Britain, 1883–1934. *Environmental Research*, 101, 395–400.

U.S. Bureau of Reclamation (n.d.). *Lake Mead at Hoover Dam, end of month elevation (feet)*. Available at: www.usbr.gov/lc/region/g4000/hourly/mead-elv.html.

U.S. Census Bureau (2015). *American community survey 1-year estimates*. Available at: https://data.census.gov/.

U.S. Census Bureau (2021). *Historical income tables: Households*. Available at: www.census.gov/data/tables/time-series/demo/income-poverty/historical-income-households.html.

U.S. Department of Agriculture (USDA) (2022). *USDA/NASS quick stats*. Available at: https://quickstats.nass.usda.gov.

Vandenabeele, W. (2009). The mediating effect of job satisfaction and organizational commitment on self reported performance: More robust evidence of the PSM–performance relationship. *International Review of Administrative Sciences*, 75(1), 11–34.

Vandenabeele, W., & van Loon, N.M. (2015). Motivating employees using public service. In J.L. Perry & R.K. Christensenc (eds.), *Handbook of Public Administration* (pp. 353–365). Jossey-Bass.

van Loon, N.M. (2016). Is public service motivation related to overall and dimensional work-unit performance as indicated by supervisors? *International Public Management Journal*, 19(1), 78–110.

Weisberg, H. (1992). *Central tendency and variability*. Sage.

Wonnacott, T.H., & Wonnacott, R.J. (1990). *Introductory statistics* (5th ed.). John Wiley & Sons.

Zahran, M., McElmurry, S.P., & Sadler, R.C. (2017). Four phases of the Flint water crisis: Evidence from blood lead levels in children. *Environmental Research*, 157, 160–172.

Zeemering, E.S. (2018). Sustainability management, strategy and reform in local government. *Public Management Review*, 20(1), 136–153.

Index